Criminal Justice

Criminal Justice

The Essentials

FIFTH EDITION

STEVEN P. LAB
Bowling Green State University

MARIAN R. WILLIAMS
Appalachian State University

JEFFERSON E. HOLCOMB
Appalachian State University

MELISSA W. BUREK
Bowling Green State University

WILLIAM R. KING
Sam Houston State University

MICHAEL E. BUERGER
Bowling Green State University

New York   Oxford
OXFORD UNIVERSITY PRESS

Oxford University Press is a department of the University of Oxford. It furthers the University's objective of excellence in research, scholarship, and education by publishing worldwide. Oxford is a registered trade mark of Oxford University Press in the UK and certain other countries.

Published in the United States of America by Oxford University Press
198 Madison Avenue, New York, NY 10016, United States of America.

For titles covered by Section 112 of the US Higher Education Opportunity Act, please visit www.oup.com/us/he for the latest information about pricing and alternate formats.

Library of Congress Cataloging-in-Publication Data

Names: Lab, Steven P., author. | Williams, Marian Rebecca, author.
Title: Criminal justice : the essentials / Steven P. Lab, Bowling Green State
    University, Marian R. Williams, Appalachian State University, Jefferson E.
    Holcomb, Appalachian State University, Melissa W. Burek, Bowling Green,
    State University, William R. King, Sam Houston State University, Michael
    E. Buerger, Bowling Green State University.
Description: Fifth edition. | New York : Oxford University Press, 2018. |
    Revised edition of Criminal justice, [2016]
Identifiers: LCCN 2018019310 (print) | LCCN 2018020905 (ebook) | ISBN
    9780190855895 (E-Book) | ISBN 9780190855871 (paperback) | ISBN
    9780190855888 (looseleaf)
Subjects: LCSH: Criminal justice, Administration of—United States. | BISAC:
    SOCIAL SCIENCE / Criminology.
Classification: LCC HV9950 (ebook) | LCC HV9950 .L33 2018 (print) | DDC
    364.973—dc23
LC record available at https://lccn.loc.gov/2018019310

9 8 7 6 5 4 3 2 1
Printed by LSC Communications, Inc., United States of America

CONTENTS

PREFACE vii

Chapter 1   Crime, Criminal Justice, and Policy   1

Chapter 2   Issues of Law   25

Chapter 3   Policing and Law Enforcement   53

Chapter 4   The Court System   82

Chapter 5   Institutional Corrections   116

Chapter 6   Community Corrections   152

Chapter 7   The Juvenile Justice System   184

Chapter 8   Conclusion   220

GLOSSARY   228

REFERENCES   249

INDEX   264

PREFACE

Changes in the criminal justice system are typically slow to take root and the basic system of justice in the United States remains fairly static. Most change comes from emerging issues in society for which the criminal justice system is tasked to address. Over the past several years, police use of deadly force and the opioid epidemic have emerged as major concerns, and the use of technology and social media in both crimes and responses to crime has persisted. This fifth edition of *Criminal Justice: The Essentials* maintains the balanced presentation of the criminal justice system found in the previous editions while adding and expanding discussions of new and emerging topics facing society and the system. We have also attempted to provide updated statistics throughout the book. Note that we consciously work to keep the footprint of the book roughly the same size as in the past. Our goal is for this book to not become an overly large, expensive tome on the criminal justice system. Instead, we are trying to provide instructors and students with a succinct text that presents the essential materials needed in an introductory course at a reasonable cost.

In this new edition, each chapter has been revised and updated. The basic organization of the book has remained unchanged. In chapters, materials that have been cut can now be found on the book's website. The website also includes a wealth of information, documents, tables, figures, websites, and some newly written material that we could not fit in the text. Although a good deal of this is referenced in the text, there are many things that are not. We encourage the reader to explore what is available on the site.

Specific changes in this edition include the following:

- Critical Thinking Exercises have been revised and new exercises added throughout the chapters.
- Each chapter includes new/updated Web Activities that direct the reader to resources either on the book's dedicated website or at a wide range of government and private sites.

- All the material has been updated to reflect the most recent data available.
- Chapter 1 has updated material on victims, social media, and the police use of force.
- Chapter 2 has a streamlined discussion on categories and degrees of offenses and added materials on excuses for criminal behaviors.
- Chapter 3 contains new discussions on the role of the police in society, deadly force, global positioning system technology, and the opioid problem.
- In Chapter 4, we have reworked the discussion of the courts and added materials on evidence in courts.
- Chapter 5 has new materials on the incarceration of women and on prisoner classification.
- Chapter 6 has been updated with new references and new web activities to reflect changes in the system.
- Materials on sexting and gangs have been updated in Chapter 7, and a discussion on the future of juvenile justice has been totally reworked.
- The final chapter has added discussions on the opioid crisis and responses of the criminal justice system and also on technology and social media.

We are hopeful that you will like the changes. Please feel free to let us know what you think and pass on suggestions for future editions. Our goal is to make the book as useful as possible without adding unnecessary pages and costs to you.

The authors wish to thank the editorial and production staff at Oxford for all their insight and assistance. We thank the reviewers for the fifth edition: Frank Ferdik (University of West Florida), Michelle L. Foster (Kent State University), Dennis McCarty (University at Albany), and J. Michael Vecchio (Loyola University Chicago). We also need to thank the reviewers of the past editions for their suggestions. The book is all the better for the efforts of these and many other individuals. Of course, the responsibility for any flaws is ours.

Steven P. Lab
Marian R. Williams
Jefferson E. Holcomb
Melissa W. Burek
William R. King
Michael E. Buerger

CHAPTER 1

Crime, Criminal Justice, and Policy

CHAPTER OUTLINE

Introduction
What Is Crime?
Criminal Justice System Policy
Criminal Justice System Philosophy
    The Classical School
    The Positivist School
    Retribution
    Deterrence
    Rehabilitation
    Incapacitation
Measuring Crime
    Official Statistics
    Self-Report Statistics
    Victimization Studies
A System of Checks and Balances
    Individual Liberty Versus Societal Civility
    Crime Control Versus Due Process
    Other Competing Ideologies
    A Loosely Coupled System
    Discretion
    The Four Cs of the Criminal Justice System
        (Citizens, Cops, Courts, and Corrections)
Recent Trends in Criminal Justice
    Victims
    Social Media
    Use of Force

Conclusion
Key Words
Suggested Readings

After reading this chapter, you should be able to:

- Define deviance
- Provide examples of informal social control
- Define and differentiate between mala in se and mala prohibita
- Define public policy
- Discuss how policies are created
- Demonstrate knowledge of the Classical and Positivist schools of criminal justice
- Define and discuss retribution
- Discuss deterrence and its different types
- Discuss the rehabilitation approach to crime
- Define incapacitation
- Identify three methods for measuring crime and discuss each
- Explain what is meant by crime rate
- Discuss NIBRS and how it differs from the UCR
- Discuss the NCVS
- Relate the differences between the crime-control and due-process models of justice
- Show how the criminal justice system is actually a loosely coupled system
- Define discretion and its importance to criminal justice
- List the four Cs of the criminal justice system
- Point out how each of the four Cs is an important decision-making component of the criminal justice system
- Tell what is the courtroom workgroup
- Identify different technologies that are affecting criminal justice and relate why they are an issue

---

INTRODUCTION

Crime and societal responses to crime present a considerable problem in most societies. This chapter introduces some fundamental concepts concerning crime and criminal justice policy. First, crime and deviance are reviewed. Policy, the method by which problems are addressed, and the notion of criminal justice policy are discussed. The chapter then presents the different and sometimes contradictory philosophies of criminal justice (the Classical and Positivist schools, and retribution, deterrence, rehabilitation, and incapacitation). The chapter then returns to the notion of crime and reviews the three primary methods of measuring crime. Next, the chapter addresses different competing tensions in the criminal justice system, such as the tension between due process and crime control in processing, discretion, and four decision points in the system. Finally, the chapter concludes with a review of some recent trends in criminal justice.

Web Activity

See a translation of the earliest written criminal code, the Code of Hammurabi, at http://avalon.law.yale.edu/subject_menus/hammenu.asp.

WHAT IS CRIME?

Understanding crime is best begun with a discussion of a concept called **deviance**. Deviance refers to human behaviors or actions that are considered by others to be wrong, bad, or inappropriate. Some inappropriate acts are relatively minor, such as spitting on the sidewalk, while others, such as killing a person, are seen as being seriously deviant. Not all deviant acts are illegal. For example, in most places it is not illegal for men to wear women's clothing in public, but a man in a dress will usually draw stares and scorn from onlookers.

Deviance is location, time, person, and event specific, meaning that some behaviors could be considered normal or deviant depending on the circumstances. For example, it is considered normal to yell at a football game but deviant to yell in a library. This simply means that deviance is more than just a particular act; the person committing the act, the surrounding events, the time, and the location all help others define if someone's behavior should be deemed deviant.

Societies rely upon **informal social control** to influence people's behavior. Indeed, throughout most of history, social control was vested in the individuals (and their families) who were harmed, and communities would take informal actions, such as shaming and ostracizing violators of the community's norms. Examples of informal social control include staring, scorn, the cold shoulder, shunning, and telling people that they are doing something wrong. Societies still rely very heavily upon informal social control to keep people in conformity. Although anyone may attempt to engage in informal social control, some common agents of informal social control are parents, schoolteachers, employers, classmates, and fellow employees.

Informal social control can be very successful in family and small group settings in which everyone knows one another. The great growth of cities and the shift to large, diverse communities have diluted the impact of informal social controls. As a response to this social change, more formal means of dealing with unwanted behavior have been developed. In addition, some deviant acts are too serious to be managed via informal social control.

Serious deviance is prohibited by societies with written laws. These laws identify the prohibited deviant behaviors, the circumstances that make such behaviors illegal, and the possible punishment for violating them. For example, it is not illegal to kill another person in self-defense, but it is illegal to do so with premeditation. In modern society, laws are generally written and approved by elected legislators at either the federal or the state level. Local governments (e.g., towns and cities) may also pass their own laws. Crimes can be classified as either **mala in se** or **mala prohibita**. Mala in se acts such as murder, robbery, and rape are viewed as inherently evil and are thus often classified as serious crimes. Mala prohibita acts are less serious offenses such as underage drinking, speeding, and loitering. Mala prohibita acts are still considered crimes, but they are not viewed as inherently bad, only as behaviors that should be prohibited by law. A law is usually classified as either a **felony**, which is a serious breach of law usually carrying a penalty of more than one year in prison, or a **misdemeanor**, a less serious crime usually carrying a sentence of less than one year in prison. When someone engages in an illegal act, and the conditions of the act are not excused by a law, that person has broken the law and thus committed a crime.

Critical Thinking Exercise

Think about a time when someone used informal social control in response to your behavior. What were you doing, and what did the agent of informal social control do? Think about a time when you applied informal social control on another person. What was that person doing, and what did you do in response?

CRIMINAL JUSTICE SYSTEM POLICY

Policies are created to set a standard of how a problem or issue will be addressed. The criminal justice system engages in policy on a daily basis. From arrest policy to prosecution policy to sentencing policy, the system engages in practices to deal with crime. Throughout the history of the criminal justice system, various policies have been supported more than others, and the justification behind these policies has varied over time.

Public policy is *"a relatively stable, purposive course of action followed by an actor or set of actors in dealing with a problem or matter of concern. This definition focuses on what is actually done instead of what is only proposed or intended; differentiates a policy from a decision . . .; and views policy as something that unfolds over time"* (Anderson 2003: 2, emphasis in original). Simply, if crime is a problem, the criminal justice system and its policies represent society's response to that problem.

Historically, criminal justice policy, or lack thereof, first centered on revenge on the part of the victim. In Europe, between the collapse of the Roman Empire and 600 AD, it was common for individuals and families to act as their own criminal justice systems (Johnson and Wolfe 1996). These societies relied upon informal social control to keep order because they lacked contemporary elements of criminal justice, such as prisons and paid, full-time police. If a person was harmed by another, the victim had to seek his or her own justice, often violently, and if a person was killed, the victim's family had to seek justice from the offender or the offender's family. Since the government was not involved in this system of justice, there was little criminal justice policy.

As society changed and became more complex, the victim-centered system of justice did not work well and was replaced by governmental control of justice. Under governmental control of justice, the government assumes the role of deciding what behaviors are considered illegal, who are considered offenders and victims, and what the punishments are. As a result, when a law is broken and a crime is committed, the government acts as the victim, as it is the government's law that has been violated.

Public policies are created at different levels of government. At the highest level are policies created by the federal government, which apply to the federal criminal justice system but could also apply to state and local systems. These are macro-level policies. Public policies at the local level, called micro-level policies, are also used to enact or change criminal justice. Thus, state laws differ in the acts they prohibit and the punishments for violating these laws. Policies may also be created by governmental entities other than federal and state legislatures. The judicial branch creates policy by issuing court rulings, and the executive branch creates policy through executive orders. Within each of these branches, various agencies are able to create policies that are far-reaching or that apply only to the agency at hand. For instance, the Ohio Public Defender Commission outlines standards and guidelines that must be followed for its public defenders. At the local level, some towns and cities create their own policies, such as local ordinances banning loud car stereos. Finally, individual criminal justice organizations like jails and prisons or police agencies create their own internal policies, such as visitation requirements or minimum education requirements for police officers.

Web Activity

You can read a description of the three branches of the federal government (judicial, legislative, and executive) at http://en.wikipedia.org/wiki/Federal_government_of_the_United_States.

CRIMINAL JUSTICE SYSTEM PHILOSOPHY

Initially, the relationship between policy and crime sounds simple. Crime is a problem, so society chooses how to solve the problem and implements policy to effect the necessary solution. Unfortunately, combating crime is not so simple. Part of this complication is caused by differences in society's philosophies about what the criminal justice system *should* do. Because society is not unanimous in how it should respond to crime, criminal justice policy becomes more complicated. In some instances, certain criminal justice organizations will implement one type of policy, while other agencies will adopt other policies. Sometimes these policies compete with or contradict each other. Part of this complication is due to different philosophies of criminal justice.

The Classical School

The **Classical school** of criminal justice stemmed from the mid-18th-century writings of Cesare Beccaria. Beccaria argued that humans possess free will, are rational, and make choices about how to behave. Human behavior is influenced by each person's weighing of the costs of an action and the benefits he or she expects to receive. For example, someone contemplating robbery will weigh the possible rewards (getting money) against the possible costs (arrest and imprisonment) and decide whether to rob or not rob. Thus, criminals choose to commit crime by a process of rational thought.

Beccaria argued that punishments should be harsh enough to deter potential offenders but not overly punitive or cruel. Laws should be clearly written in advance and should specify the punishments for each crime. Mitigating factors, such as the criminal's personality, social circumstances, or financial need, should not be weighed by a judge or jury. Simply, the law should be applied evenly to everyone who breaks it. Deterrence is the cornerstone of classicism.

The Positivist School

The **Positivist school** of criminal justice developed after the Classical view was established. Positivists claim that human behavior is influenced by conditions and situations external to individuals that are beyond their control. For example, poverty and abusive parenting influence the likelihood that a child will grow up poor and abusive as well. The law would likely hold little deterrent value for this child since he or she may have learned only deviant behaviors and never learned prosocial behaviors.

Positivists contend that preventing crime results from intervening in the conditions that cause crime and not in stricter laws. Crime can be combated best by eliminating poverty, providing opportunity, improving parenting, or reducing contact with delinquent peers. Positivists disagree about the exact causes of crime, however, so their particular prescriptions for attacking the roots of crime differ. Under Positivism, no single cause of crime exists. Rather, different factors influence different people to act in different ways. This means that no single response will be effective in solving crime. Each situation/individual needs to be evaluated for the cause, and an intervention/response needs to be implemented. Two individuals may commit the same act (e.g., robbery) but do so for different reasons (one person does it to get money to feed his family, whereas another person does it in response to a previous conflict with the victim).

The Classical and Positivist schools provide a general overview of the potential causes and solutions to crime. Although some solutions involve an overhaul of social conditions, most come in the form of punishment. There is disagreement, however, over why, how, and to what extent punishment should be used. These disagreements are illustrated in four punishment philosophies: retribution, deterrence, rehabilitation, and incapacitation.

Retribution

Retribution is a philosophy based on the belief that criminals should be punished because they have violated the law. Thus, the criminal justice system exists to punish wrongdoers. Punishment should be commensurate with the harm committed by the criminal ("an eye for an eye"), which is in accord with the beliefs of those who follow the Classical school. Retribution, however, does not punish in order to prevent potential criminals from committing crime. Rather, advocates of retribution argue that punishment is the proper and just thing for a society to do, regardless of its effectiveness in preventing crime. This is sometimes called **just deserts**.

Retributivists favor the use of incarceration as a way to punish offenders. Lesser punishments such as probation and policies such as plea bargaining may not result in the punishment fitting the crime. Retributivists also favor the use of capital punishment, in accordance with the "eye for an eye" edict.

Deterrence

Like retribution, **deterrence** is the belief that offenders should be punished; however, punishment should have some other goal besides just deserts. Proponents of deterrence contend that punishments should prevent crime by making potential offenders aware of the costs of crime. In effect, potential offenders will know that they will be punished if they commit a crime. Because of the belief that people seek pleasure and avoid pain, deterrence advocates argue that the costs of crime need to outweigh its benefits; thus, individuals will refrain from crime. This belief is also drawn from the Classical school.

There are two types of deterrence: specific and general. **Specific deterrence** refers to deterring a particular offender. For example, a juvenile punished for skipping school will not skip again in order to avoid future punishment. **General deterrence** prevents people from committing crime by showing them, through the experiences of other punished criminals, that crime does not pay. For example, fellow students at the truant's school will probably not skip school in the future if they have learned of the punishment received by their friend for skipping. Thus, general deterrence predicts that a person does not need to be directly punished in order to be deterred.

Deterrence appears to work best when the punishment is *certain*, *severe*, and *quickly applied*. Offenders must be punished every time they commit a crime (*certainty*). Furthermore, the punishment must be *severe* enough to make punishment outweigh the benefits or fruits of the crime. Finally, the punishment must be inflicted soon after the crime is committed, which is sometimes called *celerity*.

A system dedicated to deterrence would try to maximize the certainty, severity, and celerity via policy. A deterrent system would find ways to increase the rate at which crimes are reported and offenders are caught. This might involve policies requiring that crime victims report their victimizations to authorities. A deterrent system would also have to ensure that the severity of punishment was painful enough to outweigh the benefits of crime. This could entail policies and laws that limit the discretion of workers in the criminal justice system; abolish plea bargains; and apply the law evenly to everyone, no matter what their status, gender, or other non-legal factors. Finally, the system would value speedy processing of suspects. There should be little delay between arrest, trial, and punishment.

Rehabilitation

Rehabilitation, which falls under Positivism, seeks to prevent crime by rectifying individual problems that are thought to be responsible for the criminal behavior. Simple punishment is not seen as an effective solution to crime. The philosophy of rehabilitation views criminals as "broken" and seeks to "repair" them by reformation and treatment. This philosophy assumes that criminals can be reformed. Once reformed, criminals will no longer engage in crime. Examples of rehabilitation include drug treatment, mental health counseling, changing how offenders think cognitively, and job training. Prisons and jails would be structured to be more therapeutic, rather than punishment oriented.

Rehabilitation requires some flexibility in the criminal justice system that allows for an individual focus on the offender. Each offender should be held in prison or jail or kept under supervision in the community until he or she is rehabilitated. Some offenders will be quickly rehabilitated, whereas others will require long periods of treatment. This individual focus requires differential sentences based on the needs of the offender and not solely on the crime. The staff of correctional facilities should also decide when an offender is rehabilitated and can be released. Rehabilitation would also entail the use of community supervision of offenders during which they receive treatment that will assist in their rehabilitation and reintegration into society.

Incapacitation

Incapacitation is the belief that the role of the criminal justice system is to separate or segregate criminals from the rest of society in order to protect society. If known criminals are removed from society, there should be less crime. Unlike retribution, incapacitation does not view segregation as a form of punishment. Rather, incapacitation is designed to keep offenders away from society.

Incapacitation also differs from rehabilitation in that it does not necessarily advocate treating offenders.

Incapacitation comes with its own policy implications. First, it entails an emphasis on using secure facilities, such as prisons and jails, rather than community corrections such as probation. This is not to say that community corrections cannot be used as part of incapacitation; rather, pure incapacitation would emphasize physical segregation. This segregation restrains offenders from engaging in further criminal activity. Incapacitation is the goal behind laws such as habitual-offender and "three-strikes" laws that incarcerate individuals if they continue to commit offenses. The idea is that previous punishment (if any) was not sufficient to deter or reform the offenders, so the system must resort to keeping them away from society for a long time in order to prevent further crime.

Critical Thinking Exercise

Each of these philosophies entails its own policy, to impel criminal justice employees to adhere to the policy's intent. Choose one of the philosophies discussed previously and write a policy designed to implement that philosophy at a particular step of the criminal justice process (i.e., to be implemented by the police, courts, or corrections). If you find this task easy, try writing a policy that satisfies the dictates of two or three of these philosophies. Do you find this to be easy or difficult?

MEASURING CRIME

Defining crime is relatively easy compared to the task of measuring crime, but crime is central to the existence of any criminal justice system, and measuring crime accurately is important. Accurate measures of crime are important because these measures give us better insights into the nature and extent of crime. For instance, we can determine if crime is increasing or if certain types of crime are becoming less common. Furthermore, measuring crime lets us predict crime trends and plan for future demands on the criminal justice system. Valid and reliable crime statistics also permit researchers to craft better theories of crime and criminal justice, which in turn help guide the administration of justice. Finally, good crime statistics can be used to evaluate criminal justice policies and programs. For example, we could use crime statistics to determine if a mandatory minimum sentencing policy prevents crime.

It is difficult to determine the amount of crime that actually occurs because many crimes do not come to the attention of the criminal justice system. For instance, many victims do not report their victimizations to the police. In addition, some victims may not even realize that they have been victims of crime. Research reveals that, on average, less than half of all victimizations are actually reported to authorities (Maguire and Pastore 2006). Because of this underreporting of crime, criminologists often refer to the total number of unreported crimes as the **dark figure of crime** (Biderman and Reiss 1967). Underreporting means that authorities in the criminal justice system often have great difficulty producing accurate crime statistics.

Web Activity

Look at data from Americans about their crime reporting practices at the *Sourcebook of Criminal Justice* website (http://www.albany.edu/sourcebook/tost_3.html#3_l). Do rates of crime reporting differ for different types of crime? How much do reporting rates change from one year to another?

Crime is usually expressed in one of two ways. The first way of expressing crime statistics is as a count. Counts simply report the total number of crimes reported over a given time span. Thus, a city might report that it had three homicides last year. Using raw counts is not without problems. Raw counts do not facilitate comparisons of different places with different populations. For example, in 2010, New York City reported a total of 536 murders and non-negligent manslaughters. During that same year, Philadelphia reported a total of 306 murders and non-negligent manslaughters (Federal Bureau of Investigation 2012). At first blush, Philadelphia seemed like a safer city in 2010. Philadelphia, however, has fewer inhabitants than New York City, so it would seem natural for it to have fewer homicides. A raw count of homicides does not allow us to fairly compare the two.

It is sometimes better to use a **crime rate** instead of a raw count. Rates are usually expressed as the number of events per 1,000 or 100,000 people (or residents) per year. For example, a city with a population of 100,000 people where 3 people were murdered in one year would report a homicide rate of 3.0 homicides per 100,000 population. Using the New York and Philadelphia numbers, the homicide rate in New York in 2010 was 6.6 per 100,000 population, while the homicide rate for Philadelphia in 2010 was 20.1 per 100,000. Not only do rates permit better comparisons of different cities or states but also they allow better analysis of crime trends over time. Cities and states grow and shrink over time. Rates control for these differences in populations. Regardless of the measurement, there are three general sources of crime statistics: official (reported) statistics, self-report statistics, and victimization statistics.

Web Activity

The Bureau of Justice Statistics' website (http://www.bjs.gov/ucrdata) has an easy-to-use data access program. You can look at crime statistics by state, region, or city, for different years and crime types.

Official Statistics

Official statistics are gathered from criminal justice agencies and represent the total number of crimes/cases brought to or handled by the agency. The number of crimes reported to the police and the number of arrests made are the most commonly reported official crime statistics. Other official statistics include those from the courts and corrections. Although police data are the most commonly reported, it is important to recall that only about 40 percent of crime victims report their victimization to the police. In addition, research indicates that police officers do not arrest all persons they encounter who are suspected of committing a crime (Smith and Visher 1981). These facts mean that both reported crimes and arrests are imperfect measures of crime.

The largest and best-known sources of official statistics in the United States are the Federal Bureau of Investigation's (FBI's) Uniform Crime Reports (UCR). The UCR collect police data on 29 crime categories and report the numbers of crimes reported to the police and the number of arrests for many of the police agencies in the United States (Maltz 1999). The UCR also provide demographic information on arrestees and circumstances of the more serious personal crimes. Since 1985, the FBI has also collected crime data from police agencies called the NIBRS (National Incident-Based Reporting System). The NIBRS still collects data on crimes reported to the police, but it also captures data on 49 offenses, as well as detailed information on offenders, victims, and the crime incidents for all offenses (Box 1.1). Unfortunately, the NIBRS is time- and labor-intensive, and only about one-third of police agencies that report to the UCR participate in the NIBRS.

Web Activity

The textbook website (http://www.oup.com/us/labessentials) has tables from the UCR for your inspection.

Official arrest statistics or crimes reported to the police can sometimes provide a reasonable estimate of crime, but one should always be careful when interpreting these official statistics. Police agencies can change their attention to certain events, and thus change their overall number of arrests, regardless of the true crime rate. For example, a police agency may deploy many officers in a redlight district in order to crack down on prostitution. This crackdown may yield a considerable increase in arrests for prostitution, although the true incidence of prostitution has not changed. An uninformed observer might wrongly conclude that the incidence of prostitution is increasing, when in fact the increase in arrests is a result of the police initiative designed to combat prostitution.

Similarly, crimes reported to the police represent just that—crimes for which the victims have notified the police of their victimization and the police chose to record them as victimizations. If the crime is not reported, if the police do not

BOX 1.1

Information Collected by NIBRS

Offense Information	*Offender Segment*
Bias motivation	Age, sex, race, ethnicity
Location type	
Number of premises entered	*Arrestee Segment*
Method of entry	Arrest date
Type of criminal activity/gang information	Type of arrest
Type of weapon/force involved	Multiple arrestee segments indicator
	Arrestee was armed with automatic weapon indicator
Property Segment	Age, sex, race, ethnicity
Type of property loss/etc.	Resident status
Property description	Disposition of arrestee under 18
Value of property	
Date recovered	*Victim Segment*
Number of stolen motor vehicles	Type of victim
Number of recovered motor vehicles	Age, sex, race, ethnicity
	Resident status
Suspected drug type	Aggravated assault/homicide circumstances
Estimated drug quantity	Additional justifiable homicide circumstances
Type of drug measurement	Type of injury
	Relationship of victim to offender

SOURCE: Federal Bureau of Investigation (2015). *National Incident-Based Reporting System.* https://ucr.fbi.gov/about-us/cjis/ucr/nibrs/2014/resource-pages/incidents-and-offenses_f.pdf

make an arrest, or if police choose to not record an incident as a crime, official statistics will not provide an accurate estimate of the true crime rate. This problem carries through to the court and correctional statistics because courts and correctional institutions receive most of their cases from the police.

Self-Report Statistics

Self-report statistics overcome some of the limitations of official statistics. Self-report statistics are gathered from people by asking them to report the number of times they have committed a crime during a set period of time in the past.

For example, since 1975, the Monitoring the Future project has surveyed youths about a range of attitudes and activities, including alcohol and drug use and delinquent behavior. These types of surveys may ask high school seniors how many times they have smoked marijuana during the past year. The respondents are usually promised **confidentiality**, which means that the reports cannot be linked to specific individuals.

Self-report statistics avoid some problems associated with official statistics. For example, they are often better at discovering crimes that the victim did not bother reporting to authorities. Furthermore, self-report statistics are good for exploring crimes where there is no victim, called **victimless crimes**, such as illegal drug use or underage drinking. Self-reports are also good for uncovering less serious offenses such as drug use or shoplifting and for learning about crimes where an arrest is unlikely (Hindelang, Hirschi, and Weis 1979).

Web Activity

Data from the Monitoring the Future project, a major source of self-report data, can be found at http://monitoringthefuture.org.

Unfortunately, there are problems associated with self-report statistics. First, respondents may exaggerate or underreport their criminal behavior. Respondents may exaggerate their criminal activity in order to reinforce their self-concept as tough characters. Conversely, respondents may underreport because they forgot their criminal activities, because they did not know that what they had done was illegal, or because they are afraid to reveal their past criminal activities. Second, *who* is surveyed about their criminal activity is important. Most self-report surveys target high school populations since they are easily identified and available. Self-reports are much more rare from adults; thus, the data are typically useful only for understanding youthful misbehavior. Giving a self-report survey to high school seniors at their high school is also likely to lead one to underestimate the true incidence of crime committed by 17- and 18-year-olds. This is due to the fact that serious criminals in this age range are more likely to be suspended from school, might be skipping school on that day, or might be locked up in secure juvenile facilities. Thus, self-reports have limitations and do not yield a completely accurate estimate of the true crime rate.

Victimization Studies

The third type of crime statistic comes from **victimization studies**. In victimization studies, people are asked if they have been victims of crimes during a past time period. One example is the National Crime Victimization Survey (NCVS). The NCVS is a nationally representative survey of U.S. households designed to measure criminal victimization. The survey is conducted annually by the Bureau of the Census for the Department of Justice's Bureau of Justice Statistics. As with self-report studies, victimization studies sometimes encounter problems. For example, respondents may forget victimizations, lie, or fail to tell the interviewers about their victimizations. Sometimes victims will "telescope" a victimization from outside the survey time span. For example, a victimization survey may only be concerned with crimes committed during 2016, but a respondent may report that a 2015 assault occurred during 2016. The dangers of lying, underreporting, and telescoping can all be combated by various methodological techniques. For example, the NCVS uses a technique called *bounding* to mitigate the likelihood that a respondent will telescope.

Web Activity

Data from the NCVS can be found at the textbook website (http://www.oup.com/us/labessentials).

Overall, these three techniques for measuring crime provide estimates of the dark figure of crime. It is important, however, to keep in mind their limitations when using each one. Each method is subject to problems that may affect the accuracy of the estimate derived.

Critical Thinking Exercise

Which type of statistic would be best suited to study homicide in U.S. cities? What about the sexual abuse of young children? What statistic would be best suited to studying drug use by high school students? In general, for each of the three types of data (official, self-report, and victimization), what types of crime is each best suited to capture? What types of crime is each poorly suited to capture?

A SYSTEM OF CHECKS AND BALANCES

Some believe that the criminal justice system in the United States is too punitive when dealing with offenders, whereas others believe it is not punitive enough. The criminal justice system in the United States attempts to strike a balance between these two concerns.

Individual Liberty Versus Societal Civility

The first important characteristic of criminal justice in the United States is that it represents a balance between a number of opposing forces. First, the system tries to balance the rights of people to do what they want with the requirement that society remains civil, calm, and relatively crime free. Thus, the government imposes restrictions on individual behavior through laws and creates the agencies designed to enforce them in an attempt to keep society orderly. This desire for order must be balanced, however, with the public's desire for freedom to do what it wants. If there is too much governmental restriction, people are oppressed. On the other hand, society will veer toward disorder and chaos if there is too much individual freedom. The competing forces of individual liberty must be balanced with the desire for societal order at all levels of criminal justice and all stages of the system.

Crime Control Versus Due Process

Writing in 1968, Herbert Packer noted that the criminal justice system balances the competing philosophies of crime control and due process in its operations. The **crime-control model** advocates the aggressive and quick apprehension, trial, and processing of criminals. Briefly, this crime-control orientation seeks to prevent crime via a number of processes, such as deterrence and incapacitation, and cares less about ensuring that suspects are given specific legal rights. Crime control emphasizes that the system efficiently processes suspects in order to suppress crime. On the other hand, the **due-process model** is more concerned with the process of justice and grants suspects many rights to protect them from overzealous investigation and prosecution. In a due-process model, the system should carefully ensure that individual rights are not violated. In other words, a due-process perspective is concerned less with suppressing crime than with ensuring that individuals are not unfairly harmed by their government. In reality, the criminal justice system embodies a balance between these competing philosophies via the creation of policy, although the system constantly swings between these two extremes.

Other Competing Ideologies

Balancing competing ideologies also applies to the philosophies of criminal justice discussed previously. In effect, the system constantly oscillates among these four competing philosophies and, in many cases, decisions are based on satisfying two or three of these ideologies. This constant mixture of philosophies means that advocates of one philosophy are never completely happy because the system never fully implements their version of justice. Instead, the system operates under all four philosophies in most situations. A mix of philosophies is sometimes evident when individual criminal justice employees make decisions. For example, a judge might decide upon a defendant's sentence length based on the amount of time required for rehabilitation, but the judge may also want to punish the offender and send a deterrent message to the community. The criminal justice system cannot be viewed as being committed to any one philosophy; rather, the operation of criminal justice is a simultaneous combination of these different ideologies.

A Loosely Coupled System

Unlike many nations, where there is one national criminal justice system, criminal justice in the United States is composed of many loosely coupled, semiautonomous organizations. For example, instead of one national police force, there are more than 20,000 separate police agencies, each acting as a separate, independent agency. Likewise, instead of one court system, there are county, state, and federal courts, and cities and towns have municipal courts. There are thousands of local jails and hundreds of prisons (both state and federal). In addition, there are thousands of probation and parole agencies, as well as thousands of juvenile courts. Why have Americans created so many organizations to deal with crime and disorder?

This loosely coupled system reflects Americans' distrust of large government and their preference for local control. In some states, certain criminal justice positions are elected, such as sheriffs and judges, whereas other positions on parole boards are appointed. In this way, citizens exercise local control over their criminal justice system. This loosely coupled system also facilitates a system of checks and balances, where the decisions of one criminal justice agency are reviewed by later criminal justice agencies. For example, prosecutors usually conduct pretrial screenings with arrestees to decide if charges will be filed or the case dropped. In effect, prosecutors review the work of the police officers responsible for an arrest and decide if the suspect should be charged. There is less pressure for prosecutors to rubber-stamp arrests and charge suspects, for prosecutors do not work for their local police agencies.

The separation of these criminal justice components facilitates the review of decisions. Likewise, the prosecutor's decision to charge is not the final decision. Judges have the opportunity to review this decision and, if the case goes to trial, either a judge or a jury will evaluate the defendant's guilt. In this way, criminal justice in the United States embodies a system of loosely coupled agencies that check the decisions made by other agencies. Although it may appear cumbersome and inefficient at times to have so many different agencies dispensing justice, the system protects citizens from a single, all-powerful state. It allows local areas to tailor their criminal justice systems to their own local needs and permits the creation of particular balances of competing forces, such as crime control and due process and also rehabilitation and retribution.

Discretion

Discretion is an important attribute of the criminal justice system; in fact, the system could not function without it. Prior to the mid-1950s, however, few people understood or appreciated the nature or importance of discretion (Walker 1993: 6–8). Discretion involves decision-making by people involved in criminal justice— most often, but not always, employees of criminal justice agencies. These people are usually referred to as criminal justice actors. For example, a police officer decides to stop one motorist but not another. A judge imposes a longer sentence on one convicted criminal than on a criminal with a similar record who has committed the same crime. A parole board releases one prisoner early but not another. These choices represent discretionary decision-making by criminal justice actors.

Discretion involves legal and permissible decisions by criminal justice actors, including acting and choosing to not act (Klockars 1985: 93). Discretion does not include decision-making where actors break agency rules or the law, such as instances of corruption or misconduct. But within the bounds of permissible decision-making there are a wide range of possible actions available for both actors and agencies. Discretion is fundamental to the criminal justice system; it is like the thread that constitutes the cloth of the criminal justice system. The next section treats the criminal justice system as a series of four decision points that involve discretionary decisions.

The Four Cs of the Criminal Justice System (Citizens, Cops, Courts, and Corrections)

The American criminal justice system can be viewed as a conglomeration of quasi-independent organizations, each processing the outputs of the previous agency. The system can also be viewed as a process model, whereby decisions made by one system component influence the following components. This system model can be called "the four Cs of the criminal justice system." The process model highlights the importance of decision-making by individuals in the system. Figure 1.1 portrays this model of criminal justice.

Citizens

The first of the system's Cs are people not employed by the system, called citizens. The decisions made by crime victims, complainants, and offenders are crucial for understanding how the system works, for citizens provide the vast majority of inputs for the rest of the system. For example, research indicates that the majority of people arrested by the police are arrested based on the complaint of another citizen. Furthermore, as stated previously, research indicates that victims do not always call the police to report crimes. This rate of reporting varies depending on the seriousness of the crime, as victims of serious crimes are more likely to report their victimizations. Reporting rates also differ depending on the type of crime. For example, roughly 80 percent of vehicle theft victims report their loss to the police compared to 30 percent of theft victims who lost less than $50 (Bureau of Justice Statistics, 2017).

Web Activity

You can investigate reporting rates by crime types using the NCVS Victim Analysis Tool at https://www.bjs.gov/index.cfm?ty=nvat.

Figure 1.1 What is the sequence of events in the criminal justice system?

SOURCE: US Department of Justice, Office of Justice Programs, Bureau of Justice Statistics. https://www.bjs.gov/content/largechart.cfm.

Some states have responded to the underreporting of crime by using two different policies. The first policy involves passing laws that require people to report specific crimes to authorities. In many states, physicians, teachers, and social workers are mandated by law to report suspected cases of child abuse. Some states have also sought to eliminate victims' unwillingness to press charges by requiring that police officers arrest certain types of offenders, even if the victims do not request arrest. This is particularly common in domestic violence cases.

Cops

The second decision-making point of the system consists of the police and other law enforcement agents. Police officers do not patrol the streets arresting everyone suspected of committing a crime; rather, officers selectively enforce the law. In many instances, an officer chooses *not* to arrest, even when there is probable cause. Not fully enforcing all the laws all the time is a good thing; the full enforcement of every law is not possible, and society would probably not tolerate it (Klockars 1985). Again, the police exercise considerable discretion about what situations to get involved in and how to resolve these situations. The police decision to arrest is influenced considerably by the seriousness of the suspected offense, the wishes of the victim or complainant, and the demeanor of the suspect (Smith and Visher 1981). The letter of the law only plays a part in an officer's arrest decision, and in the majority of cases, the police do not make arrests.

Policies have been implemented in the hopes of controlling how police officers act. As mentioned previously, some state laws require that police officers arrest suspects who are believed to have committed domestic violence. In this way, policymakers hope to control the unwillingness of some victims to press charges. Such policies also take discretion away from police officers, who will often not arrest in such situations. Individual law enforcement agencies can also create rules and regulations to control employee behaviors. Many agencies have rules mandating when officers may use deadly force and engage in vehicle pursuits, for example (Walker 1993).

Courts

The third decision-making point is composed of court workers, such as pretrial intake workers, prosecutors, defense attorneys, and judges. This third decision point is unique, for not all of the people who work in this area are employed by a particular court, nor are they necessarily employed by the criminal justice system. For example, defendants may employ their own defense attorneys who are not employed by the government. Thus, courtroom decisions are not made by members of the same organization but, rather, by a range of actors who meet in a court "arena." This is known as the **courtroom workgroup**. The workgroup members exercise considerable discretion about a range of decisions, such as whether cases should be plea bargained, sent to trial, or dismissed. The workgroup often negotiates the charges to be brought and the possible sentences. For example, a prosecutor may negotiate a plea agreement with the defense attorney, reduce the charges against a suspect, and recommend a possible sentence to the judge. Likewise, defendants and defense attorneys can also decide to accept a plea bargain or invoke their right to a trial. Finally, judges make important decisions concerning such things as the admissibility of evidence and sentencing.

Decisions made by court workers are also affected by policy. For instance, a judge will set policy regarding the way in which his or her courtroom will operate. Further policies, in the form of laws, mandate a range of activities, such as how soon a trial must be held, how plea bargaining and trials are conducted, and how defendants are sentenced.

Corrections

The final decision-making point is composed of criminal justice system employees who work in corrections and includes probation and parole officers, correctional officers, and workers who provide services to offenders, such as social workers. Probation and parole officers are responsible for the supervision of offenders in the community, and correctional officers are responsible for maintaining security in a correctional institution, whether it is jail or prison.

The behaviors of correctional workers are also shaped and constrained by policy. For instance, state and federal laws mandate that prisoners have the right to adequate medical care while incarcerated. In other instances, the policies are created by individual correctional agencies and might cover such activities as how often probationers are drug tested or what happens to probationers who fail drug tests. Policies also cover such things as appropriate dress codes for employees and the procedures for dealing with offenders who do not follow the conditions of probation or the rules of the institution.

Each of these decision points is composed of multiple people and actors, all of whom influence the future of the criminal case, the suspect, and the victim. Thus, if a crime victim chooses to not report a crime, it is unlikely that the system will become involved. Likewise, the actors at each of these decision points interact and often negotiate the outcome of that decision point. Such negotiation is common during these discretionary interchanges. Discretion is important for running the system, and understanding discretion is crucial to understanding the system. Despite this, society has long been concerned with controlling and guiding these discretionary decisions in criminal justice (Gottfredson and Gottfredson 1988; Walker 1993). Controlling discretion is an important goal for the system, as it hopes to ensure fair and uniform processes. These attempts at controlling discretion often take the form of policies that are found throughout the system.

RECENT TRENDS IN CRIMINAL JUSTICE

The criminal justice system, like other social entities, responds to new or emerging issues in society at large. Three recent changes of note are the role of victims in the process of justice, the influence of social media, and controversies about police use of force.

Victims

Although the police are often referred to as the gatekeepers of criminal justice (because they decide about arrest), decisions made by victims are hugely important across the entire system. In some ways, victims are the true gatekeepers of criminal justice. For example, research consistently finds that victims report their victimization to criminal justice authorities only 40 percent of the time. Even after a crime is reported, victims continue to influence the process. When the police respond to the scene of a crime, research shows that officers are more likely to arrest a suspect if the victim asks for an arrest. Conversely, police are less likely to arrest when the victim asks for leniency from the police. If an arrest is made, victims still influence the process. For example, victims may help the police and prosecution by cooperating with the investigation, appearing for hearings and trial, and sometimes by prodding police and prosecutors to persist in the investigation or prosecution. On the other hand, victims may choose to slow or even halt the process—for example, by not talking with investigators or prosecutors, asking to drop charges, or disappearing (i.e., moving and not providing forwarding information). It is difficult to prosecute a case when the witness no longer wishes to cooperate with the prosecution.

After an investigation, victims may also influence the process by being visible in the media (e.g., by sitting in court during the trial and appearing on TV) and by providing victim impact statements in court during sentencing. Also, victims may continue to exert pressure during parole hearings (when offenders are eligible for release from prison). In some states, legislation requires that each victim be notified whenever his or her offender is eligible for parole or has been released from prison. Compliance with victim notification laws—that is, ensuring that prosecutors or correctional authorities notify victims—can be difficult. In some instances, the crime occurred decades prior to the offender's parole hearing or release, and authorities can no longer locate the victim.

Social Media

Advances in technology, especially personal technologies such as cell phones, have radically changed Western societies during the latter half of the 20th century. These advances, especially social media, have also influenced criminals, crime, victims, and criminal justice. For example, technology provides new avenues for criminals and for victimization, such as identity theft, revenge porn, phishing, and credit card fraud. Social media has become a common element of daily life, from texting to live streaming, Facebook, Twitter, and Snapchat. By the time this book is published, we imagine students will chuckle at our dated references to old social media formats.

Social media more closely ties individuals together in certain ways and thus has changed the nature of crime, victimization, criminal justice, and the public's perceptions of all these topics. Social media has changed crime because it introduces a range of new techniques for victimizing people. For example, criminals can now access sensitive information by hacking large databases held by social media companies, stealing a cell phone, phishing, or posting a fraudulent appeal for money on social media. Similarly, new forms of victimization have now appeared that did not exist before the spread of social media. Revenge porn, whereby one person posts embarrassing images of a victim on social media, was unheard of (and in many instances not even illegal) in pre-social media times. Terrorists may now self-radicalize themselves at home by viewing content from extremist groups online.

Social media has also become a useful tool for criminal justice. Victims have live-streamed crimes in progress and their pursuit of criminals. Police and prosecutors have used social media as evidence against criminals. For example, some police agencies monitor social media accounts associated with criminal gangs to identify who is affiliated with the gang and to gather evidence about criminal activities. Some criminals have posted pictures and video of their crimes on social media, and those posts have subsequently been used by law enforcement. At a more global level, criminal justice agencies have created social media accounts, which they use to inform the public about agency activities, to warn about ongoing incidents in real time, or to crowdsource help from the public. Social media also makes it easier for communication among employees in the criminal justice system.

Social media also greatly influences the public's perceptions of crime and criminal justice. No longer must we wait for news to be filtered through a TV station for broadcast in the evening or for the evening newspaper to land on our doorstep. With social media, just about anyone with a cell phone and a social media account can broadcast to a large audience. The ubiquity of video and pictures in social media has increased the speed at which the public expects to see events. For example, in the wake of police shootings of citizens, it is commonplace to hear calls for the immediate posting of video of the event, such as an officer's body camera video. Criminal justice agencies sometimes delay releasing evidence on social media because they are still investigating the incident or considering legal action and do not wish to (potentially) taint the process.

The increasing spread of social media has made it easier for people to communicate and has increased the amount of communication. Social media has also increased the access to, and the amount of, information available to people. At first blush, the increased amount of information appears to be a positive development for social control and criminal justice, but there are disadvantages. First, greater information is also available to criminals. Potential terrorists can learn effective methods for spreading terror. Criminals can gather information about potential victims from their profiles. The increasing amount of information readily available can also make it more difficult for people to find pertinent information and to make decisions. In other words, it is sometimes difficult to sift through all the information on social media to find exactly what one needs, and the sifting process can become overwhelming.

Critical Thinking Exercise

What new forms of social media do you think will arise in the next decade? How will these advances influence citizens, crime, social control, and criminal justice?

Use of Force

In a classic treatise, Egon Bittner (1970) argued that the only unique contribution the police (and most of the criminal justice system) make to society is that they are the system via which the state (the government) distributes non-negotiable, coercive force on its citizens. Society desires peace and finds the naked application of physical force to be intolerable. However, there are times when conditions require that someone with the authority to use force intercedes. Such situations create a tension between our desire as citizens to be free from governmental agents using force and our desire for civility and peace.

The use of force by criminal justice actors is a controversial topic in American society, and it has been controversial since the first days of the country. Periodically, public attention is riveted on use of force and widespread debate ensues, followed by reforms in criminal justice. For example, controversial police use of force in a number of large US cities in the 1960s resulted in a wave of riots and then a decade of police reform. Likewise, deadly prison riots in the 1960s, such as the riot at Attica prison in New York state, led to reforms in corrections.

Given this history, it is not wholly surprising that recent years have seen a heated public controversy about the degree, nature, and appropriateness of use of force in criminal justice. The majority of this debate has centered on publicized instances of police use of force with citizens, usually involving deadly force and often involving African American citizens. The catalyst for this debate is generally attributed to the killing (by a police officer) of Michael Brown in Ferguson, Missouri, in August 2014. The death led to weeks of public street protests in Ferguson and other communities throughout the United States. Subsequent police shootings in other cities added to the heated debate and eventually led to the creation of the President's Task Force on 21st Century Policing.

In some ways, the recent discussion about use of force seems new. The debates are often centered around very compelling video and audio of police–citizen interactions. Social media and cell phone technology have greatly increased the amount of video recorded of criminal justice employees and have facilitated the immediate sharing of such videos with others. Yet, the topics are as timeless as the controversies about use of force in criminal justice dating back to the late 1700s.

CONCLUSION

As evidenced in this chapter, the criminal justice system is a rather complex mix of philosophies and policies. These philosophies and policies cannot exist, however, without individuals whose job it is to keep the criminal justice system operational.

Individuals create policies based on their own philosophy of how they believe the criminal justice system should operate. The individuals who shape these policies represent a broad spectrum of society—legislators, judges, prosecutors, police, and victims—who have different ideas as to how to deal with the crime problem. What is evident is that no philosophy or policy is perfect for every individual, so the system must continually try to improve itself by creating and enacting more policy—a cycle that never ends.

Critical Thinking Exercise

This chapter has outlined four very large historical trends in criminal justice. What trends do you think we will see during the next 20 to 30 years? How will the system react to these larger social trends, and how will justice be affected?

KEY WORDS

Classical school	due-process model	official statistics
confidentiality	felony	Positivist school
courtroom workgroup	general deterrence	rehabilitation
crime-control model	incapacitation	retribution
crime rate	informal social control	self-report statistics
dark figure of crime	just deserts	specific deterrence
deterrence	mala in se	victimization studies
deviance	mala prohibita	victimless crimes
discretion	misdemeanor	

SUGGESTED READINGS

Bittner, E. (1970). *The functions of the police in modern society: A review of background factors, current practices, and possible role models.* Bethesda, MD: Center for Studies of Crime and Delinquency, National Institute of Mental Health.

Gottfredson, M., and D. Gottfredson. (1988). *Decision-making in criminal justice: Toward the rational exercise of discretion.* New York: Plenum Press.

Holtfreter, K., and K. A. Wattanaporn. (2013). An examination of gender responsiveness for female offender reentry. *Criminal Justice and Behavior, 41*(1), 41–57.

Johnson, H., and N. Wolfe. (1996). *History of criminal justice,* 2nd ed. Cincinnati, OH: Anderson Publishing.

Klockars, C. (1985). *The idea of the police.* Beverly Hills, CA: Sage.

Pew Center on the States. (2011). *State of recidivism: The revolving door of America's prisons.* Washington, DC: The Pew Charitable Trusts.

Walker, S. (1998). *Popular justice: A history of American criminal justice,* 2nd ed. New York: Oxford University Press.

CHAPTER 2

Issues of Law

CHAPTER OUTLINE

History of Law in the United States
Sources of Law in the United States
    Constitutions
    Legislative
    Executive
    Judicial
Substantive Law
Types of Crimes
    Crimes Against the Person
    Crimes Against Property
    Crimes Against Public Order
    Drug Offenses
    White-Collar Offenses
Defenses to Criminal Liability
    Justification
    Excuses
    Mental Capacity
Victim's Rights
Recent Trends in Substantive Criminal Law
    The Internet and Substantive Criminal Law
    Terrorism, Homeland Security, and Criminal Law
Procedural Law
    Fourth Amendment
    Fifth Amendment
    Sixth Amendment
    Eighth Amendment

Incorporation
Trends in Procedural Criminal Law
Conclusion
Key Words
Suggested Readings

After reading this chapter, you should be able to:

- Discuss the historical bases of law in the United States
- List and discuss the sources of law in the United States
- Point out the differences between constitutional, legislative, executive, and judicial sources of law
- Define substantive law and provide two examples
- Distinguish between mala in se and mala prohibita
- List and define different types/categories of crimes
- Identify two defenses to criminal liability
- Discuss how the internet has affected substantive law
- Point out how terrorism has affected criminal law
- Define procedural law
- List and discuss the amendments to the U.S. Constitution that outline criminal procedural rights
- Tell what incorporation means
- Discuss how the internet has affected procedural law

Laws are sets of rules that govern the conduct of individuals, groups, businesses, government entities, and the like. Laws are created and enforced by the power of the state—that is, local, state, and federal government bodies. The U.S. Constitution gives the responsibility of law creation to the federal legislature, the U.S. Congress. The Constitution also allows the federal court system to "interpret" the laws created by the federal legislature. In doing so, the federal courts work to ensure that the laws that are created are fair and applied equally to all citizens.

The various state constitutions also give the responsibility of law creation to their respective state legislatures. Just like the federal system, states allow their court systems to interpret the laws in much the same way as the federal courts. Within states, legislative bodies such as county commissions and city councils create laws that apply to their **jurisdiction**.

As stated previously, the federal and state legislatures create laws that govern the behavior of a variety of entities. Individuals are subject to laws that prohibit certain types of conduct, such as killing a person or burning down a house. Groups of individuals who assemble are required by law to do so peacefully and not to incite riots. The conduct of businesses is regulated so that businesses do not engage in fraudulent practices or environmental harm. Government entities are required to follow the law as well, in that they cannot engage in discriminatory practices when they enforce the law. In addition to these prohibitions, the law ensures that violators will be punished. These are just a few examples of the law, but the main point is that the law applies to everyone, even those government bodies that are responsible for law creation. This is known as the "rule of law" and is traced back to the early origins of American law (Rembar 1989).

HISTORY OF LAW IN THE UNITED STATES

American law is rooted in European, particularly English, law. Historically, English law was largely unwritten and parochial, in that communities relied on local customs and norms to guide conduct. These customs were transmitted from generation to generation and were altered occasionally if necessary. After the Norman Conquest in the 11th century, William the Conqueror instituted a practice of collecting these customs and norms and recording them so that they could be applied to the country as a whole. This practice of transforming unwritten local customs into written codes of behavior for the entire country established the English tradition of **common law**, or law that was common to all throughout the country. Local judges were responsible for applying the common law, and their decisions were recorded to help guide future judges when making their decisions. This is known as **precedent**, and this practice continues to exist today.

Over time, local English judges refined and recorded many laws, many of which were criminal laws. By the 17th century, these judges had created the crimes of murder, robbery, arson, and rape, among others. Judges also created less serious crimes, such as libel, perjury, and disturbing the peace (see generally, Blackstone 2002).

The criminal law that exists today is taken from the English tradition of common law. The United States was founded by British colonists who brought their legal tradition to American shores. After declaring independence from England in 1776, the new states incorporated the English common law and adopted many of the criminal laws that had been defined. The newly created federal government chose not to incorporate English common law. Instead, Congress established its own laws, including criminal laws, that were similar in content to common law but not directly taken from it. An exception to the incorporation of common law is Louisiana, which bases its law on the Napoleonic Code, a uniform system of laws adopted by Napoleon from ancient Roman law.

SOURCES OF LAW IN THE UNITED STATES

Although English common law is the root of most of the law in the United States, various government bodies are responsible for shaping, applying, and interpreting the law. As stated previously, the responsibility for law creation lies with legislatures, which create **statutory law**. Other government entities, however, are also involved in the creation of the law. The most important entities, state and federal constitutions, are the highest sources of law in the country. Other entities represent all branches of government—legislative, executive, and judicial.

Constitutions

Constitutions are considered the highest sources of law in the United States. All other laws that are created must abide by constitutions. Each state and the federal government has its own constitution, which outlines the structure of the government and how it will operate. These constitutions designate government power, indicating what the government can and cannot do. This is called **constitutional law**. For instance, California's constitution specifies that tax money cannot be used to support religious schools (see Constitution of California, Article 9, Section 8), and the federal constitution specifies that the federal government cannot abridge an individual's freedom of speech (see U.S. Constitution, Amendment 1). State constitutions are the highest form of law in each state, but the U.S. Constitution is the highest form of law in the country. All laws (state and federal) and state constitutions must abide by the U.S. Constitution. Any law or constitution that conflicts with the U.S. Constitution is not allowed to stand.

Web Activity

For links to and interesting facts about the U.S. Constitution, go to https://www .archives.gov/exhibits/charters/constitution.html.

Legislative

Aside from the actual legislature, the legislative branch creates government bodies that carry out some lawmaking responsibilities. These bodies are typically referred to as agencies, bureaus, and so forth. These administrative agencies include federal bodies such as the Federal Communications Commission and the Food and Drug Administration (FDA), as well as state bodies such as the Ohio Public Defender Commission. Administrative agencies have the responsibility of enforcing **administrative law**. Administrative law encompasses rules and policies that govern an agency's responsibilities. For example, the FDA establishes guidelines for allowing medicines to be available to consumers either by prescription or over the counter. The Ohio Public Defender Commission establishes guidelines for its public defenders to follow when representing poor defendants. Although created by the legislature, these agencies typically fall under the executive branch due to their regulatory and enforcement activities.

Web Activity

See https://www.fda.gov and https://www.fcc.gov for more information about the Food and Drug Administration and the Federal Communications Commission, respectively. Also, see http://opd.ohio.gov/About-Us/About-the-Office for more information about the Ohio Public Defender Commission.

Executive

The executive branch also has some law-creation responsibility. The executive branch is composed of individuals such as mayors, governors, and the president. These individuals have limited lawmaking ability, and the laws that are created are usually quite narrow and issue specific; however, they are important nonetheless. For example, a mayor may impose a curfew in a particular city, or the president may impose regulations on driving cars through national forests.

Web Activity

For more information about a particular lawmaking ability of the president—the executive order—go to https://www.archives.gov/federal-register/executive-orders/disposition.html.

Judicial

The judicial branch of government, embodied by the various state and federal courts, also engages in law creation. During the early period of common law in England, local judges were primarily responsible for creating and disseminating laws throughout the country. Today, however, judges have been stripped of most of their lawmaking authority. Whenever a judge makes a decision in a particular case, he or she is engaging in law creation. This type of law, called **case law**, is usually based on laws that were created by some other body. For instance, in the early 1960s, the state of Florida did not allow a poor defendant to have an attorney provided to him or her. In 1963, the U.S. Supreme Court ruled that Florida and other states must provide poor defendants with an attorney in certain criminal cases (*Gideon v. Wainwright* [1963]). As a result, the U.S. Supreme Court engaged in law creation by forcing the states to adopt its mandate.

Web Activity

For more information about the U.S. Supreme Court, go to https://www.supremecourt.gov.

SUBSTANTIVE LAW

Regardless of which government body creates the law, the law is either substantive or procedural in nature. **Substantive law** is often called the "what" of the law and basically defines rights and duties. On the other hand, **procedural law** describes the procedures that must be followed when carrying out the law. An example of substantive law is a law that defines first-degree murder as the deliberate, premeditated killing of another. An example of procedural law is law that states that poor defendants must be given an attorney if charged with certain crimes. Procedural law is discussed later in this chapter.

Two primary examples of substantive law are civil law and criminal law. **Civil law** deals with issues pertaining to private matters between two individuals. Civil law encompasses torts (e.g., wrongful injury), contracts and property issues, and domestic relations. Civil law allows individuals who feel wronged by another to take their cases to court for a remedy. For example, if person A is involved in an automobile accident with person B, who is uninsured, person A may sue person B in civil court for the money needed to replace the disabled car. Civil law also governs issues such as divorces, child custody, inheritance, and wills. The victim is responsible for pursuing the case against the accused.

Criminal law is another primary example of substantive law. Criminal law concerns issues between the government and individuals who are accused of violating government-created laws. Unlike civil law, in which an individual is responsible for finding a remedy to his or her problem, criminal law involves the government prosecuting an individual if that individual has committed a crime. In criminal law, the state is considered the victim and pursues the case. The actual individual who is victimized in the crime is relegated to the role of witness for the state.

Web Activity

For more information about the differences between civil law and criminal law, see the textbook website (http://www.oup.com/us/labessentials).

Substantive criminal law is defined by government bodies, and it specifies what individuals can and cannot do and the punishments for wrongdoing. This is called the **principle of legality.** This means the government cannot punish individuals for wrongdoing unless a law exists to define the conduct as a crime and to prescribe a punishment for it. Traditionally, individual conduct has been defined as **mala in se**, or inherently bad, and **mala prohibita**, or prohibited but not necessarily bad. Governments have considered acts such as murder and rape as mala in se and acts such as gambling and speeding as mala prohibita. As a result, behaviors that are considered inherently bad are typically punished more severely than others.

Critical Thinking Exercise

Develop a list of mala prohibita laws and discuss each one. Should they be prohibited? Why? What impact does enforcement of such laws have on the criminal
justice system? What value do these laws have for society in general? What negative effect might these laws have on society?

When governments specify which behaviors to deem criminal, the crimes
must have two elements: act and intent. The act, called **actus reus**, is the most
important element of criminal liability. It represents the physical action involved
in conduct. The act must be voluntary, in that it is not the result of coercion or
some condition that affects voluntary movement (e.g., a seizure). For example, for
the crime of larceny, the act would be the taking of another's property.

Although a voluntary act is needed to establish actus reus, there are instances
in which a failure to act constitutes actus reus. In these cases, an **act of omission** can
result in criminal liability. The act of omission comes into play when individuals are
required by law to act but fail to do so. For example, lifeguards are required by law to
aid drowning individuals; failure to do so can result in criminal liability. The same
is true of physicians, who are legally bound to tend to patients in their care.

Critical Thinking Exercise

Read about the story of Kitty Genovese, a very famous case dealing with individuals who failed to act (see *The New York Times* story at the time: http://www.
nytimes.com/1964/03/27/37-who-saw-murder-didnt-call-the-police.html). Some
states have proposed legislation called good Samaritan laws, which impose criminal liability on individuals who witness crimes but do nothing to stop them. This
would create a type of act of omission. What are the advantages and disadvantages of having such laws in place? What would be the difficulties in enforcing
such laws? Do you believe the individuals who did nothing in the Kitty Genovese
case should be held responsible for an act of omission?

In addition to an act, a crime must also have intent, called **mens rea**. In effect, an
individual must intend to commit the act in question—that is, the individual must
have a blameworthy state of mind. Establishing intent is rather difficult. In fact,
intent is usually inferred from the act. For example, if an individual grabs someone's
purse and runs away, we can infer that the individual intended to commit theft. This
may seem obvious, but the issue of intent is most important when an individual's
degree of liability is in question. Take the following example: Person A points a gun

at person B in an attempt to scare person B. The gun accidentally discharges, killing person B. Person A can be held liable for the death of person B, even though person A did not intend to kill person B. In effect, even though person A will be held liable for murder, he would not be held liable for the more serious crime of first-degree murder because he did not intend to commit murder in the first place.

As with actus reus, there are instances when intent need not be present in order for an individual to be held liable for a crime. This is called **strict liability**, in which liability is imposed without intent. Strict liability applies to behaviors that are typically considered mala prohibita (not inherently bad), such as serving alcohol to minors and committing traffic offenses. In these instances, it makes no difference whether an individual intended to engage in the act or not; he or she can still be held liable. A common example of a strict liability crime is statutory rape; if an individual engages in intercourse with a person who is below the age of consent, that individual will be held liable for his or her behavior, even if he or she had no intent to engage in intercourse with a minor.

Critical Thinking Exercise

With the issue of statutory rape, do you believe that individuals who unknowingly engage in intercourse with a person who is below the age of consent should be held responsible for their actions? Why or why not? Why do you think statutory rape laws are in place?

Along with the actus reus and mens rea, **causation** must also be present. In other words, an individual's conduct causes a particular result—for example, a person causes death in a homicide case. Causation can take a number of forms. The first and most obvious is called a **direct cause**, or "**cause in fact**." Also called "but for" causation, a direct cause occurs when an individual's behavior is the direct cause of harm. Essentially, but for an individual's behavior, harm would not have occurred. An example of a direct cause is an offender shooting a gun at a victim and the victim dies immediately of the gunshot wound. A second form of cause is **concurrent cause**. In this instance, two independent causes happen at the same time and either cause could have resulted in harm. For example, if two individuals shoot a victim simultaneously, either of these wounds could result in harm. Third, harm can result from a **proximate cause**. In proximate cause, something other than the individual's behavior caused the harm, but the individual began the series of events that led to the harm. For example, if an individual shoots a victim in the foot and an incompetent surgeon operates on the victim and the victim dies, an individual can still be held responsible for the victim's death, even though the individual is not the direct cause of harm.

As mentioned in the discussion of causation, the concept of **harm** must be present for criminal responsibility. Engaging in an *act* must *cause* some sort of *harm* to a protected person, place, or thing. The criminal law exists to protect people from harm (in the form of murder or robbery), to protect property (in the form of burglary or arson), or to protect a thing (in the form of larceny or shoplifting). Despite this, harm can be absent in some crimes, such as drug use, in which no other person, place, or thing is actually being harmed (beyond just the individual engaging in the behavior).

TYPES OF CRIMES

Throughout this chapter, specific crimes have been used as examples to illustrate various concepts in criminal law. The following discussion expands this, describing the various categories of crimes that exist in criminal law. This discussion will not, however, provide a detailed discussion of all of the crimes on the books; it merely provides an overview and uses a couple of states as examples.

Web Activity

For more information about your own state's laws and the laws of the federal government, go to https://www.law.cornell.edu/lii/get_the_law.

Crimes Against the Person

Personal crimes are generally considered the most serious crimes and are treated as such by the criminal justice system. Homicide, rape, assault, and kidnapping are crimes that come to mind when discussing personal crimes. Although these crimes may seem fairly straightforward, they are not so easily categorized. Each crime carries with it differing degrees of liability. For instance, killing another person could carry a sentence anywhere from probation to the death penalty. The circumstances surrounding the killing determine how an individual is to be handled by the system. In Ohio, the crime of homicide can fall into various categories, including "aggravated homicide," "second-degree homicide," "voluntary manslaughter," and "involuntary manslaughter." The most serious category, aggravated murder, is punishable by death or life imprisonment, whereas the least serious, involuntary manslaughter, results in imprisonment for up to 10 years. Unfortunately, space does not permit an examination of the different degrees of liability for each crime. Each state defines its crimes and establishes punishments for their violation. The statutes for each state are available on the internet.

Web Activity

Visit the textbook website (http://www.oup.com/us/labessentials) to read a brief discussion on the degrees of liability for the crime of homicide in Ohio and California. You can also look up the statutes for other states on the internet.

Crimes Against Property

Property crimes are not treated as severely by the criminal justice system as personal crimes, but they are considered serious nonetheless. Typical property crimes include larceny/theft, burglary, arson, embezzlement, and trespass. One type of property crime, robbery, is also considered a personal crime because force or the threat of force is used to steal an individual's belongings. Property crimes typically do not involve harm to individuals, and thus the punishments are less severe. For example, an individual cannot receive the death penalty for engaging in a property crime.

Like personal crimes, individual property crimes have varying degrees of liability. An example of this is seen with the crime of burglary. In Ohio, burglary involves trespass into an occupied structure with the intent to commit a crime. If an offender is carrying a gun or inflicts physical harm on a person within the structure, he or she is committing "aggravated burglary." If the structure is not occupied, he or she is engaged in "breaking and entering." Aggravated burglary is the most serious charge of the three, resulting in a punishment of up to 10 years in prison. Breaking and entering is the least serious charge, resulting in a punishment of up to 1 year in jail. Although intent is present, the degree of liability differs depending on specific circumstances (see generally Ohio Revised Code, §2911.11, §2911.12, 2005).

Crimes Against Public Order

Public order crimes are categories of offenses that do not necessarily harm other persons or property. These offenses are largely victimless crimes, where there is no readily identifiable victim. Public order crimes are seen as harming society as a whole, and the criminalization of such conduct aims to maintain social order. In comparison to personal and property crimes, public order crimes are committed by far more people, although they are not punished as severely. Examples of public order offenses are driving under the influence of alcohol, disorderly conduct, vagrancy, and loitering.

Critical Thinking Exercise

In 1999, Dr. Jack Kevorkian was convicted of second-degree murder in Michigan for assisting an individual with amyotrophic lateral sclerosis (ALS), or Lou Gehrig's disease, in committing suicide. To what extent do you believe Dr. Kevorkian and others should be punished for assisting ailing individuals in taking their own lives? To what extent does an individual's health status (e.g., terminally ill, in chronic pain) play a role in your decision? Also, take into account Oregon's Death With Dignity Act, enacted in late 1997, which "allows terminally ill adult Oregonians to obtain and use prescriptions from their physicians for self-administered, lethal doses of medications" (see http://www.oregon.gov/oha/ph/ProviderPartnerResources/EvaluationResearch/DeathwithDignityAct/Documents/year18.pdf).

Related to public order offenses are public morals offenses. These offenses are those that offend the morality of certain groups in society. Many public morals offenses involve sexual behavior—behavior that is not necessarily bad but is considered immoral and deviant by some. Prostitution is perhaps the most common example of a morals offense.

Drug Offenses

Laws that criminalize the use of drugs and alcohol could probably be categorized as public order offenses, but they deserve a section of their own. The reason is that the government's reaction to illegal drug use has dramatically altered how the criminal justice system deals with these offenses. The "war on drugs" has led to an increased focus on drug offenses, sometimes to the exclusion of other offenses.

Numerous criminal behaviors are associated with the use of drugs. Possession of illegal drugs, such as marijuana and cocaine, and possession of paraphernalia, such as needles, constitute perhaps the largest number of drug offenses, but laws are in place that focus on all levels of the illegal drug trade, such as trafficking, manufacturing, and selling. Punishment for drug offenses depends on a variety of factors, including the type of drug being used, the amount of drugs involved, and where a drug transaction takes place (e.g., near a school). Because of increased attention to drug offenses by both state and federal governments, the punishments for drug offenses have increased, ranging from probation to the death penalty.

White-Collar Offenses

A final category of offenses concerns those that are committed by individuals during the course of their jobs. The term *white collar* refers to the idea that individuals from a higher socioeconomic status are more likely to commit these types of crimes. It should be noted, however, that individuals of a lower socioeconomic status are capable of and do commit white-collar offenses.

The better known white-collar offenses are committed by individuals who use their job positions as a mechanism to engage in illegal behavior. Lower-level offenses such as employee theft do not receive as much attention as other white-collar offenses, although these lower-level offenses are perhaps more frequent. Tax evasion, price fixing, and insider trading are better known and more widely publicized. See Box 2.1 for an illustration of insider trading and the Martha Stewart case.

BOX 2.1

Insider Trading and the Martha Stewart Case

Although Martha Stewart was never charged with insider trading, her lawyer admitted as much during her criminal trial in 2004. In general, fair practices involve engaging in business when information is publicly known, in effect allowing the public the opportunity to compete in an open marketplace. When individuals engage in business practices based on information that is not publicly known, they are engaging in illegal behavior.

In Stewart's case, she purchased stock shares in ImClone, a pharmaceutical research company founded by her friend, Sam Waksal. Stewart's ImClone shares had returned a profit, and she continued her investment in the company. ImClone had high hopes for its cancer drug and was waiting for FDA approval in order for the drug to be placed on the market. With FDA approval, ImClone stock would rise, giving its investors a return on their investment. Without FDA approval, ImClone stock would suffer, resulting in losses on the part of investors.

In fair business practice, the FDA informs the company privately of its decision and then makes plans to announce its decision publicly so that all investors are in the same situation with regard to good or bad news. In ImClone's case, the FDA told Waksal that it would not approve the cancer drug and would make the public announcement soon. Before the public announcement, Waksal sold his ImClone stock because he knew that FDA disapproval of his company's cancer drug would result in decreased value of ImClone stock, which in turn would result in Waksal losing money on his investment. Waksal informed Stewart of the FDA's decision, and Stewart proceeded to sell her stock as well. Until the public announcement, ImClone shares were still performing well, so selling shares before the FDA's announcement allowed Waksal and Stewart to earn a profit from ImClone shares because, publicly, ImClone stock was still viable. After the public announcement, ImClone stock plummeted, and investors who were not privy to Waksal's and Stewart's information lost money on their investment. Because Waksal and Stewart had access to information on the inside—that is, nonpublic information—they were able to avoid losing money once the FDA's decision became public. This is illegal and an example of insider trading. For more information, consult the websites linked to the textbook website (http://www.oup.com/us/labessentials).

Web Activity

See http://money.cnn.com/news/specials/enron for more information about the Enron scandal, and see http://www.economist.com/node/12818310 for more information about the Bernie Madoff scandal.

Many other crimes are defined in state and federal statutes, but they are simply too numerous to mention here. All states and the federal government publish their statutes or place them online for public access. The next section deals with an issue that has already been addressed—liability—and instances in which individuals are not held liable for engaging in criminal behavior.

DEFENSES TO CRIMINAL LIABILITY

Throughout this chapter, the issue of liability has arisen to describe when an individual is held accountable for illegal behavior. The notion of criminal liability rests on the assumption that an individual knowingly commits a crime and has the intention of doing so. There are some situations, however, in which an individual is not held responsible for a criminal act and is not punished for wrongdoing. These situations constitute defenses to criminal liability.

Justification

In some situations, a crime is justified based on an individual's belief that what he or she did was the right thing to do. Perhaps the best-known **justification** is self-defense. Self-defense is used to deter an unwanted attack—force is used if an individual *reasonably* believes it is *necessary* for *protection* against an *impending* attack. The italicized words indicate what must be proven by an individual who claims self-defense. *Reasonable* means that an ordinary person would believe that force is to be used. *Necessary* indicates that force is needed to defend oneself. *Protection* suggests that the only reason that force is to be used is to protect oneself from harm, not to inflict harm needlessly on another person. *Impending* implies that an attack must be imminent and immediate—that there is no time to escape. The amount of force used must also be reasonable. For example, an individual cannot use **deadly force** if an offender merely steals a purse. Individuals who claim self-defense must prove that an ordinary, reasonable person would have acted in the same way if attacked.

Critical Thinking Exercise

One of the issues in self-defense law is the "castle doctrine," which states that individuals who are in their home or vehicle can use force, including deadly force, against an intruder. The justification is that people should not have to flee their own home and can "stand their ground" against intruders. Relatedly, "stand your ground" laws have been passed in a number of states to expand the castle doctrine to *any* place where a person can legally be. In other words, in any public place, a person can use force, including deadly force, to repel an attacker. A controversial case involving Florida's "stand your ground" law involved defendant George Zimmerman shooting and killing Trayvon Martin. (For information about this case, see http://www.cnn.com/2013/02/25/justice/florida-zimmerman-5-things/index.html?iid=article_sidebar). In your opinion, was George Zimmerman correct in "standing his ground" against Trayvon Martin? Or, do you believe that George Zimmerman was in no danger when he shot and killed Trayvon Martin?

Excuses

Sometimes, individuals are not held criminally liable because they have a legal excuse. Insanity is an example of an excuse that is recognized in the criminal law (discussed later). Other examples include intoxication, age, and duress.

Intoxication can be an excuse from criminal liability in some circumstances. **Involuntary intoxication** is a defense in all criminal offenses due to the nature of the intoxication. Generally, the law recognizes three ways to become involuntarily intoxicated. First, an individual may not know that he or she had ingested the drug. Second, an individual may be forced to consume a drug under duress. Finally, the intoxicating substance that was ingested by an individual may have unforeseeable side effects. On the other hand, **voluntary intoxication** is rarely an excuse to criminal liability. Even if it is, it is usually not a complete defense; in other words, it can be used to mitigate an individual's behavior and perhaps get charges reduced. Despite this, some states have abolished the intoxication defense completely.

Another possible excuse from criminal liability is **age**. It has been argued that younger individuals (typically younger than age 14 years) are not capable of forming intent and, therefore, cannot appreciate the gravity of their actions. After the age of 14 years, however, youths are assumed to possess criminal intent. States have the option of handling a youthful offender in adult court if the prosecution can prove that the youth has the capacity to form intent. Otherwise, youths will be adjudicated in the juvenile justice system.

Duress is another excuse from criminal liability. In this situation, a person must be under threat of death or serious bodily injury that causes the individual to commit a crime. In addition, it must be shown that a reasonable person would believe that committing the crime was the only course of action and that the individual was not responsible for the situation. Some legal theorists, however, posit that duress should not be fully recognized, as they believe that individuals should resist to the utmost when confronted with this situation. Without proof of such resistance, these theorists posit, an individual should not use duress as an excuse.

Mental Capacity

Although considered an excuse in criminal law, mental capacity deserves a section of its own. An individual can be relieved of criminal liability if his or her **mental capacity** is such that it renders the individual incapable of understanding the wrongness of his or her actions. Insanity is a common example. The term *insanity* is a legal one. It is not a medical diagnosis such as schizophrenia or bipolar disorder. The term is defined differently from state to state, so there is not one clear-cut rule that establishes whether someone was insane at the time of the offense.

Web Activity

For a list of insanity defenses used in the states, see the textbook website (http://www.oup.com/us/labessentials).

The first legal definition of insanity was known as the **M'Naghten rule**. M'Naghten was an English citizen suffering from delusions of persecution who believed it was necessary to assassinate Sir Robert Peel, the founder of the British police system and the home secretary at the time. M'Naghten did not kill Peel, but instead killed Peel's secretary, whom M'Naghten mistakenly believed was Peel. M'Naghten's lawyers claimed that he was insane at the time of the crime and should not be found guilty. As a result of this case, the M'Naghten rule was established and has become known as the "right versus wrong" rule. Under this rule, individuals must prove that they were in such a state of mind that they could not know what they were doing or that they did not know that what they were doing was wrong (see *M'Naghten's Case* [1843]).

Most states and the federal government adopted the M'Naghten rule, but other states believed that the rule should be expanded to account for issues involving self-control. The substantial capacity test was proposed in 1962, and it states that an individual

> is not responsible for criminal conduct if at the time of such conduct, as a result of a mental disease or defect, a person lacks substantial capacity either to appreciate the wrongfulness of his conduct or to conform his conduct to the requirements of the law. (Model Penal Code § 4.01)

It was thought that the M'Naghten rule was too strict, and this test provided more leeway for individuals who knew right from wrong but could not control their behavior. Today, some states and the federal government adhere to the M'Naghten rule in some form, whereas other states apply the substantial capacity test (for more information about the insanity defense, both its history and new developments, see Reider 1998).

Web Activity

See https://www.pbs.org/wgbh/pages/frontline/shows/crime/trial/history.html for a timeline of the insanity defense as well as changes to the insanity defense after the trial of John Hinckley, who was found not guilty by reason of insanity for the shooting of President Ronald Reagan in 1981.

VICTIM'S RIGHTS

An often overlooked component of the criminal justice system, victims are critically important in criminal law. Historically, victims and/or their families would exact justice for any harm committed against them. Today, the state is responsible for bringing offenders to justice. It has been argued that victims have been cast aside now that the state has assumed this responsibility. As a result, a number of programs have been created to assist victims with their cases in court as well as their recovery from the crime. A number of states have adopted constitutional amendments to protect the rights of victims; however, the federal government has yet to adopt such a provision in its constitution.

RECENT TRENDS IN SUBSTANTIVE CRIMINAL LAW

Criminal law is always changing. Government bodies propose changes to the law on a regular basis so that laws that are in place today may not be in effect next year. One of the reasons that the law changes regularly is that certain events in society result in public support for new legislation.

The Internet and Substantive Criminal Law

An ongoing problem for the criminal justice system is the use of the internet to engage in criminal behavior. Since the first webpage was launched in 1991, the internet has undergone a world of changes, making it difficult for any agency to monitor. Today, the internet is home to a host of criminal behaviors. Some of the better known violations are downloading files illegally, identity theft, posting child pornography, spreading viruses, and sponsoring terrorism. Early regulation of the internet was the primary responsibility of the federal government through the use of civil law. Many early issues dealt with copyright law and trademark protection. However, as the internet has evolved, so has its abuses, leading to a host of criminal laws to deal with this behavior. Laws against cyberstalking, unauthorized access, and theft of wireless devices did not exist 30 years ago.

Computer technology is rapidly changing, and efforts to keep up with emerging technology are ongoing and expensive. State and federal government agencies, as well as private companies, are responsible for detection and control of cybercrime. In the federal system, efforts to update legislation on computer crime are constantly being proposed to deal with the changing nature of computer crime. Recently, proposals have been made to extend the RICO (Racketeering Influenced and Corrupt Organization) statute, originally enacted to deal with organized crime, to computer-related crime. In a recent proposal, the Department of Justice noted that

> the fight against organized crime is far from over; rather, much of the focus has moved online. RICO has been used for over forty years to prosecute organized criminals ranging from mob bosses to Hells Angels to insider traders, and its legality has been consistently upheld by the courts. Just as it has proven to be an effective tool to prosecute the leaders of these organizations who may not have been directly involved in committing the underlying crimes and to dismantle whole organizations, so too can it be an effective tool to fight criminal organizations who use online means to commit their crimes. The Administration's proposal would simply make clear that malicious activities directed at the confidentiality, integrity, and availability of computers should be considered criminal activities under the RICO statute. (Downing 2011, 4)

Another problem with the internet and crime is that there are no traditional boundaries and jurisdictions. Laws vary from state to state and from country to country, but the internet is worldwide, resulting in difficulty in determining which state or country has the jurisdiction to handle internet crime. Because of this, interstate and international task forces are being created to help jurisdictions work together to deal with these issues. For example, in 2009, the U.S. Secret Service unveiled the European Electronic Crime Task Force, which involves working with European Union countries to monitor and investigate computer crime throughout Europe (Clark 2009).

Web Activity

See   https://www.dhs.gov/sites/default/files/publications/USSS_Electronic-Crimes-TaskForces.pdf for more information from the U.S. Secret Service about the creation of the European Electronic Crime Task Force.

Despite this, recent hacking incidents have illustrated the difficulty in pursuing the individuals involved. Individuals operating in foreign countries are able to hack into computer systems of international corporations and expose sensitive material. For example, hackers into Apple's iCloud storage site exposed nude photos of various celebrities. It is believed the hack occurred in China. Also, hackers into Sony Pictures' system revealed information about actors' salaries, movie scripts, and other information. It is believed that North Korea was behind the hack. Relatedly, investigations into the hacking of emails, servers, voting machines, and the spread of false information during the November 2016 election have begun. It is alleged that Russian operatives, in connection with candidate Donald Trump's campaign, were able to obtain information about the campaign strategy of the Democrat party and use this information to influence the election and elect Donald Trump. At this time, the issue is in its investigative stage.

Web Activity

For information about Russian influence in the 2016 election, see https://www.nytimes.com/news-event/russian-election-hacking.

Web Activity

For information about the iCloud breach, see https://www.forbes.com/sites/davelewis/2014/09/02/icloud-data-breach-hacking-and-nude-celebrity-photos/#89b9c52de72a.

> **Web Activity**
>
> For information about the Sony breach, see http://deadline.com/2014/12/sony-hack-timeline-any-pascal-the-interview-north-korea-1201325501.

Terrorism, Homeland Security, and Criminal Law

After the attacks on September 11, 2001 (9/11), many states and the federal government implemented laws to combat acts of terrorism. One such act was the Homeland Security Act of 2002, establishing the Department of Homeland Security as a cabinet post in the executive branch. The department's mission is to "prevent terrorist attacks within the United States; reduce the vulnerability of the United States to terrorism; and minimize the damage, and assist in the recovery, from terrorist attacks that do occur within the United States" (see https://www.dhs.gov/xabout/laws/law_regulation_rule_0011.shtm). The department sponsors legislation that "combats terrorism and enhances security" (see https://www.dhs.gov/mission). Examples of legislation include regulations that allow the department to monitor and regulate high-risk chemical facilities (Department of Homeland Security Appropriations Act of 2010) and enhancing port security (Coast Guard Authorization Act of 2010).

States also implemented homeland security and/or emergency response departments similar to the federal Department of Homeland Security. These agencies are responsible for implementing laws passed by the state legislatures for combating domestic terrorism. The U.S.A. Patriot Act defines domestic terrorism as

> activities that involve acts dangerous to human life that are a violation of the criminal laws of the United States or of any state; appear to be intended to intimidate or coerce a civilian population; to influence the policy of a government by mass destruction, assassination, or kidnapping; and occur primarily within the territorial jurisdiction of the United States. (see Section 802, https://www.gpo.gov/fdsys/pkg/BILLS-107hr3162enr/pdf/BILLS-107hr3162enr.pdf)

Critics of this definition claim it is too broad and could net those who engage in ordinary street crime. In fact, a number of states have used their terrorism legislation to cover gang activity or any other activity that could fall within the wording of the statute. This legislation, as well as enhanced investigative techniques, has resulted in the convictions of more than 35,000 individuals worldwide since 9/11 (Mendoza 2011; for more information about international cybercrime laws, see Treglia 2011).

Recent events have highlighted breaches in security regarding sensitive data. For example, WikiLeaks is an online organization devoted to publishing news leaks and classified information. It has been implicated in the release of U.S. State Department information about detainees at the Guantanamo Bay Naval Base after 9/11. Julian Assange, the founder of WikiLeaks, is being investigated by the United States as possibly violating numerous federal laws, including the

Espionage Act of 1917. Also, Edward Snowden, a former contractor for the National Security Agency, leaked classified information about global surveillance systems, endangering intelligence operations. Snowden escaped U.S. custody and sought asylum in a number of countries; currently, he resides in Russia. The U.S. government has filed charges against Snowden, including theft of government property and violation of the Espionage Act of 1917.

Web Activity

For more information about WikiLeaks, see https://www.huffingtonpost.com/news/wikileaks.

Web Activity

For more information about Edward Snowden, see https://www.theguardian.com/us-news/edward-snowden.

PROCEDURAL LAW

Thus far, this chapter has provided a general overview of many of the aspects of substantive criminal law. This section focuses on an equally important component of the law—procedural law. As stated previously, procedural law describes the procedures that government bodies must follow when carrying out the law. Most of the procedural law in the United States is rooted in the U.S. Constitution, which has articulated policies that federal, state, and local governments must follow.

The federal Constitution is essentially composed of two parts: the body of the Constitution, which outlines the structure and function of the federal government, and the amendments, which involve changes to the original document. The body of the Constitution is largely a blueprint for the federal government. It defines the three branches of government and specifies the role and responsibilities of each. When the Constitution was being drafted in 1787, the Framers were divided over whether the document should contain provisions that protected the rights of citizens from a newly created federal government. This division was the result of some of the Framers not trusting the new government because they believed that a strong federal government would infringe on the rights of citizens. These individuals likened the new federal government to England's government, from which the United States had recently achieved independence. Prior to the American Revolution, the English government had infringed on the rights of the American colonists, abridging their freedom of speech and press, not allowing representation in the English government, and engaging in the practice of entering homes without cause to search for seditious material. Those skeptical of the new federal government wanted to ensure that it would not be another England and pushed for the Constitution to include these protections (Schwartz 1992). As such, the body of the Constitution contains four protections of individual rights: a prohibition against ex post facto laws, a prohibition against bills of attainder, the right to habeas corpus (all found in Article I, Section 9), and the right to a trial by jury (found in Article III, Section 2).

The **ex post facto** provision prohibits retroactive laws; in effect, a law that is passed tomorrow cannot be applied to behavior that one engages in today. The provision against **bills of attainder** is in place to prohibit the imposition of punishment without trial. The right to **habeas corpus** allows an individual to challenge illegal confinement by the government. Finally, the right to a **trial by jury** guarantees that individuals are judged by a jury of their peers instead of one or two individuals who may not be neutral. These rights were considered important enough to be placed in the body of the Constitution. Despite this, some of the Framers insisted that these provisions did not go far enough and demanded that more rights be included. These rights were created and passed as the Bill of Rights in 1791.

The Bill of Rights is composed of the first 10 amendments to the Constitution, which were passed *en masse* in 1791. Since then, the Constitution has been amended 17 times, bringing the total number of amendments to 27. The Bill of Rights (Box 2.2) was passed to allay the fears of those skeptical of the new federal government, and the provisions found in the Bill of Rights encompass a wide range of protections (Schwartz 1992). For procedural criminal law purposes, this section focuses on the Fourth, Fifth, Sixth, and Eighth Amendments. The Fourteenth Amendment, passed in 1868, is discusses later in the chapter.

Box 2.2

The Bill of Rights and the Fourteenth Amendment

First Amendment: Congress shall make no law respecting an establishment of religion, or prohibiting the free exercise thereof; or abridging the freedom of speech, or of the press; or the right of the people peaceably to assemble, and to petition the government for a redress of grievances.

Second Amendment: A well-regulated militia, being necessary to the security of a free state, the right of the people to keep and bear arms, shall not be infringed.

Third Amendment: No soldier shall, in time of peace be quartered in any house, without the consent of the owner, nor in time of war, but in a manner to be prescribed by law.

Fourth Amendment: The right of the people to be secure in their persons, houses, papers, and effects, against unreasonable searches and seizures, shall not be violated, and no warrants shall issue, but upon probable cause, supported by oath or affirmation, and particularly describing the place to be searched, and the person or things to be seized.

Fifth Amendment: No person shall be held to answer for a capital, or otherwise infamous crime, unless on a presentment or indictment of a grand jury, except in cases arising in the land or naval forces, or in the militia, when in actual service in time of war or public danger; nor shall any person be subject for the same offense to be twice put in jeopardy of life or limb; nor shall be compelled in any criminal case to be a witness against himself; nor be deprived of life, liberty, or property, without due process of law; nor shall private property be taken for public use, without just compensation.

Sixth Amendment: In all criminal prosecutions, the accused shall enjoy the right to a speedy and public trial, by an impartial jury of the state and district wherein the crime shall have been committed, which district shall have been previously ascertained by law, and to be informed of the nature and cause of the accusation; to be confronted with the witnesses against him; to have compulsory process for obtaining witnesses in his favor, and to have the assistance of counsel for his defense.

Seventh Amendment: In suits at common law, where the value in controversy shall exceed twenty dollars, the right of trial by jury shall be preserved, and no fact tried by a jury, shall be otherwise reexamined in any court of the United States, than according to the rules of the common law.

Eighth Amendment: Excessive bail shall not be required, nor excessive fines imposed, nor cruel and unusual punishments inflicted.

Ninth Amendment: The enumeration in the Constitution, of certain rights, shall not be construed to deny or disparage others retained by the people.

Tenth Amendment: The powers not delegated to the United States by the Constitution, nor prohibited by it to the states, are reserved to the states respectively, or to the people.

Fourteenth Amendment (Section 1 only): All persons born or naturalized in the United States, and subject to the jurisdiction thereof, are citizens of the United States and of the state wherein they reside. No state shall make or enforce any law which shall abridge the privileges or immunities of citizens of the United States; nor shall any state deprive any person of life, liberty, or property, without due process of law; nor deny to any person within its jurisdiction the equal protection of the laws.

Web Activity

For links to and interesting facts about the U.S. Constitution, see https://www.archives.gov/exhibits/charters/constitution.html

Fourth Amendment

The *Fourth Amendment* is in place to protect against unreasonable searches and seizures by government entities. In colonial times, the colonists were growing increasingly weary of an overreaching English government. Colonists began to speak out and criticize the English government's implementation of strict policies, such as expansive taxation, and the English government itself. In response, the English government considered this criticism seditious libel and authorized the use of general warrants to break into homes and businesses, not only to search for evidence of seditious libel but also to search for individuals who were disobeying English law, such as those who refused to pay taxes. These warrants permitted government officials to ransack homes and businesses without just cause, and this was the reason for the creation of the Fourth Amendment (Zalman and Siegel 1997).

The Fourth Amendment protects individuals from unreasonable searches and seizures by the government, but not all searches. If government officials wish to search an individual's home, they must secure permission to do so from a judge. This comes in the form of a **warrant**. The warrant contains the name and address of the individual or home to be searched, as well as a specific description of the person or items to be seized. This information must be justified by a standard known as **probable cause**. This standard is difficult to define, but the U.S. Supreme Court, in *Brinegar v. United States* (1949), provided a definition: Probable cause exists when "the facts and circumstances . . . [and] . . . reasonably trustworthy information [are] sufficient in themselves to warrant a man of reasonable caution in the belief that an offense has been or is being committed" (p. 176). In effect, more evidence must exist than not that an individual has committed a crime. Once government officials have provided this information, they must get a warrant approved by a judge before a search may take place.

At times, government officials engage in unreasonable searches and seizures. For whatever reason, a warrant may not be secured if probable cause does not exist. As a result, the U.S. Supreme Court ruled in *Mapp v. Ohio* (1961) that searches and seizures that violate Fourth Amendment provisions are subject to the **exclusionary rule**; that is, illegally seized evidence is excluded from a prosecution. The exclusionary rule helps to ensure that government officials conduct their procedures in a legal manner and provides a penalty when they do not.

Since its inception, the Fourth Amendment has been the subject of numerous court cases that have attempted to modify it to account for changing times and circumstances. The amendment's provisions now go beyond someone's home and office to include such things as vehicles, drug tests, telephones, and computers— none of which existed at the time of the creation of the Fourth Amendment. In addition, there are circumstances that do not require the use of a warrant or the standard of probable cause. It is beyond the scope of this book to examine the various permutations of the Fourth Amendment. For more information about the Fourth Amendment, see Hemmens, Worrall, and Thompson (2004).

Critical Thinking Exercise

Today, the Fourth Amendment has been utilized to protect individual privacy in an age of rapidly advancing technology. A recent U.S. Supreme Court case, *United States v. Jones* (2012), dealt with the use of a global positioning system (GPS) tracking device on a suspect's car so police could monitor his whereabouts. The U.S. Supreme Court ruled that this constituted a search under the Fourth Amendment, thereby violating the U.S. Constitution. Read the case at https://www .supremecourt.gov/opinions/11pdf/10-1259.pdf. Do you agree with the Court that this is a search under the Fourth Amendment? What is the harm in tracking a suspect's movements in this way? Should police be able to use GPS tracking systems to follow suspects?

Fifth Amendment

The *Fifth Amendment* features an amalgam of provisions that include a broad range of procedural rights. One of the most important provisions is the due-process clause, which forces government officials to abide by fair procedures when an individual is subject to the criminal justice process. The due-process provision encompasses all other procedural rights, as they are simply specific forms of due process.

Perhaps the best known provision of the Fifth Amendment is the **self-incrimination** clause. This specifies that an individual cannot be compelled to confess involvement (or noninvolvement) in criminal activity. Historically, the English government, dating back to the 1200s, used torture and psychological coercion to elicit confessions from accused individuals, many of whom were innocent. As a result, the self-incrimination clause of the Fifth Amendment was created to prohibit government officials from compelling individuals to confess to something they did or did not do.

Another important provision of the Fifth Amendment is the protection against **double jeopardy**. The double-jeopardy clause prohibits the government from prosecuting someone again after that individual has been acquitted or convicted. In essence, the government does not get "two bites at the apple" if it is not happy with a particular verdict.

Another provision of the Fifth Amendment is the right to a **grand jury** proceeding. A grand jury consists of a number of ordinary citizens who review the charges against an individual and decide if the charges warrant a trial. The grand jury requirement was deemed important by the Framers of the Bill of Rights because they believed that a prosecutor, who is a government official, would have too much power in making charging decisions (Zalman and Siegel 1997).

Sixth Amendment

The *Sixth Amendment* is often called the "trial rights amendment" because of its provisions regarding aspects of the trial process. The first provision is the right to a **speedy trial**, which benefits both the defense and the prosecution. A speedy trial helps the defense by minimizing the amount of time that an accused individual must endure until his or her case is resolved. This is especially true if the accused is jailed prior to trial. A speedy trial assists the prosecutor because it ensures quick justice, provided the accused is guilty.

The right to a **public trial** ensures that trials are open to the public. English courts were notorious for secret proceedings, and the Framers of the Bill of Rights wanted the public to act as a watchdog over government proceedings to ensure that illegal procedures were not being used against the accused.

An accused individual also has the right to an **impartial trial**. This means that judges and juries are to be unbiased and neutral when making decisions about an accused individual's case. To ensure this, juries are selected through a fairly rigorous process with the goal of drawing out any biases that individual jury members may have.

Relatedly, the right to a trial by jury is included within the Sixth Amendment's protections. Although specifically listed in Article III, Section 2 of the Constitution, the right to a trial by jury has been interpreted as a Sixth Amendment right as well, since a jury trial is inferred by the other trial rights listed within the Sixth Amendment. This right seeks to safeguard the right to a jury of one's peers in place of a government trial.

The Sixth Amendment provides that an accused individual has the right to be prosecuted in the state and county where he or she allegedly committed the crime. This was incorporated in response to the English practice of taking colonists who allegedly committed crimes to England for trial, which hurt the accused because many English citizens were biased against colonists. In addition, accused individuals have the *right to know what they are being charged with* (in order to establish a defense against those charges), the *right to know who their accusers are* (to ensure that these witnesses are not fabricating the charges), and the *right to call witnesses to testify on their behalf*. Early English practice did not allow accused individuals to know the charges, to question witnesses, or even to put on a defense.

The final provision in the Sixth Amendment is the **right to counsel**. Most accused individuals do not know the intricacies of the law and need skilled attorneys to assist them. In addition, attorneys are able to offset any questionable governmental actions that could possibly harm the accused, such as trying to elicit confessions. Attorneys are present to ensure that due process is followed. Initially, this provision was interpreted to mean that if individuals could afford attorneys they could use them, but the poor were denied representation. This has since changed, and individuals who cannot afford attorneys can be provided them at the government's expense.

Eighth Amendment

The *Eighth Amendment* is considered the "punishment amendment" because two of its three provisions deal with criminal punishment. The first provision, the right against **excessive bail**, was created to restrain the government from detaining individuals before they were found guilty. During a bail decision, a judge is prohibited from imposing a bail amount that is too high in relation to the accused individual's crime, flight risk, or threat to the community. The right against excessive bail does not guarantee that the bail amount must be affordable to the accused individual, nor does it guarantee the right to bail in general.

The right against **excessive fines** was created to prevent the government from imposing financial penalties that did not accord with an individual's charge. The **cruel and unusual punishment** clause has a varied history, with lawmakers and judges still trying to decide what the clause actually protects. Some U.S. Supreme Court rulings declare that the clause prohibits not only barbarous modes of punishment, such as the rack and thumb screws, but also any punishment that is grossly disproportionate to the crime at hand (see *O'Neil v. Vermont* [1892]). U.S. Supreme Court decisions, however, have backed away from the disproportionality argument. In *Harmelin v. Michigan* (1991), Justice Antonin Scalia declared that the cruel and unusual punishment clause says nothing about proportionality and, in effect, only protects against certain forms of punishment that are not regularly used. Despite this, some judges do consider proportionality to be an Eighth Amendment issue and will overturn a punishment if they believe the punishment is too severe for the offense charged.

Another issue involving the Eighth Amendment is the use of the death penalty. Although the use of the death penalty per se is not unconstitutional (*Gregg v. Georgia* [1976]), the U.S. Supreme Court has ruled that its use for certain offenders or offenses is unconstitutional. For instance, the Court ruled that the death penalty for rape was cruel and unusual (*Coker v. Georgia* [1977]), as was the use of the death penalty for those who are mentally retarded (*Atkins v. Virginia* [2002]) or who were younger than age 18 years at the time of their offense (*Roper v. Simmons* [2005]).

Web Activity

For these and other U.S. Supreme Court cases, search the Cornell Legal Information Institute's website at https://www.law.cornell.edu/supremecourt/text/home.

Web Activity

See the textbook website (http://www.oup.com/us/labessentials) for an illustration of states and their use of the death penalty.

INCORPORATION

The previous discussion outlined the primary criminal procedure rights found within the U.S. Constitution and the Bill of Rights. Since these are federal documents, these provisions protect individuals from violations of rights by the federal government. Protection against state and local encroachment on procedural rights was not guaranteed, and individuals had to rely on state constitutions to provide these protections. Some state constitutions followed the federal lead and provided extensive procedural rights to their citizens, while others did not. This was problematic because it resulted in an unfair and unequal application of the laws (Zalman and Siegel 1997).

The ratification of the *Fourteenth Amendment* in 1868 was the catalyst for extending the reach of the U.S. Constitution and the Bill of Rights to the states. The Fourteenth Amendment consists of five sections, but the first section is most relevant here. This section outlines a due-process clause that applies to states. As mentioned previously, the Fifth Amendment contains a due-process clause as well; however, because it is in the Bill of Rights, it only applies to the federal government. The Fourteenth Amendment's due-process clause specifies that no state shall "deprive any person of life, liberty, and property without due process of law." Since 1868, the U.S. Supreme Court has issued a number of decisions that have used this clause to justify forcing the states to adopt the procedures found in the U.S. Constitution and the Bill of Rights. The U.S. Supreme Court was given this authority in the cases *Marbury v. Madison* (1803) and *Fletcher v. Peck* (1810). In these cases, the practice of **judicial review** was established, in which the U.S. Supreme Court has the power to review federal and state laws to ensure that they comply with the U.S. Constitution.

Using its power of judicial review, the U.S. Supreme Court has incorporated, or made applicable to the states, most of the procedural rights found in the U.S. Constitution and the Bill of Rights. This process of **incorporation** was selective and time-consuming because the Court had to wait for cases to come before it before it could issue a ruling. Initially, the Court only incorporated the procedural rights it thought were "fundamental" and "essential" (see *Palko v. Connecticut* [1937]), but over time, the Court came to realize that all rights found within the U.S. Constitution and the Bill of Rights were fundamental; if they were not, they would not be there. Today, all states and the federal government abide by the provisions in these documents. In fact, some states have gone beyond what these documents specify, providing more rights to their citizens than is required.

Despite the fact that federal and state governments must recognize these procedural rights, none of these rights is absolute. As stated previously, there are scenarios involving searches and seizures that do not require a warrant or probable cause, as specified in the Fourth Amendment. The same is true for the other procedural rights articulated previously. Over time, the provisions found in the U.S. Constitution and the Bill of Rights have been modified to account for circumstances that simply did not exist when these documents were created.

For example, the number of accused individuals who come into contact with the criminal justice system is much larger than the number in 1791. The system has had to accommodate these numbers without collapsing. As a result, accused individuals are asked to waive many of their rights, including their right to a speedy trial, their right to have an attorney, and their right against self-incrimination. Courts have also scaled back many of these procedural rights. For instance, only individuals who face more than 6 months' incarceration are given the right to trial by jury. For more information about the extent of procedural rights in the United States, see Samaha (2012) and Zalman and Siegel (1997).

TRENDS IN PROCEDURAL CRIMINAL LAW

As noted previously, courts have restricted many of the procedural rights found in the U.S. Constitution and the Bill of Rights. In many cases, this restriction is the result of security issues that place public safety on a higher ground than individual rights. For instance, because of the potential danger of police work, courts have allowed police to engage in searches without a warrant and arrests without probable cause to ensure that police officers are not placed in precarious situations.

As mentioned previously, the internet has exploded with new technologies and new ways to conduct criminal behavior. As a result, the criminal justice system has had to improve its investigation techniques to stay ahead of cyber-criminals. When the U.S. Constitution was written, the Framers had no idea about the possibilities of internet technology. As a result, the Constitution and the criminal justice system have had to adapt. Although laws are in place to protect the privacy of individuals from electronic surveillance (e.g., see the Electronic Communications Privacy Act of 1986), the realities of the internet have stretched the original purpose of many of these laws. The use of cell phones and email, as well as the participation in third-party sites such as Facebook and YouTube, has placed the Constitution in "a complex, often convoluted area of law" (*United States v. Smith* [1998]). Lower courts have upheld searches of a suspect's cell phone text messages soon after arrest (*United States v. Finley* [2007]) as well as the seizure of subscriber information given to a third-party internet provider (*United States v. Perrine* [2008]).

The U.S.A. Patriot Act, passed after 9/11, has allowed federal authorities to engage in more expansive wiretapping and electronic surveillance of telephone and internet service providers, as well as voicemail and email communications. Any activity that federal authorities deem is related to even a remote threat to national security is subject to increased surveillance and fewer constitutional protections. This is something that many view as important for the safety of the nation. Others, however, believe the federal government has given itself too much authority to investigate such activity because the government alone defines what is a threat to national security.

CONCLUSION

Both substantive law and procedural law are critical to the function of society and all entities that exist within it. This chapter provided a general overview of the numerous aspects of substantive and procedural law and the information needed to understand the presence of the law in society, particularly in the criminal justice system. The criminal justice system exists because of the law. Something or someone must be responsible for the enforcement of the law as written. The criminal justice system, moreover, does not exist in a vacuum. It must abide by the law just as individuals, groups, and corporations must. The reader is encouraged to consult the sources of information provided throughout the chapter to gain a more thorough understanding of both substantive and procedural law.

KEY WORDS

act of omission
actus reus
administrative law
age
bills of attainder
case law
causation
cause in fact
civil law
common law
concurrent cause
constitutional law
criminal law
cruel and unusual
   punishment
deadly force
direct cause
double jeopardy

duress
ex post facto
excessive bail
excessive fines
exclusionary rule
Fourteenth Amendment
grand jury
habeas corpus
harm
impartial trial
incorporation
involuntary intoxication
judicial review
jurisdiction
justification
mala in se
mala prohibita
mens rea

mental capacity
M'Naghten rule
precedent
principle of legality
probable cause
procedural law
proximate cause
public trial
right to counsel
self-incrimination
speedy trial
statutory law
strict liability
substantive law
trial by jury
voluntary intoxication
warrant

SUGGESTED READINGS

Friedman, L. (1993). *Crime and punishment in American history.* New York: Basic Books.

Ross, D. (2009). *Civil liability in criminal justice,* 5th ed. Cincinnati, OH: Anderson.

Scheb, J., and J. Scheb. (2011). *Criminal law and procedure,* 7th ed. Florence, KY: Cengage.

Singer, R., and J. LaFond. (2010). *Criminal law: Examples and explanations,* 5th ed. New York: Aspen.

Walker, S. (1980). *Popular justice: A history of American criminal justice.* New York: Oxford University Press.

CHAPTER 3

Policing and Law Enforcement

CHAPTER OUTLINE

Introduction
    Law Enforcement
    Order Maintenance
    Service
The Role of Police in Society
    Intelligence-Led Policing
Structure
    Local
    Sheriff
    County Police
    Constables
    Special Police
    State
    Federal
    Tribal
    Private Police
Organization
    Sworn Versus Civilian
    Specialization
    Geography
    Time
Police Work and Career Paths
    The Hiring Process
    Field Training
    Promotion
Enduring Elements and Issues
    Police Subculture
    Police Corruption

Harassment
Improper Use of Force and Police Brutality
The Blue Wall of Silence
Policing the Police
Special Constituencies
Future Issues
Conclusion
Key Words
Suggested Readings

After reading this chapter, you should be able to:

- Distinguish between the law enforcement, order maintenance, and service functions of police work
- Identify key developments in the professional police era
- Discuss the "broken windows" theory of policing
- Explain the difference between problem-oriented policing and community-oriented policing
- Identify and discuss what is meant by intelligence-led policing
- List and discuss different levels/types of police structure (e.g., local and county)
- Briefly discuss different federal law enforcement agencies and their mandates
- Point out various aspects to police organization
- Distinguish between single-entry and dual-entry tracks
- Identify different stages of the hiring process
- Discuss issues related to police subculture
- Define and discuss police corruption
- Outline the use of force continuum
- Point out various emerging issues for police

INTRODUCTION

We commonly speak of the police as the "gatekeepers" of the criminal justice system because the vast majority of criminal cases brought before the courts result from decisions made by the police. Although the police are thought of as *law enforcers*, arresting criminals is only a small portion of police work. The police also foster **law compliance** and provide an array of services that are not *directly* linked to crime. Almost 80 percent of a patrol officer's time is devoted to activities other than law enforcement. However, the law enforcement image dominates the public face of the police.

Because the law reflects the collective will of a people, the police are the "muscle" behind that society's law. Those who do not voluntarily obey the law will have it imposed upon them; the police are the primary means by which the law is imposed. Egon Bittner described the role of the police as "a mechanism for the distribution of non-negotiably coercive force employed in accordance with the dictates of an intuitive grasp of situational exigencies" (1970: 46). Although other occupations and social institutions have the right to use force in a limited set of circumstances (e.g., to restrain a patient who may hurt himself or to discipline children), only the police have a general mandate to use force for the common good.

The police may use force to ensure that the law is obeyed and public order preserved. When the police actually use force is the essence of police **discretion** (Brown 1981). It is not possible to write a law, or a rule, that will cover every possible situation the police might encounter. Nor will the police necessarily know with certainty every factual matter that attends every call they answer. The police combine their knowledge with the array of verbal and nonverbal information that attends each unique situation, make an accurate judgment about what is going on (the "situational exigencies"), and decide on the proper response.

Not every police action is a coercive one, of course. The right to use force on behalf of society lies behind many of the other things police do. In broad terms, there are three primary responsibilities of police work: **law enforcement**, **order maintenance**, and **service**. These aspects were first explored by James Q. Wilson in his 1968 book *Varieties of Police Behavior*.

Law Enforcement

"Enforcing the law" by apprehending criminals after crimes occur is an important part of police work, but it is only one element of the law enforcement mission. The entertainment media portray policing as an exciting career of hunting criminals, thwarting robberies in progress, engaging in high-speed car chases, making dynamic entries, and apprehending desperate criminals. In truth, these events happen infrequently. The police are far more likely to deal with crimes committed by people who are drunk, depressed, mentally ill, or simply overwhelmed by life stresses than they are with crimes committed by so-called master criminals.

Tense confrontations, take-down moves, and an enticing array of high-tech weaponry and science seem to be the tools of the trade. Although these are important, by far the most important tools are patience, good communication skills, and knowledge of human psychology. The ability to enforce the law by bringing criminals to justice rests in large part on the willingness of the public to cooperate with the police (Black 1981; Mastrofski, Snipes, and Supina 1996). The foundation for that is laid in the routine interaction between police and citizens in the course of everyday, non-emergency activities.

Crime prevention has been a prime function of police work, ensuring the safety of the community by denying criminals the opportunity to commit crime and by defusing volatile situations before they reach the point of violence (Lab 2016). Visible **patrol**—on foot, in motor vehicles, on bicycles, or on horseback—is seen as a means of preventing crime by **deterrence**. Active patrol raises the possibility that a criminal will be seen and apprehended. The impression that the police are always around and ever vigilant discourages criminals from committing crime—that is the essence of police deterrence. Often, the presence of authority, backed up by powers of arrest, will scatter potential troublemakers or quiet boisterous behavior.

Police foster crime prevention in other, less flashy ways as well. Officers help organize and support community-based self-help activities, such as **Neighborhood Watch**, to observe and report suspicious activity in the neighborhood (Garofalo and McLeod 1988; Rosenbaum 1987). Community involvement may range from supplemental **citizen patrols** to initiating court action against landlords of properties where drug sales take place. A wide range of anti-crime activities take place at the block level. Citizen patrols, **property marking** projects, **safe havens** for children, looking after each other's property when people are away, and block parties can all be organized under the umbrella of Neighborhood Watch.

Patrol officers, **school resource officers**, Police Activity League volunteers, and others participate in a wide variety of community-building activities, both on and off duty, to keep youngsters safe and to encourage law-abiding activities (Bond 2001; Newman et al. 2000). Gang intelligence helps defuse feuds that otherwise might turn violent, and skilled officers sometimes negotiate truces between rival gangs. Officers host self-defense workshops and conduct property surveys to help reduce individuals' risk of victimization, and they make numerous referrals to social service agencies across a wide spectrum of problems they encounter.

Order Maintenance

Crime is not the only thing in modern life that can cause concern. All sorts of conflicts can create alarm, concern, fear, or inconvenience. Loud and boisterous groups of teenagers, heated bar arguments, and noisy arguments over finances between a husband and a wife in an adjacent apartment all disturb the peace and tranquility of neighbors. Those who call for police interventions do not necessarily expect the officers to make arrests, as long as they restore order. Although arrests are possible, most incidents are resolved through other means: mediation, referral, or the mere threat of arrest. In some cases, such as a dispute between a landlord and a tenant over the payment of rent, the police may have no legal authority in the matter (rent disputes are a matter of civil law), but they may serve as referees. Their presence and authority act as a safety valve: Both parties can back down without losing face.

Service

Service, the third function of the police, takes a wide variety of forms depending on the location. Directions, assistance to disabled motorists, funeral escorts, administration of various kinds of permits, emergency relays of blood, checking vacant residences or looking in on vulnerable adults, aiding with traffic control at road construction and emergency scenes, and many more services are provided by local police and sheriffs' deputies.

Because of this wide diversity of tasks, police officers are trained to be generalists. Most officers begin their careers doing uniformed patrol work. They will be called upon to answer an almost unimaginable array of different needs. These include assisting in childbirth, breaking up fights, talking down suicidal "jumpers," interviewing abused children, trading gunfire with desperate criminals, intervening in domestic arguments, assisting mentally ill and confused persons, and investigating corrupt police officers.

Police officers frequently describe their work as "long hours of sheer boredom, punctuated by moments of sheer terror." In contrast to Hollywood portrayals, the reality of police work is that exciting events happen infrequently and favorable results can be elusive. Those who expect exciting careers in law enforcement are likely to find that much of their time is devoted to social work, helping people cope with life, occasionally resolving low-level problems, and building interpersonal relationships with the community.

THE ROLE OF POLICE IN SOCIETY

Throughout history, the police in Anglo-American society have reflected the conditions and needs of the dominant society, even though periodically the police have been slow to recognize and adapt to legitimate social change. The police must operate in the tension between rapidly changing social conditions and a conservative, slow-to-change legal environment. Individual, organizational, and subcultural changes usually develop more slowly than the larger social ones, often creating visible tensions between the police and parts of the community. That was true of the civil rights movement of the 1950s and 1960s, and certain aspects of present conditions seem to be harbingers of a reprise of that era.

Web Activity

Students who are interested in the historical development of the English and American police, as well as a discussion of different American police eras, can find material on the textbook's website (http://www.oup.com/us/labessentials).

At the same time, the police today are far more professional than their generational predecessors of earlier eras and in general much less "tools" to be wielded by local politicians. For instance, when President Trump made off-hand remarks to the effect that arrestees should be roughed up, the police were generally outspoken. Many chiefs and departments made public statements to the effect that such behavior was neither legal nor ethical, and that the standards of behavior expected under the law would continue to be observed (Berman, 2017).

That is not to say that police do not have to respond to the direction of local officials: far from it. In the wake of the shooting death of Michael Brown in Ferguson, Missouri, in August 2014, an investigative report revealed that police enforcement of minor violations was viewed as a revenue-generating device by the city authorities. Those enforcement activities were focused overwhelmingly on lower-income residents with fewer resources to respond legally (U.S. Department of Justice, 2015).

As America moves toward the third decade of the 21st century, a number of social tensions have burst into the public view and directly or indirectly involve the police. One movement demands the removal of Confederate statues that, in the minds of its proponents, indirectly glorify slavery and treason. In doing so, it gives rise to the resurgence of a resistance movement that insists the statues commemorate states' rights, honorable soldiers who fought for what they believed in, and an honorable history. Although those two opinions have clashed in public space, they have provided a vehicle for far-right groups such as the Nazi Party and its various analogs to assert White supremacy, among other beliefs noxious to most Americans. They, in turn, have provoked the rise of equivalent groups on the far left, such as the Antifa movement (antifascist). Both sides wear masks, brandish and sometimes use weapons, and engage in provocational activities just short of—and sometimes boiling over into—outright violence. The police are caught in the middle, obliged to defend the right of all sides to free expression but also charged with protection of target from assailant, regardless of political beliefs.

The politically fired debate over immigration control also has an impact on the police, as well as on jails and holding facilities under police control. Long-standing precedents have created set requirements for the detention and conditions of release of detained persons. Attempts to add federal-level immigration charges on detained persons must conform to legal strictures as well, and state prisoners cannot be detained for federal convenience without authorizing paperwork. Such paperwork is often slow to materialize. In response, the federal government has moved to try to create incentives for such activities. A November 20, 2017, press release from the Office of Justice Programs' Office of Community Oriented Policing Services (OJP OCOPS) noted that

> in September, the Justice Department announced additional priority consideration criteria for FY2017 COPS Office grants. Applicants were notified that their application would receive additional points in the application scoring process by certifying their willingness to cooperate with federal immigration authorities within their detention facilities. Cooperation may include providing access to detention facilities for an interview of aliens in the jurisdiction's custody and providing advance notice of an alien's release from custody upon request. Eighty percent of the awarded agencies received additional points based on their certifications of willingness to cooperate with federal immigration authorities.

"Willingness to cooperate" does not mean "defy the requirements of law" in practical terms. The limitations of federal agencies such as Immigration and Customs Enforcement (ICE) and the U.S. Border Patrol can lead to a gap between willingness and actual practice. At the street level, as well, the impression that local police are the agents of federal immigration authorities can mean a loss of valuable trust and cooperation from whole communities of those who are in the United States legally, either as naturalized citizens or on visas. The police can ill afford to be viewed as targeting the loved ones of their citizens, particularly against the backdrop of unsettled law.

Shifting social conditions are not the only focus of police activity, of course. The predominant part of police work remains the enforcement of the criminal law and the maintenance of social order, as it has been for decades. The various initiatives of previous decades, such as "**broken windows,**" **problem-oriented policing**, and **community-oriented policing** (see the web material), have coalesced under the current heading of "intelligence-based policing."

Web Activity

Explore influences on the development of community policing on the textbook website (http://www.oup.com/us/labessentials).

Intelligence-Led Policing

Drawing upon the example of "intelligence-based medicine," the police of the modern era are increasingly basing decisions on crime analysis and other data systems. With roots in the **Kansas City Preventive Patrol Experiment**, the **Minneapolis Domestic Violence Experiment**, and the other evaluative projects of the 1970s and 1980s, crime analysis has become more than the mere production of year-end statistics. New York's CompStat process was the first contemporary use of integrated statistics in real time. Advances in computer technologies have made it possible to do far more. Mapping tools and analytic software not only manage crime data but also incorporate trend data from other functions that might affect police operations, such as land use, economic development, and demographic trends.

The expansion of criminal enterprises in a global economy has created demands for better information about conditions beyond local boundaries. The war on terror has led to the creation of fusion centers to collect, assess, and coordinate information about possible terrorist activities. The centers also track the connections among other criminal enterprises: guns, drugs, gangs, human trafficking, child pornography, and many others. Police professional associations also update their members across jurisdictional lines on topics such as tactics, new threats, new technologies, and legal developments in the various federal districts.

Web Activity

The Society of Police Futurists is an offshoot of the World Futures Society. You can read more about its work at http://www.policefuturists.org.

STRUCTURE

Police agencies have different mandates depending on their level of political authority, region of the country, and specific charter. Government police agencies are authorized at the local, tribal, county, state, and federal levels. In addition, various special police forces may be authorized. Based on 2013 data (the most recent available), more than 12,000 police and law enforcement agencies exist in the United States employing roughly 605,000 officers and agents (Reaves 2015).

Local

The blue uniforms and patrol cars of the nation's municipal police forces are the image most associated with the police. Their legal jurisdiction is usually limited to the borders of the town or city that hires them, although there are exceptions. Fresh pursuit of a suspect, **mutual aid** compacts among municipalities, and being sworn in as special officers or deputies for other agencies all may extend police officers' local authority.

Most municipal police agencies are small. Uniformed generalist patrol work is a universal entry point, and many officers spend most of their careers doing patrol work. In larger departments, increased specialization in the form of detectives, juvenile officers, SWAT (Special Weapons and Tactics) team members, and the like is possible in later career steps, as are promotions to supervisory positions.

Sheriff

The county **sheriff** is one of the oldest police offices and in many states is authorized by the state constitution. Unique among law enforcement personnel, sheriffs serve all three branches of criminal justice: policing, courts (sheriffs provide security to courtrooms and serve civil and criminal writs), and corrections (sheriffs run most county jails). Deputy sheriffs often start their careers in jails as correctional officers and work their way up to uniformed patrol and investigations.

Sheriffs are elected officials in 48 of the 50 states, but the duties of sheriffs' departments vary regionally. In the South and West, they are the primary law enforcement services for many rural and unincorporated areas. In the urban centers of the Northeast, sheriffs tend to be court officers but provide only limited law enforcement because most of their jurisdictions have full-time municipal police.

County Police

In some densely populated urban areas, county police departments have taken over the law enforcement duties of the sheriff. Organized like large municipal departments, county departments are responsible to the county executive or county council rather than to an elected sheriff. County police may have concurrent jurisdiction with municipal police agencies located within the county. In such instances, like the sheriffs' offices and state police, the county police tend to concentrate on areas without other police resources, cooperating with the municipal departments when the need arises.

Constables

In many areas of the country, the old office of **constable** has been abolished or restricted to minor court and service duties. In Texas, the office of constable is comparable in many ways to the sheriff or the county police, generally serving court writs but also providing patrol services in some areas.

Special Police

State laws authorize police forces for special limited purposes, such as railroads (which run through multiple jurisdictions), college campuses, school districts, mass-transit systems, and parks and woodlands. The best known is the Port Authority of New York and New Jersey Police, which lost many officers in the September 11, 2001, attack on the World Trade Center.

A variation on the "special police" concept is the part-time officers (variously called "reserves," "special officers," or "auxiliary officers," among other titles) who work for municipal, county, and sheriffs' departments in addition to their regular jobs. They may work on either an hourly paid basis or as volunteers, depending on the agency and the state's authorizing statutes. With proper training, they may perform full police duties, especially in rural areas. Otherwise, they supplement regular police in support roles: directing traffic, providing crowd control at major events such as concerts and fairs, and assisting in a variety of roles. Many sheriffs' departments have "sheriffs' posses" who can be called upon for additional staffing of special events and search-and-rescue operations. Their powers usually are less than those of full-time officers, but they provide valuable resources and expertise.

State

State police functions take one of two forms. **State police** have standard law enforcement duties and general jurisdiction throughout the state. **State patrols** or highway patrols primarily enforce traffic laws on state highways; they have police powers and training but no general police jurisdiction. States with highway patrols may also have an independent bureau of criminal investigation that provides criminal investigation and crime lab services throughout the state. Other elements of state government may employ investigators and officers with special police powers, such as the welfare, motor vehicle, revenue, alcoholic beverage control, and natural resources departments. Some jurisdictions grant police powers to corrections employees, especially probation and parole officers.

Federal

Federal agencies have specific powers and jurisdiction under federal law and do not enforce state or local laws. There are more than 90 federal law enforcement agencies, including the Border Patrol, Customs Service, Federal Protective Services, U.S. Mint Police, and smaller police forces for various parts of the federal government (e.g., the Capitol, Supreme Court, and the Environmental Protection

Agency). In many cases, federal and state jurisdictions overlap because drugs, firearms, explosives, and bank robberies may all be part of an interstate or even international criminal enterprise. For these and emerging problems, such as human trafficking and international internet fraud, federal and state agencies coordinate their investigations through **multi-jurisdictional task forces**, usually under the direction of the regional U.S. District Attorney. Although almost every federal agency has some kind of investigative service specific to its mandate, federal criminal justice agencies are grouped in three cabinet-level departments: Justice, Homeland Security, and Treasury.

Web Activity

Visit https://www.justice.gov/agencies/alphabetical-listing-components-programs-initiatives to explore information on the wide range of federal agencies that are involved in enforcing the law.

Many agencies were incorporated into the new Department of Homeland Security (DHS) in the wake of the September 11, 2001, attacks against American targets. To coordinate the nation's defenses and deal more effectively with the threat of international terrorism, agencies with relevant missions were brought under the direction of a single agency. The creation of the DHS at the cabinet level combined many smaller federal enforcement functions under a single office.

Among the components of the new DHS are the Secret Service; the Border Patrol, renamed Customs and Border Protection; the Immigration and Naturalization Service, renamed Immigration and Customs Enforcement (ICE); the U.S. Coast Guard; the Federal Law Enforcement Training Centers (FLETC), which trains the agents for all but two of the federal enforcement agencies; and the Transportation Safety Administration. Other components relating to nuclear detection, threat assessment, intelligence, animal research, and similar functions were brought under the DHS umbrella selectively from their former homes in other federal agencies.

Web Activity

Investigate the different components of the DHS at https://www.dhs.gov/department-components.

Created in 1908, the Federal Bureau of Investigation (FBI) has a mandate to investigate approximately 200 federal crimes, including bank robbery and kidnapping, unless Congress specifically designates jurisdiction to another agency. Criminal acts and conspiracies that cross state lines usually fall to the FBI, the enforcement arm of the Justice Department. The FBI crime lab provides forensic support for investigators throughout the nation, and the National Academy provides advanced training for state and local officers. Recognizing the emerging needs created by globalization, the FBI has established offices in foreign countries and has been involved in the training of police forces in emerging nations and the countries of the former Soviet bloc. In 2005, the FBI began training all new agents to be intelligence-gathering officers, both in anti-terror investigations and in the investigation of transnational enterprise crime.

The Drug Enforcement Administration (DEA) was established in 1973, combining several existing antidrug offices under the Justice Department. The DEA has primary responsibility for coordinating national drug enforcement efforts and is the sole agency authorized to pursue overseas drug investigations.

The Alcohol, Tobacco, Firearms and Explosives Bureau (still referred to as the ATF or BATF) is an enforcement arm of the Treasury Department. Created in 1972 when it was split from the Internal Revenue Service, ATF has powers based in the tax laws and other federal laws and regulations relating to alcohol, tobacco products, firearms, explosives, and arson. Another Treasury function, the Secret Service, was created in 1865 to investigate money counterfeiting. Protection of the president of the United States was added after the 1901 assassination of President McKinley. Fraud in commerce and fictitious securities documents also lie within its investigative mandate.

The U.S. Marshals Service is the oldest federal law enforcement agency, created by the Judiciary Act of 1789. Marshals protect the federal judiciary, transport federal prisoners, and protect endangered federal witnesses (the Witness Protection Program). In addition, marshals manage assets seized from criminal enterprises and may even run businesses until their sale under the asset forfeiture laws.

Tribal

The U.S. Constitution recognizes Indian tribes as sovereign entities, and tribal lands may have their own police forces. The Navajo nation is representative of the more developed agencies. The federal Bureau of Indian Affairs also has a separate police force for tribal lands, whose territorial dimensions may cross municipal, county, and even state lines. Like their municipal and state counterparts, tribal police have jurisdiction over anyone on tribal land, whether Native American or not. Tribal jurisdiction over its own members may include traditional methods of dispute resolution (community circles, banishment, and property exchanges) as well as the contemporary criminal and civil courts.

Critical Thinking Exercise

What advantages would there be to having a national police force with centralized, universal training standards and common equipment, salaries, and benefits?

Private Police

During the past several decades, the United States has seen a growth in special **private police** forces. Most are not "police" in the same sense as state or municipal officers because they do not have the authorization of law or general police powers that come with a sworn position. However, a small but growing number of private police forces now have state-authorized jurisdiction in some privately controlled places such as vacation resorts. They are uniformed and equipped in much the same way as their municipal counterparts, and many have completed preservice police training.

Private police forces are an augmented form of private security, with powers derived from the property rights of the corporate and incorporated entities that employ their services. They are **first responders** for alarms (intrusion, fire, and health emergencies), exercise a qualified set of access-control powers to limit visitors to the properties under contract, and sometimes handle disputes in much the same way that police patrol officers would. Professional organizations make a point of coordinating and interacting well with local police agencies, although there are fly-by-night, disreputable agencies as well.

Private police provide a more systematic patrol presence for those who can afford their services. In addition, they relieve the pressure on local agencies to answer alarm calls, the vast majority of which are false alarms (accidental activations or equipment malfunctions). The modern equivalents of the ancient night watchman and the store detective, their level of training and range of duties are considerably greater than those of their predecessors, reflecting the more complex requirements of asset protection and personal security in the modern age.

The former sharp distinctions between public and private policing have blurred in recent years. Electronic commerce has created new challenges and opportunities. The need for the physical security of locked doors has not disappeared, but it has been augmented by demands for protection of the electronic infrastructure (data), intellectual property (trade secrets), and goods in transit. Corporations now address the issues of asset protection, including electronic surveillance, personnel background checks, process integrity, data protection and verification, and the personal protection of corporate personnel.

Critical Thinking Exercise

Is the cause of justice served by having private police to protect the wealthy? What conflicts are possible when private police and public police jurisdictions overlap?

In addition, private security forces now often work under contract for public police agencies, providing security at crime scenes, guarding prisoners in hospitals, and even conducting background checks on potential new employees. Their relationship to the formal police authority is similar to that of private security contractors in military zones overseas.

Critical Thinking Exercise

What are some of the positive and negative consequences of having American law enforcement fragmented among so many different jurisdictions?

ORGANIZATION

Sworn officers in American police and law enforcement agencies are organized in a hierarchical form, with a **chain of command** conveying information from the front line to the administrative decision-makers and conveying orders and information back down. In larger departments, patrol officers report to shift supervisors (sergeants), who report to shift commanders (lieutenants), who in turn report to precinct commanders (captains). Precinct and unit commanders report to divisional heads (deputy chiefs). Police work is organized by task requirements (sworn or civilian) as well as by geography and by time.

Sworn Versus Civilian

For many years, almost every position in a police department was held by a uniformed police officer or a plainclothes detective. Women held only secretarial jobs and "matron" positions in jails. Support positions could be those to which officers were assigned as a punitive measure or "plum jobs" that offered a daytime Monday-to-Friday refuge from rotating shift work.

In modern times, many departments employ civilians (also called nonsworn or contract employees) to perform tasks that do not require the extensive training and experience of a sworn officer. Records, dispatching, fleet maintenance, personnel and budget, and even crime scene investigations may be staffed by nonsworn personnel. They are trained only for their special function, do not have police powers or carry weapons, and generally are paid less than sworn officers. Some agencies practice "outsourcing," contracting with private security agencies to perform many services formerly done by uniformed police officers: guard crime scenes, transport prisoners, and guard prisoners while they are in medical facilities.

Specialization

Patrol officers have general duties attending to a wide variety of calls and situations. In order for police departments to function efficiently, however, a number of specialist positions must be filled. Best known are the detectives or investigators, who do not answer calls. Their time is spent interviewing witnesses and following up on leads in unsolved crime cases. Detectives may specialize in a certain type of crime (homicide, burglary, robbery, sex crimes, etc.) or conduct all kinds of criminal investigation. Crime analysis, gang intelligence and intervention, school resource officers, training coordinator, **HAZMAT** (hazardous material), and high-risk warrant service, among others, are task-specific functions for sworn officers. Supervision is also a specialty job: As a rule, once promoted to sergeant or above, police officers do not handle calls unless circumstances force them to take police actions. Their primary responsibilities are to observe and assist patrol officers or investigators and to coordinate efforts. The farther up the hierarchy one rises, the more the duties are managerial and administrative in nature, except in small agencies, in which everyone is a generalist.

Geography

In the smallest local departments, officers are responsible for covering the entire town or village. Elsewhere, officers patrol specific areas of town called **beats**. They are responsible for answering all calls within their beats, as well as for preventing crimes and resolving problems.

Larger agencies are organized into **precincts** containing several beats. There are, for instance, 76 precincts in New York City; 6 in Austin, Texas; and 4 in Minneapolis, Minnesota. It is easier to manage smaller areas within a large city, enabling the precinct commander to be more responsive to citizens' concerns.

Sheriffs' departments may also be divided into different districts or may operate out of a central office. In addition, sheriffs' offices may assign deputies to local municipalities, known as **contract cities**, for a specified number of hours according to a contract negotiated between the city and the sheriff. Contracts guarantee basic police services while relieving smaller cities of part of the expense of maintaining their own departments.

The term **beat integrity** refers to a policy of keeping officers assigned to one specific beat consistently in order to develop knowledge about the players and build relationships with the community. This represents a significant change from the pre-1960s policies that moved officers frequently to different areas of a city in an effort to thwart corruption. However, officers may cross beat boundaries to assist other officers, if necessary, and to cover high-priority calls if the beat officer is tied up with a previous call.

State police agencies must cover entire states, and they organize into **troops** for the same reasons that police departments organize into precincts. In rural areas, troopers may operate out of their homes (e.g., the Connecticut Resident Trooper program) but are responsible to a troop-level administration.

Federal agencies responsible for national coverage organize into administrative regions and generally maintain offices in major cities. Federal agencies also work cooperatively with local and state agencies through **regional task forces** for various purposes, recognizing that crime does not confine itself to jurisdictional boundaries. Short-term task forces may devote their efforts to tracking down a serial rapist or a prolific bank robber. Long-term resources are devoted to organized crime such as racketeering, insurance fraud, illegal drug importation and distribution, human trafficking, and smuggling.

Time

Because crime and public emergencies occur around the clock, dispatch services and police coverage must be available 24 hours a day, 7 days a week. Police agencies tend to staff their shifts differently according to the volume of activity expected for various times of the day. There are many different shift schedules, ranging from the standard 40-hour workweek of five 8-hour days to the popular 4–10 and 3–12 shifts (four 10-hour or three 12-hour days). The two basic models are **rotating shifts**, in which officers periodically change from days to evenings to nights, and **steady shifts**, in which work hours are determined by a seniority system or a bid lottery.

Overlapping shifts and "**power shifts**" provide extra police presence during the active evening hours and on weekends. More officers are available to handle the call load and provide backup in dangerous situations. Depending on the nature of union contracts or other work rules, the power shifts may be staffed by officers who volunteer to work the evening hours on a regular basis, without rotating to day and midnight assignments.

Smaller agencies may provide nighttime coverage by an "on-call" arrangement. Officers work their shifts and return home to sleep but can be called out again for an accident or some criminal incident. Another agency, such as the sheriffs' office or state police, also may provide after-hours coverage.

Investigators and crime scene technicians generally work day and evening shifts, with either minimum staffing or on-call status for the overnight hours. Other support positions, such as records, planning and research, personnel, and purchase and supply, usually do not work around the clock or on weekends. They tend to be Monday-to-Friday jobs because their work entails interaction with other public- and private-sector offices on the standard work schedule.

POLICE WORK AND CAREER PATHS

Municipal policing remains a single-point-of-entry career. Officers working in municipal departments begin in patrol, doing shift work and answering a wide variety of calls. The diversity of patrol activities provides a learning base of experience. After that, three basic career paths are possible: Officers may remain in patrol for their entire careers; they may move from patrol into some specialty role, typically as investigators or detectives; or they may follow a mixed career of supervisory promotions and specialty assignments that lead to administrative posts.

Sheriffs' departments may have single- or dual-entry tracks. **Single-entry tracks** mean that deputies begin their careers working in the jails, unarmed, supervising prisoners. When a patrol position becomes available, jail deputies have the first opportunity for the slot, subject to seniority and testing rules. The emerging professional movement in corrections has led some sheriffs to create **dual-entry tracks.** Deputies hired for corrections functions are hired with an understanding that they will be working only in jails, and those seeking law enforcement positions apply directly for patrol positions. Jail deputies may apply for patrol slots later if they wish, but they do so on a level playing field, with no seniority advantages or "inside track" compared to outsiders.

Federal agencies have different requirements, depending on their needs and mandates. Some have uniformed branches as well as investigators; others tend to be exclusively investigative in nature. The FBI is one of the investigative agencies, and because of the sensitive nature of its work, it generally does not hire persons right out of college. The FBI searches for candidates who have established a solid work record and credit history, among other qualifications, so many aspiring FBI agents work in uniformed police service until they meet the eligibility requirements. By contrast, the Border Patrol has expanded rapidly to meet the demands to secure the nation's borders; many college students have stepped directly into Border Patrol slots upon graduation.

The Hiring Process

The older police career model, which endures in many areas, began with candidates being hired by an agency. At that point, the town or city sent them to a **police academy** for training and state certification as a police officer. As police training and education requirements expanded, other options developed. Today, persons seeking a police career may pay for their own **preservice training** before being hired, which may give them a competitive edge in the job market.

In some states, candidates can pay to attend a regular police academy. In others, alternative police certification processes are integrated into academic programs at two-year, community, and vocational colleges. Students graduate with an associate's degree and state certification as a police officer, although they have no police powers until an agency hires them. It is not a guarantee that they will be hired, and certifications often expire after a specified period of time if the graduate has not obtained work in an authorized agency. Nevertheless, preservice certification represents a savings for the municipality, which can put the officer to work immediately without having to pay for training.

Police recruits must pass a battery of tests to be hired, even with preservice certification. Written, psychological, and physical tests, as well as **background checks** for character and conduct, are standard in most areas. Some agencies require polygraph exams; still others put candidates through assessment centers to test their skills and instinctive reactions in various situations.

No preservice training options exist for those seeking federal law enforcement jobs. The FBI and DEA maintain their own specialized academies in Quantico, Virginia. All other federal agencies train their agents and officers at the FLETC in Georgia or Arizona.

There are two primary models for police training academies. **Stress-based academies** are run similar to military boot camps: They are residential and isolated from other groups; they tend to concentrate heavily on physical fitness as both a goal and a form of punishment for minor infractions or errors; they incorporate military trappings such as marching in formation; and they interweave classroom instruction with practical, hands-on exercises. **Campus-based academies** are run in two-year and technical college campuses, and the police academy curriculum is often part of an accredited associate's degree. Classroom instruction is augmented by practical exercises similar to those in stress academies, including mandatory state certification in firearms use and defensive/pursuit driving. Because of the setting, where trainees intermingle with students from numerous other academic disciplines, the boot-camp trappings are generally absent. Each model has strong proponents, primarily based in philosophical preferences rather than scientific evaluation of the effectiveness of the model.

Critical Thinking Exercise

What are the relative merits of the stress academy model of training and the campus academy model? How might each be changed to provide even better preparation for street duty?

Field Training

Most departments have a full-time **field training officer (FTO)** program that provides the bridge between academy learning and autonomous authority in the field. Officers-in-training ride with experienced officers who have a mandate to expose the rookies to as many situations as possible, evaluating and critiquing the trainees' responses as part of the field learning process. Once the FTO program is complete, rookies may work independently, but most undergo an additional period as probationary employees. If their performance is poor, they can be released without any further action. If they pass their probationary period, they become full-fledged members of the agency, accorded all civil service and bargaining unit protections where applicable.

Promotion

The requirements for being promoted to supervisory rank or to specialty positions vary widely. At the low end, seniority is still found in some departments. The person who has been in the department the longest gets the next open position, regardless of his or her training, education, or general fitness for the job. At the other end of the spectrum are batteries of written tests, oral interviews, and assessment center tests. A few departments also incorporate a "promotability score" based on past performance and supervisors' assessments of the individual's skills that will be necessary for the new job.

Criminal investigation often requires a long-term commitment to cases, interviewing people, following up leads, assessing physical evidence, and preparing affidavits for warrants and cases for court. It is difficult to conduct investigations if one is frequently being called off to answer another call for service, so most police agencies have an investigative specialist position, usually called **detective.** In some agencies, detective is a rank and is considered a promotion above patrol officer. In others, it is considered an assignment and holds the same rank within the organization as a patrol officer.

Because of its high profile and clarity of focus, criminal investigation, or detective work, is a prized assignment for many police officers. In smaller organizations, detectives are investigative generalists. In larger agencies, detectives are specialized, devoting their time to a single category of crime. They may work in several different investigative units over the course of their careers.

Undercover assignments are a special type of investigation, in which the officers pretend to be criminals or "fringe players" in order to gather intelligence on criminal networks or to buy drugs and stolen merchandise. Undercover officers differ from plainclothes officers, whose police status is known or acknowledged; an undercover officer's police identity is secret. Occasionally, undercover police run **sting operations** in which officers pose as criminal fences or drug dealers; **john details** are a variation used against street prostitution and cruising activities. Police officers (usually women, although similar operations are conducted in gay male cruising areas) pose as prostitutes in order to arrest "johns" who solicit them for sex.

Internal Affairs, now often called the Office of Professional Responsibility or a similar title, is the most specialized investigative function. It has the responsibility for investigating allegations of crime and misconduct by other police officers in the organization. Juvenile Investigations is both an investigative unit specializing in juvenile crime and a support unit that works with social service agencies to get juvenile offenders back on the straight and narrow.

Other specialties exist. Only a few cities have full-time SWAT or SRT (Special Response Team, a more contemporary appellation) squads, but many have trained personnel who can be mobilized into a team at need; smaller cities and towns often participate in regional SWAT or SRT teams. Hostage negotiations and barricaded persons situations are typical situations for SWAT/SRT. HAZMAT is a similar specialty, requiring additional training and equipment for dealing with incidents such as toxic waste or chemical spills, volatile chemicals in clandestine drug labs, or accidents in legitimate business and manufacturing sites. Agencies near large bodies of water often have marine units for monitoring water traffic and for rescue; many densely populated urban areas have police helicopter units for surveillance, search, and rapid deployment across wide-flung areas.

Training is a vital element of any agency for preparing new recruits, updating veterans on changes in law and procedure, and introducing new techniques and technologies to all members of the agency. School resource officers are similar to juvenile officers but work exclusively in schools, providing a combination of security, investigation, and public relations. They may deal exclusively with students or may have responsibilities for both student and staff conduct. Drug Abuse Resistance Education (D.A.R.E.) is a special form of school liaison, a national antidrug curriculum taught by uniformed police officers. In some departments, crime scene technicians are sworn officers; in others, they are civilians.

Police officers are often supervisors for civilianized support units, such as Dispatch or Records. In addition to knowledge of the various police jobs that the unit supports, they have the legal authority to handle difficult questions and requests, and they can provide technical knowledge of the criminal and procedural laws when needed.

ENDURING ELEMENTS AND ISSUES

Across the multiple types and approaches to policing, there are certain themes common to the American police. Many of them center on what scholars call the **police subculture**, the views of the world shared by many police officers. Police discretion, the **use of force**, corruption, handling of special constituencies, and relations with the community, particularly minority citizens, are all intertwined with this difficult-to-define concept.

Police Subculture

The idea of a police subculture at odds with mainstream society stemmed from the politically charged era of the 1960s. Two schools of thought emerged to explain the adversarial relationships of the day. Police opponents viewed the overwhelmingly Caucasian, almost entirely male police as racist, ignorant, authoritarian, and thuggish, completely out of touch with a changing society. In this viewpoint, police work attracted mean-spirited bullies.

The other school of thought held that people were drawn to police work out of a sense of altruism, but the nature of police work transformed them. The major scholars of the police of the 1960s drew a picture of police whose "working personality" was marked by concepts of danger, authority, and cynicism (Niederhoffer 1967; Skolnick 1966). The nature of their work meant dealing with people at their worst, handling problems of abuse and death on a regular basis, being personally reviled, and having their motives questioned. These combined to harden police officers, bringing about a defense mechanism. Those scholars also noted that the police were given to the use of stereotypes as a "perceptual shorthand" to discern and minimize danger.

The wider admission of women and minorities to policing has had some impact on police culture, but certain common themes are still recognized. Police officers work within a moral framework as much as a legal one, assessing situations on the basis of their assessment of the persons with whom they interact. A feeling of "us against them" predominates in many areas, although community policing has broken down that attitude in many others. Crank (1998) summarized many of the themes of police culture: the necessity and righteousness of force; reliance upon an undefined "common sense" and personal bravery in the face of sudden and potential danger; and a moral division of the world into "good" and "bad" people, with the police as a "thin blue line" between civilization and chaos. Others include solidarity in the face of opposition, individualism and personal autonomy, unpredictability, and survival.

Because most officers are socially and politically conservative, the police culture adapts slowly and sometimes grudgingly to changes in the social and legal environment. Guyot (1979) likened the process of creating change in police organizations to "bending granite." This resistance often puts the police at odds with large segments of the public, as it did in the 1960s, and gives rise to a series of concerns about police behavior. Common to all of the concerns is the manner in which police exercise their discretion.

Police Corruption

Corruption is the use of the police position for personal gain. Although it is common to refer to police powers as those of arrest and the right to use force, police discretion also gives the police the power *not* to arrest, and indeed not to take action at all. In the 19th and early 20th centuries, with police salaries as low as the hiring standards, police were susceptible to bribes to "look the other way," "lose" evidence, or focus their enforcement efforts on criminals' or politicians' business competitors. During Prohibition, bootleggers bribed police in cities on a widespread basis. In modern times, higher standards and better salaries have improved the police as a whole, but pockets of corruption are revealed periodically.

More problematic than the bribing of police by organized crime are cases in which the police themselves become criminals. The classic case in modern times was "The Pad" in New York City, revealed by Frank Serpico to the Knapp Commission in the early 1970s. Systematic police corruption shook down merchants for protection money like the racketeers of earlier periods. Police shaking down drug dealers, confiscating their drugs, and selling the drugs themselves has been a problem in several cities, as uncovered by the Mollen Commission's investigation of New York Police Department (NYPD) corruption in the 1980s and the Los Angeles Rampart Division CRASH scandal of the late 1990s. More contemporary research by Stinson has revealed fewer instances of organized police crime but has brought to light a far larger number of individual cases.

Harassment

The clear-cut moral division of the world focuses police attention on those they deem "bad." Anyone whose appearance or behavior signals "trouble" is likely to be subjected to scrutiny, usually in a field interrogation contact to determine who they are and what they are up to. Constant police pressure on violent street gangs and drug dealers is considered a good thing, serving law-abiding citizens by reducing the opportunity for criminals to act out. When the net is widened to include law-abiding citizens whose demeanor is without reproach and who bear only a superficial resemblance to the criminals, the police affront the autonomy and personal dignity of citizens. If that happens on a regular basis, the perception grows that the police are merely harassing people they do not like for reasons with little or no relation to the police mission.

Racial profiling remains a continuing concern, arising from police efforts to intercept bulk drugs before they can be marketed in the cities but also extending to weapons crimes. Cases in New Jersey and Maryland documented that state police stopped and searched minority motorists' vehicles in numbers far greater than their proportion of highway users. The underlying assumption equating race with criminality—the belief that African Americans and Hispanics are more involved with drug trafficking than Whites—was not borne out by the search results: Drugs were found at equal rates in minority and White motorists' vehicles. Other jurisdictions have found similar patterns of racial disparities in stops, although in less dramatic numbers. The fundamental objection is to the use of race rather than behavior as a reason for initiating a police inquiry. Other objections arise from the manner in which minority motorists are treated during contact.

Web Activity

The city of East Haven, Connecticut, came under scrutiny for its police department's treatment of Hispanic citizens. You can read about this at http://www.nytimes.com/2012/01/25/nyregion/connecticut-police-officers-accused-of-mistreating-latinos.html?pagewanted=all. More recently, the NYPD's "stop and frisk" program was discontinued after it came under intense criticism for targeting young African American and Latino males.

Improper Use of Force and Police Brutality

The power to use "non-negotiable coercive force" in defense of the law and social order is vital to the police role. In the vast majority of police–citizen interactions, police use force properly, if at all—most incidents are resolved without force. Like any other power, however, it can be subject to abuse. There are two primary categories of abuse. *Wrongful* use involves using force for the wrong reason, such as to retaliate against a person for "disrespect" to the officer. *Disproportionate* use occurs when the level of force far exceeds the level of resistance or aggression of the subject. The police are also required to protect the life and safety of those they use force against once the situation is brought under control.

Web Activity

You can find one presentation on the use-of-force continuum on the National Institute of Justice's website at https://www.nij.gov/topics/law-enforcement/officer-safety/use-of-force/Pages/continuum.aspx.

Legitimate force may be used to bring resisting subjects into compliance. This usually means submitting to arrest, although people may also be forced out of areas where they are trespassing. Police are trained and equipped to employ force in accordance with the **force continuum**, which links the level of police force to the aggressiveness and resistance of the citizen (Figure 3.1).

The force continuum begins with the authoritative presence of the officer and moves through commanding voice and directions to the first actual application of physical force, a guiding push or firm grip to steer a person away from a particular point. Physical resistance from a citizen is required for higher levels of force, including pain compliance holds (wristlocks and other pressure-point techniques), devices such as pepper spray and electrical shocks from stun guns, and the use of impact weapons such as nightsticks. Deadly force is the final step, reserved for a narrowly defined set of circumstances.

Federal funding has promoted the development of less lethal weaponry to assist the police in their mission while minimizing the risk of harm to officers, suspects, and bystanders. Incapacitating chemical agents such as pepper spray, beanbag rounds that knock a person down but do not penetrate the skin, capture nets fired from shotguns, sticky foam, disorienting lights and stun grenades, and other weapons still in the development stage all seek to provide safer alternatives to gunfire.

Police have the power to use deadly force only to save their own lives or those of a third party. A common-law "fleeing felon" rule allowed the use of lethal force to apprehend any accused felon. In 1985, the U.S. Supreme Court in *Tennessee v. Garner* restricted the use of lethal force to situations of imminent and articulable danger. Although police sidearms are the most obvious instruments of lethal force, blunt objects such as a baton or nightstick are also capable of inflicting deadly harm if used improperly or against the wrong target, such as a blow to the head.

Periodically, the issue of the use of force is brought to the public's attention by a high-profile case. In late 2014, a series of use-of-force events leading to the deaths of civilians occurred over a compressed period of time: Many of those

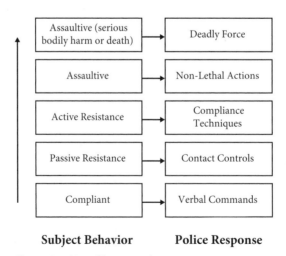

Subject Behavior   **Police Response**

Figure 3.1 Use of force continuum.

incidents were captured on video, either through bystanders' cell phone recordings or officers' dashboard or body-worn video cameras.

The shooting death of Michael Brown in Ferguson, Missouri, is widely acknowledged as the starting point for the Black Lives Matter movement protesting police shootings in particular and any use of force in general. "Hands up! Don't shoot" was one slogan of the protests, arising from early claims that Michael Brown had his hands in the air in surrender as he was shot. Unlike some of the later incidents, no video evidence of the encounter emerged. A grand jury heard substantial conflicting eyewitness testimony: Some reported the "hands up" story, but other testimony substantiated the officer's claim that Brown had attacked him, had tried to take the officer's sidearm, and was charging at the officer when he was shot. Forensic evidence supported the officer's account of the incident, and the grand jury returned "no bill" on the charge of murder against the officer.

A seemingly rapid series of similar events followed, adding fuel to the flame. The wrongly named "chokehold" death of Eric Garner in New York City led to "I can't breathe" as another slogan, as Garner's last words were recorded on a bystander's cell phone video during his arrest. The shooting deaths of Tamir Rice in Cleveland, Ohio, John Crawford in Beavercreek, Ohio, Laquan McDonald in Chicago, and a drug raid on the wrong house in Atlanta that led to the shooting death of a 92-year-old woman all followed a series of contested shootings, including several in Albuquerque, New Mexico.

The outcry led to protests against police throughout the country and was directly responsible for the assassination of two New York City police officers by a mentally disturbed Maryland man who set out to "put wings on pigs" by killing two officers for every citizen who died as a result of police action.

Web Activity

Additional examples of events involving the use of force can be found on the textbook website (http://www.oup.com/us/labessentials).

A number of secondary issues attend the public debate about the police use of deadly force. Police and their conservative supporters assert that shootings are more likely to occur because of the violence in high-crime areas (the residents of which are disproportionately minority); criminologists who have investigated the claim find no substantiation for it across the range of shootings, although individual incidents do fall under that heading. Defenders claim that the numbers of Whites and Blacks shot by the police tend to be roughly equal, including both armed and unarmed suspects. Critics of the police note that although the raw numbers are approximately the same, Blacks are a distinct minority in the population, and the "equal" numbers actually represent a disproportionate number of Black victims. Very few police officers are held criminally liable, even in highly questionable shootings, because judges and juries are reluctant to second-guess the potential for danger. Even when officers are fired for misconduct, appeals boards often require their reinstatement.

Critical Thinking Exercise

What can be done to mend relations that are damaged by a good-faith erroneous shooting? If a member of your family, a close friend, or even someone you knew casually were shot and killed by police officers under comparable circumstances, what would you expect to happen?

The Blue Wall of Silence

The cultural theme of feeling unappreciated and under fire combines with themes of danger and solidarity to create the **blue wall of silence.** Some police officers who know of wrongdoing by other police will not take action against them or provide information against them to investigators for two reasons. First, police mistrust their superiors and fear being given disproportionately harsh punishment to set an example or to alleviate political pressure on their administrators. Second, they fear alienating their brother and sister officers, upon whom they depend for backup assistance in dangerous situations. Unions also fear that employee rights will be abrogated under political pressure, so they intervene as advocates and lawyers for officers accused of wrongdoing. To the public, it appears that "the police protect their own," even against legitimate grievances and complaints of the community. The blue wall is no longer as strong as it was once thought to be, as professional and community-oriented officers realize that the police must clean their own house for legitimacy and that a rogue officer is as much a danger to them as are criminals. Nevertheless, it is still entrenched in some agencies, and the issues that give rise to it remain salient.

Policing the Police

The periodic scandals that arise from police misconduct are followed by public cries for police reform. In the past, most reforms were promises of better internal management by the police agency. In effect, clear rules would be written, better training would be devised, and supervision would be stricter. Police agencies asserted that the illegal behavior featured in the headlines was solely confined to "bad apples" who were not representative of the majority of police officers, who were honest, fair, and devoted to the public good.

More recently, the cyclical nature of police scandals has led people to question the ability of the police themselves. Because criminal convictions of police officers are difficult to obtain, aggrieved citizens and advocacy groups have pursued lawsuits against police agencies, asserting a pattern and practice of denial of civil rights. In addition, the federal Justice Department has moved against some police departments, using lawsuits to craft **consent decrees** that articulate specific changes the departments must make. Typically, those changes are monitored by outside entities that report to the federal court; the issue of racial profiling by the New Jersey State Police resulted in one such consent decree.

Federal intervention depends on the willingness of the current administration to intervene. Lawsuits can also take years to settle. At the local level, residents concerned with police misconduct have begun to call for **civilian review** of police. Allegations of police misconduct are heard by boards composed entirely of residents or a mixture of residents and police officials. Conduct is judged based on community expectations rather than just police practice. In the best models, police experts identify the acceptable standards and types of training that support police policy. The judgments made are then based on whether or not the officers' conduct was in accordance with law, policy, and community expectations of conduct. If discipline is recommended, typically the police chief is responsible for its administration.

Critical Thinking Exercise

Should citizens have the power to judge the actions of a police officer via civilian review boards or other mechanisms? Or is it necessary to have been a police officer in order to determine that a police officer's decision in any matter was correct or incorrect? Is it necessary to be a doctor in order to judge medical malpractice?

Special Constituencies

Police often face issues regarding communities with special needs. The mentally ill are much more prominent on the streets of the nation in the wake of the deinstitutionalization movement in the 1950s that closed asylums and hospitals. Their behavior may be frightening to citizens, and some are potentially dangerous. Immigrant communities bring new languages, different social customs and expectations, and often antagonism toward the police based on their experiences with extremely corrupt and brutal police in their homelands. Police often lack the language skills and social understanding to make contact with the communities, thus hindering service. In both cases, individuals are also vulnerable targets for criminals who take advantage of their inability or reluctance to communicate with the police. In addition, community policing attempts to establish positive relations with immigrants are often in conflict with the federal laws and enforcement mandates to deport those illegally in the country. Some local agencies do not cooperate with ICE because cooperation would inhibit their ability to protect the legitimate immigrant community. Other agencies complain that when they do apprehend illegal immigrants, the understaffed ICE cannot take them into custody and the police are forced to release them. The elderly are also emerging as a new concern for police, who have to deal with issues such as Alzheimer's disease, dementia, isolation, and loneliness.

FUTURE ISSUES

Currently, challenges facing the American police include a combination of older and emerging issues. Terrorist attacks emanating from al Qaeda and other Middle East terrorist organizations have provoked calls for racial profiling of Arabs, despite the continuing problems of African American and Hispanic profiling domestically. Immigration rules are in a state of flux, but the same problems remain for police who must deal with local immigrant communities. Civil liberties are perceived to be threatened in exchange for what is believed to be greater security against terror.

Critical Thinking Exercise

How do you think the recent national attention to terrorism will affect law enforcement practices in the United States? How will it affect the daily activities of local police agencies and officers?

Technology also poses many new challenges for the police. Computer fraud and identity theft are new forms of theft for which most police agencies are not prepared to handle. They lack the necessary state-of-the-art equipment, and only a handful of officers have the necessary skills to track cyberspace looters, hackers, and other electronic predators. The very notion of jurisdiction changes in cyberspace, and American laws may conflict with laws of the European Union, China, and others.

Invasive technologies may soon be widely available, threatening traditional expectations of privacy. The case of *Kyllo v. United States* (2001) required the police to observe privacy as it existed in 1789 when the Constitution was adopted, banning police use of any new technologies that revealed intimate details of a house (e.g., thermal imagers, which were used in the *Kyllo* case). That technology may soon be widely available to the public and to the criminal element, however, requiring both new investigative skills and new countermeasures to protect police resources. Implanted chips, cloning, live human–computer interface, augmented reality systems, and many other issues will result in long-term and potentially profound changes that the police will have to face. The most recent development is the widespread availability of quadcopters, known colloquially as drones. Drones raise considerable concerns over privacy, as legitimate uses clash with potential illegal activities: The same flyover cameras that permit monitoring of crops, remote facilities, and potential hazards can also be used to surreptitiously record private citizens' activities, both outside and inside the home. Despite a relatively low weight-bearing capacity at the present time, drones have a proven capacity to transport uncut drugs across borders and to carry contraband of various types (including cell phones and guns) over prison walls. The recent discovery of a crashed drone on the grounds of the White House has raised alarms about the delivery of improvised explosive devices (IEDs) or biological weapons packages. Other robotic constructs could use the ground or even underground tunnels for similar types of deliveries.

Global Positioning Satellite (GPS) technology is developing rapidly, and it is already a feature in newer automobiles. This greatly increases the ability of the police to track known or suspected criminals and to recover stolen vehicles and other goods. However, the courts still require the police to obtain a warrant before placing a GPS device on a target's vehicle or to piggyback on corporately maintained vehicle-monitoring services such as OnStar. The same is true for accessing information on individuals' cell phones and other portable devices: The Supreme Court unanimously ruled in *Riley v. California* (573 U.S. _2014) that the search of cell phones seized incidental to arrest required a separate warrant, protecting the personal privacy of the information on a basis comparable to personal papers and effects.

Although body-worn cameras are increasingly sought by the police and demanded by their critics, comparable privacy issues attend their use. When the cameras are turned on (particularly on calls in private dwellings), how long recordings are maintained (as well as the conditions for their editing and disposal), as well as to what uses their content may be put for analysis work are all considerations that are being worked out.

Nanotechnology is developing at a rapid pace, with positive implications for medicine already demonstrated, but negative possibilities abound. The public is most familiar with three-dimensional (3D) printing—rapid layering of plastics to form solid objects. A 3D printed firearm has already been claimed, and widespread manufacture of cheap, anonymous, one-use firearms represents a potential threat to the public. As nanotechnology develops further, computer codes for constructing designer drugs, poisons, and explosives through molecular assembly are a different threat.

Economic issues at the state level are undermining the incapacitation model that has held sway over correctional policies for several decades. Faced with rising prison costs and court mandates against overcrowding, legislatures have changed their mandate to the euphemistic "community control," releasing thousands of prisoners well before their sentences have been completed. Without corresponding resources devoted to probation and parole, prisoner reentry is largely unmonitored except by the police. At the same time, the knowledge that conviction will lead to either less time in "the joint" or perhaps even no time at all undermines whatever efficacy remained in the concept of deterrence. Although the long-term impacts are not yet recognized, it is a reasonable expectation that the main burden of "community control" will fall to the already overstretched police.

Social expectations are also changing. The nation's punitive drug laws are under attack as too harsh, wrongly applied, and the wrong approach to the problems of drug abuse. Although the trend toward decriminalizing marijuana—and even legalizing it at the state level—is no longer viewed as dangerous as it once was, the opioid epidemic sweeping the nation has created new demands on the police. Families encourage the use of Narcan and other naloxone treatments, which reverse the effects of potentially fatal drug overdoses, in order to give addicted loved ones a second chance. On the other side of the debate, experiences of law enforcement and emergency medical services personnel suggest that for many addicts, the "second chance" is simply to get high again. They report giving repeated doses to the same individuals, sometimes only hours after a revival, and openly question the wisdom of providing a "fail-safe" to continued self-destructive behavior.

The addition of fentanyl, and now carfentanyl, to the opioid crisis is also changing police procedures. At least two officers have died as a result of inadvertent exposure to the drug while trying to revive an overdose victim or searching a crime scene. Gloving and double-gloving are increasingly the rule for officers in such cases, and many agencies no longer do field testing of suspected drugs. Instead, they treat them as potentially toxic substances and refer them to crime laboratories as such.

The nature of privacy in public spaces is being redefined by closed-circuit TV, social media, GPS tracking, and other technologies. The line dividing federal and state rights is being redefined in the states' favor by the Supreme Court at the same time that many state crimes are being "federalized" in hopes of securing harsher penalties. The impact of globalization on the economy, laws, and social expectations of the nation—indeed, in a longer view, even on the concept of the nation state and sovereignty—has not fully been realized. Globalization is a long-term force with short-term ripples. The "war on terror" may be a short-term problem, but it has long-term implications for civil rights and civil liberties. Technology has implications for both and presents an even more uncertain future as the definition of what it is to be human is determined. All of these present the possibility of another period of radical change for the police, adjusting to new factors in the human and social condition.

CONCLUSION

The police represent a constantly evolving network of agencies and individuals who are empowered to use force but are also expected to use knowledge, insight, and understanding to solve a wide variety of problems that afflict American society. Because of their power to arrest, the police are the gatekeepers of the rest of the criminal justice system, but the greater impact of police work lies in situations that are resolved without arrest. Changes in police work are driven by changes in law, evolutionary changes in social attitudes, and emerging technologies. New challenges, such as the impact of globalization and the intersection of American law with foreign law, will be added to the ongoing challenges of proper selection, training, inculcation of values, and guidance.

KEY WORDS

background checks

beat integrity

beats

blue wall of silence

broken windows

campus-based

   academies

chain of command

citizen patrols

civilian review

community-oriented

   policing

CompStat

consent decrees

constable

contract cities

corruption

crime prevention

detectives

deterrence

discretion

dual-entry tracks

exclusionary rule

Field training officer

   (FTO)

first responders

force continuum

HAZMAT

Internal Affairs

john details

Kansas City Preventive

   Patrol Experiment

law compliance

law enforcement

Minneapolis Domestic

   Violence Experiment

multi-jurisdictional task

   forces

mutual aid

Neighborhood Watch

order maintenance

patrol

police academy

police subculture

power shifts

precincts

preservice training

private police

problem-oriented

   policing

property marking

racial profiling

regional task forces

rotating shifts

safe havens

school resource officers

service

sheriff

single-entry tracks

state patrols

state police

steady shifts

sting operations

stress-based academies

troops

use of force

SUGGESTED READINGS

Police Culture

Crank, J. P., and M. A. Caldero. (2000). *Police ethics: The corruption of noble cause.* Cincinnati: Anderson.

Muir, W. K., Jr. (1977). *Police: Streetcorner politicians.* Chicago: University of Chicago Press.

Community-Oriented and Problem-Oriented Policing

Goldstein, H. (1979). Improving policing: A problem-oriented approach. *Crime and Delinquency* 25:236–258.

Greene, J. R., and S. D. Mastrofski (Eds.). (1988). *Community policing: Rhetoric or reality.* New York: Praeger.

Sparrow, M., M. H. Moore, and D. Kennedy. (1990). *Beyond 911: A new era for policing.* New York: Basic Books.

Trojanowicz, R., and B. Bucqueroux. (1990). *Community policing: A contemporary perspective.* Cincinnati: Anderson.

Modern Reform: Initial Studies

Klockars, C. (1985). *The idea of police.* Beverly Hills, CA: Sage.

Reiss, A. J., Jr. (1971). *The police and the public.* New Haven, CT: Yale University Press.

CHAPTER 4

The Court System

CHAPTER OUTLINE

Basic Tenets of the Court System
History of the Courts
    History of Federal Courts
    History of State Courts
Actors in the Court System
    Judges
    Prosecutors
    Defense Attorneys
    Other Court Actors
Movement of Cases Through the Court System
    Initial Stages to Formal Charging
    Trial
    Sentencing
    Appeals
Trends in the Court System
    Specialized Courts
    Increased Victim Involvement
    Court Technology
    Use of Jury Consultants
Conclusion
Key Words
Suggested Readings

After reading this chapter, you should be able to:

- Explain what is meant by a dual court system
- Discuss the adversarial nature of the court
- Point out key points in the history of federal courts
- Discuss the U.S. Courts of Appeal
- Discuss the history and types of state courts
- Compare and contrast trial courts of limited and general jurisdictions
- List and define the various actors in the courtroom, including the distinctions between federal and state
- Outline the typical movement of cases through the court system
- Discuss the selection of jurors
- Explain the difference between indeterminate and determinate sentences
- Discuss the appeals process
- Identify and define different types of specialized courts
- Give examples of how courts have increased victim involvement

The court system is often referred to as the link between police and the correctional system, although this is something of a misnomer. While it may be true that the court system is, in effect, the second primary aspect of the criminal justice system, its role spans the entire system. In many cases, the court system is involved in criminal cases before police make an arrest and after a person has been subject to some form of correctional sanction. Generally, the court system has two basic functions: to adjudicate defendants charged with crimes and to ensure the entire criminal justice system is engaging in fair procedures as the law is enforced. This is a major undertaking, which is why the court system is viewed as a complex, and often misunderstood, component of the criminal justice system.

BASIC TENETS OF THE COURT SYSTEM

The United States has what is called a **dual court system**, which simply means that the federal government has its own court system and the states have their own court systems. This may seem obvious, but when it comes to the enforcement of the law, having 51 different court systems can become quite complex. The federal court system is responsible for violations of federal law, and state court systems are responsible for violations of the laws in their respective states. It becomes complicated, however, when state and federal laws conflict with one another and the court system must get involved. An example of this is seen with the use of medical marijuana. As of 2017, 29 states had passed laws allowing for the medical use of marijuana for various illnesses. Federal law, however, prohibits the use of medical marijuana. Thus, an individual in California, which authorizes the use of medical marijuana, could be held liable in federal court for use of the drug, even though it is allowed under state law. Because of this conflict between laws, the court system has to get involved to resolve the issue. Numerous individuals have challenged the federal law prohibiting the use of the drug for medical purposes, and perhaps as many have challenged state laws allowing for its use. As a result, state and federal courts have both become involved in these cases, illustrating the complex nature of a dual court system.

Web Activity

For more information on the dual court system, see http://www.uscourts.gov/about-federal-courts/court-role-and-structure/comparing-federal-state-courts
For more information about the conflict between federal and state law regarding medical marijuana, see http://www.ncsl.org/research/health/state-medical-marijuana-laws.aspx.

Another issue involving both federal and state court systems is jurisdiction. The term **jurisdiction** in the court system does not refer to a specific geographic area but, rather, to the authority of courts to hear certain types of cases. For instance, the federal court system only has jurisdiction to rule on cases involving federal law. It does not have the ability to rule on cases involving state law, unless the state law conflicts with federal law or the U.S. Constitution. Appellate courts do not have the jurisdiction to conduct trials. This is the jurisdiction of lower state and federal trial courts. Finally, juvenile courts do not have jurisdiction to hear issues involving divorce or custody issues. In effect, each court, whether at the state or federal level, is limited in the types of cases it is allowed to rule upon. A defendant cannot simply go to any court he or she wishes in order to be heard. He or she must go to the court that specializes in the particular issue at hand.

Another tenet of state and federal court systems is the **adversarial system of justice**. An adversarial system relies on two opposing parties. In criminal cases, this involves a defendant versus the state (in the form of a prosecutor). In addition, this system involves a neutral body, in the form of the judge or jury, that decides the outcome of the case. Generally, it is the responsibility of the state to prove its case against the defendant. This reflects the presumption of innocence. A defendant is presumed innocent until proven guilty by the state. On the other hand, a defendant must challenge a state's case and question the evidence that the state brings forward. It should be known that a defendant is not responsible for proving his or her innocence at trial—the state must prove guilt.

When adjudicating cases, the court system often must balance the needs of the state versus the rights of the defendant. This is sometimes referred to as the crime-control versus due-process model of justice. Packer (1968) developed models to illustrate how the criminal justice system must try to accomplish its goals while ensuring the fair and equal application of the law. The **crime-control model**, as its name implies, focuses on the reduction of criminal behavior. It stresses the swiftness and certainty of case outcomes, suggesting that any delay in the adjudication of criminal cases undermines the ability of the system to reduce crime. The crime-control model posits that many defendants who are arrested are factually guilty, so the court system should waste no time convicting and sentencing them. On the other hand, the **due-process model** emphasizes the protection of rights of defendants. This model is concerned about the violation of rights in the name of crime control and works to ensure that the criminal justice system does not violate the law in order to enforce the law. It views swiftness in the administration of justice as a concern because it increases the likelihood of mistakes being made and innocent people being punished. The criminal justice system has tried to strike a balance between these two competing models, although, at times, one or the other predominates. The court system is the primary component of the system that is charged with ensuring that the law is enforced in a fair and equal manner.

Critical Thinking Exercise

Which model (crime control or due process) do you believe is dominant in criminal courts? Is this appropriate? Should it be changed? What are some examples of the crime-control model in action? The due-process model?

HISTORY OF THE COURTS

Chapter 2 discussed the origins of criminal law in the United States, and the court system has largely been responsible for ensuring that the law is enforced fairly and equally. It is important to understand the history of both federal and state court systems in order to appreciate the role of the courts today.

History of Federal Courts

During the Constitutional Convention in 1787, two competing plans were proposed to establish the federal court system. The New Jersey Plan called for the establishment of one federal court, a Supreme Court, with state court systems playing an active role in adjudicating federal matters. Proponents of the New Jersey Plan were skeptical of a strong, centralized federal judiciary and wanted the states to maintain some control over federal court matters. Under this plan, state courts would conduct trials and other lower-level federal court proceedings, and the process of appeal would take the case to the one federal Supreme Court. An alternative, the Virginia Plan, proposed a broader and more centralized federal court system with the establishment of a Supreme Court and various lower federal courts. Proponents of this plan argued that states should not be involved in federal court matters and that the federal government should have a judiciary system just as states do.

A compromise between the New Jersey Plan and the Virginia Plan was reached, and the result is found in Article III of the U.S. Constitution: "The judicial power of the United States, shall be vested in one supreme court, and in such inferior courts as the Congress may from time to time ordain and establish." In essence, this created the one Supreme Court that both plans advocated, but it allowed Congress to create lower federal courts when necessary. At first, this compromise seemed to benefit the proponents of the New Jersey Plan because no vast federal court system was created. However, over time, the compromise greatly favored the proponents of the Virginia Plan, who eventually saw the creation of a centralized federal court system.

Because the U.S. Constitution allowed Congress to establish lower federal courts, it was only a matter of time before these courts were created. One of the first concerns of the first Congress was the creation of the federal court system. This system consisted of three areas: the U.S. District Courts, the U.S. Courts of Appeal, and the U.S. Supreme Court.

U.S. District Courts

The trial courts of the federal system, the **district courts**, were established by the Judiciary Act of 1789. The 11 states in the union at the time and the territories of Maine and Kentucky were considered districts, so the organization of the federal trial courts was entirely state-contained; that is, no federal district crossed state lines. Each district court was staffed by one district court judge who also had a role in hearing appellate cases. As new states entered the union, more district courts were created.

After the creation of the lower federal courts in 1789, each state was considered a district with one district court. Today, some states are divided into multiple districts because they are simply too populated to have just one district court. There is at least one district court in every state. There are currently 90 district courts in the 50 states and the District of Columbia and 4 others in Guam, Puerto Rico, the U.S. Virgin Islands, and the Northern Mariana Islands.

As noted previously, district courts are the trial courts of the federal system. U.S. District Courts have **original jurisdiction**, which means that these courts have the authority to hear cases for the first time and decide an outcome. Almost 80,000 criminal cases are filed in district courts every year, mostly for federal drug violations and various white-collar offenses (Neubauer and Fradella 2014). Civil cases comprise the bulk of cases that move through the district courts.

U.S. Courts of Appeal

The Judiciary Act of 1789 also established the **appellate courts** of the federal system. The country was divided into three federal court circuits—southern, middle, and eastern—and an appellate court was established for each. The courts were staffed by two U.S. Supreme Court justices and a "district judge" from the U.S. District Courts. The district judge was responsible for establishing the court's caseload, and the Supreme Court justices traveled to each circuit to hear cases at the appellate level—a practice known as "circuit riding." This practice was grueling for the justices and the caseload of the appellate courts increased, especially after the Civil War, making the existing system ill equipped to handle a mounting workload. This system of hearing appellate cases continued until 1891, when Congress passed the Evarts Act. This act created nine federal appellate courts, one for each judicial circuit at the time, that were to hear appeals from the lower federal trial courts. Each appellate court, called a "circuit court," was staffed by newly created circuit court judges, thereby relieving the U.S. Supreme Court justices of their circuit-riding duties. This created a more uniform system of hearing appeals.

The U.S. Courts of Appeal have **appellate jurisdiction**, which means that cases do not originate there and these courts only hear cases that are brought up on appeal, after a lower court has decided an outcome. When federal appellate courts were established in 1789, the country was divided into 3 appellate circuits. Today, there are 11 appellate circuits, and each circuit consists of multiple states.

There is one U.S. Court of Appeals in each of these circuits, and these courts are identified by their circuit—for example, the U.S. Court of Appeals for the Eighth Circuit. There are two other federal appellate courts. One represents the D.C. Circuit (Washington, DC), and one represents the Federal Circuit, which handles cases involving international trade and federal administrative law.

Web Activity

For an illustration of the boundaries of the federal courts, see the textbook website (http://www.oup.com/us/labessentials).

According to Neubauer and Fradella (2014), approximately 60,000 cases are filed each year in the courts of appeal. Of these, only about 20 percent involve federal criminal law issues. Although decisions by the U.S. Courts of Appeal may be petitioned for review by the U.S. Supreme Court, these federal appellate courts are often the "court of last resort" for federal law because the U.S. Supreme Court rarely reviews decisions made by these courts.

Most of the cases heard by the courts of appeal come from the federal district courts. Defendants must appeal their cases in the courts that cover their states. The federal courts of appeals have no control over the cases they hear; that is, there is no discretionary authority to reject appeals. When deciding cases, the courts of appeal usually utilize three-judge panels, which rotate membership periodically.

A majority of the panel is sufficient for a ruling. In rare instances, all of the judges in a circuit may sit to hear a case. This is called an *en banc* proceeding.

U.S. Supreme Court

The final court created by the Congress in 1789 was the Supreme Court. The Supreme Court was to consist of one chief justice and five associate justices. In its first decade of existence, the Court floundered, not really knowing or understanding its role in a federal system of government. According to Carp et al. (2017), the Court did not rule on a case in its first three years of existence and decided only approximately 50 cases during its first decade. This situation was greatly altered, however, with the appointment of John Marshall as the third chief justice in 1801. Marshall is credited with giving the Supreme Court its vision and establishing rules and guidelines that governed the Court's procedures. One of these guidelines was the issuance of a single opinion of the Court. Until this point, each individual justice issued his own ruling with his own rationale. These multiple rulings made it quite difficult for those responsible for enforcing the rulings to know what to do. Marshall created the practice of allowing one opinion of the Court (now called the ruling of the Court or the majority opinion) in order for the Court to present an air of unification around a particular ruling. During Marshall's tenure, the Court was involved in a number of rulings that are considered some of the most important decisions in judicial history (see the textbook website (http://www.oup.com/us/labessentials) for key rulings from this term), including *Marbury v. Madison* (1803) and *McCulloch v. Maryland* (1819).

Web Activity

For a list of all U.S. Supreme Court Justices, including Chief Justices, see the textbook website (http://www.oup.com/us/labessentials).

Web Activity

For access to full opinions by the U.S. Supreme Court, visit its website at https://www.supremecourt.gov/opinions/opinions.aspx.

The U.S. Supreme Court is considered the final arbiter for issues involving federal law and the U.S. Constitution. Once the U.S. Supreme Court has made a decision in a case, that decision is final and cannot be reviewed by any other court. Although the Court has primarily appellate jurisdiction, it does have original jurisdiction in some cases. For example, the Court is the first and only court to hear cases involving disputes between two states, such as boundary disputes.

Today, the U.S. Supreme Court is composed of one chief justice and eight associate justices. When deciding to hear cases, the U.S. Supreme Court has a large amount of discretion, unlike the courts of appeal. The Court hears oral arguments in only a fraction of cases petitioned for review each year. In fact, out of approximately 7,000 cases on the Court's docket each year, only about 100 are selected for oral arguments.

Web Activity

For more information about the U.S. Supreme Court's caseload, see https://www .supremecourt.gov/about/justicecaseload.aspx

---

The U.S. Supreme Court only hears cases that involve what it considers to be the most important policy issues. Cases that come to the Court come from the U.S. Courts of Appeal (for cases involving federal law) and state supreme courts (for cases involving conflicts with federal law or state violations of the U.S. Constitution).

Web Activity

For more information about the history of the U.S. Supreme Court, visit http://www .supremecourthistory.org

---

History of State Courts

The federal court system is probably better known to the public, but state court systems were in existence before the federal court system was established. In colonial times, local courts, often called justice of the peace courts or magistrate courts, handled lower-level court matters. County courts were the trial courts of the colonies, and appeals were handled by the royal governor (Carp et al. 2017). After the revolution, state court structure was largely the same as that of the colonial courts, although the royal governor was no longer present.

The various states had largely been left to their own devices when it came to the creation and administration of their court systems. Most states had systems for handling various levels of court procedures, such as trials and appeals, but encountered problems as industrialization and population increased after the Civil War. Local courts began to struggle with increased caseloads and different types of cases, which involved newly created laws dealing with issues such as business and child labor. As a result, state courts were forced to find innovative ways to deal with these issues, including creating more courts and specialized courts, although some states are still facing some of the same problems today.

Trial Courts of Limited Jurisdiction

Trial courts of limited jurisdiction comprise the lowest level of courts in the state court system. These courts go by a variety of names, including "magistrate," "municipal," "city," and "justice of the peace" courts. They have limited jurisdiction because they are restricted to handling only certain types of matters—in effect, minor matters. In criminal cases, these minor matters include misdemeanors, but they also include the early stages of felony cases, such as first appearances, bail hearings, and appointment of counsel. These courts also handle cases involving traffic and small claims issues.

Although trial courts of limited jurisdiction are restricted in the types of matters they can handle, they constitute approximately 85 percent of all judicial bodies in the country. As such, the number of cases that are handled by these courts has grown over time, and they now handle roughly 70 million cases per year (Neubauer and Fradella 2014). Most of the cases are traffic offenses (more than 40 million). This has resulted in overcrowding problems, and courts do not have the resources to handle the increasing numbers of cases coming into the system. The number of each of these courts varies from state to state, and more populated areas have numerous courts of limited jurisdiction in certain counties.

Web Activity

The National Center for State Courts monitors courts throughout the states. Its report on limited jurisdiction courts illustrates challenges that these courts face. See http://www.ncsc.org/sitecore/content/microsites/future-trends-2012/home/Courts-and-the-Community/3-6-Limited-Jurisdiction-Courts.aspx.

State courts vary in organization and structure. Box 4.1 offers a brief summary of the structure of three different court systems. California has a streamlined and organized court system. Throughout the state, all courts of limited and general jurisdiction are called "superior courts." California's intermediate appellate courts are called "courts of appeal," and its court of last resort is called the "supreme court."

Ohio has four types of limited-jurisdiction courts, each handling similar cases. Counties and cities in Ohio vary as to which type of limited-jurisdiction court they will use. For example, municipal courts are found in 128 municipalities (cities) in Ohio, but there are only 38 county courts statewide. Generally, a particular county will have only one or the other operating within the county. In addition, Ohio's trial courts of general jurisdiction are called "courts of common pleas," which is a unique name for this type of court. This name is a holdover from British common-law courts in existence in England until the 1800s. Most states call these courts "superior courts," "district courts," "circuit courts," and the like. Ohio's court of last resort is called the "supreme court."

BOX 4.1

The Structure of Three State Court Systems

California

    Superior courts (58 counties)

    Courts of appeal (six districts)

    Supreme court

Ohio

    Limited-jurisdiction courts (four types: mayor's courts, county courts, municipal courts, and courts of claims)

    Courts of common pleas (88 counties)

    Courts of appeal (12 courts)

    Supreme court

New York

    Limited-jurisdiction courts (eight types)

    General jurisdiction courts (city and county)

    Appellate courts (one for New York City counties; one for outside New York City)

    Court of appeals

Web Activity

Figures depicting the structure of the California, Ohio, and New York courts can be seen on the textbook website (http://www.oup.com/us/labessentials).

Finally, New York provides a good illustration of a state court structure in need of organization. New York has eight limited-jurisdiction courts, and the county or city determines which court it will use. In addition, New York has two trial courts of general jurisdiction—called a "supreme court" and a "county court"—with county courts operating outside of New York City. New York also has two intermediate appellate courts. Counties in New York are combined into "departments," and each department has an appellate court that serves those counties. The first intermediate appellate court, the "Appellate Divisions of Supreme Court," serves departments outside of New York City. The second appellate court is called the "Appellate Terms of Supreme Court," and this court handles appeals from departments representing the counties encompassing New York City. Finally, New York's court of last resort is called the "court of appeals." As demonstrated by this discussion, states differ widely in the way they structure their courts.

Web Activity

The National Center for State Courts provides court structure charts for all 50 states. See http://www.courtstatistics.org/Other-Pages/State_Court_Structure_Charts.aspx.

Trial Courts of General Jurisdiction

A second form of state courts is **trial courts of general jurisdiction**. These are considered the major trial courts at the state level and handle the more serious criminal and civil cases that arise in state courts. The actual names of these courts vary depending on the state, but most trial courts of general jurisdiction are called "district," "circuit," or "superior" courts.

Generally, each state is divided into districts, usually counties, and each district employs one major trial court. In rural areas, these districts may encompass several counties and judges will travel to each county in the district to hear cases. In other areas, judges are assigned to specific courthouses and cases come to them. According to Neubauer and Fradella (2014), more than 18 million cases are filed each year in these courts, vastly outnumbering the number of cases filed in federal trial courts. Of these, most are traffic offenses (3 million), civil cases (6.6 million), and criminal cases (3.8 million).

State Courts of Appeal

The next set of courts are **state courts of appeal**, which are often called "intermediate courts of appeal" because they comprise the middle level of the court system between trial courts and the state supreme courts. Eleven states do not have intermediate courts of appeal, largely due to the fact that the appeal load is so low that this level of court is not needed. In these situations, the state supreme court is the only state appellate court. State courts of appeal primarily have appellate jurisdiction.

State courts of must hear all appeals that are filed with the court and provide a resolution to each. As such, the state supreme court is able to exercise much discretion because many appeals are resolved at the intermediate level. In states that do not employ intermediate appellate courts, state supreme courts must hear all appeals and provide resolutions.

The number of judges serving on state courts of appeal varies depending on the state. Like the federal courts of appeal, cases at this level are typically heard by three-judge panels. As stated previously, most appeals end at this stage because the state supreme court is highly discretionary when selecting appeals to hear.

State Supreme Courts

State supreme courts are the courts of last resort for issues involving state law. Although most states call these courts "supreme courts," a few designate them as "courts of appeals" or other names. In states with state courts of appeal, the supreme court has the discretion not to take a case because the other courts are required to provide some resolution. The number of judges who serve on state supreme courts varies depending on the state, but the judges hear cases *en banc*. These courts have original jurisdiction in some matters but largely have appellate jurisdiction.

ACTORS IN THE COURT SYSTEM

Each level of the court system in state and federal courts consists of individuals who are responsible for processing defendants through the system. This chapter has already mentioned judges with regard to their presence at the various levels of the court system, and the judge is perhaps the most visible actor in court. There are two other prominent actors, the prosecutor and the defense attorney, who occupy equally important positions. The judge, prosecutor, and defense attorney compose the courtroom workgroup, a concept used to illustrate how each individual actor works with the other actors to move cases through the court system. Although the criminal justice system is considered an adversarial system, there are no true adversaries in practice. Generally, prosecutors and defense attorneys work together to create mutually beneficial case outcomes, and judges are on hand to assist in the negotiations. This process is typically seen in overcrowded court systems, when all participants are eager to move cases off of their dockets and out of the system quickly through the use of practices such as guilty pleas or dismissals. In addition to the major actors in the court system, there are other actors such as clerks of court, court administrators, bailiffs, probation officers, and others who serve important functions in the court system.

Judges

As mentioned previously, **judges** are perhaps the most visible actors in the court system. They are also considered the most powerful because they make many important decisions at all levels of the court system. They also exercise a large amount of discretion, as evidenced by the many roles that judges undertake. In lower courts, judges conduct bail hearings, assign counsel, accept guilty pleas, conduct misdemeanor trials, sentence defendants, conduct preliminary hearings, issue warrants, and rule on the admissibility of evidence. In trial courts, judges preside over felony trials and sentence defendants. At the appellate level, judges review decisions of lower courts and issue rulings based on the merits of the case. Judges are present at every level of the court system and issue important rulings on every aspect of a case.

Federal Judges

The path to becoming a judge in the federal court system is fairly straightforward. Federal judges are called "Article III" judges because their appointment is outlined in Article III of the U.S. Constitution. The president nominates a person for a federal judgeship, and that person must be confirmed by the Senate. Federal judges serve no specified terms of office. They have life tenure and leave the federal bench through retirement, death, or impeachment. There are no formal qualifications for becoming a federal judge, such as a minimum age requirement or minimum experience practicing law. There are, however, informal qualifications that can determine whether an individual is appointed to the federal bench. Typically, nominees have distinguished law careers or have actively supported the political party in office. As such, federal judges are considered political appointees and must endure a highly political process to be confirmed by the Senate.

An advantage of judicial appointment is that it leaves the decision of who becomes a judge to individuals who are able to judge the qualifications of a particular candidate. It also allows judges to make their decisions a little more freely, in that they are not subject to the will of the public and election cycles. A disadvantage is that the appointment is quite political, with ideology overshadowing qualifications in some cases. In addition, federal judges who make unpopular decisions cannot be removed from the bench easily. Life tenure enables judges to stay on the bench for an extended period of time.

Web Activity

A recent report indicated that more judges are needed in federal district courts. For information on how this affects the federal court system, see https://www .brennancenter.org/sites/default/files/analysis/Federal%20Judgeship%20Act%20 Testimony.pdf.

State Judges

There are varying routes to becoming a state judge. The three primary methods are by election, merit selection, and appointment. More than half of the states utilize an election process, in which voters decide who will be the next judge in their community. Elections can either be partisan or nonpartisan. In a **partisan election**, candidates declare a political affiliation and campaign as a party member, typically with support from the party. In a **nonpartisan election**, the candidates' political affiliations are not specified, although the candidates' party affiliation usually becomes known because the state's political parties contribute money to their candidates' campaigns. Elected judges usually serve a term of office and must be reelected after the term is complete.

An advantage of judicial elections is that the public can choose judges it believes are best qualified to serve. Also, judges can be held accountable for their rulings and voted out of office if the public believes they are not performing well. A disadvantage of judicial elections is that they are often not as publicized as other elections, and the public may not educate itself on the qualifications of a particular candidate, voting instead on criteria that have little to do with a judge's ability to serve.

A second method, **merit selection**, typically involves three steps. First, recommendations are made to the governor by a group of lawyers and citizens about qualified nominees. Second, the governor appoints the judge to a specified term of office (often a year or less). Third, the new judge is placed on the ballot for a "retention election." This retention election asks voters if they wish to retain the judge for a full term of office. The vast majority of judges are retained by voters.

An advantage of merit selection is that it takes partisan politics out of the process: Lawyers and citizens hold the cards in the selection. Also, merit selection gives voters a chance to see a judge in action before he or she is retained, and voters do not have to wait for a full judicial term (usually six years) to vote someone out of office. A disadvantage is that although power is taken away from political parties, it gives more power to the legal profession, which may reward its own.

The third selection method for state judges is **gubernatorial or legislative appointment**. Only a handful of states allow either the governor or the legislature to appoint judges. In this system, the governor or the state legislature has the sole authority to appoint judges. There is usually no other entity (e.g., the Senate in federal cases) to approve the choice of the governor or legislature. The governor or legislature is also responsible for reappointment after the term of office is complete.

As with the federal system, politics comes into play with gubernatorial and legislative selection. Governors may give appointments to those who have supported their campaigns or those who could help them politically. According to Carp and Stidham (1990), legislatures often appoint former lawmakers to the post. In fact, the authors claim that legislatures appoint their former members as judges in 80 percent of cases.

Web Activity

For more information about the selection of judges in various states, see the website of the American Judicature Society at http://www.judicialselection.us/judicial_selection/methods/selection_of_judges.cfm?state.

Critical Thinking Exercise

What do you think is the best method for selecting judges? Do you believe judges are influenced by their chances of being reelected? Should judges be concerned about voters when making their decisions?

Prosecutors

Whereas judges are considered the most visible actors in the court system, **prosecutors** often work behind closed doors. Much of what prosecutors do is not readily visible to the public. As a result, the role of the prosecutor is cloaked in mystery. Prosecutors are most often seen by the public in courtrooms arguing cases on behalf of the state, but this constitutes only a small portion of their time. In criminal cases, prosecutors make bail recommendations to judges, file charges against defendants, conduct preliminary hearings and grand jury proceedings, file motions with judges, engage in plea agreements, represent the state at trial, and make sentencing recommendations. Due to these actions, prosecutors exercise a tremendous amount of discretion in the court system. Some argue that prosecutors have more discretion than judges, particularly since judicial discretion has been curbed by sentencing guidelines.

Federal Prosecutors

Prosecutors in the federal court system work for the U.S. Department of Justice. As head of this department, the U.S. Attorney General is nominated by the president, is confirmed by the Senate, and serves as a member of the president's cabinet. The position of Attorney General is largely an administrative one, directing the work of those who work for the department. As such, he or she is not involved in everyday federal court matters. This responsibility is given to U.S. Attorneys and their assistants.

As mentioned previously, the United States is divided into federal court districts, and each district is assigned a U.S. Attorney and multiple Assistant U.S. Attorneys. U.S. Attorneys are nominated by the president and confirmed by the Senate, and Assistant U.S. Attorneys are appointed by the Attorney General. These individuals have the responsibility of prosecuting cases in federal court and defending the United States when it is sued in civil court. U.S. Attorneys are able to exercise tremendous discretion in their jobs. There is no real formal oversight of U.S. Attorneys in their respective districts.

State and Local Prosecutors

The role of prosecutors at the state and local levels is not much different from their role at the federal level, although the route to becoming a prosecutor at the state level differs. Like the federal system, states have attorneys general, who are usually selected by voters in statewide elections. The role of the state attorney general differs from state to state, but one main characteristic is the lack of authority over local prosecutors. In effect, the state attorney general does not have much authority to get involved in matters at the local level, limiting his or her role to providing legal advice and defending the state when it is sued in civil court. In recent years, state attorneys general have become increasingly involved in civil matters, especially matters that involve consumer protection.

The individuals responsible for prosecuting violations of criminal laws are the local prosecutors. Local prosecutors are usually elected at the county level, and they represent the county in which they are elected. These prosecutors are called by a number of titles; the most common are "district attorney," "chief prosecutor," and "county attorney." The chief prosecutor's job in a county is both administrative and prosecutorial, in that he or she organizes and directs the responsibilities of assistants as well as goes to court and prosecutes criminal defendants in higher-profile felony cases. The assistants, often called assistant district attorneys or assistant prosecutors, are largely responsible for the early stages of a criminal case and minor criminal offenses. These assistants are typically hired by the chief prosecutor and are not subject to election by voters. Neubauer and Fradella (2014) noted that assistant district attorneys are usually hired right out of law school, work only a few years at a prosecutor's office, and use the office as a stepping stone into private practice or upper-level positions in the criminal justice system (e.g., judge).

Web Activity

The Bureau of Justice Statistics conducted a survey of prosecutors in 2007. To view the report, see the textbook website (http://www.oup.com/us/labessentials).

Defense Attorneys

Defense attorneys have the job of defending the accused against prosecution by the government. Although defendants in the criminal justice system have the right to be represented by an attorney, many cannot afford the services of an attorney. As a result, the U.S. Supreme Court has ruled in a number of decisions that poor individuals have the right to an appointed attorney in certain cases. The various forms of defense attorneys are discussed next.

Private Attorneys

Private attorneys, or **retained counsel**, are hired by defendants, who pay for the attorneys' legal services. Defendants who can afford them may have their attorneys represent them in any type and at any stage of a criminal case. In these instances, defendants literally get what they pay for and are able to have continuous representation if they can afford it. However, the bulk of criminal defendants cannot afford to pay for their own attorneys and must use attorneys provided by the government. In fact, in some areas, up to 80 percent of felony defendants are considered too poor to hire an attorney (Smith and DeFrances 1996).

Appointed Attorneys

As mentioned previously, a number of U.S. Supreme Court rulings have insisted that defendants can have appointed attorneys represent them if they cannot afford one. In *Gideon v. Wainwright* (1963), the Court ruled that poor defendants charged with felonies have the right to court-appointed counsel. In the subsequent cases *Argersinger v. Hamlin* (1972) and *Scott v. Illinois* (1979), the Court extended the right to court-appointed counsel to defendants who face imprisonment. Although this seems like a victory for poor defendants, in reality, defendants do not have the right to court-appointed attorneys if they do not face imprisonment. Thus, defendants who are subject only to probation or fines are not entitled to court-appointed counsel. In addition, whereas private attorneys can represent their clients at any stage of a criminal case, court-appointed counsel is generally not guaranteed at stages that are not deemed "critical," such as lineups, grand jury proceedings, and some appeals.

At both the state and the federal level, the methods of providing and appointing counsel vary. At the federal level, Congress is responsible for organizing and appropriating funds to the various districts for provision of counsel. In the states, most methods are organized and financed by the state and/or county. In general, there are three methods of providing counsel to poor defendants: assigned counsel, public defenders, and contract systems.

One of the appointed counsel systems involves the appointment of private attorneys who volunteer their services to the court. This **assigned counsel** system is primarily utilized in areas with smaller caseloads because it is more economically feasible to provide counsel on a case-by-case basis. Typically, a judge maintains a list of eligible attorneys and chooses one when a case arises. These attorneys are usually paid on an hourly or per-case basis, but the rate of compensation is generally low and critics question the ability of assigned counsel to provide effective representation. In 2000, the New York County Lawyers' Association successfully sued the city of New York to increase the compensation of court-appointed attorneys.

A second type of appointed counsel system is the **public defender**. A public defender's office is usually a state- or county-administered organization staffed by attorneys who are paid a yearly salary for their services. This system is typically found in medium- and large-sized urban areas that have considerable caseloads and specialize in defending the poor. Some proponents of a public defender system claim that the attorneys are able to provide expert criminal defense because it is the only thing they do. Despite this, public defender systems have long been criticized for providing inadequate representation due to the large numbers of cases they handle. Although they may be experts in their field, public defenders may not have the time to concentrate on cases the way they should.

Web Activity

For the Bureau of Justice Statistics' report on state public defender systems, see the textbook website (http://www.oup.com/us/labessentials).

A third type of appointed counsel system is called the **contract system**. In this type of system, private attorneys bid to represent poor defendants for a fixed fee and a specified period of time. This method is seen as a way to save money on indigent defense because the state or county will likely choose the attorney who submits the lowest bid. A downside is that the quality of representation may be low because the attorney has only a set amount of money to use when defending clients.

Although not considered a formal, government-sponsored method of providing indigent defense, **legal aid** societies are found in many larger cities. Legal aid societies are usually supported by private contributions that provide payment for the services performed by the attorneys who work for the organization. In addition, some attorneys work **pro bono**, donating their services out of what they view as a professional obligation. Finally, criminal defendants are allowed to represent themselves (called **pro se**), provided they meet certain requirements established by the judge in a particular case.

Web Activity

For an examination of indigent defense systems in the United States, see https://www.bjs.gov/content/pub/pdf/idsus0812.pdf.

Regardless of the type of criminal defense, all attorneys are required to provide effective assistance of counsel, according to the U.S. Supreme Court's ruling in *McMann v. Richardson* (1970). Since this ruling, the U.S. Supreme Court has established guidelines for defendants to meet if they claim that their attorney provided ineffective assistance of counsel. In general, defendants must prove that the outcome of their case would have been different if their attorney had been effective, which is extremely difficult to prove (see *Strickland v. Washington* [1984]).

Critical Thinking Exercise

Debate over the quality of legal representation often involves the relative merits of hired vers'us appointed counsel. Many critics claim that those who can afford to hire their own counsel fare better in court. Do you believe that this is true? Investigate this claim. What evidence is there to support this position? What evidence is there that this position is false?

Other Court Actors

Many other individuals besides attorneys work in the courtroom. **Bailiffs** are responsible for maintaining order in the courtroom, and law enforcement officers—usually deputies—transport detained defendants between the courthouse and jail. Probation officers work with the court to monitor individuals who are sentenced to probation. In addition, probation officers are often responsible for completing a presentence investigation of a defendant. This involves providing the sentencing judge with detailed information about the defendant and the crime before the judge imposes a sentence.

There are numerous individuals who are responsible for the administrative aspects of the court. Clerks of court are the record keepers of the case files. Court reporters create a transcribed record of proceedings as they occur. Court administrators are responsible for supervising court staff and working with the judge on issues such as budgets and personnel.

Besides formal court personnel, there are others who appear in court from time to time. Victims and witnesses often come to court for official proceedings or to inquire about the state of their cases. Victims may also utilize victim advocates, who assist victims when their cases are processed by the criminal justice system. In addition to victims and witnesses, jurors play a pivotal role in the court system. Jurors are responsible for assessing the evidence against the accused and determining if the state, in the form of the prosecutor, met the burden of proof in establishing guilt. The process of selecting jurors is discussed later.

MOVEMENT OF CASES THROUGH THE COURT SYSTEM

Most criminal cases follow a general trajectory as they move through the court system. As mentioned previously, the court is involved in many cases before official arrests have been made, so the court's role is not relegated to dealing with cases after the police have completed their tasks.

Initial Stages to Formal Charging

One of the constitutional requirements of police work is to secure a warrant prior to making an arrest. Despite this, the U.S. Supreme Court has authorized many types of arrest without a warrant. These are typically reserved for circumstances in which it is not feasible to take the time to secure a warrant. In other circumstances, police must secure a warrant from a judge in order to make an arrest. Police must go to a judge in a limited-jurisdiction court and support the information in the warrant (e.g., probable cause and evidence). Once the judge approves the warrant, the police may make a formal arrest. Police may also ask a lower-court judge to approve a search warrant in order to search a specific place for evidence.

After an arrest has been made, suspects are brought before a lower-court judge for their **initial appearance**. At this stage, defendants are informed of the charges against them, a bail decision is made, representation by a defense attorney is arranged (if applicable), and a date is set for the next stage in the case. In most misdemeanor cases, defendants plead guilty to the charges against them and are sentenced immediately. In many states, those charged with felonies are not allowed to plead guilty at this stage. Instead, they plead not guilty and await the next stage of their case.

Web Activity

You can examine the process of cases through the federal system at https://www.justice.gov/usao/justice-101/steps-federal-criminal-process.

When a **bail** decision is made, the judge examines a number of variables to determine if a defendant is to be released into the community pending the resolution of his or her case. The primary variables are seriousness of the offense, prior record, and flight risk. Generally, the more serious the offense, the more extensive the prior record, and the higher the flight risk, the greater the likelihood that bail will be high or will be denied altogether. For some offenses, such as first-degree murder, bail is denied outright and a defendant has no chance to secure release. The U.S. Supreme Court has upheld the denial of bail for purposes of **preventive detention** (*United States v. Salerno* [1987]). Regardless of the offense, prior record, or flight risk, if a defendant is deemed by the judge to be too dangerous to be released into the community, bail is denied.

For most offenses, bail is granted. If a defendant pays the amount (called a **bond**), he or she is released and must return to court when his or her next court date is scheduled. Upon return, the bond is refunded to the defendant. If the defendant does not return to court, the bond is forfeited. Some courts will accept only a cash bond, whereas others will accept a collateral bond. In these cases, the defendants put up assets, such as cars or property, as collateral in return for release. In most cases, however, defendants are unable to pay the bail amount, so they use the services of bail bondsmen. Bail bondsmen usually require that the defendants pay a fee of 10 percent of the bail amount to the bondsmen. In return, the bondsmen pay the rest of the bond to the court, usually in the form of insurance, and guarantee the court that the defendants will appear for the next scheduled court date. The bondsmen keep the 10 percent of the bail amount as payment for services and can utilize any legal means at their disposal to ensure that the defendants appear for court.

Critical Thinking Exercise

A number of states have embarked on bail reform on the premise that lower-income individuals are disadvantaged in a monetary bail system. A *Washington Post* article from 2015 highlights some of the problems with the bail system. What are some ways to fix these problems? See https://www.washingtonpost.com/posteverything/wp/2015/07/20/theres-never-been-a-better-time-for-bail-reform/?utm_term=.d1c542e515b7.

The next stage of a case is usually a **preliminary hearing**. This occurs when a lower-court judge (not the judge at the initial appearance) views the evidence against the defendant to determine if there is enough probable cause to proceed to trial. In many states, the preliminary hearing is the only chance for a judge to view the evidence before a trial. In these cases, a prosecutor will issue an **information** to indicate that probable cause has been met and the defendant is formally charged with a crime.

In other states, a grand jury hearing takes place after the judge has ruled in a preliminary hearing that a case will proceed. A grand jury hearing is required in all federal prosecutions but not state prosecutions, although 19 states require the procedure in felony cases. A **grand jury** is composed of citizens who serve for a set period of time during which they consider numerous cases. The prosecutor alone provides evidence of the crime—the defendant has no right to present a case—and the grand jury must find that there is probable cause to proceed to trial, usually by majority vote. If probable cause has been met, the grand jury issues a **true bill of indictment** (or simply referred to as an indictment), the equivalent of a prosecutor's "information." If probable cause has not been met, then a "no true bill" is issued. The idea behind a grand jury is that the public is allowed to provide a check on the power of the prosecutor and judge—in effect, to be a watchdog over the courts to prevent malicious prosecutions. However, most states do not utilize a grand jury because it has not been required by the U.S. Supreme Court, and the vast majority of cases brought before grand juries end with indictments.

After formal charges have been filed, the next stage of a case is the **arraignment**. At this stage, the defendant is required to enter a plea to the formal charges against him or her. Defendants who have not yet pled guilty are likely to do so at this stage because formal charges send a message that the criminal justice system has a strong case against the defendant. If a defendant pleads guilty, a sentence is then imposed. For those pleading not guilty, a trial date is set.

Plea Agreements

It is necessary to discuss plea agreements in a separate section due to the frequency of the practice in the court system. It has been estimated that 90 percent of cases in which charges are filed result in plea agreements (Covey 2008). Plea agreements are often viewed as a necessary evil in a system that is ill equipped to take every case to trial. Plea agreements are a method of disposing of a court's caseload while trying to dispense justice at the same time.

A defendant can engage in a plea agreement at most stages of a criminal case. With few exceptions, such as felony defendants at first appearance, a defendant can decide to plead guilty if he or she believes it is warranted. As mentioned previously, most misdemeanor defendants plead guilty and are sentenced at their initial appearance. Other defendants may plead not guilty and wait and see how their case progresses. There is always a chance (however slim) that the case will be dismissed later. Regardless of when the plea agreement occurs, most charged defendants plead guilty before a trial commences.

Plea agreements typically involve some sort of leniency on the part of the prosecutor and judge. Thus, a **plea bargain** occurs when the defendant makes a deal with the court to plead guilty in exchange for a charge/count reduction or a sentence reduction. In a charge/count bargain, a prosecutor may agree to reduce the charge from a felony to a misdemeanor or reduce the number of counts for which a defendant is charged. In a sentence bargain, the prosecutor may agree to argue for a more lenient punishment at sentencing, provided the defendant pleads guilty as charged. Some plea agreements involve no bargain at all, and defendants plead guilty as charged and are sentenced without any promised leniency.

Some argue that plea agreements, particularly plea bargains, allow defendants to "get off the hook" because their punishments do not fit their crimes. In fact, some communities have proposed or enacted bans on plea bargaining because of the sense that it allows criminals to escape harsher punishment. Critics also argue that plea agreements negate the adversarial process that is the cornerstone of the criminal justice system. In effect, plea agreements are orchestrated by the courtroom workgroup because the agreements are beneficial to everyone involved. Supporters argue that plea agreements are needed to help dispose of cases in crowded courts and that they result in sure convictions and punishment for defendants whom everyone knows are guilty. Regardless of the views on the practice, the use of plea agreements will continue in the court system for a long time.

Web Activity

The state of New Jersey has placed its plea agreement form online. To view it, see https://www.judiciary.state.nj.us/forms/10079_main_plea_form.pdf.

Assembly-Line Justice and Case Attrition
In the early stages of a criminal case, the court system is often accused of engaging in **assembly-line justice**, a term used to illustrate the movement of cases through the courts. In areas with large caseloads, it may not be possible for the courtroom workgroup to spend much time on cases, so each case is handled in a quick and efficient manner in order to move on to the next. This is especially seen in the lower courts, where initial appearances and plea agreements are handled much like a manufacturing assembly line. Ordinary, run-of-the-mill cases are handled this way in order to concentrate on other, more serious cases, such as those that go to trial.

The handling of cases as if on an assembly line is one of the reasons for **case attrition**, or the filtering out of cases from the court system. Case attrition is likened to a funnel, such that, as cases progress through the criminal justice process, the number of cases decreases. Although case attrition is most visible in the court system, police also engage in the practice. For instance, police may choose not to arrest or file charges against a suspect. As a result, these cases are filtered out of the courts even before they enter it. Largely, however, case attrition occurs during the court process. Prosecutors may choose not to formally charge a suspect with a crime, due to lack of evidence or witness problems. In addition, plea agreements contribute to attrition when cases are settled at the initial appearance. As a case progresses, defendants may choose to plead guilty at a later stage, such as at arraignment, or a prosecutor may dismiss the charges. In effect, attrition for whatever reason is necessary because the court system is simply not equipped to take every case to trial. Figure 4.1 provides an illustration of case attrition (http://nhw.ozpanda.com/tag/crime-funnel).

Critical Thinking Exercise

Due to the increasing number of cases coming into the criminal justice system, the court system has become overcrowded and assembly-line justice has resulted. What are some mechanisms to reduce the influx of cases into the system?

Trial

After formal charges have been filed, a defendant enters a plea to those charges. If a defendant pleads not guilty, a trial date is set. According to the U.S. Constitution, a defendant has a right to a jury trial, but this right is limited to defendants who are charged with "serious" offenses—those that authorize a punishment of six months' or more incarceration. Defendants who are eligible for jury trials may opt for bench trials instead. A **bench trial** occurs when a judge alone hears the evidence against a defendant and renders a verdict. According to Neubauer and Fradella (2014), a defendant may prefer a bench trial when the trial involves complex issues or when the case is emotionally charged.

If a jury trial is on the docket, the first step is to conduct jury selection. A **master jury list** is composed to identify potential jurors who are eligible to serve on a jury, usually people who are registered voters or who possess valid driver's licenses. Once the master jury list is created, a sample of potential jurors is selected from the list. This list is called the **venire,** or jury pool, and these individuals are notified by mail to report for jury duty. Once at the courthouse, the jury pool is questioned during a process called **voir dire**, in which the prosecutor and defense attorney (and sometimes the judge) question the individuals on their knowledge about the case or potential biases they may possess. If the prosecutor or defense attorney wishes to exclude an individual from jury duty, he or she may dismiss the juror using one of two methods. The first method, called a **challenge for cause**, allows attorneys to dismiss an unlimited number of jurors for legal reasons specified in state and federal statutes. An example of a challenge for cause would be that a potential juror is related to someone involved in the case.

A second method of dismissing jurors is called a **peremptory challenge**, in which lawyers may dismiss a limited number of jurors based on reasons that do

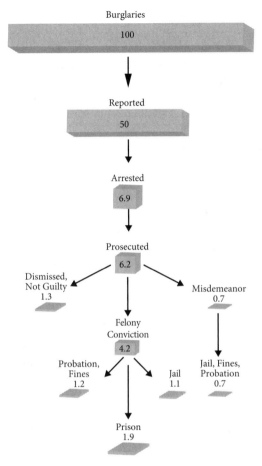

Figure 4.1 Crime funnel for burglars.
SOURCE: Calculated from Bureau of Justice Statistics (BJS), Sourcebook of Criminal Justice Statistics, 1995, p. 250; FBI Crime in the United States 1997, p. 213; and BJS, Tracking Offenders, 1990, pp. 2, 5, 8.

not need to be specified to the court. A lawyer may not believe that an individual juror "looks right" and may dismiss the juror based on a mere hunch. The use of peremptory challenges has long been challenged in the courts because it provides opportunities for both the prosecution and defense to "stack the jury" in their favor. Historically, the use of these challenges allowed both sides to engage in discriminatory practices by removing jurors based on race or gender (see *Batson v. Kentucky* [1986]). Courts therefore have imposed a limit on the number of peremptory challenges, making it more difficult for either side in a case to stack the jury.

Once jury selection is complete, the trial begins. The trial starts with opening statements by the prosecutor and defense attorney, each telling the jury what he or she hopes to show with regard to the evidence. The prosecution presents its case first, and the defense has an opportunity to cross-examine the prosecution's witnesses. In a trial, the prosecution has the burden of proving the defendant is guilty beyond a reasonable doubt. This is called the **burden of proof**. The defense, on the other hand, only has to question the prosecution's case enough to instill doubt in a juror's mind—the defense does not have to prove a defendant innocent. In fact, the defense does not have to present any evidence at trial if it believes that the prosecution has not met the burden of proof. In reality, defense attorneys usually provide some sort of defense, calling witnesses who can support its case or call into question any evidence the prosecution presents. Like the defense during the prosecution's case, the prosecutor is able to cross-examine defense witnesses at this time. Both sides then have another chance to refute any evidence given by the other side—a process called **rebuttal**.

During the trial process, both the prosecution and the defense present **evidence**. For the prosecutor, this evidence points to the guilt of the defendant. **Direct evidence** is the strongest form of evidence. Examples of direct evidence include a confession by the defendant, eyewitness testimony, or the defendant's fingerprints at the crime scene. **Circumstantial evidence** is indirect evidence. This type of evidence implies or infers guilt on the part of the defendant. An example of circumstantial evidence would be a defendant being in the vicinity of a crime when it took place. In other words, there is no direct evidence that the defendant committed a crime; however, the defendant's presence in the area implies that the defendant is involved in the crime. For the defense, the evidence presented can accomplish two things. First, it can discredit evidence provided by the prosecutor. For example, if a defendant has confessed to the crime, the defense can argue that the defendant was coerced or threatened by police into confessing. Second, defense evidence can refute evidence provided by the prosecutor. For example, if an eyewitness testifies that he or she saw the defendant at the crime scene, the defense can counter that the defendant was nowhere near the crime scene at the time, providing an **alibi** for the defendant.

Once both sides have presented their cases, they are allowed to make closing statements to the jury. The prosecution emphasizes the evidence against the defendant and tries to convince the jury of the defendant's guilt. The defense also emphasizes its evidence but stresses that the prosecutor must meet the burden of proof. After closing arguments, the judge provides instructions to the jury that outline the legal issues in the case (e.g., burden of proof, elements of the crime, and possible verdicts). After instructions, the jury begins to deliberate the case. A unanimous vote is required for a verdict of guilty or not guilty. If the vote is not unanimous, there is no verdict, and a **hung jury** is declared by the judge. If this occurs, the defendant may be prosecuted again on the same charge.

Sentencing

If a defendant has been found guilty by a judge or jury, the next stage is sentencing. Although the judge has formal sentencing responsibility, punishments for offenses are created by state legislatures and Congress (for federal cases). The various legislatures have adopted a number of sentencing schemes to achieve the goals that they consider important, whether they are retribution, deterrence, incapacitation, or rehabilitation. These schemes are addressed next.

Indeterminate Sentencing Schemes

In the past 100 years of punishment, **indeterminate sentencing** was the primary method utilized in the states. Indeterminate sentencing is usually associated with the goals of rehabilitation and incapacitation, tailoring sentences to the needs of individual offenders. In this scheme, a judge sentences a defendant to a minimum and maximum range of time. Some states utilize indeterminate sentencing for incarceration sentences only, whereas others use it for incarceration and community supervision. The exact amount of time that is actually served by the offender is not specified at sentencing. Instead, the parole board determines when and if an offender is eligible for release after the minimum term has been served.

Determinate Sentencing Schemes

In the late 20th century, there was a shift away from indeterminate sentencing schemes due to an increased "law-and-order" approach to crime. In this scheme, a judge sentences an offender to a punishment for a specific period of time. Also referred to as "flat" or "fixed" sentences, **determinate sentencing** results in a defendant knowing how long his or her sentence will be when a judge imposes it. In effect, a judge declares at sentencing that a defendant will serve X number of months or years of incarceration, probation, and so forth. In some states, prisoners can earn good-time credits for good behavior that decrease the amount of time spent in prison. Other states have abolished these credits in the hope that defendants will serve their full sentences. Determinate sentencing schemes came about because many became skeptical of the rehabilitative aspects of indeterminate sentencing, believing that defendants were not being sufficiently punished for the crimes they committed.

Sentencing Guidelines

Regardless of the type of sentencing scheme, many states and the federal government have implemented **sentencing guidelines** to help curb what was considered to be inconsistent decision-making on the part of judges and parole boards. In many areas, guidelines were established by a sentencing commission or a legislative body to assist judges and others in providing appropriate sanctions for similar defendants. The varying guidelines range between "suggested" sentences and mandated sentences (specific sentences with little or no variation). Usually, the guidelines consider the seriousness of the offense and prior record, but some guidelines may take into account a defendant's legal status at the time of the crime (e.g., if the defendant was on probation or parole) and victim injury. Some guidelines allow limited judicial discretion by allowing a judge to impose less or more severe punishment on a defendant if circumstances warrant it.

More recent additions to sentence guidelines include habitual offender and mandatory minimum punishments. With **habitual offender** punishments, states allow judges to sentence offenders to a more severe punishment if the offender has prior felony convictions. An example of a habitual offender punishment is a "three strikes" punishment. This occurs when a defendant has received a third felony conviction, and the sentence for the third conviction is increased to reflect the habitual offender status. In California, this punishment states that "the requirements for sentencing a defendant as a third strike offender . . . require . . . the new felony to be a *serious or violent felony* with two or more prior strikes to qualify for the 25 year-to-life sentence as a third strike offender" ("California's Three Strikes Sentencing Law," http://www.courts.ca.gov/20142.htm; emphasis in original). With **mandatory minimum** punishments, judges *must* sentence a defendant to a minimum amount of punishment for certain types of offenses. Georgia's "Seven Deadly Sins" law is an example of a mandatory minimum punishment. This law specifies that for a first offense of kidnapping, armed robbery, rape, aggravated sodomy, aggravated sexual battery, or aggravated child molestation, the minimum punishment is 10 years in prison with no chance of parole. The minimum punishment for a first offense of murder is life with a possibility of parole after 25 years. A second offense for any of these seven crimes is life without the possibility of parole ("'Truth in Sentencing' in Georgia," http://www .dcor.state.ga.us/sites/all/files/pdf/Research/Standing/Truth_in_sentencing.pdf).

Critical Thinking Exercise

The use of sentencing guidelines in some states has reduced the discretion exercised by judges with regard to imposing punishments for crimes. As a result, sentences have become offense based rather than offender based. Do you think that a judge should be able to consider the circumstances of the offender when imposing a sentence? In effect, should an offender's lack of education, home life, history of abuse, and so forth play a role in punishment? Explain.

Available Sanctions

State legislatures and Congress have authorized a number of sanctions that may be imposed by judges. Although prison is often the first punishment that comes to mind, it is not the most common punishment used for law violators. Jail, probation, fines, and other sanctions are far more common than prison. **Prison** is reserved for the more serious (i.e., felony) offenders. The United States has the highest incarceration rate in the world, housing more than 1.5 million inmates in state and federal prisons in 2015 (Kaeble and Glaze 2016). In recent years, legislatures have authorized longer and mandatory prison sentences for some offenses, including drug-related offenses. This has resulted in a dramatic increase in the incarceration rate (Blumstein and Beck 1999). Prisons are typically state controlled, but private prisons have been constructed in some states with the hope of defraying some of the costs of operating state prisons. One sanction that is reserved for the most serious offenders is the **death penalty**, which is utilized in 31 states and in the federal system. The death penalty is rarely imposed, as it is restricted to individuals who have committed the highest form of murder, variously called first-degree, aggravated, or felony murder. At the federal level, the death penalty may also be imposed on those convicted of treason and on drug kingpins. Four states currently have a gubernatorial moratorium on the death penalty (Death Penalty Information Center 2017).

Jail is a form of incarceration for individuals who have been convicted of misdemeanors. Approximately 728,000 people are housed in jails (Kaeble and Glaze 2016). Jails also house those who are awaiting trial (known as pretrial detention). In the states, jails are typically operated at the county level. The federal government operates its own jails.

The primary alternative to incarceration is probation. Almost 3.8 million offenders are on probation at the federal and state level (Kaeble and Glaze 2016). The justification for probation is that incarceration is too much punishment for some offenders, but they simply cannot be released back into the community unpunished. Lower-level felony offenders and upper-level misdemeanor offenders are those typically placed on probation. Probation allows an offender to remain in the community as long as he or she abides by certain conditions, such as finding or maintaining employment, avoiding alcohol, submitting to drug tests, and meeting with a probation officer for a specified period of time.

For some offenders, probation is not a severe enough punishment, but incarceration is considered too harsh. A remedy to this is the use of **intermediate sanctions**, so named because they lie somewhere between prison and probation. Various intermediate sanctions include intensive supervision probation, electronic monitoring, house arrest, and boot camps. Intermediate sanctions tend to be used less frequently than regular probation, although the exact number of offenders serving intermediate sanctions is not known.

Fines are one of the oldest types of sanctions used and are typically reserved for traffic offenses or in conjunction with other types of punishment, usually probation. Fines are not utilized as extensively in the United States as in other countries, simply because most offenders in the U.S. criminal justice system cannot afford to pay them.

Regardless of the types of sentencing schemes and available sanctions, there has been a trend of increased legislative involvement in the sentencing of offenders. This involvement has led to reduced discretion on the part of judges, who were often viewed by legislators and the public as being too lenient in their sentencing practices. This law-and-order approach to crime and justice has led to increased supervision of more offenders by the criminal justice system, which has cost considerable sums of money.

Appeals

After an offender has been convicted and sentenced, he or she has the right to one **appeal**. This means that the offender has the opportunity to have his or her case reviewed by an appellate court in order to fix any problems that may have occurred during the case. These problems typically involve issues such as improper jury selection, defects in jury instructions, or admission of illegally seized evidence. Prosecutors, on the other hand, cannot appeal a finding of not guilty.

The right to one appeal carries with it certain constitutional requirements by which the state or federal government must abide. Offenders who appeal have the right to free transcripts of their trials and the right to appointed counsel. Despite this, many offenders do not appeal their convictions or sentences simply because they view it as a waste of time and energy, especially when they will have completed their sentences before their appeals get through the appellate stage. In addition, appeals are rarely successful. Neubauer and Fradella (2014) estimate that less than 10 percent of defendants win on appeal. Most of these victories are minor, however. Convictions are typically upheld and sentences may be modified only slightly, or offenders are subjected to retrial only to be reconvicted the second time around.

After the first appeal is finished, offenders have the opportunity to file other appeals if they wish. Called **postconviction review** or a **collateral attack**, prisoners can challenge their convictions or sentences in a different proceeding. Collateral attacks are typically filed in federal court and are civil matters, not criminal appeals. They raise constitutional questions only, not errors in interpretation or application of the law, which are seen mostly in the first right of appeal. Offenders are not given free trial transcripts and are not provided with appointed counsel in these appeals. As a result, few offenders take advantage of the opportunity to file a collateral attack. A common type of collateral attack is **habeas corpus**, in which prisoners claim that they are being detained illegally. In recent years, Congress and the U.S. Supreme Court have greatly restricted the filing of habeas corpus appeals in a number of ways. Now, offenders have a one-year deadline to file an appeal and are limited in the number of appeals that can be filed, among other things (see the Antiterrorism and Effective Death Penalty Act of 1996).

TRENDS IN THE COURT SYSTEM

Due to increasing numbers of individuals coming into the criminal justice system and also increasing problems involved with it, the court systems in many areas have developed new ways and methods to handle cases. Among the methods are the development of specialized courts, increasing victim involvement, adopting new technologies, and employing jury consultants.

Specialized Courts

Special-needs offenders are those who are repeatedly seen in the system due to issues such as drug and alcohol abuse and mental illness. Court systems have created specialty courts that deal exclusively with certain types of offenders.

Drug Courts

Court systems have become bogged down with large numbers of relatively minor drug offenders. As a result, many court systems have created drug courts to process these cases efficiently without taking up the time and resources of the lower courts. Drug courts have been in existence since the mid-1980s and are in operation or are being planned in every state. Despite this, drug courts are not utilized statewide, either because particular areas have no need for them or because states simply cannot afford to operate them.

Drug courts emphasize treatment of lower-level drug offenders. A lower court typically identifies these offenders and transfers the cases to a drug court. The drug court then establishes a treatment program that entails drug treatment, counseling, employment, and life skills training. The offenders are usually released into the community and must meet with judges periodically, often weekly. This is similar to probation, but it is not a probation sentence. The offenders are monitored by judges, not probation officers, and the judges ensure that the offenders are progressing through the treatment program. The success of drug courts has been mixed. The research that has been conducted has found that offenders who successfully completed their treatment programs have lower recidivism rates compared to offenders who were not processed through drug courts. This success is tempered, however, by the fact that being processed through drug courts and undergoing treatment is largely voluntary. In effect, the success of drug courts could be explained by the possibility that offenders who volunteer to go through the drug court process want help for their problems and are willing to go through treatment (Arnold et al. 2000).

Web Activity

For more information about drug courts, visit the website of the National Association of Drug Court Professionals at http://www.nadcp.org/.

Mental Health Courts

It has been estimated that 5 to 15 percent of incarcerated offenders suffer from some form of mental illness. Many jails and prisons do not provide adequate treatment of mental illness while offenders are incarcerated, and fewer establish procedures for aftercare once the offenders are released. As a result, the mental illness, which may have contributed to the offenders' criminal behavior, remains untreated and the offenders are in no better position than they were before incarceration. This has led to the creation of mental health courts in some areas. These courts establish guidelines for mental health treatment in lieu of other punishments. Typically, **mental health courts** place restrictions on the types of offenders whom they process, such as prohibiting violent offenders from participation.

Mental health courts work with community treatment programs to establish appropriate procedures for both the treatment of the offenders and the safety of the community. Offenders are closely monitored throughout their treatment programs, which usually consist of not only mental health treatment but also life skills and vocational training. If an offender successfully completes the program, some courts authorize removal of the original criminal charges from the offender's record (Slate 2000).

Research on the effectiveness of mental health courts has found some success. An assessment of Seattle's mental health court found that the court is successfully identifying offenders in need of treatment and that the treatment program itself has reduced recidivism (Trupin 2001).

Web Activity

For more information about mental health courts, see the textbook website (http://www.oup.com/us/labessentials).

Domestic Violence Courts

Due to the increasing number of domestic violence cases in the criminal justice system (including repeat offenders and victims), **domestic violence courts** have been created to address the unique issues in these cases. For example, many domestic violence cases involve divorce proceedings as well as child custody and other issues, which can result in numerous cases being brought before different judges. The domestic violence courts would combine these cases in one court, with a judge overseeing all aspects of the case. The court also advocates early intervention and the use of community agencies in order to coordinate services for both victims and offenders.

Research on the effectiveness of domestic violence courts is mixed. Although Casey and Rottman (2005) argued that the courts increase the satisfaction of victims and offenders, Scott and Kunselman (2007) noted that although the motives of these courts are noble, they have not been successful in providing the needed services and reducing recidivism.

Web Activity

For more information about domestic violence courts, see the textbook website (http://www.oup.com/us/labessentials).

Increased Victim Involvement

In addition to making changes to address special-needs offenders, courts are increasingly allowing victims to become involved in the resolution of their cases. The criminal justice system views crime as an offense against the state or federal government, not against an individual victim. The victim is basically a witness for the state. Because of this, victims have felt excluded from the criminal justice process, believing that their interests are not taken into account during the course of the case. During the past 30 years, the court system has become more sensitive to the needs of victims and has devised new methods of taking victims into account.

Restorative Justice

One major philosophical change has been that the criminal justice system needs to address all the victims of crime—the actual victims, the offenders, the family members, and the community. The idea is that crime affects more than the government entity whose laws have been broken. The system must, in effect, restore the injured parties to where they were before the crime occurred. **Restorative justice** enables offenders to understand the harms they have caused and gives them the chance to try to make things right. Victims are able to provide input and participate in the process, meeting with criminal justice personnel and community leaders to outline the best course of action for a particular victim. One common requirement in restorative justice is victim restitution, which involves the offender offering monetary compensation for the harm caused. In addition, the criminal justice system works with community programs to address offenders' needs, reintegrate offenders into the community, and reduce future criminal conduct.

Alternative Dispute Resolution

Alternative dispute resolution (ADR) seeks to settle disputes in ways besides the formal court process. Although it is more common in civil cases, it is also used in criminal cases, usually misdemeanors. One common form of ADR is mediation, which involves a neutral individual (not a judge) who works with the parties involved to come to a mutual agreement as to a resolution. For example, in civil cases, lawsuits may be settled through mediation without ever having to go to court. In criminal cases, mediation resembles aspects of restorative justice, in that the victim and offender can work out their issues to the benefit of both. Victim restitution is a common outcome of mediation. Some argue that ADR is a form of restorative justice; however, offender reintegration does not occupy as predominant a position in ADR as it does in a true restorative justice program.

Court Technology

Many courts are using new and updated technology to assist with court operations. One of the uses of technology is to create a more efficient case management process through an increased use of computerized files, in essence creating an "e-court." Case files move among many individuals and offices within a court, so the use of case management technology is essential to keep the flow of cases moving. Although the court system is a long way from becoming paperless, case management technology allows all individuals involved in a case (e.g., the judge, prosecutor, clerk of court, defense attorney, and probation officer) 24-hour access to case files. Thus, there is no longer the need to wait for a file as in a traditional paperwork scheme. In addition, courts can measure their performance with the use of CourTools, an online measure instituted by the National Center for State Courts. These tools include such measures as access to the courts, fairness, length of case, and reliability of case files, among others. These tools allow courts to measure their performance and enact changes, if necessary.

Another use of technology is through the establishment of video arraignments and hearings. Rather than transport offenders to the courtroom, the parties to the proceedings, which include the accused/offender, the attorneys, and the judges, can convene online using video streaming technology. Such activity can save a great deal of time and expense compared to bringing everyone to the physical courtroom. It can also allow for processing of more cases in a shorter period of time at a lesser cost to the system.

Use of Jury Consultants

The selection of jurors is a key step in many cases. In general, the jury selection process involves the prosecutor and defense attorney choosing a jury that would favor their side. In doing so, they will choose or dismiss jurors based on their evaluation of a juror's perceived bias toward their case. To better assist in the jury selection process, jury consultants have been utilized to assess the characteristics of offenders, victims, cases, and jurors that are associated with a particular outcome. With the use of mock trials, jury consultants are able to determine what factors will influence a juror's vote. For instance, a jury consultant may determine that those with a higher income are more likely to vote to convict a lower-income defendant. With these conclusions, the jury consultant will advise attorneys on the juror characteristics that will be favorable to their side. Jury consultants are mostly hired by defense attorneys as opposed to prosecutors, and they are being increasingly used throughout courtrooms today.

Web Activity

For more information about trends in state courts, visit the website of the National Center for State Courts at http://www.ncsc.org/sitecore/content/microsites/trends/home/Annual-Publication.aspx.

CONCLUSION

The court system is involved in many aspects of the criminal justice system. Courts can become involved in cases before an arrest is made and after an offender has served a sentence. The courts are primarily responsible for ensuring that the laws are followed properly, both by citizens and by government entities, and that law violators are punished. Although many cases never formally enter the criminal justice system, the number of cases that courts have to process has increased in recent years due to law-and-order policies that have brought more offenders and different types of offenders to the attention of the system. State and federal legislatures have also reduced the discretion of judges by authorizing longer and mandatory prison sentences, which has dramatically increased the incarceration rate. Courts are trying to find a balance between the demands that offenders should be punished and the pressure on the courtroom workgroup to get cases out of the system quickly and efficiently. This can be an incredibly difficult task. Actors in the court system must measure the ideological goals of retribution and deterrence against the practical goals of not allowing the courts to fall apart as caseloads mount.

KEY WORDS

adversarial system of justice
alternative dispute resolution
appeal
appellate courts
appellate jurisdiction
arraignment
assembly-line justice
assigned counsel
bail
bailiffs
bench trial
burden of proof
case attrition
challenge for cause
collateral attack
death penalty
defense attorneys

determinate sentencing
district courts
domestic violence courts
drug courts
dual court system
fines
hung jury
indeterminate sentencing
initial appearance
intermediate sanctions
jail
judges
legal aid
master jury list
mental health courts
merit selection
nonpartisan election
original jurisdiction
partisan election

peremptory challenge
plea bargain
postconviction review
preliminary hearing
preventive detention
prison
pro bono
pro se
prosecutors
public defender
rebuttal
restorative justice
sentencing guidelines
trial courts of general jurisdiction
trial courts of limited jurisdiction
venire
voir dire

SUGGESTED READINGS

Carp, R., R. Stidham, K. Manning, and L. Holmes. (2017). *Judicial process in America.* Thousand Oaks, CA: CQ Press.

Eisenstein, J., R. Flemming, and P. Nardulli. (1999). *The contours of justice: Communities and their courts.* Lanham, MD: University Press of America.

Hemmens, C., D. Brody, and C. Spohn. (2013). *Criminal courts: A contemporary perspective.* Thousand Oaks, CA: Sage.

Mays, L., and P. Gregware. (2008). *Courts and justice: A reader.* Prospect Heights, IL: Waveland.

Spohn, C., and C. Hemmens. (2012). *Courts: A text/reader.* Thousand Oaks, CA: Sage.

Tarr, A. (2003). *Judicial process and judicial policymaking.* Belmont, CA: Wadsworth.

CHAPTER 5

Institutional Corrections

CHAPTER OUTLINE

History of Punishment
History of Incarceration for Women
    The Neglect Response
    The Differential Response
    The Equalization Response
Eras of Punishment
    The Era of the Penitentiary
    The Era of Reform
    The Era of Industry
    The Era of Rehabilitation
    The Era of Retribution
    The Era of Reentry
Size and Costs of Imprisonment
Jails
Modern Prisons
    Prison Types
    Custody and Security Within Institutions
    Prison Violence and Prison Discipline
    Prison Life
Special Offender Populations
    Inmates and HIV/AIDS
    Inmates and Substance Use
    Aging and Elderly Inmates
    Inmates and Mental Illness
Problems, Rights, and Implications in Modern Prisons
    Inmate Rights
    Crowding

Violence
Solutions
Principles of Effective Classification
Future Directions for Institutional Corrections
Conclusion
Key Words
Suggested Readings

After reading this chapter, you should be able to:

- Identify different eras of punishment and point out highlights of each
- Understand the three responses to female imprisonment
- Discuss the recent trends in the philosophy of corrections
- Report on the size and costs of imprisonment
- Define jails and detention centers and relate their features
- Compare and contrast different types of prisons
- Discuss issues related to privately operated prisons
- Compare and contrast the deprivation and importation models of prison
- List different special offender populations
- Discuss the problem of HIV/AIDS in prison
- Point out issues and responses to an aging prison population
- Discuss the problem of handling inmates with mental illness
- Note milestone cases in the rights of prison inmates
- Discuss the advantages and disadvantages of technological innovations in corrections
- Illustrate the problems inherent in prison overcrowding
- Discuss future concerns and directions for institutional corrections

---

Institutional correctional facilities have been used for centuries, ever since the Roman Catholic Church made use of confinement at the abbey during the Middle Ages. Even though there were precursors to the modern jails and prisons, corporal punishments such as flogging, branding, and other forms of torture were widespread throughout the world. The American colonists followed suit with these punishments throughout the centuries but soon came to realize that such sanctions were inhumane and inappropriate for some behaviors. Soon thereafter, the penitentiary became the primary method by which convicted offenders would be punished.

HISTORY OF PUNISHMENT

Punishment for the violation of group norms, rules, and laws is a common element across human history and societies. Whether the response is informally handed out by the head of a household or reflects the official commands of a modern-day court, social life imposes various restrictions on behavior, and violations carry the possibility of a negative response. Punishment may be justified for a variety of social, political, moral, or religious reasons. In ancient times, punishment for a violation of a social norm or law was often handled locally, by the family, clan, or head of the community. Larger and more organized societies typically used more formal procedures for investigating, prosecuting, adjudicating, and punishing offenders. There was considerable variation, however, in the response depending on the type of law or custom that was violated, who the offender and victim were, the specific geographic location of the incident, and the exact historical time period.

Nearly every society has had some arrangements for the temporary confinement of offenders. Some ancient civilizations, such as the Greeks and Romans, also had facilities designed to hold offenders for longer periods of time. In general, however, punishment in premodern Western societies and colonial America primarily involved the use of monetary compensation or corporal punishments. This is not to suggest that imprisonment did not occur, but it was far from the most common or most important form of punishment. When incarceration did occur, it was for the purpose of holding the offender until the corporal or capital sentence was to take place, usually within a day or two.

Modern societies are structured by the formal organization and routinization of social tasks and social life. One of the social tasks that has been increasingly controlled and managed has been the enforcement of laws and punishment of law violators. With the spread of democratic values and market capitalism came growing criticism of the use of physical punishment. In the late 1700s, severe forms of punishment were being questioned by those adhering to the Classical school. Furthermore, existing punishments and facilities of the day were perceived as ineffective and counterproductive. As society shifted from a top-down power structure to one based on the sovereignty of the people, new forms of punishment were needed to reflect these new social relations. It was during this time that the modern-day penitentiary was born, and with it the beginning of formal organizational structures designed to carry out punishments (Morris and Rothman 1995; Rothman 1971).

Several major penal institutions were created in the United States between 1790 and 1830. Although there were differences in the design and operation of these early penitentiaries, they were more similar than not. In less than 100 years, punishment changed from the rather arbitrary use of physical punishment to a model emphasizing the confinement and correction of individual offenders through segregation, regimentation, and control. Offenders were increasingly separated based on personal characteristics. As a result, female offenders, juvenile delinquents, and the mentally ill were placed in facilities independent of male adult criminal offenders.

HISTORY OF INCARCERATION FOR WOMEN

Compared to male offenders, females have historically been less frequently convicted of crimes and sentenced to prison. The main reason noted by some scholars is that women were presumed to be treated more leniently by prosecutors and judges. During the past 35 years, however, there has been a large increase in the percentage of women who are incarcerated, especially for drug and property crimes. In fact, according to the Bureau of Justice of Statistics (Carson 2015), the number of women in prison has outpaced men by more than 50% since 1980, when women made up more than 26,000 of the U.S. prison population. By 2014, their numbers had increased to well over 215,000. Justice system reactions to female offending can be understood in three stages, or historical responses: the neglect response, the differential response, and the equalization response.

The Neglect Response

After the 1820s, penal codes of most states were changed to indicate that imprisonment would be the primary form of punishment for criminals. Before this time, however, state prisons often housed only 50 inmates. During most of the 20th century, the percentage of female inmates hovered around 4 percent of the total prison population (today, women comprise approximately 7 percent of state and federal prison populations). There were no national statistics on inmate demographics until approximately 1910, but there is little reason to think that the percentage of women incarcerated during the 18th and 19th centuries was higher than the 4 percent figure. Thus, prisons in the late 17th and early 18th centuries likely had approximately 1 or 2 female inmates housed in their facilities.

Given these low numbers of women in prison, interest in the treatment of women in prison was lacking and few discussions were held on building separate institutions for female offenders. Women who were sentenced to incarceration were actually placed in the same large rooms that held male inmates. It was not until the 1820s that segregating the sexes into separate cells occurred. Furthermore, it was not until the 1830s that same-sex facilities became standard practice.

Housing females along with males in institutions that were designed to serve male offenders created a number of problems for female inmates:

1. The obvious—issues of privacy.
2. Women were lonelier than men while incarcerated.
3. Females were more vulnerable to sexual exploitation by male correctional workers and inmates. The idea of women supervising women inmates seldom, if ever, was realized during the neglect stage.
4. Women tended not to receive much needed support from visitors, medical personnel, and chaplains in these co-ed facilities.

One prison in New York circa 1825 attempted to ameliorate some of these problems in the Auburn prison by keeping female inmates in a third floor attic above the prison kitchen instead of housing them in the cell block with male prisoners. A prison matron (i.e., a female correctional officer who was more of a mother hen-type figure) was hired in 1832, but before her appearance, the female inmates had no supervision. An agent of the prison delivered food to the women and removed the waste once daily, but other than that, these women were expected to take care of themselves. The conditions in the attic were quite deplorable and overcrowded, making the cell blocks where the males were housed look like a luxury hotel in comparison.

Although it would seem like any type of separation in housing for men and women would improve the daily lives of female inmates, new problems surfaced. As women were given their separate units, they were often far away from the prison's center where the programs and other opportunities for betterment were held. Women were seldom able to access the health care, religious services, or exercise facilities. Thus, in seeking equal treatment, what women received was the appearance of equality with inferior conditions. Enter the reformatory era.

The Differential Response

During the reformatory era (discussed later), which began in the 1860s, concern for both male and female prisoners became evident. Feminists at this time campaigned in earnest to encourage male legislators to fund separate reformatory institutions for female offenders. Their arguments surfaced around three major ideas: (1) Males are not to blame for female criminality; females should be responsible for their own actions; (2) rehabilitation would be more effective if women were not subjected to the negative influences of men; and (3) women have the ability to control and reform their sisters and should be given every opportunity to do so (Freedman 1984). In essence, female inmates and male inmates require different responses in punishment and treatment, and the best way to achieve this goal is for women to be separated from men in their own facilities operated by women.

As one might imagine, these ideas did not go over very well with the men of the day. Yet, in 1873, Indiana opened the first women's prison, followed by Massachusetts in 1877, with other states soon following their lead. The facilities were administered and run by women for female offenders. The architectural style of these institutions differed a great deal from the typical male prison. Female prisons were constructed in a cottage plan, with inmates living in small units (hence, the cottages) that had a home-like atmosphere rather than a cell block. It was believed that this environment would enable the women to understand and accept their expected role in society. The main elements of treatment that incarcerated women received at the time were training in sewing, cooking, washing and ironing clothes, gardening, and farming.

Thus, separate and differently designed prisons, different programs, and different labor assignments were just some of the ways in which the differential response to female offenders became evident. Of course, in any number of ways, this differential treatment was an improvement over the neglect of the previous stage when women were housed with men and supervised by male guards. However, in focusing on the special needs of females and creating this differential response, the reformers (mostly middle-class women intent on molding female offenders into homemakers despite the reality that most of these women would have to support themselves upon release from prison) "created a new set of problems by assuming that all women inmates, as women, could be treated alike, by methods aimed at reinforcing true womanhood in an era in which a new woman was emerging" (Freedman 1984: 90).

The Equalization Response

It took nearly 100 years for the women's movement to have any success in demonstrating that restricted opportunities created by an overemphasis on domestic skills and imprisoning women on minor charges (men were often not subjected to such terms) was a misguided pursuit in the quest for equality. Thus, pleas for equal treatment for both male and female inmates were made. One mechanism that jump-started the equalization response was the use of legal action by and for female inmates in the late 1960s. Such issues as sentencing disparities between men and women wherein women were serving longer, indeterminate sentences were brought before the courts.

In the 1970s, conditions of confinement were the equalization issues brought forth for the courts to rectify. The decisions handed down held that there must be substantial equivalence between men and women across a number of practices. For example, men and women must be given similar opportunities to participate in work-furlough programs, assignment to minimum-security institutions should be available to both men and women, and the distance between the location of sentencing and the prison should be equivalent for men and women. These last two holdings were driven by the fact that most states only have one prison for all female inmates and thus it must house all security levels. Outcomes from other cases resulted in the development and implementation of quality treatment and vocational programs equal to those delivered in male prisons. Furthermore, courts held that women must have access to adequate law facilities and legal assistance in their prisons as well.

Critical Thinking Exercise

After reading about the three responses, which one do you think best explains the large increase in the number of women imprisoned compared to their male counterparts? Detail your reasons.

ERAS OF PUNISHMENT

The purpose of punishment and the use of different types of punishment have largely reflected the needs of a particular society. As a result, there have been different eras of punishment in the United States that used varying mechanisms for punishment.

The Era of the Penitentiary

Incapacitation and deterrence were the philosophies that dominated the purposes for confinement in the 1800s to 1860s. This was known as the **penitentiary era**, so called because of the development of a formal penal system and a heavy reliance on incarceration. Two different styles of penitentiaries became symbols of this era: separate and congregate. These styles are more commonly known as the Pennsylvania and Auburn systems, respectively.

The Eastern State Penitentiary in Philadelphia, Pennsylvania, was said to be a separate system because of its heavy reliance on silence and the separation of inmates from one another in individual cells. Eating, working, and sleeping were performed in the confines of the cells. The purpose of silence and solitude was reflected in the belief that the only way to repent and reform for one's wrongdoings was to reflect silently on one's deeds. Inmates were also denied visits from family members and friends and access to newspapers, and correspondences of any kind were forbidden (Rothman 1971).

The Auburn Prison in New York also operated under the rule of silence, but it differed from the Pennsylvania prison in that inmates could congregate with one another during the day while eating or working. Auburn prisoners returned to separate cells at night, and silence, even while in the presence of other inmates, was strictly enforced. Inmates in New York were also secluded from the outside world; there was no sight, sound, or contact with anyone or anything beyond the prison walls (Rothman 1971).

Penitentiaries sprang forth in other areas of the United States following the procedures and philosophies of their predecessors, despite the criticisms lodged against the imposition of silence, corporal punishments to keep inmates under control, and restriction of access to the external society. This so-called old prison discipline led some inmates to suffer from mental, emotional, and physical illness and, in some cases, even death.

The Era of Reform

The Civil War detracted attention from the plight of prisoners housed in the penitentiaries that were built in the 1800s. By 1870, however, the harsh environment of these institutions again came to be scrutinized. A more humanitarian approach to the practice of incarceration was advocated based more on the philosophy of rehabilitation rather than pure incapacitation or deterrence. The National Prison Association, which is known today as the American Correctional Association, was formed in 1870 to address the problems of the penitentiary system. Prison administrators, members of Congress, and prominent citizens from the United States and abroad gathered in Cincinnati, Ohio, and issued a set of declarations by which prisons would be reformed. These principles emphasized the value of treatment for inmates based on their individual needs, an indeterminate sentencing scheme by which inmates could earn their way out of prison, vocational and educational training, labor that was purposeful rather than punishment oriented, and noncorporal methods of discipline that made use of rewards rather than punishment for conformity (Pisciotta 1994). In addition, the reformers abolished the rule of silence. A system whereby released inmates could continue their treatment in the community was also introduced during the **reform era**. Today, this practice is better known as parole, and it is discussed in more detail in Chapter 6.

The Elmira Reformatory in New York was the prototype institution whose mission was to carry out these principles. Inmates were classified based on their conduct and success in the interventions available at the facility, such as training for trade and academics. Similar to Elmira's predecessors, the reformatory was criticized for the means used to control inmates, inhumane working and living conditions, and rigid order. Thus, the intentions of the reforms appeared to be sound but, in the end, poor implementation and a lack of funding required a new approach to the use of institutions for punishment.

The Era of Industry

The idea of convict labor was not new to the world of incarceration: The Pennsylvania and the Auburn systems required inmates to engage in craft-oriented or factory-oriented labor, respectively (Conley 1980). The goods produced by inmates were often sold in the open market. Inmates at the Auburn prison actually built Sing Sing Prison, New York's second state institution for the incarceration of convicted offenders. Chain gangs were developed during this era, with inmates working on road or canal projects and prison construction for the states. Inmates were also tied to the private sector by being employed contractually with private-sector businesses in the making of furniture, clothing, brooms, baskets, and hosiery. In addition, some inmates were contracted out to work in stone quarries and coal mines (Mancini 1978; Sellin 1976).

These latter practices, known as **convict leasing**, were a Southern development, and some authors have suggested that convict leasing was basically another way to enslave Blacks following the Civil War (Johnson 2002; Sheldon 2001). Convict leasing of inmates often led to illness, suffering, and even death. For example, in Georgia, convicts were beaten if they did not produce the designated amount of coal per day (Mancini 1978).

Despite such horrific consequences associated with convict labor during the **industrial era**, states and their officials continued their labor programs for inmates until the 1930s, when state legislatures and Congress passed a number of measures banning the sale of inmate-produced goods to the public (Sexton 1995). The major impetus for such legislation was complaints advanced by workers in the organized labor force that inmate-made goods undercut the price at which free-market products could be sold. Once the Great Depression hit in the 1930s, pressure from workers increased considerably to prohibit inmate labor from interfering with their profits; thus, inmate labor was curtailed.

Legislation was reintroduced in the late 1970s that permitted products produced by prison industries to be sold in the open market once again. Today, inmates continue to work while doing their time in various industries connected to the private and public sectors. Inmates have been involved in such jobs as assembling graduation gowns for Jostens, making embroidered emblems for Lyon Brothers Manufacturing Company, and even sewing garments that were later purchased by J.C. Penney and Victoria's Secret for retail sale for Third Generation. (Sexton 1995).

The Era of Rehabilitation

By the early 1930s, there was a strong sense of urgency that something needed to be done about the harsh punishments faced by inmates in U.S. penal institutions. The Depression contributed to discontent among the general public, and dissatisfaction in prisons was also on the rise. Several major prison riots in Illinois, Colorado, New York, and Kansas City prompted the government to take notice. Even prison officials began to understand the hopelessness that prisoners experienced. With a report issued by the Wickersham Commission in 1931, inmate grievances were officially recognized. State prisons did not provide anything more than capricious rules and coercive punishments for inmates, and meaningful programs to assist inmates in their reformation were lacking. In fact, inmates spent most of their time inactively engaged in simply doing their time.

The Wickersham Commission called for a new philosophy to guide the prison system; the philosophy of **rehabilitation** soon replaced the philosophies of deterrence and incapacitation that had dominated since the inception of the penitentiary. The major players in the move toward more rehabilitative efforts were the progressives, who were most active during the first couple of decades of the 20th century. The progressives were known for their indeterminist view that social problems, including crime, were often beyond an individual's control, much like having a disease that needs treatment. The medical model dominated the **rehabilitation era** with a focus on the needs of the individual offender and less reliance on prisons to carry out the criminal sanction. Probation, indeterminate sentences, classification systems, vocational and educational training, and release from prison based on treatment success were some of the significant practices devised and implemented to carry out the goal of rehabilitation. Many of the recommendations from the 1870 National Prison Association finally came to fruition.

Corrections would follow the rehabilitation philosophy for more than 40 years, with reported success in some jurisdictions and failure in others. It appeared that states were just not equipped to carry out the rehabilitative ideals. This latter statement especially held true for prisons in which the correctional officers were mandated to keep order within the institution while simultaneously attempting to create an environment that was amenable to treatment (Rothman 1980). It soon became clear that the premise of rehabilitation could not climb over the hurdles blocking its proper implementation.

When we couple these ideological struggles with the social and political context of the 1960s and 1970s, it should come as little surprise that the philosophy of rehabilitation would soon be replaced with a more punitive philosophy, better known as the "get-tough" movement. Student uprisings over Vietnam, civil rights demonstrations, increases in poverty and crime rates, and the Watergate scandal led people to question the government, social institutions, law enforcement, courts, and corrections. The catalyst that provided further justification for abandoning the philosophy of rehabilitation was the publication of a report by Robert Martinson finding that "with few and isolated exceptions, the rehabilitative efforts that have been reported so far have had no appreciable effect on recidivism" (Martinson 1974: 25).

The Era of Retribution

The "nothing works" doctrine associated with Martinson's (1974) publication provided the impetus to close the book on rehabilitation. During this era, and even in the 2010s, some sanctions and criminal justice practices continue to reflect correctional policies that were based on more punitive ideals such as an increased reliance on secure confinement for more offenders for longer periods of time, determinate sentencing models, and the abolition of parole. Offenders are now sentenced to a finite amount of time, and release is not necessarily tied to reformation or rehabilitation. Under the auspices of "get-tough" practices, offenders who commit crimes will get their just deserts.

Now in the **retributive era**, during the past 35 years, there has been a general trend in the United States and western European countries to respond to law violators with more severe penalties and a decreasing support for rehabilitative efforts. In the United States, this has resulted in most jurisdictions enacting lengthier prison sentences, more punitive sanctions (e.g., "three-strikes" policies that stipulate life sentences for offenders convicted of their third felonies), and attempts to limit the discretion of judges or correctional administrators to reduce sentence lengths. Although these changes apply to a wide variety of behaviors, violent crimes and drug law violations have been particularly affected by these changes (Blumstein and Beck 1999). Perhaps most important has been the "war on drugs" that has been fought during the past 30 years. As a result, drug law violators make up a significant percentage of offenders in criminal courts and under correctional supervision. This is a considerable change from just 30 years ago (Blumstein and Beck 1999).

The Era of Reentry

Although not a traditional purpose of punishment like many of the eras explored previously, the reentry movement was a necessary response to decades of sanctioning practices based on retributive and incapacitative philosophies whereby increasingly more persons were behind bars for lengthier periods of time, which is a costly enterprise. The release of inmates will happen regardless of sentencing motivations. Consider that at a minimum, 95 percent of state inmates will be released from incarceration at some point (Hughes and Wilson 2002). In 2010, more than 700,000 inmates were released from state prisons; in 2011, the number was nearly 689,000 (Carson and Sabol 2012). **Reentry** is the transition period of persons who are soon to be released or have recently been released from prison or jail back into the community. It involves providing services and assistance to these individuals and their families. After the terrorist attacks on September 11, 2001, states were in debt, the economy was souring, and unemployment was fairly high compared to that during the booming years of the late 1990s. When the recession hit between 2007 and 2009, states had to devise ways to defray costs, and imprisoning offenders is very expensive. Couple the budget cuts with the fact that the "get-tough" policies in the 1980s led to overcrowded prisons, and states had to come up with alternative models to save money while trying to maintain the relatively low crime rates the nation had been experiencing for several years.

In general, there are two mechanisms to reduce prison crowding and its cost. **Front-door options** involve community-based sanctions such as probation instead of prison or jail. **Back-door options** involve early release mechanisms such as parole, transitional placement in a community-based correctional facility, or simply being released from prison without any assistance or supervision. The focus on reentry programs and services, most notably in the areas of employment, housing, and behavioral health, becomes important when back-door options are implemented. Given that 4 in 10 offenders return to prison within three years after release, concentrated reentry efforts are vital (Pew Center on the States 2011). Of specific concern are individuals with substance abuse and/or mental health disorders, who have an even greater risk of recidivism. It is estimated that more than 70 percent of state prisoners have struggled with either one or both of these conditions (James and Glaze 2006). Research has shown that without appropriate community-based treatment, employment, housing, and other relevant support systems in place, rearrests and reincarcerations of this population are highly likely, especially in the first few months after discharge (Fontaine et al. 2012; Hartwell 2010; Lurigio, Rollins, and Fallon 2004).

Web Activity

Two exceptional documentaries on the issue of mental illness in state prison systems are *The New Asylums* (https://www.pbs.org/wgbh/frontline/film/showsasylums/) and the follow-up production *The Released* (https://www.pbs.org/wgbh/pages/frontline/released/view).

Offenders face a multitude of barriers, such as finding employment, obtaining stable housing, adjusting to life outside prison/jail, and repairing broken ties with friends and family members. Numerous local, state, and federal agencies and nonprofit organizations throughout the country provide reentry programming and assistance. Reentry efforts that make connections even before inmates return to the community and that continue during the first year after release are essential. Fortunately, there are more formalized reentry programs today than there were even five years ago, and there is more financial support through grant funding with the passage of the 2008 Second Chance Act.

Web Activity

For a snapshot of some promising programs and the populations served, see https:// csgjusticecenter.org/wp-content/uploads/2013/11/ReentryMatters.pdf. You might find your state is doing something noteworthy for offender reintegration.

SIZE AND COSTS OF IMPRISONMENT

In total, there are more than 6.7 million individuals under some form of correctional supervision in the United States, be it prisons, jails, probation, or parole (Kaeble and Glaze 2016) (Figure 5.1 shows trends in populations between 2000 and 2015). Perhaps the figure that stunned the nation about a decade ago, and

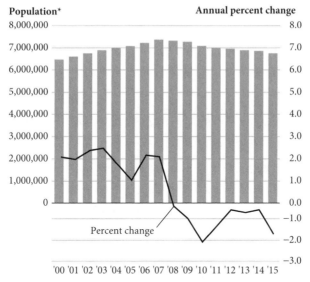

Figure 5.1 Total population under the supervision of adult correctional systems and annual percent change, 2000–2015.
*Estimates include offenders in the community under the jurisdiction of probation or parole agencies as of December 31, under the jurisdiction of state or federal prisons as of December 31, or in the custody of local jails as of the last weekday in June.
SOURCE: Bureau of Justice Statistics, Annual Probation Survey, Annual Parole Survey, Annual Survey of Jails, Census of Jail Inmates, and National Prisoner Statistics program, 2000–2015.

still resonates with us today, was the following: One out of nearly 100 adults is in jail or prison at the state and federal levels (Pew Center on the States 2008). This figure was released in early 2008 and made history because it was the first time the United States has ever witnessed such an alarming incarceration rate. Today, the figure is 1 out of 108 adults. Since 2002, the United States has had the highest incarceration rate of all industrialized countries.

To keep up with the constant flow of offenders formally processed in the criminal justice system and serving longer prison terms as a result of the adoption of determinate sentencing models by state and federal governments, jurisdictions have had to increase their funding for various justice agencies. Although the funding for all aspects of the criminal justice system has increased, the increase for correctional spending has been the most dramatic. To illustrate, recent cost analyses from the U.S. Department of Education's Policy and Program Studies Service (2016) for 2013 (the most recent year available for comparison at the time of writing) found that state and local correctional budgets in the United States totaled more than $70 billion, which is an increase of 324 percent since 1980 when costs hovered around $17 billion. For pre-kindergarten through 12th grade education, corresponding increases from 1980 to 2013 were only 107 percent. For higher education, during this same period, funding per full-time equivalent student decreased by 28 percent, yet for corrections, per capita costs increased by nearly 45 percent. Corrections is a costly business, and as noted previously, states are grappling with both a large institutional population and the budget crises (Pew Center on the States 2008). To reduce prison overcrowding, many states and the federal government have greatly increased the bed space within their prison systems through massive prison construction programs. The rationale behind the boom in building more secure places of confinement is the idea that, eventually, the more offenders we incarcerate, the less crime we will have (Austin and Irwin 2001). Unfortunately, it also appears that even with such a high incarceration rate, recidivism and crime rates have not been reduced as significantly as many policymakers and the public had expected. Indeed, we continue to incarcerate people at levels disproportionate to actual offense counts (Pew Center on the States 2008).

Critical Thinking Exercise

Corrections has witnessed several eras in terms of the punishments used and the purposes for which they were instituted. What do you think the next era of corrections will be like? For example, will there be an even greater reliance on institutions for punishment? Will more rehabilitation programs be developed? Will special offender populations be effectively served? Will we see more technological advances and less human interaction between corrections officers and inmates? What will our future prisons look like? Who will be housed in them? How can you be confident that your predictions are accurate?

In 2010, the mean cost of incarcerating one person in prison for one year was $31,286 (Mai and Subramanian 2017). Figured into these costs are expenditures for housing, feeding, clothing, and supervising inmates. If capital expenses and employee wages and benefits are included in the calculation, the total annual cost per inmate could run as high as $65,000 in a medium-security prison. To put these numbers in perspective, consider that in the academic year 2014–2015, per-pupil expenditures in state schools averaged $11,709 (National Education Association 2016). As can be seen, states spend anywhere from three to six times the amount per inmate as per pupil in a given year.

On a global scale, the United States, although it is the number one country in incarceration, spends fewer dollars per inmate on average (using the $31,286 figure) compared to other Western nations. For example, to date, Australia's average per-person incarceration cost is $105,742 a year, followed by Canada at greater than $91,000 and then England with a mean value of $41,258. Other than England, these other nations greatly outspend the United States per inmate, yet these three nations' total prison populations combined do not even compare to that of the United States: 125,282 versus 1,526,800, respectively. Indeed, the United States prevails as the "winner" in the total number of persons imprisoned and expenditures on incarceration.

By this point in our discussion, it is obvious that corrections is "big business," with high overhead and human costs. Some states are beginning to realize that something must be done to curb the amount of money allocated to institutional corrections, especially with the serious state budget crises that have occurred during the past few years. For example, Massachusetts, Michigan, Missouri, Arizona, New Mexico, and Mississippi legislators either repealed minimum mandatory sentencing laws that were the cornerstone of the "get-tough" era in the 1980s and 1990s or have considered modifications to existing legislation. Although many of these laws targeted drug offenders, few, if any, states have observed significant decreases in the number of drug crimes occurring with the adoption of minimum mandatory sentences for these offenders. The proposed changes to these types of sentencing systems involve either a reduction in time spent in prison or widening the eligibility standards for parole. Thus, "get-tough" stances are being replaced by "smart-on-crime" strategies that enable states to conserve both monetary and material resources for already taxed social systems (Shy 2004: 1).

JAILS

Currently, there are more than 3,300 jails in the United States. **Jails** and **detention centers** are facilities designed to hold a variety of offenders for a relatively brief period of time, usually less than one year. The size of a jail varies depending on the geographic and legal jurisdictions it serves. Whereas jails in rural areas and small communities may hold relatively few prisoners, those in cities can be immense. Counties or municipal governments operate most jails, while some jurisdictions such as the federal government have special facilities for their own detainees in certain areas of the country.

Jails perform several important functions. First, jails are where most offenders are housed following arrest. After arrest, a local judge or magistrate reviews the offenders' charges and flight risk and sets a bail amount, orders the offenders held without bail, or releases the offenders on their own recognizance until their next court date. Second, jails house defendants who have been sentenced to less than one year of incarceration. Some jail sentences are served on weekends, or the offenders may be released to the community for work while residing in the jail. Finally, jails may serve as detention centers to temporarily confine a variety of offenders until their cases are resolved or until authorities from the proper jurisdiction assume custody. Therefore, juvenile and adult, misdemeanor and felony, and state and federal offenders may all be housed briefly in the same facility, but sometimes in different units within that facility.

Although there are exceptions, jails tend to be chaotic environments and face a number of problems. Jails have historically been the "dumping grounds" for the poor, deviant, and marginalized individuals in a community (Sheldon 2001). They seem to be continually under pressure from overcrowding, a lack of resources and training, and the issue of local politics. Many individuals processed into the jail are intoxicated or under the influence of behavior-altering substances, highly agitated, suicidal, or mentally unstable when they arrive. Jail personnel often do not have adequate information on an arrestee's needs and risks when he or she is first booked into the facility. This lack of knowledge may lead to otherwise preventable problems. Finally, the continuous movement of prisoners in and out of the jail presents logistical and safety challenges to jail staff and administration. Inmates are frequently moved for court hearings, community service work, and other activities. The high volume of visitors can also provide opportunities for violence or smuggling of contraband.

Jail administrators are constantly facing a number of problems in the management of their facilities. Jails are often impersonal, with little contact between the guards and the inmates. Jails also lack necessary services such as medical, psychological, and substance abuse treatment for inmates. It should come as no surprise that stress levels are often heightened in the jail setting, with violence and safety issues in constant need of resolution. To overcome some of these problems, there has been a movement to replace existing jails with what are known as **new-generation jails (NGJs)**. These are built to house fewer inmates in what are known as pods or modules that contain 16 to 30 separate cells, with one or two inmates per cell. Inmates do not have access to other pods in the jail, and the staff does not have to be concerned with managing more than 60 inmates at any given time. In other types of jails, staff may have to monitor hundreds of inmates at once, thereby decreasing safety for all involved. In the NGJs, inmates eat, sleep, make phone calls, and engage in activities such as playing games or watching television in the pod (Zupan 2002). The staff is in closer contact with the inmates and consistently monitors inmates' behavior, which not only attenuates problems among the inmates and within the facility but also can provide inmates with more positive social exchanges between inmates and staff (Bayens, Williams, and Smykla 1997). One earlier evaluation of an NGJ found that recidivism did not increase and, for some offenders, actually decreased compared with that of inmates housed in traditional jails (Applegate, Surette, and McCarthy 1999).

According to a recent report (Austin 2014), compared to state prisons, with more than 1.3 million persons incarcerated and serving an average of 2.5 years, jails house 55 percent fewer individuals, with an average length of stay of approximately 23 days. The majority of jail inmates have not been convicted, meaning they have yet to plead or be found guilty of any offense (i.e., they are in the pretrial process). With rare exceptions, offenders go to prison only after they have been convicted. Demographically, nearly 46 percent of jail inmates are White males; in contrast, African American males are the most represented racial/ethnic group in prisons.

A major concern facing our nation's jails is the increasing number of individuals with mental illnesses and how jail administrators and staff can effectively deal with this population. Approximately 80 percent of jails conduct mental health exams upon intake (James and Glaze 2006), and it is through this initial screening that persons with mental illnesses are identified. These assessments find that 23 percent of inmates had been treated for a mental illness the year preceding arrest, 17 percent used medication that affected their mental illness, and 7 percent had at least one overnight stay in a psychiatric hospital (James and Glaze 2006). Other than some jails providing psychotropic medications, most facilities lack appropriate treatment for affected inmates, and the political, physical, and administrative realities of jails are often counterproductive to any treatment efforts that might be effective (Treatment Advocacy Center 2014).

Critical Thinking Exercise

Given the problems faced by jail administrators and staff, what approaches and strategies could be tried to better manage the needs of the jail population both while incarcerated and after release? What are some strengths and weaknesses of your recommendations? Why would some strategies work better than others?

MODERN PRISONS

Although felony offenders in the United States are more commonly sentenced to community supervision rather than incarceration, prisons are financially and symbolically important forms of punishment. Prisons are also socially and politically important because they are used to house those individuals who are determined to be unresponsive to community supervision, who pose a considerable risk to the community, or who have committed offenses so serious that they deserve to have their freedom taken away for a given period of time. Prisons are also known as penitentiaries, correctional institutions, and penal institutions. To reduce confusion, the term *prison* is used in this section.

Prison Types

In most American criminal justice systems, offenders who have been convicted and sentenced to more than one year of incarceration for a felony offense are generally held in **prisons**. Although many jurisdictions have a juvenile version of a prison system, the majority of prisoners are adults held in state or federal institutions. At any one time, the prison population is composed of offenders sentenced for a variety of offenses as well as those sentenced to prison for probation violations and those returned for parole violations. Individual states and the federal government tend to have a number of prisons within their prison systems. Each prison has certain features that make it more suitable for particular types of offenders. Once an inmate is sentenced to prison, personnel from the corrections department usually conduct an initial **classification** review, in which they evaluate the needs and risk of the offender to determine the best placement for him or her within the prison system. Common topics evaluated in this assessment are the danger posed by the prisoner, the length of sentence, any gang affiliation, physical or mental health needs, and whether treatment programs are available and considered important for the prisoner. Based on this assessment, prisoners are sent to an institution that is classified by its security type.

Critical Thinking Exercise

Prisons house offenders who have committed a variety of different offenses. Research the types of crimes for which offenders have been incarcerated and the demographics of offenders (the textbook website has some suggestions on where to look; see http://www.oup.com/us/labessentials). Describe the types of offenses and offenders in prison. What does this suggest about crime that is committed and who commits it?

Most American jurisdictions have three to five different types of prisons, distinguished by their security level. **Supermax prisons** are primarily found in the larger jurisdictions and represent the most restrictive and secure prisons in the country. Because of their extremely high cost of operation and strict limitations on the number of prisoners they can hold, supermax prisons are generally reserved for the most incorrigible and dangerous prisoners in a correctional system. Prisoners in these facilities tend to be continuously confined to their cells except for very brief periods of exercise. Supermax prisons use the most sophisticated security systems and most rigorous safety procedures.

Maximum-security prisons represent the highest level of security in many states. These facilities tend to hold the most violent and disruptive prisoners in those jurisdictions without supermax facilities. Inmate movement within the prison is restricted by numerous checkpoints and gates. External barriers such as walled perimeters, several rings of razor-wired fencing, or armed guard towers are also common.

Some jurisdictions use a third security classification known as **close security**, which lies between maximum- and medium-security prisons. Such facilities may house individuals convicted of violent offenses who do not require a maximum-security setting or disruptive inmates who do not pose as great a physical threat to inmates or staff. **Medium-security prisons** hold a diverse inmate population and can have a variety of architectural styles. Inmates may have some degree of movement within the institution during certain times of the day and participate in a range of activities. However, the specifics of inmate life and the amount of security can vary considerably, even within different prisons in the same jurisdiction.

Finally, **minimum-security prisons** represent the most open and least restrictive type of institution. These can house prisoners convicted of nonviolent offenses, those who pose a minimal security risk, or those nearing final release. Minimum-security prisons tend to allow the greatest freedom of movement and offer inmates a range of services and programs in which to participate.

Some jurisdictions have **specialized prisons** that primarily house inmates with specific characteristics that pose unique challenges to institutions. These facilities offer treatment programs or services that are tailored to meet the needs and risks posed by particular populations. Examples of these institutions include those dedicated to substance-abusing prisoners, sex offenders, and mentally handicapped or psychiatric prisoners. Each jurisdiction typically has a facility dedicated to housing prisoners with severe psychological disorders because of the unique problems such inmates present to the operation of an institution.

Female offenders may be held in jails that house both males and females, but prisons are typically separated by sex. This was not always the case, however. Historically, females, juveniles, and adult male inmates were often housed in the same facility and perhaps even the same cell. Although females make up approximately 6 or 7 percent of all prisoners and approximately 15 percent of all offenders under community supervision, in the past decade females have been one of the fastest-growing correctional populations (Glaze and Kaeble 2014). If this trend continues, correctional systems will have to respond to the increasing proportion of female offenders with more designated institutions and additional resources to serve this population.

Another characteristic that can distinguish prisons is whether they are privately operated or managed and staffed by a jurisdiction's own personnel. Historically, it has not been uncommon for some degree of private interest to be involved in the operation of jails and prisons. Since the birth of the modern penitentiary around the turn of the 19th century, American correctional systems have had a variety of relationships with private for-profit businesses and non-profit agencies. However, during the 20th century, the funding and operation of most American prisons has primarily been the responsibility of the public sector. During the push for increasing privatization of government services in the 1980s, American jurisdictions began increasingly to contract out some of their correctional services (Gowdy 2001).

To date, treatment services, community service, and smaller residential programs are more commonly privatized than major prisons. With rising incarceration rates, prison overcrowding, and increasing operating costs during the 1980s, governments were interested in alternatives that could increase the cost-effectiveness of correctional budgets. Although the term "**private prison**" is often used to indicate a correctional facility that is managed and operated by a private corporation, the privatization of correctional services can take a number of forms. The authority to operate these facilities is granted through a contract awarded by a jurisdiction's government. There is considerable debate about the validity of incorporating a profit motive in the punishment of offenders (Gowdy 2001). There are also real questions about whether private prisons are actually more cost-effective and about the quality of services they provide. Despite this, punishment is a major for-profit enterprise, and several states have private prisons that are used in conjunction with the state-run institutions. Only time will tell whether privatization becomes a permanent and growing feature of American corrections or a passing trend that is remembered primarily in history books.

Critical Thinking Exercise

Investigate the use of private prisons in your state. How many people are in private institutions (nationally and in your state)? Should states be turning over control and supervision of prisoners to for-profit companies? What advantages and disadvantages do you see?

Custody and Security Within Institutions

The primary goal of a prison is maintaining custody of inmates within the institution. In fact, nearly every decision affecting the operation of a prison must take into account the safety and prison control consequences. Even within the most secure facilities, inmates outnumber the **correctional officers** (or guards) who supervise the prisoners. This is particularly true in large, lower-security facilities.

Secure custody of inmates involves several components. First, prisons must ensure that they are physically secure and can prevent escape and the introduction of contraband into the institution. Second, prison officials want to reduce the occurrence of inmate assaults on staff. Limiting the frequency of inmate-on-inmate violence is another important goal for both the safety of the inmates and the impact such events have on institutional operations. Finally, prison administrators want to secure the efficient functioning of the institution. Procedures such as head counts and activities such as feeding, clothing, and work details create a structure to prison life. The smooth operation of these activities is vital to a manageable environment.

A symbiotic relationship is thought to exist among prisoners, correctional officers, and prison administrators. Although prison personnel have official (and unofficial) mechanisms at their control to ensure discipline, prisoners can create considerable disruption in the operation of a facility. Therefore, all sides tend to engage in activities and relationships that will maintain the status quo and reduce disruptions to daily life and routines. Clearly, the most destructive and disruptive event is a prison riot. In riots, prison officials lose all but the most basic control over some or all inmates and institutional operations. As a result, staff and inmate safety can be in serious jeopardy, and considerable damage can be done to the physical structure of the institution.

Prison Violence and Prison Discipline

Violence, or at least the threat of violence, is a common concern among both inmates and staff. After all, prisons tend to be filled with people who have already demonstrated a willingness to engage in violent or otherwise unlawful acts. Knowledge about violence within prisons is limited by concerns over the validity and reliability of prison records and the limitations of other methodologies used to study **prison violence**. The level and extent of violence will greatly vary from prison to prison and for different prisoners. Different features of the prison, such as its architectural design, inmates' freedom of movement, and group and individual dynamics, can affect the level of prison violence (Adams 1992; Bottoms 1999).

Research suggests that most prisons are not characterized by the systematic and rampant violence often portrayed in the popular media (Bottoms 1999). Of course, there have been and continue to be prisons and prison systems that are plagued by higher levels of violence. Coercion and the threat of violence appear to be more common than actual physical assaults. Coercion may be used by physically dominating inmates to obtain items such as food, money, personal services, and sexual favors. This threat of violence, including sexual assault, is very real to prisoners. Furthermore, prisoner assaults on staff and other prisoners do occur and can result in serious injury or death. Female prisons tend to have less explicit violence compared to male prisons, although violence and the threat of violence are clearly a reality in women's prisons as well. Similar to male prisons, there tend to be female convicts who are more willing to use instrumental violence and cause disruptions within the facility (Johnson 2002).

Prison officials have a number of tools to deal with violence and other violations of institutional rules. For violations that are criminal offenses, administrators can refer the matter for criminal prosecution. However, the difficulty in obtaining a conviction in many of these cases and the logistical problems involved often discourage such attempts (Jacobs 1982). A more common response is to use one or more of the sanctions that prison officials have at their disposal, including the loss of certain privileges such as visitation, solitary confinement (often called segregation) for a period of time, or a change in the inmate's classification status or location (Jacobs 1982). Prison officials may also have the discretion to reduce an inmate's good-time credit. In jurisdictions with indeterminate sentencing, parole officials will examine an inmate's behavior and may reject a parole application if an inmate has a history of disruptive behavior while incarcerated.

Prison Life

Prison life can be stressful for both inmates and staff. Research indicates that the unique nature of prison life results in a distinct subculture within prisons. Prison life can be both stressful and monotonous, and new inmates must adapt to the environment if they are to cope with the demands of prison. Perhaps the most important initial concern is an inmate's personal safety and how to deal with the violence that occurs in an institution.

Prison Subculture and Coping

Most of the research on prison subculture is from the study of maximum-security prisons (e.g., Sykes 1958), but there is reason to believe that elements of a unique prison subculture exist even in less secure facilities. Based on the premises of the **deprivation model** used to explain the formation of prison subcultures and adaptation to the prison environment, the nature and impact of an individual prison's culture over its residents will vary across prisons and among residents (Adams 1992; Bottoms 1999; Johnson 2002). In an important work, Sykes (1958) identified several characteristics of prison life that contribute to the development of the prison culture and individual responses to imprisonment. These **pains of imprisonment** included the loss of liberty, deprivation of goods and services, the barring of heterosexual relations, limitations to a prisoner's autonomy, and concerns over personal security. These pains are thought to be central features of prison life and require adaptations by individual prisoners if they are to cope with their new environment in any positive manner (Johnson 2002).

The first pain, the deprivation of liberty, refers to the fact that inmates are confined to the institution and within the institution. The second pain is the deprivation of goods and services, in which inmates are deprived not only of individual dress but also of amenities such as televisions, radios, and favorite foods. The third pain is the lack of heterosexual relationships, which makes inmates experience a loss of identity. The fourth pain is the deprivation of autonomy, or the lack of freedom to make choices for oneself. The final pain is the deprivation of security, in which inmates are housed together, constantly living in fear of victimization.

Since Sykes's (1958) publication, the degree to which inmates experience these deprivations has changed. Some deprivations, such as the deprivation of goods and services, have been lessened somewhat with the opportunity to purchase some goods in the commissary. The deprivation of heterosexual relationships can be attenuated if prisoners are allowed conjugal visits with significant others. For example, some women's facilities have provided family "homes" in which family members can visit over a couple of days. These facilities, while still located on prison grounds, are usually set apart from the general prison population. This opportunity is a privilege, not a right; therefore, corrections officials can withhold these visits from inmates in order to gain compliance with directives.

Researchers also believe that individual characteristics, as opposed to the characteristics unique to the prison as detailed in the deprivation model, will affect a particular prisoner's ability to adjust. The **importation model** suggests that the skills, experiences, and attributes that individuals bring with them into a prison environment affect the prison culture and the ability of an individual to adjust to that environment (Adams 1992). Increasingly, researchers recognize that it is likely the interaction of individual attributes and the unique physical and social dynamics of a given institution that will determine the nature of the prison culture and how an individual is able to cope within that setting (Adams 1992). Whatever the specifics of a given institution's subculture, it is important that a prisoner become socialized into this environment by learning the norms or expectations of behavior and various techniques to cope and adapt to this environment.

Prison Programs

With the exception of the highest-security prisons, most prisons offer some **prison programs** promoted as helping with offender rehabilitation and increasing the structure and activities involved in an inmate's daily routine. The number and types of programs vary in different institutions and jurisdictions. In some jurisdictions, inmates can receive good-time credits by productively participating in approved activities. In states with indeterminate sentencing, inmates may consider that participation in certain programs improves their chances of an earlier parole release. Prisoners may be given a particular work assignment that constitutes a major part of their day. Many basic prison operations, such as food service, laundry, and groundskeeping, are carried out by prisoners with varying degrees of staff supervision. Other prison programs may be of a more voluntary nature. Activities such as religious groups, substance abuse and counseling programs, educational classes, and charity and self-help groups may be offered for interested and eligible prisoners. Although the funding for such programs tends to be a relatively low priority, many scholars and practitioners consider these types of activities important in helping prisoners cope with the stresses of prison life and improving their likelihood of successful reintegration after release (e.g., Gaes et al. 1999).

Web Activity

An important influence on corrections has been the emergence of technology. For a discussion of this issue, see the textbook website (http://www.oup.com/us/labessentials).

SPECIAL OFFENDER POPULATIONS

Similar to the general public, the prison population includes individuals with substance abuse problems, mental illness, physical disabilities, and diseases. There has also been an increase in the number of aging offenders in correctional institutions due to the "get-tough" sentencing policies adopted and implemented during the 1980s. Inmates are a unique population in that they are one of two groups in society that are entitled to medical treatment based on decisions handed down by the U.S. Supreme Court (the other group is the military).

Inmates and HIV/AIDS

Since the 1980s, the prison population, like the general population, has witnessed an explosion of individuals diagnosed as HIV positive or with full-blown AIDS. Today, there are approximately 24,000 inmates in state and federal prisons who are HIV positive, and one-fourth of that number have confirmed cases of active AIDS (Maruschak 2004). Prior to 1999, it was estimated that prisoners were seven to nine times more likely than the general population to have confirmed cases of AIDS. The good news is that since 1999, the number of inmates who have HIV/AIDS has been decreasing.

The most common method of transmission of HIV in the United States is through the sharing of needles or other equipment used to ingest illegal substances. The increase in mandatory minimum-sentencing practices arguably led to an increase of substance users in prison, many of whom had already been exposed to HIV. In secure facilities, HIV is most often spread through sexual contact between inmates, who were most likely exposed prior to their incarceration via unclean drug-taking methods.

Correctional administrators and staff throughout the country have implemented several approaches to decreasing the number of new cases within prisons. Some institutions focus on education in terms of how the disease is contracted and treatment options available. A few institutions have provided condoms for those inmates engaged in sexual activities; however, this option is controversial because sex between inmates is usually prohibited. Voluntary or mandatory testing to determine who is infected with HIV has also been used. Special housing for inmates at different stages of the disease has also been attempted. It has been proposed that, at a minimum, infirmaries should be established where inmates already confirmed to have AIDS can be held to protect them from airborne infections such as tuberculosis and pneumonia.

Web Activity

You can explore more about HIV in prisons and women and HIV in prisons on the textbook website (http://www.oup.com/us/labessentials).

Many state corrections systems have been proactive in collaborating with public health agencies to increase knowledge about how to take care of not only HIV/AIDS in the prison but also other sexually transmitted diseases and tuberculosis, which are widespread among correctional populations disproportionate to the general population (Hammett 1998). Given that many inmates will eventually be released into society and the gravity of these communicable diseases, there is a definite need to provide appropriate treatment, prevention, and post-release programs to curb further transmission of these conditions. Thus, it would be remiss to ignore what goes on in the prison merely because the population affected is made up of offenders.

Critical Thinking Exercise

What should be the response of prisons to HIV/AIDS and other sexually transmitted diseases? What alternatives make the most sense? What do institutions in your state do to deal with these problems?

Inmates and Substance Use

Nearly half of offenders housed in jails and prisons throughout the United States admit to having been under the influence of alcohol or drugs when they committed the offense that led to their incarceration. Drug and property offenders are more likely than other types of offenders to engage in crime to acquire money to feed their substance addiction. The mentally ill are more likely to be under the influence at the time of their offenses compared to those who are not mentally ill. Overall, approximately 70 to 80 percent of incarcerated offenders report that they have used drugs in the past. Younger offenders, particularly those who are first-time or minor drug offenders, make up a significant proportion of jail populations. Since the war on drugs in the 1980s, the United States has seen unprecedented increases in incarceration rates for drug crimes that carry longer sentences than was typically the case prior to "getting tough."

Given that "kicking the habit" is difficult for those seeking treatment in the general population and their success rates are low, the environment of the prison often complicates effective service delivery for inmates who want to rid themselves of their substance addictions. Treatment in correctional facilities can involve counseling, therapeutic communities, detoxification, and 12-step programs such as Alcoholics Anonymous or Narcotics Anonymous. Of these treatment options, recent research shows that in-prison therapeutic community interventions, especially if coupled with continued treatment after participants are released from prison, are especially effective (Galassi, Mpofu, and Athanasou 2015). The introduction of drug courts as alternatives to incapacitation since the late 1980s has provided yet another avenue for handling offenders with substance abuse problems.

Overall, some treatment programs have been found to be ineffective in reducing recidivism. However, only approximately 20 percent of inmates in secure confinement actually participate in the alcohol- or drug-treatment programs that are offered; in contrast, more than 70 percent of inmates in state prison have substance abuse problems with and without co-occurring mental health disorders (James and Glaze 2006). Recidivism rates are two to four times higher for individuals who abuse substances compared to those who do not, so providing and encouraging completion of effective treatment programs while incarcerated increases the probability of higher success rates after release (Bennett, Holloway, and Farrington 2008).

If inmates do participate, they usually do so during the last 6 months of their sentences. The length of time in treatment could be one of the hurdles standing in the way of reducing recidivism. In fact, a review of the literature demonstrates that programs that do work are intensive, last 9 to 12 months, focus on offenders who are younger and more at risk, and maintain services after release. They actually work quite well and save money, too. Several recent studies have observed that offenders who participate in treatment programs both in prison and in the outside community have a lower incidence of drug use relapse and criminality (McCollister et al. 2004).

Aging and Elderly Inmates

One prominent issue in the United States during the past 10 to 15 years has been a surge in the percentage of the population older than age 55 years. News reports and politicians have often highlighted this fact with an emphasis on government programs in need of reform such as Social Security and Medicare, long-term care, and prescription drug costs. Special housing such as assisted-living communities and retirement communities has been a significant moneymaker for construction companies, investors, and real estate developers alike. Few cities larger than 50,000 residents are without such properties.

Recall that what happens in the general society soon occurs inside the prison walls. With the mandate to provide medical treatment for inmates, the costs and unique problems posed by an aging prison population are an ever-pressing dilemma for an institution that traditionally held convicted offenders between the ages of 18 and 49 years. The number of state and federal prisoners aged 55 years or older is growing at twice the rate of their younger counterparts. Between 1980 and 2010, inmates aged 55 years or older increased by nearly 1,400 percent. According to the American Civil Liberties Union (2012), if this rate of growth continues, inmates aged 55 years or older will make up 33 percent of prison populations throughout the country by 2020. Figure 5.2 displays the distribution of state and federal prison populations, indicating that nearly 11% are 55 years of age or older. There is no epidemic of older persons committing crimes; rather, the increase in this age group is a result of longer sentences, life-without-parole sanctions, and mandatory minimum provisions. As a result, state and federal corrections systems need to allocate three times the expenditures to care for aging inmates compared to their younger counterparts (Faiver 1998). Some state prisons have created special wings that are essentially nursing homes to provide for older prisoners.

Age Distribution of Sentenced Prisoners 2015 Yearend

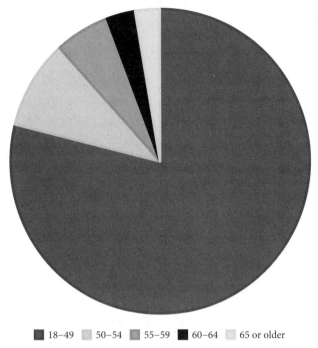

■ 18–49   50–54   ■ 55–59   ■ 60–64   65 or older

Figure 5.2 **Age distribution of sentenced prisoners, 2015 year end.**
SOURCE: Carson, E. A., and Anderson, E. (2016). *Prisoners in 2015.* Washington, DC: Bureau of Justice Statistics. Retrieved from https://www.bjs.gov/content/pub/pdf/p15.pdf.

When people age, in or out of prison, they change physically, socially, and mentally. For offenders who are aging behind bars, however, many of the issues associated with aging are aggravated. Although aging inmates are entitled to health care, the quality of that care may not be sufficient to take care of many of the problems associated with old age, such as dementia. In addition, older inmates may not be able to take care of themselves if they are harassed or assaulted by younger inmates.

Possible solutions to these problems involve early release on medical parole, also known as compassionate release; sentences served in the community for older offenders who do not pose a significant risk to the community; increases in funding to serve aging inmates; and the creation of geriatric units within existing and proposed facilities. Certainly, the former two alternatives would be the most cost-effective for the administration of corrections, considering that offenders serving their time in the community are responsible for their own housing, medical treatment, and daily care. Government allocation of more funds to correctional budgets would be helpful but is not practical or economical based on the fiscal crises during the past several years. In general, most states already spend more on corrections than on education and other social programs.

Web Activity

To learn more about compassionate release for elderly inmates, see https://www
.youtube.com/watch?v=GGGI11LAnK4.

Creating geriatric units and even geriatric prisons is becoming the major approach for dealing with the aging inmate population. These facilities look like mini-hospitals that are staffed with registered nurses and are equipped with appropriate medical devices, which are more readily available than they would be in the typical prison infirmary. Some states have developed prison hospice facilities. Similar to hospice facilities in the community, prison hospices care for terminally ill inmates who are not eligible for or who were denied medical parole. Certainly, as the prison population continues to gray, different approaches, programs, and facilities will be needed to house this population, especially if other back-door options are not available.

Inmates and Mental Illness

Historically, asylums held society's misfits, whether they were insane, poor, or criminal. In 19th-century America, asylums were institutions where the mentally troubled were held until a cure for their sickness could be found. Once tranquilizers became available, asylum patients were basically sedated into a stupor. Essentially, this practice continued into the 20th century. Long-term institutionalization in a secure hospital setting became the primary method of care in the United States until the early 1970s.

With the passage and implementation of community mental health acts by states throughout the country, patients housed in the asylums who were no longer considered to be a threat to themselves or others were released into general society, a process called **deinstitutionalization**. Soon, many city streets in America were occupied by thousands of mentally ill former hospital patients, many of whom were unable to function in ways that were deemed appropriate law-abiding behaviors. Most jurisdictions responded to the problem by confining these "offenders" in correctional institutions. This process is known as **transinstitutionalization**; the mentally ill were first placed in secure confinement in a hospital setting, then they were released, and then they were reconfined, this time under the auspices of the criminal justice system.

Web Activity

Mental health among the offending population and those in correctional facilities is a growing concern. More information can be found on the textbook website (http://www.oup.com/us/labessentials).

Currently, it is estimated that 15 to 20 percent of inmates housed in jails or prisons can be classified as having a mental disability (Pollock 2004; Treatment Advocacy Center 2014). Symptoms of mental health disorders most commonly observed in jails and prisons are mania, followed by major depressive disorder and psychotic disorder. Nearly all of the state public and private correctional facilities in the United States have reported that they provided some sort of treatment to meet inmates' mental health needs (Beck and Maruschak 2001). Treatment forms range from therapy or counseling services to psychotropic medications and separate care units within the facility.

Inmates with mental disabilities are often at most risk for victimization, both physically and psychologically. These inmates are also found to be difficult for staff to control because many correctional officers do not have the training or educational background to deal with the compounded problems inmates with mental illness face in correctional facilities, especially when officers must give inmates orders of compliance to maintain security and control within the institutions. For example, correctional officers may be required to distinguish between those inmates who truly do not understand the orders that they are given, and as a result act out irrationally, and those who understand the expectations but become upset because they do not want to comply (Pollock 2004).

Dual-disorder inmates are also becoming a major concern for management issues in the nation's prisons and jails and then for communities after release. These inmates are those who can be classified as having both substance abuse and mental health problems. These inmates are especially problematic for jails because the majority of these offenders are purportedly arrested more frequently for less serious offenses (Alemagno et al. 2004). In addition, some of these dual-disordered individuals may seek treatment in a traditional psychiatric center for their mental illness, but they are often turned away because some centers or programs prefer not to deal with patients who also have drug addictions. Whatever the reason, a large number of individuals will return to the community still needing treatment to improve their chances for successful reentry. Further complicating matters, mentally ill offenders are more likely to be homeless, jobless, and alcohol or drug dependent during the year preceding their offense (Ditton 1999).

Critical Thinking Exercise

To what extent should correctional institutions be responsible for handling mentally ill individuals? Why does the criminal justice system assume responsibility for these individuals? Should it continue? What alternatives exist (or should exist) for handling these individuals?

Secure institutions in the criminal justice system have been facing an increase in the number of inmates with characteristics that require special assistance and programming. There has been progress in providing services for the mentally ill in terms of screening for problems and treatment availability, but more needs to be done. The same can be said for aging inmates; inmates with diseases, particularly HIV/AIDS; and inmates with substance abuse issues. These special populations, however, will continue to grow as long as legislation increases sentence lengths for various offenses and broadens the types of offenses punishable by incarceration.

PROBLEMS, RIGHTS, AND IMPLICATIONS
IN MODERN PRISONS

In addition to the challenging composition of inmate populations, institutional corrections will continue to deal with the problems of crowding, violence, and decreased availability of effective programs to reduce recidivism. Of course, these issues existed in the past and, given the heavy reliance on institutional facilities for punishment during the past few decades, will most likely persist in the future. Many of these issues have been brought to the attention of the courts by prisoners seeking to lessen the impact that the unique features of prison have on their lives. Even though many decisions set forth by the courts could be considered in favor of such solutions as reducing inmate crowding, the reality is that changes to rectify these problems have been more the exception than the rule. Indeed, some argue that problems surrounding inmate rights, crowding, violence, and inmate social systems have actually worsened over time.

Inmate Rights

Traditionally, appellate courts took a hands-off approach to the problems and grievances of those incarcerated (Haas and Alpert 1989). The reasons for this hands-off approach were that (1) the courts believed that they should not interfere with the operations of the prisons, (2) the judiciary offered a type of checks and balances, and (3) the judiciary could not possibly understand the problems of prison administrators because judges lacked a coherent knowledge of penology (Haas and Alpert 1989). In 1941, the Supreme Court ruled in *Ex parte Hull* that the Fifth and Fourteenth Amendments to the Bill of Rights granted everyone, even inmates, access to the courts (Haas and Alpert 1989). However, not until 1964 did the courts really begin to lift the hands-off policy with the *Cooper v. Pate* decision.

Until the mid-1960s, most prisons were homogeneous institutions in which strict control, sometimes rehabilitation, and structure were the rule (Sykes 1958). With the advent of the civil rights movement, many groups began to seek legitimacy for their grievances and remedies to their problems through court decisions. The courthouse door opened for inmates and granted them access to address their grievances similar to that of other groups in society. This hands-on approach to inmate rights has led to lessening a number of deprivations but also paved the way for inequitable sentences, which could undermine other goals or philosophies of the criminal justice system in general and the corrections system in particular.

The prisoners' rights movement led to the establishment of certain new privileges. For instance, inmates now could buy televisions or radios, wear what they wanted in some prisons, or have visitors bring in amenities (Carroll 1974). This led to a situation of the "haves" versus the "have nots" in which the "have nots" could burglarize or victimize the "haves" to obtain what they wanted. The purpose of using correctional facilities for incapacitation is to prevent offenders from committing any further crimes. If crime continues in the prison, the goal of incapacitation is weakened.

Another result of the prisoners' rights movement is increased freedom of movement and the elimination of the requirement that inmates must participate in treatment programs. Lack of structure means idle time for some inmates, which occasionally leads to violence (Wooldredge 1994). This means that some inmates will experience a rougher time in prison compared to others because they are being victimized. Therefore, the philosophy of retribution is undermined in that no longer will punishment for similar crimes be the same for all inmates (Hawkins and Alpert 1989). Rehabilitation as a goal may be impossible to meet because inmates must be able to concentrate on their treatment; if they are constantly worrying about being victimized, they cannot actively participate in their own reformation. Deterrence—the idea that imposing severe punishments will create enough fear that the costs will outweigh the benefits of committing crime—may also be undermined because some inmates will be victims and some will continue to be offenders. Correctional officers often look the other way for most infractions because they do not want to attract the attention of administrators who are primarily concerned about the effective control of prisons (Zimmer 1986).

Legislation passed by Congress in 1995, however, may change the current state of affairs for both correctional philosophies and prisoners' rights. The Prison Litigation Reform Act (PLRA) establishes that inmates must exhaust the internal prison grievance procedures before accessing the federal courts. The PLRA also requires inmates to pay their own court filing fees, thereby further limiting access to judicial review of complaints by inmates. In addition, the PLRA reinforces the right of the courts to dismiss any lawsuit deemed by judges to be frivolous or malicious or to state an improper claim. An inmate who receives three such determinations (i.e., three "strikes") regarding his or her petitions is restricted from filing further lawsuits without paying court fees in advance. Prisoners also face the possibility of losing good-time credit if judges find that the purpose of their grievances was harassment or a presentation of lies or false information. Furthermore, the PLRA has a provision mandating that inmates must show physical injury in order to file a claim for mental or emotional injury. State inmate petitions filed in U.S. district courts, for both civil rights and prison-conditions grievances, did decline after the passage of the PLRA. Despite these reductions in inmate lawsuits, several key cases did make their way to the U.S. Supreme Court and further affected life in prison and correctional operations.

Crowding

Due to the growing trend of incarcerating and managing large numbers of offenders because of the fall of rehabilitation, more punitive sentencing policies, and increasing the number of offenses eligible for incarceration, prison crowding has become an endemic problem in the United States. For example, it is estimated that 44 percent of the prison population can be accounted for due to the war on drugs (Blumstein 1995). The rise in prison populations is indicative of the trends that can be attributed to judges and prosecutors in convicting more persons and sending them to prison. Prison populations will vary according to (1) how many people are sentenced to prison, (2) how long offenders are sent to prison, and (3) the rate at which they return (Joyce 1992).

Crowding leads to a number of problems within the institution, such as elevated blood pressures, more trips to clinics, difficulty sleeping, suicides, homicides, and other types of assaultive behaviors (Gaes and McGuire 1985; Harer and Steffensmeier 1996). In addition, crowding adds to the uncertainty, apprehension, and cognitive overloads of inmates. These emotional difficulties can interfere with treatment because inmates need to concentrate on their reformation; if they are constantly living in fear, this becomes a near-impossible task. Crowding can also undermine rehabilitation, in that classification of inmates into appropriate housing, programs, and the like is made more difficult and can deplete resources, leaving some inmates to be placed on treatment waiting lists or leading to the elimination of rehabilitation programs altogether.

In addition, crowding can undermine incapacitation due to the early release mechanisms that are relied on to reduce the population. In effect, inmates are on the streets sooner and may return to crime due to shorter sentence lengths. Inmate crowding can also weaken the goal of general deterrence because would-be offenders see that crowding has led to limited space in facilities, which means that they may not receive prison sentences at all. Crowding can also weaken the objectives of specific deterrence due to the harsh living conditions of the prison environment. Finally, crowding can negatively affect retribution because no two sentences will be served equitably due to crowding.

Violence

As noted previously, violence in prison has become increasingly more pervasive due to the ever-changing composition of the prison population, such as the entrance of gangs and the mentally disordered, and the pervasive impact of the prisoners' rights movement (Irwin 1980). Inmates are free to move around the facilities, which leads to more opportunities for victimization. In addition, due to increased crowding, classification efforts may be ineffective at separating violent inmates from the nonviolent (Van Voorhis 1994). Furthermore, because inmates are not required to participate in treatment programs, they have plenty of free time. It has been found that inmates who spend less time in educational activities are more likely to commit personal crimes (Wooldredge 1994). In addition, the impact of determinate sentencing, the entrance of younger inmates into the prison, decreases in furloughs, lack of visitation, and longer time until parole dates can lead to increases in violence (Burke 1995).

Violence undermines retribution because some inmates are offenders and some are victims; this is not equal time for equal crimes. Violence weakens the goals of deterrence and incapacitation because the mere existence of violence in prison means that threats of punishments and preventing further crimes are ineffective at suppressing violence. Rehabilitation efforts may also be unsuccessful because some inmates live in fear of being victimized, and inmates must feel in total control of their being and safety in order to gain anything from treatment efforts.

Critical Thinking Exercise

You are the director of the Department of Corrections for your state. The governor has just informed you that you need to devise a plan to reduce prison crowding by 30 percent in year one, by 40 percent in year two, and by 10 percent each year thereafter until prison crowding in your state's facilities is near 0 percent. How will you accomplish this task? What policies would you propose to reduce incarceration rates? Why do you think these would work? What are some of the problems you might face when implementing your policies? Remember to take into account special offender populations when designing your plan.

Solutions

Possible solutions to these problems have been studied and found to be promising. For example, smaller, more efficiently designed prisons are better able to alleviate the problems posed by violence, inmate subcultures, and crowding. New designs are being used in jails such as the new-generation or direct-supervision jails. Such facilities make better use of design to promote a safer and more controlled environment for correctional officers. Smaller facilities may also encourage inmates to engage in activities such as treatment, vocational training, or education in a manner that can be replicated on the outside when they are released. Housing inmates in huge, dark, noisy prisons is not beneficial for any goal, let alone the well-being of inmates.

If classification systems, which have been found to be valid in dividing prison populations into manageable subgroups, are used more effectively, there may be reductions in violence, crowding, and favorable offender treatment outcomes (Makarios and Latessa 2013; Van Voorhis 1994). Arguably, some inmates do not belong in prison in the first place, and classification systems can dictate which offenders would be better served in the community. More emphasis might be placed on separating the violent from the nonviolent, the aging from the young, and the mentally disabled from the general prison population. These types of separation could reduce levels of violence and other misconduct, dilute the inherent inequities that resulted from the prisoners' rights movement, and counterbalance the challenges of housing such varied groups in correctional institutions. More adequately classifying inmates can also increase successful treatment outcomes, thereby increasing the probability of decreases in future reoffending after release from custody (Latessa, Listwan, and Koetzle 2013). To achieve such positive outcomes, however, we need to ensure we are targeting the (1) right offenders and (2) their criminogenic needs who are (3) amenable to the elements of matched treatment programs. This triad is best known as risk, need, and responsivity, respectively, and together are known as the "principles of effective classification."

Principles of Effective Classification

As originally developed by Andrews and Bonta (2006), there are three principles of effective classification: risk, need, and responsivity.

The **risk principle** states that we only target offenders who are medium-high to high risk in terms of their propensity to reoffend. Often, individuals of low risk are placed in institutions and programs with more serious offenders. Low-risk, often situational (i.e., first crime committed is likely the last), offenders in these settings will be influenced by the higher-risk individuals in terms of the justifications and rationalizations—"tools and tricks of the trade," so to speak—for behaving in antisocial, criminal manners. In turn, this exposure can increase the chances that the low-risk offenders will engage in future crimes because low-risk individuals will learn from their more "experienced" counterparts. In order to reduce the chances of these negative influences on those who are and will likely be law-abiding, a one-size-fits-all approach is not advised. Rather, we should concentrate our efforts on those most likely to recidivate.

The **need principle** focuses on two types of needs. One is **general needs**. Think of these as more like deficiencies in conduct or life, such as lack of employment or educational skills, substance abuse problems, and relationship issues. The second category is **criminogenic needs**, which are antisocial attitudes, antisocial friends, substance abuse, lack of empathy, and impulsive behavior. We will surely see greater failure rates if we do not address the factors that have been repeatedly shown to lead to offending. Successful programs will target the individual needs of each offender relative to those variables that influenced his or her law-violating behaviors.

The third principle is the **responsivity principle**. Many offenders are assessed for risk and needs, but few are assessed relative to how responsive, or amenable, they will be to any given treatment or programmatic approach, as well as to correctional placement. In other words, the responsivity principle tells us that we should determine how amenable a person will be to a specific program or practice before we subject him or her to it. Aspects to consider when addressing responsivity are a person's personality, maturity level, intelligence, psychological state, learning style, cognitive abilities, and other interpersonal qualities.

To illustrate, let us assume there is a program for offenders that requires a journaling component, but several of the individuals the Department of Corrections would like to place in this program are unable to read or write past a third grade level. These individuals will likely not be as successful in this type of program and, therefore, we will not see promising outcomes for these offenders. Often, we hear that programs do not work when in reality they do work for some offenders but not for others, but because we are comparing all of the participants to one another, the successes are often masked, or canceled out, by the failures when the program is evaluated.

Instruments are available to assess the three principles of effective classification. Most jurisdictions consider offenders' risk and needs, albeit frequently neglect criminogenic needs, but few assess for responsivity. This situation is unfortunate, especially given that studies have shown for more than 25 years what programs can work, for what types of offenders, and in what types of settings.

In addition to classification systems, alternatives to incarceration such as community-based correctional facilities, intensive supervision probation, and home confinement coupled with treatment interventions could also be used. Better use of administrative "good time" and sentencing guidelines to reduce sentence lengths may also help alleviate crowding as well as violence and other problems (Joyce 1992). Perhaps limiting parole supervision to one year could be implemented if prison is used as the sanction of choice or if community corrections are used. The conditions required of offenders could be limited to those that are necessary to ensure public safety.

FUTURE DIRECTIONS FOR INSTITUTIONAL CORRECTIONS

Like all components of the criminal justice system, correctional systems reflect the characteristics and environment of the society they serve. It is only natural that as society changes, so will the institutions designed to reinforce and protect it. Although there is inadequate space to cover the considerable number of important issues facing corrections in the next few decades, the following discussion briefly touches on some of these issues.

Perhaps the most compelling issue is what will happen with the prison population and incarceration rate, which has seen a fourfold increase during the past 30 years. The wars on crime and drugs have taken an enormous toll on government budgets, often to the detriment of other human services such as education and social services. It is unclear whether jurisdictions can maintain the level of spending on corrections indefinitely or whether public and political support will continue for such expenditures. The wars on crime and drugs have also had a considerable impact on the social fabric of communities and society in general that we are only beginning to understand (Hagan and Dinovitzer 1999). Removing such a large number of persons from society will have an observable impact on the children, families, and communities of offenders. This impact will likely include a number of negative consequences. Expanding the prison population also increases the number of prisoners who will eventually return to the community with additional burdens, especially when mental illness and substance dependency issues are present. The steps that are taken to reintegrate this population into the community and the success of those efforts will be important issues for the country as a whole.

A second major issue is how institutional supervision will deal with the special-needs offenders who are increasingly becoming part of the correctional population. One population demanding special attention is the growing number of substance abusers and addicts in jails and prisons. Although prisons have always had a disproportionate number of substance abusers among their populations, quality drug-treatment programs have never been a high priority within correctional budgets. Most programs tend to be understaffed, underfunded, poorly designed and implemented, and simply too short in duration to adequately address the multifaceted problem of substance abuse. The relatively high percentage of HIV-positive inmates presents another set of unique legal, medical, and operational challenges to correctional institutions. How prisons respond to HIV-positive inmates and the measures they take to limit the spread of the virus within institutions will require balancing the needs and rights of the individual with the needs of the other inmates and the institution. Medication and treatment for illnesses related to HIV also increase medical costs for correctional budgets.

A third population that will increasingly become a fixture in institutions is the elderly. As jurisdictions have increased sentence lengths and decreased the discretion to reduce those sentences, the percentage of older inmates has increased. Incarcerated elderly inmates will require additional medical resources and have special physical and psychological needs.

CONCLUSION

Clearly, there are problems and challenges that correctional systems face. The nature of the problems is a function of the society that a correctional system serves. Exploring alternatives to secure confinement and methods to improve existing conditions within institutions should be seriously considered. Currently, it could be argued that none of the goals of the criminal justice system has been achieved due to the problems and characteristics of current correctional environments. Crowding, violence, gangs, and even the unforeseen consequences of the prisoners' rights movement have helped diminish further the prospects for effective rehabilitation, retribution, incapacitation, and deterrence. These realizations should be at the heart of policies and reforms; there are no short-term solutions to problems that have lasted for decades, especially when they were exacerbated during periods when crime rates were decreasing.

KEY WORDS

back-door options
classification
close security
convict leasing
correctional officers
deinstitutionalization
deprivation model
detention
detention centers
dual-disorder inmates
front-door options
importation model
industrial era
jails

maximum-security
  prisons
medium-security prisons
minimum-security
  prisons
need principle
new-generation jails
  (NGJs)
pains of imprisonment
penitentiary era
prison programs
prison violence
prisons
private prison

punishment
reentry
reform era
rehabilitation
rehabilitation era
responsivity principle
retributive era
risk principle
secure custody
specialized prisons
supermax prisons
transinstitutionalization

SUGGESTED READINGS

Bernstein, N. (2007). *All alone in the world: Children of the incarcerated.* New York: New Press.

Jacobson, M. (2005). *Downsizing prisons: How to reduce crime and end mass incarceration.* New York: New York University Press.

Latessa, E. J., S. J. Listwan, and D. Koetzle. (2013). *What works (and doesn't) in reducing recidivism.* New York: Routledge.

Mears, D. P., and J. C. Cochran. (2014). *Prisoner reentry in the era of mass incarceration.* Thousand Oaks, CA: Sage.

National Center for Education Statistics, U.S. Department of Education. (2008). *Digest of education statistics, 2007* (NCES 2008–022), Table 171.

Petersilia, J. (2003). *When prisoners come home: Parole and prisoner reentry.* New York: Oxford University Press.

Pew Center on the States. (2008). *One in 100: Behind bars in America in 2008. Public Safety Performance Project.* http://www.pewtrusts.org/en/research-and-analysis/reports/2008/02/28/one-in-100-behind-bars-in-america-2008

Pew Center on the States. (2009). *One in 31: The long reach of American corrections. Public Safety Performance Project.* http://www.pewtrusts.org/en/research-and-analysis/reports/2009/03/02/one-in-31-the-long-reach-of-american-corrections

Pratt, J. (2002). *Punishment and civilization: Penal tolerance and intolerance in modern society.* Thousand Oaks, CA: Sage.

Pratt, T. C. (2009). *Addicted to incarceration: Corrections policy and politics of misinformation in the United States.* Thousand Oaks, CA: Sage.

Prendergast, M. L., E. A. Hall, H. K. Wexler, G. Melnick, and Y. Cao. (2004). Amity prison-based therapeutic community: 5-year outcomes. *Prison Journal, 84*(1), 36–60.

Santos, M. (2004). *About prison.* Belmont, CA: Thomson/Wadsworth.

Terry, C. (2003). *The fellas: Overcoming prison and addiction.* Belmont, CA: Thomson/Wadsworth.

CHAPTER 6

Community Corrections

CHAPTER OUTLINE

History of Community Corrections
Contemporary Community Corrections
Probation and Intermediate Sanctions
    Probation
    Intermediate Sanctions
Post-Release Supervision and Reintegration
    Types of Release
    Prisoner Reentry and Reintegration
Community Supervision
    Offender Responsibilities
    Officer Responsibilities
    Supervision Violations
Special-Needs Populations and Community Supervision
The Effectiveness of Community Corrections
Incorporating "Best Practices" into Community Corrections
Conclusion
Key Words
Suggested Readings

After reading this chapter, you should be able to:

- Provide a brief history of community corrections
- Explain different correctional sanctions used in the United States
- Relate how restorative justice fits into a community supervision approach
- Discuss the extent and operation of probation
- Define net widening and discuss why it is problematic

- Define and discuss intensive supervision probation
- Discuss home confinement and issues in using electronic monitoring
- Differentiate day reporting centers and residential centers
- Outline the issues related to the use of boot camps
- Discuss the responsibilities of community supervision officers
- Identify different types of supervision violations
- Describe swift–certain–fair policies, their justification, and criticisms
- Discuss the effectiveness of probation and intermediate sanctions
- List and define different forms of prison release
- Discuss issues related to reentry and reintegration
- Identify different special-needs populations
- Relate what is meant by "best practices"

Community corrections constitute the various punishments and forms of supervision that occur within the community rather than in an institutional setting. Contemporary forms of community corrections include probation, **intermediate sanctions**, and parole supervision. Although some types of intermediate sanctions, such as boot camps and community residential programs, occur in institutional settings, stays in such facilities are generally brief and often include an element of community supervision. Therefore, they are typically included in discussions of community corrections. While jails and prisons may be the most familiar forms of punishments in the United States, far more offenders are supervised in the community than in institutional settings (Glaze and Kaeble 2014). In fact, almost 70 percent of the American correctional population is in the community (Glaze and Kaeble 2014). Thus, community corrections is an important aspect of the criminal justice system that requires further discussion.

Correctional agencies and institutions are responsible for administering the penalties imposed on convicted offenders by the courts. Thought to be the end of the criminal justice process, correctional agencies actually provide a range of services to the criminal justice system and participate in collaborative activities with a variety of criminal justice and human service agencies. For example, probation officers in many jurisdictions are responsible for conducting court-ordered presentence investigations and submitting reports to assist in judicial decision-making. In their community supervision efforts, community correctional officers may have informal or formal arrangements with drug treatment programs, area schools and aftercare programs, and local law enforcement.

A number of different agencies may provide community correctional services depending on the legal and geographic jurisdiction. There are community correctional programs at the local, state, and federal government levels. Furthermore, local and state governments have community correctional programs for both juveniles and adults. The decentralized nature of criminal justice in the United

States makes it difficult to generalize about specific practices and policies. The purpose of this text is to introduce readers to the essential features of the criminal justice system. Therefore, this chapter discusses community corrections generally, with an emphasis on sanctions and supervision of adults in the community (see Chapter 7 for discussion about penalties imposed on juvenile offenders). Although specific practices and the types of sanctions that are available will differ across jurisdictions, many of the underlying principles and issues are quite similar.

HISTORY OF COMMUNITY CORRECTIONS

For most of human history, punishment has been "community" based. With the exception of banishment, most punishments were carried out in a public setting or in a manner that involved community members, especially victims, to a far greater extent than today. Punishing offenders by removing them from the community and incarcerating them for a specified period in a facility built specifically for that purpose is largely a modern practice. Chapter 5 described the numerous changes in the late 18th century and early 19th century that were associated with the birth and development of the penitentiary and its use. However, by the middle of the 19th century, additional changes were occurring that also led to an increased use of **community supervision** for offenders (Vanstone 2008). Many of these community correctional practices had their roots in historical practices, such as judicial reprieve and release on recognizance, that were designed to mitigate the severity of criminal punishment (Clear and Dammer 2003).

By the 19th century, the ideas of the Enlightenment, the growth of capitalism, and democratic values were influencing attitudes about crime and punishment. These changes led to new approaches to dealing with problems of social order in the new American republic. In particular, the social environment was increasingly identified as an important contributor to crime and disorder (Rothman 1971). Within this context, the notion of individual reform, whether based on moral repentance or changing environmental factors, influenced attitudes on what to do about criminal behavior, especially among less serious offenders. Such ideas would have a direct impact on the development of two of the major forms of community corrections: probation and parole.

Of increasing concern in the new republic were drunkenness and the perceived problems associated with it (Rothman 1971). During the 19th century, those arrested for public drunkenness were frequently sentenced to periods of confinement in local jails, which were often overcrowded and characterized by filth and disease. It was in just such a case that John Augustus, a Boston bootmaker and philanthropist, asked a Boston court to release an offender into his custody in 1841. Motivated by humanitarian interests, Augustus allowed the defendant to reside in his home and assisted him in securing employment while requiring that the offender abide by certain conditions. It was from this humble beginning that **probation** started. After Augustus returned to court with the defendant several weeks later, the court was impressed with the apparent change in the offender and agreed to continue to suspend his sentence as long as he remained in good conduct. Augustus soon returned to court to select additional offenders whom he supervised under certain conditions in exchange for the court delaying the imposition of their original sentences (Abadinsky 1997).

For the next 18 years until his death in 1859, Augustus developed a set of procedures that remain essential features of probation today: interviewing defendants to determine their suitability for release, requiring conditions for offenders to obey in exchange for their release, and notifying the court if an offender violated a condition of his or her supervision (Clear and Dammer 2003). In 1878, the Massachusetts legislature created a paid position for a probation officer assigned to the Boston court (Abadinsky 1997). By the early 20th century, formal probation organizations existed in numerous local, state, and federal jurisdictions. By the middle of the 20th century, probation was available for adult felony offenders in all U.S. states and all federal jurisdictions and could be found, in some version, in many countries throughout the world (Abadinsky 1997; Vanstone 2008). Dissatisfaction with the newly created penitentiaries to achieve their intended goal led to the development of both probation and parole, in the United States as well as internationally (Rothman 1971; Vanstone 2008). Innovations by prison administrators in Australia and Ireland had a considerable impact on the development of parole. In 1840, Alexander Maconochie became administrator of the Norfolk Island penal colony off the coast of Australia (Abadinsky 1997). Maconochie arrived at a penal colony that had experienced a number of disruptions and set about instituting changes to encourage individual reform. He developed a system based on "marks" that prisoners earned toward early release. Prisoners would pass through stages of increasing liberty on the island after periods of good conduct. Eventually, prisoners could earn an early conditional release from the colony (Abadinsky 1997).

Maconochie's mark system was politically controversial and lasted for only a few years (Abadinsky 1997). News of his experiment and its apparent success, however, eventually reached Britain. Soon after, laws were passed that allowed for awarding "tickets of leave" to prisoners, during which time they were to be supervised by the local police. In 1854, Walter Crofton became head of the Irish prison system and instituted policies based on Maconochie's earlier experiment. Under the Irish system, prisoners progressed through four stages of incarceration, each providing a greater level of freedom within the institution, resulting ultimately in early release through a ticket of leave. Importantly, released prisoners were given conditions of release and were supervised by either local police or a civilian who was assigned this responsibility (Abadinsky 1997).

The policies implemented by Maconochie and Crofton were rooted in a penal philosophy emphasizing individual reform that held prominence among many leading American prison experts during this period. The notion of individualized punishment by use of an indeterminate sentence was promoted at an important conference of the National Prison Association in 1870 (Clear and Dammer 2003). Dissatisfied with the current state of prison operations, scholars and practitioners called for a system of incarceration that encouraged reform through offering incentives for early release dependent upon evidence of good conduct and individual reform (Clear and Dammer 2003). Based on these ideas, New York passed an indeterminate sentence law in 1876 for inmates sentenced to the Elmira Reformatory (Abandinsky 1997). The superintendent, Zebulon Brockway, assisted in drafting legislation that imposed sentences with a maximum term of incarceration but allowed inmates to earn early release after demonstrating good conduct and accumulating a specified number of marks by participating in various activities. This became the first official version of parole in American corrections. Appointed guardians, rather than the police officers of the Irish system, supervised released prisoners, and failure to abide by certain conditions of release could result in their return to prison (Abadinsky 1997).

The notion of the indeterminate sentence spread slowly to other states, most of which used it initially only for youthful offenders and those sentenced for less serious offenses. By the early part of the 20th century, the majority of states used indeterminate sentences for at least some types of offenders (Bottomley 1990). As Rothman (1980) notes, the growth of the use of parole was likely as much a matter of convenience as principle. Urbanization, the increasing immigrant population, and the Great Depression contributed to prison overcrowding and strains on correctional resources (Abadinsky 1997). The increasing use of parole, while consistent with penal theories of the day, was also a useful mechanism for controlling both inmate behavior and prison overcrowding (Bottomley 1990). By the middle of the 20th century, the indeterminate sentence and parole had become standard features of American criminal law and corrections.

CONTEMPORARY COMMUNITY CORRECTIONS

Although there are a number of community correctional programs, offenders on regular probation and those under parole supervision constitute the largest portion of the community correctional population. Approximately 6.7 million people were under some form of correctional supervision in 2015 (Kaeble and Glaze 2016). Of this total, slightly more than 4.6 million people were under community supervision—approximately 3.8 million on probation and 900,000 under parole supervision (Kaeble and Bonczar 2016). After several decades of increasing correctional populations, the United States has recently experienced a period of little or no growth in this population. In fact, the number of persons under probation, jail, or prison supervision has decreased each year since 2008. These numbers, however, must be interpreted cautiously. It is far too early to determine whether this trend will continue. Furthermore, recent decreases have been relatively small, especially when considered in the context of more than 25 years of annual growth.

Web Activity

Detailed information on correctional populations in the United States can be found in the Bureau of Justice Statistics reports *Correctional Populations in the United States, 2015* and *Probation and Parole in the United States, 2015*, which are available on the textbook website (http://www.oup.com/us/labessentials).

Although there may be similarities, each jurisdiction has its own model for organizing its criminal justice system. The federal government has a specific criminal justice system for defendants arrested and prosecuted for violating federal criminal statutes and a correctional system to carry out the punishments ordered by the federal courts. When it comes to violations of state law, the picture becomes more complex, as each state has its own criminal justice system and various subsystems within that larger framework. Defendants convicted of state felony statutes and sentenced to prison are sent to facilities run by state correctional agencies. Defendants convicted of misdemeanors and sentenced to time in jail are held primarily in facilities funded and run by city or county governments. The responsibility for supervising defendants convicted of misdemeanor or felony offenses and sentenced to nonprison sanctions, however, varies greatly. In some jurisdictions, supervision of defendants sentenced to community supervision is the responsibility of court employees, whereas other jurisdictions use state agencies, such as the state departments of corrections, to handle supervision duties. There are also combination or hybrid models of organizing correctional services in which the sanction imposed or the jurisdiction determines who supervises an offender. In addition, the supervision of parolees or those on supervised release may be the responsibility of a department that also supervises probationers or an agency that exclusively handles parolees. The diversity of organization and practice of community corrections in the United States requires that the following discussion emphasize the most common features and general principles of community corrections.

Jurisdictions vary greatly in the number and types of sanctions that they can use for law violators. The term "sanction" is often used interchangeably with "punishment" and refers to a specific punishment (e.g., fine, probation, and prison) imposed by a court. Although prison is the first punishment that comes to mind for many Americans, it is not the most common punishment used for violations of the law. Incarceration in a state correctional institution is reserved typically for the most serious or habitual offenders and those who cannot abide by the rules of other previously imposed penalties. On a daily basis, courts that deal primarily with misdemeanor crimes handle a far greater volume of offenders than do courts that deal exclusively with felony offenders. However, even among offenders convicted of felonies, a probation sentence is imposed in more than one-fourth (28 percent) of all such cases (Reaves 2013).

Available sanctions for felony offenders include a range of penalties that vary in severity. Table 6.1 provides a brief description of the most common sanctions found in the United States. Although not all of these sanctions are available in every jurisdiction, the variety of sanctions in most jurisdictions has increased in the past several decades. Courts may also use a combination of punishments rather than simply relying on one sanction. Parole supervision is not a sanction imposed by a court; instead, prisoners are released from incarceration to parole supervision by a correctional agency (e.g., a parole board). Perhaps the most important distinction is that parolees typically remain under

Table 6.1 Types of Correctional Sanctions

Fines	Fines are often a part of a larger probation sentence. Some jurisdictions have developed more rigorous monetary penalties called "day fines" that require payment of a percentage of an offender's income over time rather than a flat fee.
Community service work (CSW)	CSW requires that a set number of volunteer hours be completed within a specified period of time. Some jurisdictions use CSW as a stand-alone punishment, especially for misdemeanor offenders. CSW for felony offenders is most commonly a special condition of a probation sentence.
Probation	A term of court-ordered supervision during which offenders remain in the community provided that they follow certain conditions.
Day reporting center (DRC)	A form of community supervision requiring offenders to report to a DRC on a daily or near-daily basis. DRCs may house a variety of services and programs in which offenders are required to participate, such as drug testing, GED courses, and counseling.
Intensive supervision probation (ISP)	A form of supervision involving frequent contact, perhaps several times a week, between offenders and probation officers. Some jurisdictions may require offenders' confinement to their residence (i.e., "house arrest") when not engaged in approved activities. ISP may involve electronic monitoring or global positioning system (GPS) devices in some jurisdictions.
Community correctional facilities	Refers to a wide variety of facilities designed to hold offenders for relatively brief periods of time. May serve as a work-release facility in which offenders go into the community for work or other approved activities but are otherwise required to remain in the facility. Such facilities can be used for residential treatment programs for special-needs offenders. They may also serve as halfway house facilities for recently released prisoners.
Jail	Offenders who are sentenced by the court to less than a year of incarceration (the maximum may be less in some jurisdictions) usually serve their sentences in jails or detention centers run by the county or municipality. Jail sentences may involve work-release provisions or be followed by a period of community supervision.
Shock incarceration	Some states give judges or correctional authorities the authority to grant early conditional releases to eligible offenders sentenced to a period of regular incarceration. This release typically follows a brief period of confinement (30–180 days) and is conditional upon the offender remaining on community supervision for a specified time upon release. Also known as "shock probation" in some jurisdictions.
Boot camps	Also referred to as shock incarceration programs in some jurisdictions, boot camps involve a brief (less than six months) confinement in a secure facility in which inmates go through a period of drill and instruction modeled on basic military training. Common features include the use of physical exercise and instruction to instill discipline and self-control and encourage prosocial behavior. Most boot camp programs now include varying degrees of rehabilitative interventions such as educational and drug treatment programs. Typically followed by a period of community supervision.
Prisons	Also referred to as penitentiaries or correctional institutions. Typically hold felony offenders sentenced to incarceration for more than one year and those returned to prison for parole violations. Security levels and the types of services and offenders they are designed to accommodate vary among prisons. Prisoners under sentences of death may be held on "death row," a wing in a high-security institution in or near where executions are carried out.

the jurisdiction of the correctional system, whereas probationers and others on community supervision remain under the legal jurisdiction of the original sentencing court. In practice, parolees and probationers may have many of the same conditions and may even have the same officer in a given jurisdiction. Violations of the conditions of supervision for either group may result in the offender answering to the authority that retains jurisdiction in his or her case. Parole is considered a form of community corrections because it involves the supervision of the offender in the community or a community-based facility and may require the use of community resources. Therefore, parole supervision is included in this chapter.

Beginning in the 1980s, many jurisdictions began to create new sentencing options that are less expensive than incarceration but more punitive than regular probation. Often referred to as intermediate sanctions, these provide an alternative to either traditional probation or prison. As shown in Table 6.1, sanctions such as intensive supervision probation and community residential centers are forms of intermediate sanctions increasingly used for a variety of offenders. Such programs are touted as more cost-effective than prison, more restrictive and punitive than regular probation, and offering a better opportunity for a rehabilitative or deterrent impact on offenders (Tonry and Lynch 1996). In addition, courts and correctional departments have begun increasingly to use sanctions and programs consistent with restorative justice. Box 6.1 describes the role of restorative justice in community corrections.

BOX 6.1

Restorative Justice and Community Corrections

Restorative justice represents an alternative vision of the purposes and goals of criminal punishment. Although not incompatible with retribution, deterrence, or rehabilitation, restorative justice focuses on repairing the harms associated with criminal offending. The key attributes of restorative justice are its emphasis on holding offenders accountable by requiring them to take meaningful steps in the healing process for victims and the community to which they may eventually return. Restorative justice has its roots in the treatment of deviant community members by indigenous populations. Restorative justice has become increasingly important as a method of conflict resolution and responding to criminal offenders and their victims. Restorative criminal justice policies have become institutionalized in many Western countries, such as Canada, New Zealand, and Australia, especially for cases dealing with youthful offenders (Prison Fellowship International 2012). Restorative justice practices in the United States appear to be expanding beyond the juvenile justice system and are increasingly being used in cases with adult offenders. Today, many adult correctional departments highlight the role of restorative justice in their supervision of convicted offenders.

There is both a theoretical and a practical basis for a continuing relationship between community corrections and restorative justice. The nature of community corrections has made its mission susceptible to changing trends and pressures. As such, the focus of community corrections frequently shifts to differ-ent responsibilities and practices depending on the sociopolitical environment (Duff 2003; Pease 1999; Tonry 1999). Restorative justice can be used in a manner that is consistent with holding offenders morally accountable, improving public safety, as well as providing meaningful opportunities for rehabilitation (Duff 2003). Although there are a number of challenges to restorative justice becom-ing a central theme of community supervision (R. E. Smith 2001), advocates see promise in the role that community corrections can have in creating a more just response to law violations—for offenders, victims, and the community (Duff 2003; R. White and Graham 2010).

From a practical standpoint, many restorative justice interventions take place in a community setting. Restorative justice programs can be found in in-stitutional settings, but they remain most common for offenders whose punish-ment would traditionally take place in the community under the supervision of community corrections. Common restorative justice programs, such as family group conferencing, victim–offender mediation, sentencing circles, and forms of community or victim service, often take place in a community setting (Na-tional Institute of Justice n.d.; Prison Fellowship International 2012; R. White and Graham 2010). As a result, community correctional officers may have the responsibility of ensuring that offenders under supervision comply with the conditions of a restorative justice program. At a minimum, agencies and super-vising officers can have a significant impact on the organizational and public support for restorative justice programs.

Critical Thinking Exercise

Examine the different types of criminal sanctions in Table 6.1. Identify which phi-losophy of punishment—retribution, deterrence, rehabilitation, incapacitation, or restorative justice—is the best justification for each of these sanctions. Is there more than one possible justification for some of the sanctions? If yes, how might having multiple justifications be a potential benefit or problem?

Web Activity

There are some excellent resources on the internet about restorative justice pro-grams with criminal offenders. Students are encouraged to visit the Prison Fellow-ship International Centre for Justice and Reconciliation at http://www.pficjr.org/ and materials in their library about probation at http://restorativejustice.org/rj-library/. In addition, the National Institute of Justice offers information about restorative justice at https://www.ncjrs.gov/pdffiles1/nij/242196.pdf.

PROBATION AND INTERMEDIATE SANCTIONS

Probation

All forms of probation represent a term of conditional supervision imposed by a sentencing court. The frequency of contact required between the offender and the probation officer varies depending on the jurisdiction, the offender, and the specific type of probation supervision that the court imposes. Although traditional probation is often the subject of political and media criticism, it remains the most frequently imposed penalty for criminal offenders (Petersilia 1997). In 2015, there were approximately 3.8 million adult offenders under some form of probation supervision in the United States (Kaeble and Bonczar 2016). Almost 60 percent of those on probation were convicted of a felony (Kaeble and Bonczar 2016). Only a small fraction of all offenders sentenced to community supervision are placed on intermediate sanctions, although the exact number is not known. For example, Florida has approximately 90,000 offenders on regular probation compared with only 9,000 on intensive supervision probation—a ratio of 10 regular probationers for every offender on intensive probation (Florida Department of Corrections 2017).

Web Activity

To learn about New York's probation population, including demographics, original offense, and type of discharges from probation, see http://www.criminaljustice.ny.gov/pio/annualreport/nys_probation_report2007_profile.pdf.

In recent decades, a recurring theme has been the lack of proper funding for regular probation that has resulted in increasing caseload sizes and a reduction in the amount of contact between offenders and officers (Jacobson et al. 2017; Kleiman 2015; Petersilia 2002). Although there is no universal level of supervision for offenders placed on regular probation, a common practice is that offenders must report once a month to their probation officers. In addition, officers may be expected to have direct contact with offenders at least once a month, whether in the office or in the field. However, due to budgetary constraints and concerns about officer safety, officers may go several months between direct contacts with offenders in some jurisdictions. Furthermore, some departments use a form of unsupervised probation that does not require personal contact between offenders and officers except for special problems or concerns. Scholars and practitioners criticize the deterrent or the rehabilitative function of probation when so little supervision actually takes place or when there are few consequences for technical violations (Alm 2015; Jacobson et al. 2017; Kleiman 2015; Petersilia 1997, 1998).

Intermediate Sanctions

Intermediate sanctions claim to achieve a number of often competing goals (Tonry 1990). These include decreasing costs, increasing offender accountability and public safety, and increasing rehabilitative effectiveness (Tonry 1999;

Tonry and Lynch 1996). Intermediate sanctions can also be justified by both retributive and utilitarian penal philosophies; however, the targeted population and function of the sanctions may differ depending on the perceived value of these goals (Harris 1996; von Hirsch 1998). Although scholars and critics are correct to point out the challenges intermediate sanctions face, support for alternatives to traditional probation and reducing our overreliance on prison remains strong (e.g., Klingele 2015; Larkin 2015; Petersilia 1997, 2002; Tonry and Lynch 1996). The following sections discuss some of the more important intermediate sanctions currently used (see Clear and Dammer 2003, Chapter 7). Community service work and fines, although potentially important forms of intermediate sanctions, are more commonly used as a special condition of community supervision rather than as a stand-alone penalty as many advocate (e.g., Morris and Tonry 1990).

Intensive Supervision Probation

After early experiments with intensive supervision in the 1960s, the notion of **intensive supervision probation (ISP)** gained increasing support in the 1980s (Clear and Dammer 2003). Today, ISP is perhaps the most common intermediate sanction and is available, in some form, in most U.S. jurisdictions. Some jurisdictions use intensive supervision primarily for parolees, whereas other jurisdictions have ISP available as both a sentencing option for the courts and a form of early release (Clear and Dammer 2003). Most ISP programs have several common features. A central premise of ISP is that it provides closer supervision by frequent contact between offenders and officers and greater restrictions on the freedom of offenders. Offenders on ISP have far more contact with their officer than do those on regular probation. They may be in contact several times per week, with interactions at the probation office and the offender's home and place of employment. Due to the increased supervision, ISP officers have smaller caseloads compared to officers with a regular probation caseload. Although the exact number may vary, ISP officers typically have fewer than 40 offenders under their supervision, whereas regular probation officers may supervise more than 100 offenders. ISP conditions are more restrictive, and violations tend to be dealt with in a more immediate and punitive manner.

ISP is promoted by supporters as a "real" form of supervision and contrasted with the comparatively lenient requirements of regular probation. A primary goal of many ISP programs is the reduction of institutional overcrowding by diverting appropriate offenders from prison and jail. Proponents claim that ISP can improve community safety by increasing surveillance and contact with offenders and providing a more meaningful opportunity for rehabilitation. Research indicates that it is the ability of ISP to ensure participation in more intensive treatment, and not merely enhanced surveillance, that is critical to reducing recidivism and increasing offender success (Lowenkamp et al. 2010; Paparozzi and Gendreau 2005).

Critical Thinking Exercise

Intensive supervision programs are more restrictive and provide much greater contact and oversight of offenders. One result from this closer supervision is that more technical violations are discovered. As a result, a higher percentage of ISP offenders fail to complete their supervision. If a goal of ISP is to keep offenders out of prison, what should officers and courts do in response to technical violations?

House Arrest and Home Confinement

In some jurisdictions, ISP may also involve a period of home confinement and/or electronic monitoring. Other jurisdictions may use these as penalties independent from ISP. Also referred to as **house arrest**, **home confinement** is a specified period of time during which offenders may not leave their places of residence except for previously approved activities such as work, treatment programs, food shopping, and visits to the doctor or the probation office. Offenders are typically required to submit a weekly schedule in advance, and any activities outside the home must be approved by supervising officers. Officers can use this schedule to make random field contacts to verify that offenders are at home or at an approved activity. The rationale behind the use of home confinement is fairly simple: The likelihood of offenders violating their supervision can be reduced by greatly restricting their movement and freedom by confining them to their residences. Thus, offenders are essentially incarcerated, except for approved activities, without accruing the costs associated with incarceration. Of course, like any form of community supervision, offenders can easily choose to ignore the requirements of the program. In particular, home confinement (and electronic monitoring) cannot prevent crimes and violations that occur within residences. Confined to their residences, however, offenders are less likely to have access to targets and opportunities for many types of crimes.

Electronic monitoring seeks to improve compliance with home confinement, whether as a form of pretrial release, court-ordered supervision, or as a condition of parole release (DeMichele and Payne 2009) (Box 6.2). The primary types of electronic monitoring systems currently used are programmed contact or continuous signaling devices (Clear and Dammer 2003). Programmed contact devices use random automated telephone or beeper calls that require offenders to contact a centralized call center within a limited period of time. Offenders then must verify their identities by video or voice identification or use special bracelets that either attach to their legs or wrists and transmit a signal over the telephone line or are inserted into special receivers placed in the offenders' homes that transmit a signal to verify their presence. Continuous contact devices use bracelets that emit a continuous signal to receivers placed within offenders' residences. Such bracelets typically have a limited range (e.g., 200 feet), and once a bracelet leaves that area, the receiver automatically contacts a centralized computerized system to note the offender left the premises. The computer system is thus able to keep records of when offenders leave their residences and when they return, which officers can compare against approved schedules (DeMichele and Payne 2009). Bracelets are typically tamperproof and send an automatic notification to the computer system if removed.

BOX 6.2

Technology and Community Supervision

Early technologies used in the community supervision of offenders, such as defensive weapons and communication technology, were typically adapted from their initial use in law enforcement. The use of alcohol- and drug-testing equipment became more common as policymakers supported efforts to enhance surveillance and enforce compliance with supervision conditions. For example, some jurisdictions use remote alcohol detection devices. These require the offender to submit to random alcohol tests, and the results are transmitted electronically over phone lines to a computer monitoring system (DeMichele and Payne 2009). Most significantly, however, community corrections' increasing emphasis on public safety has led to dramatic increases in the use of technology to verify the location of an offender under community supervision (DeMichele and Payne 2009).

The most significant increase in technology-enhanced supervision has been with the use of a global positioning system (GPS; DeMichele and Payne 2009). Such systems use satellite technology to monitor the specific location of offenders and communicate that information to a computer monitoring system (Brown, McCabe, and Wellford 2007). These systems are increasingly sophisticated. Programmed with information about the community, they can indicate whether offenders are entering prohibited areas, such as when sex offenders approach schools. One of the more common uses of GPS supervision (and electronic monitoring in general) is for sex offenders under community supervision (Button, DeMichele, and Payne 2009). The use of GPS technology for supervising offenders grew from less than 500 in 2000 to 90,000 in 2009 (DeMichele and Payne 2009). It is likely that nearly 150,000 offenders are currently supervised with the use of GPS technology.

GPS technology is still being refined, and various options can be added to the programs by third-party vendors (Brown et al. 2007). GPS shares some problems and challenges with electronic monitoring but has its own unique technological, liability, and privacy concerns as well (Brown et al. 2007; DeMichele and Payne 2009). There are legitimate concerns about the unforeseen social consequences of such invasive surveillance in a democratic society. For example, even before the development of GPS and the widespread use of electronic monitoring, von Hirsch (1998) argued that there are ethical limits to the intrusiveness of community supervision of offenders. Simply because community supervision is less intrusive than prison does not justify any possible intrusion into offenders' lives. It is important to consider whether the level of intrusiveness is proportional to the seriousness of the original crime as well as the impact on the privacy of third parties (von Hirsch 1998). However, there appears to be considerable political support for the use of GPS and other technologies to enhance the surveillance of offenders in the community. As a result, it is likely that they will continue to grow in importance as an option for courts and correctional agencies.

Web Activity

For a detailed discussion of the different technologies, options, and challenges associated with electronic monitoring, see DeMichele and Payne (2009) on the textbook website (http://www.oup.com/us/labessentials).

Web Activity

To read the American Probation and Parole Association's official position on electronic monitoring, see http://www.appa-net.org/eweb/Dynamicpage.aspx?site=APPA_2&webcode=IB_PositionStatement&wps_key=ae001bce-6268-46a6-aba3-3ea1d0710e8c.

Critical Thinking Exercise

Considerable research has supported the practice of reserving intensive supervision, especially electronic monitoring and GPS, for high-risk offenders. The intensive supervision or treatment of low-risk offenders is associated with *worse* outcomes for those offenders. Therefore, the targeting of appropriate offenders for intensive supervision programs is critical. What criteria do you think are important to consider when determining whether a specific offender is appropriate for such supervision? Are there any factors that should exclude an offender from intensive supervision? Why are these important and what should be the alternative form of supervision for these offenders? Remember that an important goal for these programs is to reduce the use of incarceration.

Web Activity

For an in-depth discussion of the issues associated with GPS, including different technologies and important implementation issues, see Brown, McCabe, and Wellford's (2007) report on the textbook website (http://www.oup.com/us/labessentials). Pay particular attention to the figures on pages 1-2, 1-3, and 1-6.

Day Reporting Centers

Day reporting centers were first established in Great Britain and followed by programs in Massachusetts and Connecticut beginning in 1985 (Clear and Dammer 2003). Today, day reporting centers can be found in a number of jurisdictions. Similar to other community correctional programs, they can be used for a variety of populations. For example, Cook County (Chicago) created a day reporting program as a condition of pretrial release (Martin, Olson, and Lurigio 2000; McBride and VanderWaal 1997). In addition, there are day reporting centers used as intermediate sanctions intended to divert appropriate offenders from incarceration as well as those that serve offenders recently released from prison (Marciniak 1999; Osterman 2009; Vaas and Weston 1990).

Despite the variety of populations they serve, most day reporting centers have several common features. First, they are nonresidential programs that require offenders to report on a daily or very frequent basis to a reporting center. The specific frequency of reporting may vary across programs and individual offenders, but offenders report to their centers far more frequently than probationers or parolees report to their supervising officers. Second, these centers house a number of the required programs and services for offenders, such as drug testing, substance abuse treatment, job training, and education courses. Probation or parole officers are frequently stationed at the centers as well. Thus, day reporting centers can serve as a centralized location for offenders to fulfill a variety of their court-ordered conditions, such as drug testing, restitution payments, community service orders, and treatment programs (Clear and Dammer 2003). The amount of contact between participating offenders and program staff tends to be quite high, and the emphasis of many day reporting centers is to provide a range of services to offenders with identified treatment needs.

Residential Programs

Residential programs that serve as temporary housing for released inmates as they adjust to living in the community are referred to as "**halfway houses**" because they serve offenders who are halfway between prison and complete freedom in the community. Although the public is familiar with such programs, similar programs exist for offenders as an intermediate sanction. The term **residential community correctional program** (Latessa and Travis 1992) is increasingly used to designate residential programs serving a variety of offender populations for a relatively short period of time, typically less than one year. These programs are designed to assist in offender reintegration into the community by targeting particular offender needs with intensive services. For example, some programs focus on substance abuse treatment, mental health counseling, or serve as a work-release center that assists offenders in securing employment and making payments toward court-ordered financial obligations.

The freedom of movement for offenders and the level of security in residential correctional programs vary. Some programs require offenders to remain at the facility except for approved activities, whereas others allow more freedom of movement. The types and intensity of the services provided at these facilities depend to some extent on the population they serve. It is common for education and employment training, cognitive thinking and life skills courses, and substance abuse treatment services to be available. Residential programs, especially those emphasizing employment, are frequently located in urban or suburban areas with accessible employment opportunities and public transportation. Most residential programs serve a relatively high need population that is at greater risk for substance abuse and/or recidivism than comparison populations (Latessa and Travis 1992). Furthermore, there is evidence that residential community correctional programs may have the most benefit for those at highest risk for substance abuse and recidivism (Lowenkamp, Latessa, and Holsinger 2006). Therefore, the targeting of appropriate offenders for these programs appears to be critical to their overall effectiveness (Lowenkamp and Latessa 2005).

Boot Camps

One of the more publicized and better known of the community correctional programs, **boot camps** have been subject to critical scholarly attention since they began as a correctional sanction in the late 1980s. The use of boot camps for offenders has intuitive appeal for American society. Most adults are familiar with the basic premise of a military boot camp, and many American men can relate their own military experience with numerous benefits. Some jurisdictions and scholars identify boot camps with **shock incarceration**. Not all shock incarceration programs, however, incorporate a boot camp experience (Clear and Dammer 2003). Some jurisdictions retain the option of early release to community supervision for eligible inmates. The idea is that offenders' brief experience in prison will "shock" them into a desire to abide by community supervision requirements and remain crime-free. Programs that use a boot camp experience have been subject to far more public and scholarly attention. Therefore, the following discussion focuses on boot camp programs.

Although there are considerable differences, the central premise is that the highly structured environment of military-like training can provide a unique experience for offenders. The emphasis on discipline, strict adherence to program rules, and physical conditioning is thought to provide an opportunity for constructive change in offenders' attitudes and behavior (National Institute of Justice 2003). The most characteristic feature of boot camps is the quasi-military atmosphere created by physical conditioning, drills, and manual labor enforced with strict rules and program staff who act in a manner consistent with military boot camp training. Recent modifications to early programs have included incorporating more rehabilitation and treatment services for inmates and increasing educational and life skills training components (Kempinen and Kurlychek 2003; National Institute of Justice 2003).

The physical nature of the boot camp experience naturally limits such programs to eligible youthful offenders. Some boot camps are exclusively for juvenile offenders, whereas other programs accept young adult offenders. Many programs target offenders with a history of substance abuse, and most exclude offenders with a significant history of personal violence. The vast majority of boot camp programs are designed for male offenders (Clear and Dammer 2003). The high prevalence of past physical, sexual, and emotional abuse among female offenders makes boot camps for this population very questionable (MacKenzie and

Donaldson 1996; National Institute of Justice 2003). A common research finding has been that boot camps with longer and more intensive aftercare services yield more positive outcomes in their graduates, although these differences tend to be rather modest (Kempinen and Kurylchek 2003; National Institute of Justice 2003).

Widely popular when initially created, support for boot camps has somewhat diminished. Considerable evidence suggests that they do little to reduce recidivism rates and may actually result in higher technical violations and other problems (National Institute of Justice 2003; Wilson, MacKenzie, and Mitchell 2005). Furthermore, incidents of abuse and poor treatment by staff leading to injuries and even deaths of residents have led to public criticism. Some jurisdictions, most notably the federal government, have closed their boot camp programs. Boot camps for offenders, however, remain popular in some jurisdictions, especially for juvenile offenders.

Web Activity

Review the assessment of juvenile boot camps on the National Institute of Justice's Crime Solutions website at https://www.crimesolutions.gov/PracticeDetails.aspx?ID=6.

Critical Thinking Exercise

Despite the considerable evidence that boot camp graduates do not have lower recidivism rates, such programs remain popular with some politicians and the public. Why do you think this is the case? What explains the apparent disconnect between research on the value of such programs and continuing support for them? What is the impact of such factors on criminal justice policy in general?

Net Widening

A frequent goal of intermediate sanctions is to divert offenders from a sentence considered too severe or expensive for a particular offender. In fact, a number of intermediate sanctions are justified on the premise such programs can divert less serious offenders from prison into less expensive sentencing options. However, scholars have questioned how new sanctions are used by the courts in practice. Research indicates that intermediate sanctions are often applied to offenders who would have received a less severe penalty prior to the availability of the intermediate sanction. As a result, some offenders receive a more severe sanction than they originally would have received prior to the creation of this new sanction. Meanwhile, many offenders who were the targets for diversion by the new intermediate sanction continue to be sentenced to the more punitive sanctions that existed prior to the new program. In other words, the new program is used for less serious offenders rather than the originally targeted population. This is referred to as **net widening**—when a punishment is used on a larger or different population than the one originally intended.

Although some may view net widening as simply an appropriate increase in the severity of punishment for offenders, this ignores a primary rationale for intermediate sanctions and poses a problem for several reasons. First, net widening increases costs rather than decreasing them by placing offenders who would have received a less expensive sanction (generally, the closer the supervision, the higher the costs) on a more expensive form of supervision without similarly diverting prison-bound offenders. Second, because closer supervision programs generally have higher revocation rates for technical violations (Petersilia and Turner 1993), a percentage of the offenders who might have succeeded under a less restrictive program will likely end up in prison because of violations of the stricter rules of the intermediate sanctions. This could add to operating costs rather than reduce them. A third major concern is the larger issue of social control. By using new sanctions to impose more severe penalties on offenders rather than diverting those who do not require a prison sentence, the criminal justice system is further expanding its intrusiveness into and control over the lives of members of the community (Cohen 1985; von Hirsch 1998).

POST-RELEASE SUPERVISION AND REINTEGRATION

Types of Release

More than 90 percent of all prisoners will eventually be released from prison (Petersilia 2003). Over 500,000 prisoners are released each year to the community. This means that a significant number of convicted offenders will need to make the transition from the highly structured prison environment to the relative freedom of open society. Upon release, most prisoners must identify new ways to meet basic needs such as food, shelter, employment, and clothing that were previously provided by the institution. Failure to secure these decreases the likelihood that a released prisoner will be able to successfully reintegrate into the community (Petersilia 2003).

Depending on the jurisdiction and the particular inmate, prisoners may be released from prison in four ways. Perhaps the most important distinction is whether the prisoner will be under any form of supervision after release. First, a small portion of offenders serve their maximum sentences and are released when the sentence expires. Such inmates, who may be in either indeterminate or determinate sentencing systems, have "maxed out" their sentences, and all supervision is terminated upon release from the institution. Although only approximately 20 percent of inmates are released without any supervision, this is a dramatic increase from 30 years ago, when only 5 percent of prisoners were released in this manner (Petersilia 2003; Pew Charitable Trust 2014). Second, some prisoners may be sentenced to **split sentences**, in which they serve a period of probation following their release. Third, several jurisdictions with determinate sentencing models have created a period of supervision for released prisoners called **supervised release**, or post-release supervision.

Such prisoners are required to report to community supervision offices located near where they will reside and assigned to a supervising officer. Similar to probation and parole, these former prisoners are required to abide by certain conditions following their release to the community. The length of supervision may vary depending on the conviction offense or the length of incarceration. A violation of these conditions may result in offenders' return to prison. Finally, prisoners given an indeterminate prison term may be eligible for release to **parole supervision** by the parole authority once they have served their minimum sentence. Prisoners must agree to abide by parole conditions in order to obtain their release. Community supervision may continue until the expiration of the released prisoner's original maximum sentence or until the parole authority terminates its supervision. Failure to comply with the conditions of release may result in the parolee's return to prison until the parole authority grants a new parole release or until the expiration of the original sentence. In some jurisdictions, officers who supervise probationers are also responsible for supervising parolees in their geographic area. In other jurisdictions, distinct agencies provide parole officers who supervise only parolees and those released from prison to mandatory supervised release.

Prisoner Reentry and Reintegration

The sheer number of prisoners returning to American communities each year has forced correctional administrators and policymakers to reevaluate efforts to improve the successful reintegration of prisoners. Prison has not demonstrated itself as being very effective at preventing future criminal behavior by offenders either through its rehabilitative efforts or through its deterrent capacity. It is an unfortunate reality that a significant percentage of released prisoners will eventually return to prison. Approximately 60 percent of released prisoners are rearrested for serious misdemeanors or felonies within three years of release, and half of released prisoners return to prison within three years (Langan and Levin 2002). The consequences of America's imprisonment binge are becoming apparent in the reallocation of public resources and the problems that high recidivism rates cause the criminal justice system (Austin and Irwin 2001; Travis 2004). In addition, scholars are increasingly discovering the often unintended negative consequences of mass incarceration and failed prisoner reentry on communities (Rose and Clear 2003), families (Travis and Waul 2003), and offenders themselves (Maruna and Immarigeon 2004; Petersilia 2003).

Web Activity

The Urban Institute has been a leading public voice in addressing the challenges of prisoner reentry and developing sound policies in response to this problem. For an example of a collaborative community effort to improve prisoner success upon release, see https://www.urban.org/research/publication/framework-safer-return-research-based-community-initiative/view/full_report.

Prisoners face a multitude of problems and challenges that they must overcome if they are to avoid returning to prison (Visher and Travis 2011). Research indicates that lack of adequate and meaningful employment is one of the major characteristics associated with a return to prison (Petersilia 2003; Travis 2005). In addition, offenders may face difficulties because of the "ex-con" label that can have a negative impact on their occupational and housing opportunities. A lack of sufficient education, job skills, or life skills may present difficulties in obtaining basic amenities, services, and material goods. Another major concern is reestablishing family and social networks. Offenders may be estranged from family and friends who could assist with reintegration into the community (Hagan and Dinovitzer 1999). Although not all former associates will have a positive influence on offenders' lives, social isolation can lead to stress and negative behaviors such as substance abuse and crime. Research indicates that an increasing percentage of inmates have histories of substance abuse and/or mental health problems. At the same time, the availability of prison programs and the level of participation in such programs have been diminishing (Petersilia 2003). Therefore, prisoners increasingly need access to meaningful treatment services inside prison and upon release.

Prisoner reentry (also referred to as **prisoner reintegration**) is the process of adjusting to a law-abiding lifestyle after returning to the community from prison (Petersilia 2003). A variety of programs to improve prisoner reentry are currently in operation throughout the country. Some of these are informal programs run by nonprofit and faith-based agencies, whereas other jurisdictions have very structured government programs that may involve a variety of organizations, including correctional staff and resources (Petersilia 2003; Travis and Waul 2003). To reduce the stress and problems of release, many offenders are released into halfway houses, which may be privately operated or run by correctional departments. Similar to the community residential programs discussed previously, there is considerable diversity in the types of halfway houses. They typically provide inexpensive housing and offer only basic amenities. Prisoners may be placed in these facilities as a condition of their release or may elect to reside there because of a lack of housing options and a shortage of money. More structured facilities may provide a range of services and resources such as substance abuse counseling, life skills training, or other relevant services and may place a number of restrictions on residents.

Web Activity

Visit the National Reentry Resource Center website at http://csgjusticecenter.org/nrrc. This is a clearinghouse of information sponsored by the Department of Justice and the Council of State Governments Justice Center and is an excellent resource for information, statistics, and tools for criminal justice and community agencies, as well as the general public.

COMMUNITY SUPERVISION

Offender Responsibilities

Offenders placed under some form of community supervision or in an intermediate-sanction residential program are given a list of conditions that they must comply with in order to remain in good standing with the court or parole board. These **conditions of supervision** state the expectations for offenders while under supervision. Failure to conform to these rules constitutes a violation of the offenders' supervision and may result in a supervising officer or staff member submitting a violation report to either the court of jurisdiction or the parole board. As a consequence, offenders' supervision may be revoked, and they can receive more severe sanctions or be returned to prison.

Conditions of supervision can be divided into standard or special conditions. **Standard conditions** are rules that all offenders placed on this type of supervision must follow. Standard conditions represent the minimum expectations for offenders to obey while under supervision. The most prevalent standard condition requires offenders to obey all laws. Other common standard conditions include informing a supervising officer of a change in address or work, not leaving the state or jurisdiction without the approval of a supervising officer, and, in some jurisdictions, submitting to drug testing.

Courts and parole boards impose **special conditions** depending on the nature of the crime or characteristics of the defendant. Such conditions are based on the needs and risks of a particular offender. Examples of special conditions include sex offender treatment, substance abuse counseling, work toward the completion of a GED, and the payment of restitution to a crime victim.

Web Activity

Examples of standard conditions of probation for federal probation can be found at https://www.dcp.uscourts.gov/Supervision/Conditions_English.pdf and for the state of New Mexico at http://www.corrections.state.nm.us/ppd/ppd.html.

Officer Responsibilities

In many jurisdictions, officers who supervise offenders in the community perform a range of duties. The two major responsibilities are conducting investigations and supervising offenders. The most important investigation conducted by probation officers is the court-ordered **presentence investigation**, which is typically completed after a defendant has pleaded or been found guilty. It summarizes facts about the offender, the offense, and other relevant information used by the court to determine an appropriate sentence. It is common to include information about the defendant's prior criminal and substance abuse history, employment, and education as well as the financial or emotional harm caused to any victims. Through their investigation, probation officers may identify special conditions that the court should consider imposing if the offender is sentenced to a form of community supervision. Although the courts are not required to follow either the sentencing or the special condition recommendations found in the presentence investigation report, there tends to be a close association between the probation officer's recommendations and the final sentence (Abadinsky 1997). Supervising agencies frequently use presentence reports to assist in the needs and risk assessment for the offender. Other investigations conducted by community supervision officers include helping the court determine if it is appropriate to reduce a defendant's bail and verifying an offender's plans for transferring supervision to or from another location.

Web Activity

Several Web-based resources exist that outline the use of and information to be included in presentence investigations in different jurisdictions. These training manuals are an interesting tool to help understand the content and purpose of presentence investigations. Actual reports from the federal courts are on the textbook website (http://www.oup.com/us/labessentials). Presentence reports in the juvenile justice system are called "predisposition reports."

The most important role of a community supervision officer is to ensure that offenders abide by the conditions of supervision. Depending on the type of supervision and jurisdiction, officers may have little personal contact with offenders, or they may have regular office, work, or home contacts. Officers are responsible for verifying that offenders are attending all required programs; making regular payments toward their court costs, fees, and restitution; and abiding by the law while under supervision. Officers may also conduct drug tests on those offenders who are required to submit to drug testing as a condition of their supervision.

Probation officers may also be given the responsibility to supervise offenders who have been placed in diversion programs prior to adjudication of guilt. **Diversion programs** offer offenders the opportunity to temporarily halt the prosecution effort against them. Some jurisdictions have a special form of probation imposed prior to adjudication of guilt. If the offender completes the requirements of the program, the prosecutor's office dismisses the charges against the offender, avoiding an official conviction on his or her record. Violation of the conditions of the program can result in the prosecutor deciding to proceed with a criminal prosecution against the defendant. Diversion programs are typically reserved for juveniles, youthful offenders, or first-time offenders. Offenders with previous felony convictions or those arrested for violent or serious offenses are typically not eligible for participation in diversion programs.

Supervision Violations

Supervision violations are violations of probation, parole, or an intermediate sanction's program conditions. Supervision violations may be either new-offense or technical violations. **New-offense violations** occur when offenders under supervision commit a new crime. For new-offense violations, the offender has to appear before the appropriate court for the new crime as well as the court or parole board with jurisdiction for his or her community supervision to address the violation of supervision conditions (i.e., violation of the condition to obey all laws). **Technical violations** are violations of conditions of supervision that do not involve violations of criminal statutes. Positive drug tests, failure to attend treatment meetings, absconding from supervision (i.e., fleeing supervision), and failure to make a good-faith effort toward paying restitution are common technical violations.

How officers respond to a violation of supervision conditions depends on the nature of the violation, the offender, and the officer's perception of the appropriate response (Clear, Harris, and Baird 1992; Jones and Kerbs 2007) (Box 6.3). Minor technical violations are often handled informally, perhaps with verbal or written warnings to the offender. More serious violations require officers to consider the nature and context of the violations, the probationer's progress and likelihood of successfully completing supervision, and organizational and office dynamics (McCleary 1992). New-offense violations, especially felonies, are almost always reported to the court or parole board. Serious technical violations, such as those that potentially represent a threat to public safety, may also be reported to the appropriate agency. Prosecutors, judges, and parole boards have considerable discretion in their response to condition violations, but supervising officers' recommendations can play an important role in the final disposition of the case. For new-offense violations or serious technical violations, offenders' supervision can be revoked. As a result, an offender may be sentenced to a new term of supervision, a more restrictive form of community supervision such as an intermediate sanction, or a term of incarceration in jail or prison.

BOX 6.3

Swift–Certain–Fair Responses to Probation Violations

One of the most widely discussed innovations in community supervision in the past several decades has been efforts to create a process in which officers and the courts respond quickly to probation violations. These are often referred to as "swift–certain–fair" policies or HOPE-style probation because HOPE is the name of Hawaii's program, which has been the most prominently discussed (Kleiman 2016; Larkin 2015). Although there are numerous variations across jurisdictions, a common goal is to respond to technical violations, especially failed drug tests, with a judicial hearing within 72 hours of the violation and impose a modest but meaningful sanction at that time (Klingele 2015). HOPE probation began in Hawaii in 2004 after Judge Steven Alm decided that "probation-as-usual" was not working (Alm 2015). A major problem with "probation-as-usual" is that it often takes several violations before an officer may decide it is necessary or worth the effort to seek a revocation hearing with the court (Alm 2015). Furthermore, violation hearings under traditional probation may take several weeks or months to resolve (Kleiman 2015; Larkin 2015). This greatly diminishes the purported deterrent value of punishment for violations. In response to this problem, some jurisdictions have created mechanisms for mandatory reporting of violations to the court for immediate action. The most common sanction is a brief jail sentence (typically one to five days), but judges may have the option to impose other sanctions, such as community service, curfew restrictions, or residential drug treatment. The response to violations under these programs is argued to be swift, certain, and fair.

Swift–certain–fair programs have been widely touted as a way to make probation supervision meaningful once again (Alm 2015). Furthermore, early evaluations of HOPE and similar programs reported significant reductions in recidivism and revocation rates (Hawken and Kleiman 2009; Larkin 2015). More recent evaluations of these programs, however, have found little or only modest long-term reductions in recidivism and revocation rates (Lattimore et al. 2016; O'Connell, Brent, and Visher 2016). Such results are not surprising to those critical of exclusively deterrent-based strategies with offenders. Some have questioned the effectiveness of merely relying on the threat of additional penalties as a means to change offender behavior, even when those penalties are imposed swiftly and with a degree of certainty (Cullen, Manchak, and Duriez 2014; Klingele 2015). Although swift–certain–fair programs have intuitive and political appeal, they largely ignore the numerous cognitive and social challenges that affect the lives and decision-making of many offenders. Furthermore, the attention paid to such programs seemingly minimizes the existing evidence about what actually works to reduce recidivism and revocation rates. Numerous studies have found that incorporating core correctional practices, such as targeting offender risk, reserving intensive programs for high-risk offenders, and utilizing cognitive behavioral strategies, can result in significant reductions in offender recidivism and revocation rates (Gleicher, Manchak, and Cullen 2012; Lowenkamp et al. 2010; Paparozzi and Gendreau 2006; Taxman 2008a; Trotter 2006). The challenge seems to be how to respond in a timely and effective manner to significant violations while minimizing the use of incarceration for all but the most necessary cases (Corbett 2015; Kleiman 2016; Klingele 2015). Significant justice reforms frequently require revision and modification in light of practical concerns and evidence of their effectiveness. It remains to be seen whether and how swift–certain–fair policies will be revised in light of recent evidence.

SPECIAL-NEEDS POPULATIONS AND COMMUNITY SUPERVISION

Many offenders have characteristics that place them at considerable risk for recidivism or create additional barriers to successful reintegration. Scholars have identified several characteristics that pose unique or particularly difficult challenges for offenders, often referred to as "special-needs populations," and those responsible for supervising them. Research has begun to focus on how these traits affect offenders' behavior and their ability to meet the conditions of supervision (National Institute of Corrections 2011). Examples of such groups include substance abusers (Center for Substance Abuse Treatment 2005), elderly persons under supervision (Aday 2003), female offenders (Belknap 2001; Sheenan, McIvor, and Trotter 2011), and offenders with mental health problems (Prins and Draper 2009). Although not all individuals with these traits experience difficulty in completing their sentence, research has found these populations have a variety of problems that can contribute to higher rates of recidivism and other negative outcomes. Those responsible for the supervision of these offenders should be aware of these problems and challenges.

One special-needs population that the criminal justice system has been increasingly responsible for supervising includes offenders with mental health problems. The percentage of the correctional population with identifiable mental health disorders has been growing during the past 30 years (Ditton 1999; James and Glaze 2006; Prins and Draper 2009). To date, correctional agencies have been unable to meet the increasing demand for mental health services for institutional or community-based offenders (Ditton 1999). Offenders with mental health problems have considerable challenges in abiding by the conditions of their supervision. In addition to the challenges of obtaining and maintaining a stable residence and employment, mental health problems can make it difficult to comply with even seemingly simple conditions of supervision, such as reporting to the probation office. Furthermore, these offenders often have co-occurring disorders of mental health and substance abuse problems. Such conditions exacerbate already difficult circumstances and place real constraints on offenders' personal and social resources and their ability to use those limited resources.

The criminal justice system has taken steps to improve the success of offenders with mental health problems. Many probation departments have officers with special training who are responsible for supervising such cases. Also, some communities have mental health courts, which are designed to provide a holistic response to the challenges facing these offenders (Justice Center 2008). Although considerable variation exists, mental health courts seek to coordinate the variety of social services thought necessary to improve the lives of individuals with mental health problems who come to the attention of authorities. They often use a problem-solving and team approach to providing services and supervision. For those cases under community supervision, the probation officer may have an active role in case management (Justice Center 2008). Although many mental health courts are in the experimental stage, results are encouraging. Furthermore, the use of evidence-based treatment strategies and protocols has been found to reduce a variety of negative outcomes for this population (Justice Center 2008; Prins and Draper 2009).

THE EFFECTIVENESS OF COMMUNITY CORRECTIONS

Research has found that community supervision programs have varying degrees of success in reducing recidivism (Paparozzi and DeMichele 2008; Petersilia 1997; Tonry and Lynch 1996). Given the wide variety of sanctions discussed and the meaningful differences in the same type of sanction across jurisdictions, any conclusions about the impact of various sanctions should be tempered with caution. Furthermore, some programs have been found to be more successful with particular types of offenders. Despite these caveats, there appear to be some common themes in the research on a variety of community correctional sanctions. Interested readers are encouraged to see more comprehensive reviews of the research literature found in Gray, Fields, and Maxwell (2001), Petersilia (1997), and Tonry and Lynch (1996).

Depending on the jurisdiction and the exact outcome measure, research has found considerable variation in the effectiveness of community supervision. In general, research has found that probation and intermediate sanctions are moderately effective at achieving several goals. A major issue in evaluation research is determining how program effectiveness will be measured. Measurements of offender success could include the number of offenders who successfully complete supervision, the number of new-offense or technical violations during supervision, or the number of new arrests following the completion of their supervision. How "success" is measured will greatly affect how successful a program appears.

Morgan (1996) reported that studies have found that 15 to 50 percent of probationers "failed" under community supervision. A report on probationers in the state of New York found that of the 40,000 probationers discharged throughout the state in 2006, 22 percent had their probation revoked for a technical violation and 9 percent had it revoked for new offenses, resulting in a total "failure" rate of approximately one-third of probationers (New York State Division of Criminal Justice Services 2008). Other studies have found evidence of comparable success in other jurisdictions (e.g., Gray et al. 2001). The majority of probation failures are the result of technical violations and new misdemeanor offenses. Most studies have found that violations for new felony offenses are far less common than other violations (e.g., Gray et al. 2001). Those on misdemeanor probation appear to have a much higher success rate compared to offenders placed on probation for felonies, but this could be due to the lower risk posed by misdemeanor defendants or the less intense nature of the supervision for those convicted of misdemeanors (Petersilia 1997).

An important question in evaluating the effectiveness of intermediate sanctions is "In comparison to whom?" Determining the appropriate comparison group for offenders sentenced to intermediate sanctions is often a challenge and may affect conclusions about the utility of such sanctions. To some extent, the identification of a comparison group depends on the goals of a specific program (Lurigio and Petersilia 1992). One goal that most intermediate sanctions achieve is closer supervision and control over offenders compared with regular probation

(Petersilia 1998). In many jurisdictions, intermediate sanctions have been incorporated into structured sentencing and provide more proportional sentencing options between probation and prison (Harland 1998). Another common finding is that offenders sentenced to intermediate sanctions generally have higher levels of participation in treatment programs compared to those on regular probation or imprisoned (Tonry and Lynch 1996). This is significant because programs that emphasize treatment services are more effective at reducing recidivism compared to similar programs that focus primarily on surveillance and control (Lowenkamp et al. 2010).

Intermediate sanctions, however, suffer from a number of problems that challenge their ability to reduce recidivism or correctional costs. Perhaps the most significant problem is that net widening plagues intermediate sanctions (Tonry and Lynch 1996). Despite efforts to structure sentencing decisions to reduce net widening, many offenders sentenced to intermediate sanctions were not the originally intended population, resulting in higher costs, limited impact on prison overcrowding, and expanded social control over offenders.

Generally, most evaluations have found only modest differences in the recidivism rates of similar offenders who receive intermediate sanctions versus those who receive either probation or imprisonment. Probationers tend to have the lowest recidivism rates, followed by offenders placed on intermediate sanctions. Released inmates have the highest recidivism rates. However, when offense seriousness and other relevant characteristics are taken into account, the difference in recidivism rates between intermediate sanctions and other populations becomes marginal (National Institute of Justice 2003; Petersilia and Turner 1993; Tonry and Lynch 1996). Whereas the bulk of research on boot camps finds little impact on recidivism (National Institute of Justice 2003; Wilson et al. 2005), studies on the impact of electronic monitoring on recidivism are mixed (Bonta, Wallace-Capretta, and Rooney 2000; Padgett, Bales, and Blomberg 2006). Research indicates that community correctional programs with an institutional and staff commitment to treatment and that adhere to demonstrated effective practices have much better success rates (Lowenkamp et al. 2006; Paparozzi and Gendreau 2005; Taxman 2008a; Trotter 2006). Unfortunately, these qualities are not found in every program or jurisdiction, and making such changes is not easy.

Although probationers and those on intermediate sanctions may have comparable new-offense violations, offenders on intermediate sanctions typically have higher revocation rates. The increased restrictions and closer supervision involved in intermediate sanctions have resulted in considerably higher technical violation rates for regular probation. The stronger control and surveillance orientation of most intermediate sanction programs also means that such violations may be dealt with more severely and result in revocation and possible imprisonment (Tonry and Lynch 1996). As a result, research has questioned the ability of merely surveillance-focused intermediate sanctions to reduce offender recidivism or correctional costs (Lowenkamp et al. 2010; Tonry and Lynch 1996).

Critical Thinking Exercise

Although intermediate sanctions do not appear to have met many of their utilitarian goals (cost-effectiveness, reduction of prison overcrowding, and reduction of recidivism), some argue that such penalties may serve a retributive function of simply being a more appropriate (i.e., deserved) punishment and sentencing option. However, a consequence of this is the increased costs to the criminal justice system. Is it appropriate to spend more money on the criminal justice system, especially given the fact that states have struggled with their budgets and reported crime rates have been stable or declining? How do we balance the budgetary needs of the criminal justice system and other public goods (e.g., education, health care, and highways) that governments provide?

Perhaps the clearest measure of the effectiveness of parole and post-release supervision is whether an offender returns to prison following release. Although there is evidence that prisoners who participate in targeted, problem-specific prison programs have significantly lower recidivism rates upon release, the percentage of offenders participating in such programs is rather minimal (Petersilia 2003). Many of the recent reentry programs have not yet been subject to thorough evaluation. However, released prisoners who participate in long-term, well-designed, and well-implemented post-release programs tend to have lower recidivism rates compared to inmates released without such services (Andrews 2006; Paparozzi and Gendreau 2005). The extent to which reentry continues to be a politically viable investment remains to be seen (Wodahl, Ogle, and Heck 2011). The history of criminal justice policy suggests caution in assuming long-term commitments to particular policy initiatives, especially those emphasizing rehabilitation. Research indicates that continuing allocation of sufficient resources and proper implementation greatly affect the overall effectiveness of such programs (Wilson and Davis 2006). It is too early to determine how such issues will affect the future of reentry efforts. Given the tremendous number of inmates released each year and the direct and collateral consequences of imprisonment, however, the benefits of improving prisoner reintegration could be tremendous. On the other hand, the failure of the criminal justice system, social service agencies, and communities to assist this population could have serious long-term negative implications that we are only beginning to appreciate.

Critical Thinking Exercise

Many studies find that most violations of supervision are for technical violations and not for new offenses. How should technical violations affect the perceived success or failure of a program? What are the justifications for sanctioning an individual for a technical violation, especially when the violation does not pose a threat to public safety? What should the courts or parole boards do in such cases?

INCORPORATING "BEST PRACTICES" INTO COMMUNITY CORRECTIONS

Responding to criticisms about the effectiveness of correctional interventions, a growing body of research has focused on those practices that have demonstrated success in reducing recidivism (e.g., Andrews and Bonta 2006; Bernfeld, Farrington, and Leschied 2001; McGuire 2001). Based on evaluations of a wide range of correctional practices, scholars have identified important principles for correctional treatment programs (Andrews and Bonta 2006), examples of programs and programmatic elements associated with offender change (Lowenkamp, Latessa, and Smith 2006), and insights into implementing these in real-world settings (Bernfeld et al. 2001; McGuire 2001). For example, studies have demonstrated that intensive programs should be reserved for higher risk offenders (Lowenkamp, Latessa, and Holsinger 2006). The use of intensive programs for low-risk offenders can actually increase offender recidivism rates, thereby decreasing public safety and increasing costs. Correctional agencies are increasingly developing and implementing programs consistent with these correctional best practices and effective correctional interventions. Websites for many community correctional agencies highlight initiatives organized around the principles of "what works" (Crime and Justice Institute 2004; Ohio Department of Rehabilitation and Corrections 2007; White 2005).

Although some offenders will fail to respond positively to even the best-designed programs, the knowledge base about how to improve program success rates has grown considerably in the past two decades. The challenge is how to translate this knowledge into politically, fiscally, and operationally meaningful action (Taxman 2008b). Politically, public officials remain very cautious about supporting policies that may be interpreted as "soft on crime." The use of correctional resources has historically been focused on control and surveillance activities. Even within community corrections, where officer caseloads are often high and resources limited, there is often real skepticism about the development of and resource allocation to new programs and strategies. Finally, research has demonstrated that new programs are rarely implemented in a manner consistent with important underlying principles. Whether the result of budget shortfalls, a lack of staff training or commitment, or changes in administrative philosophy, it is difficult, although not impossible, to maintain long-term program integrity in human service organizations.

Web Activity

Visit the National Institute of Corrections' website on incorporating evidence-based practices into community corrections at https://nicic.gov/evidencebasedpractices.

CONCLUSION

Ongoing efforts in the international war on terrorism, concerns about homeland security, and continuing economic problems have put a strain on public resources. Recent state budget crises have resulted in many government agencies, including corrections, making budget cuts. In corrections, resources dedicated to rehabilitation efforts typically suffer most during periods of budget problems. It is unclear what long-term impact these forces will have on criminal justice policy. History suggests, however, that the economic implications and political feasibility of any changes will be more important than philosophical considerations of criminal justice policy. As a result, criminal justice reformers are using this context to call for less ideological and more evidence-driven policies. For example, there has been increasing attention to the problems associated with mass incarceration and prisoner reintegration (Maruna and Immarigeon 2004; Petersilia 2003; Travis and Waul 2003). Evidence of the financial costs associated with mass incarceration and the failure to provide resources to assist in reentry may lead to meaningful policy changes, but that is far from certain.

Although community corrections is increasingly recognized as a vital component of American criminal justice systems, it continues to be viewed by the public and political decision-makers as of secondary importance compared with institutional corrections (Paparozzi and DeMichele 2008). A result has been that community correctional programs have been required to do more with less: supervise more offenders without a similar growth in the funding to provide adequate supervision and services to those populations. Every day, thousands of community correctional professionals try to achieve the difficult balance of helping offenders maintain a crime-free lifestyle and reintegrate into the community while identifying and responding to supervision violations and threats to public safety.

The trend appears to be to increase both the surveillance and the treatment requirements for offenders placed under community supervision. It is unclear if the funding necessary to sustain such changes will continue to be available. Recent attention to the challenges and long-term consequences of prisoner reentry may provide an opportunity for meaningful dialogue about offenders in the community and efforts to reduce their likelihood of recidivism. There have also been calls to reduce the use of supervised probation by focusing on moderate- to high-risk offenders who actually require supervision (Jacobson et al. 2017). Furthermore, scholars have questioned the necessity of extensive restrictions and impositions on offenders that are unrelated to their criminal behavior and seemingly do more harm than good (Corbett 2015; Horwitz 2010; Klingele 2013, 2015). It is unclear whether such arguments will make much progress in reversing long-standing practices and trends in community corrections. It is certain, however, that community corrections will continue to be an important component of American criminal justice and the community it serves.

Critical Thinking Exercise

The recent economic crisis has required many state and local governments to make significant cutbacks in services. Although the criminal justice system is often protected from substantial cutbacks, this has not been the case in all jurisdictions. As noted previously, community corrections is often far more susceptible to cutbacks, due to fewer fixed costs, compared to institutional corrections. Imagine you are the administrator of a large community corrections agency and are required to make substantial cutbacks to next year's budget. Where would you try to save money and why? How might you save money in those areas? What services would you consider essential? What arguments would you make to protect resources for those activities?

KEY WORDS

boot camps
community corrections
community supervision
conditions of supervision
day reporting centers
diversion programs
electronic monitoring
halfway houses
home confinement/house
   arrest

intensive supervision
   probation
intermediate sanctions
net widening
new-offense violations
parole supervision
presentence investigation
prisoner reentry/prisoner
   reintegration
probation

residential community
   correctional program
shock incarceration
special conditions
split sentences
standard conditions
supervised release
supervision violations
swift–certain–fair
   policies
technical violations

SUGGESTED READINGS

Crime and Justice Institute at Community Resources for Justice. (2009). *Implementing evidence-based policy and practice in community corrections*, 2nd ed. Washington, DC: National Institute of Corrections.

Kurki, L. (2000). Restorative and community justice in the United States. In M. Tonry (Ed.), *Crime and justice: A review of research*, vol. 27, 235–303. Chicago: University of Chicago Press.

Maruna, S., and R. Immarigeon (Eds.). (2011). *After crime and punishment: Pathways to offender reintegration*. New York: Willan.

McNeil, F., P. Raynor, and C. Trotter (Eds.). (2010). *Offender supervision: New directions in theory, research and practice*. New York: Willan.

Sheenan, R., G. McIvor, and C. Trotter (Eds.). (2011). *Working with women offenders in the community*. New York: Willan.

State of Ohio. (2002). *The Ohio plan for productive offender reentry and recidivism reduction*. http://www.drc.ohio.gov/web/ReentryFinalPlan.pdf

Tonry, M. (1998). Intermediate sanctions in sentencing guidelines. In M. Tonry (Ed.), *Crime and justice: A review of research*, vol. 23, 199–253. Chicago: University of Chicago Press.

Travis, J. (2005). *But they all come back: Facing the challenges of prisoner reentry.* Washington, DC: Urban Institute Press.

Trotter, C. (2006). *Working with offenders: A guide to practice.* Thousand Oaks, CA: Sage.

White, R., and H. Graham. (2010). *Working with offenders: A guide to concepts and practice.* New York: Willan.

CHAPTER 7

The Juvenile Justice System

CHAPTER OUTLINE

The Development of Juvenile Justice
  The Growth of Juvenile Institutions
  The Juvenile Court
  The Philosophy of the System
Defining Delinquency
Measuring Delinquency
  Official Measures
  Self-Report Measures
The Juvenile Court Process
  Detention
  The Intake Decision
  The Transfer (or Waiver) Decision
  Adjudication
  Disposition
Due Process for Juveniles
Institutional Corrections
  Institutional and Residential Interventions
  Alternative Interventions
  Deinstitutionalization
Community Interventions
  Probation
  Aftercare
  Reentry Concerns
  Issues in Supervision
Special Topics
  Gangs
  Restorative Justice
  Capital Punishment and Juveniles

The Future of Juvenile Justice
Conclusion
Key Words
Suggested Readings

After reading this chapter, you should be able to:

- Provide a brief history of the development of juvenile justice
- Compare the terminology of the juvenile and adult justice systems
- Identify and define the philosophy of the juvenile justice system
- List key contributions to the growth of *parens patriae*
- List and discuss the different types of general-purpose clauses
- Compare and contrast different definitions of delinquency
- Define and discuss the issue of sexting
- Define transfer or waiver provisions
- List different forms of transfer
- Tell the differences found using different ways of measuring delinquency
- Outline issues involved in detention
- Talk about the intake decision and alternatives
- Identify different roles assumed by attorneys in juvenile court
- List and discuss key court cases in juvenile procedural rights
- Define "state training school" and discuss programming in such institutions
- Discuss the move toward deinstitutionalization
- Identify different issues in community supervision of youths
- Demonstrate knowledge of reentry concerns
- Discuss the gang problem and talk about different efforts to deal with gangs
- Identify restorative justice and family group conferencing and discuss their impact on youths and recidivism
- List different forms of restorative justice
- Address the issues related to capital punishment for juveniles

---

Dealing with juvenile offenders poses unique problems for society, and an entire system has been established to address juvenile concerns and issues. Where it is possible to talk about a "criminal justice system" that attempts to coordinate the efforts of the police, courts, and corrections into a functional whole, the juvenile justice system is often viewed as only an appendage to that system. This is largely due to the fact that juvenile justice was founded on a different set of assumptions about the nature of juvenile misbehavior and the proper responses to deal with juvenile transgressors.

THE DEVELOPMENT OF JUVENILE JUSTICE

The history of juvenile justice is a relatively short one. Until the mid-1800s, there was no separate legal status of "juvenile," nor was there a separate system for dealing with youthful offenders. Throughout most of history, there was no such status as "child." Youthful members of society were considered either property or people. When very young, from birth to age five or six years, they held the same status as property. They could be bought, sold, and disposed of according to the needs of the owners (the fathers) just as a cow or other belonging. Once youths turned five or six years old, they became full-fledged members of society and were expected to act the same as any adult.

Web Activity

A list of common practices for dealing with the very young can be found on the text-book website.

The general view that children were the same as adults extended to the realm of legal sanctioning. Children were subject to the same rules and regulations as adults. There was not a separate system for dealing with youthful offenders. The law made no distinction based on the age of the offender. In fact, youths could be sentenced to death for various criminal actions. Although harsh punishments, including the death penalty, were imposed on youthful offenders, few received the sanction and there was a de facto process of **nullification**, or a refusal to enforce the law and sanctions against children.

The concept of childhood began to emerge in the 16th and 17th centuries as medical advances expanded youthful life expectancies. Youths began to be viewed as in need of protection, assistance, and guidance in order to grow up uncorrupted. This was largely led by clergy and scholars. Protecting children was a means of ensuring a more moral and productive society in the future.

The beginnings of the juvenile justice system are found in the policy changes directed at dealing with poverty and the potential threat the poor posed to society (Table 7.1). A primary response undertaken by many communities and religious groups was to take the poor off the streets and provide religious and vocational training, with the expectation that they would eventually be released so they could assume jobs and care for themselves and their families. Many groups focused their attention on dealing with poor children because they were viewed as better candidates for education and training.

Table 7.1 Major Milestones/Events/Dates in Juvenile Justice, 1800–1899

1825	Houses of Refuge established
	New York, 1825
	Boston, 1826
	Philadelphia, 1828
1838	*Ex parte Crouse* rules in favor of *parens patriae*
1841	Probation initiated in Boston
1848	Lyman School for Boys established
mid-1800s	Institution of reformatories
1855	Chicago Reform School Act established reform schools in Chicago
1869	Massachusetts State Board of Charities takes control of juvenile probation
1870	*People v. Turner* rules against *parens patriae*
1892	New York separates trials of juveniles and adults
1899	First juvenile court established in Cook County (Chicago), Illinois

The Growth of Juvenile Institutions

Various institutions were established to assist with the policy of helping the poor while protecting society. The earliest such institutions were the **houses of refuge**, the first of which was established in New York in 1825. This was quickly copied in Boston (1826) and Philadelphia (1828). These institutions handled both adults and juveniles in need of assistance. Central aspects in the handling of youths were education, skills training, hard work, religious training, and parental discipline. Unfortunately, the houses of refuge quickly became overcrowded and failed to provide the training and assistance they promised.

By the mid-1800s, the houses of refuge gave way to a new set of institutions— the **reformatories**. Although the basic goal of the reformatories was the same as that of the houses of refuge—education, training, and parental discipline—the reformatories followed a cottage design that closely resembled homes, each with a set of surrogate parents and a small number of youths. Unlike houses of refuge, the reformatories focused exclusively on youths. The parental figures would provide the love and care needed by the youths. Unfortunately, the reformatories suffered from many of the same problems as the houses of refuge. What makes them important is the fact that they started to recognize the unique needs and issues of young people in society.

Throughout the development of these new institutions, there remained a single system for dealing with criminal behavior by individuals of all ages in society. Youths who broke the law were still taken before the same courts as adults and subjected to the same penal code as anyone else in society. Although the houses of refuge and the reformatories handled youths sent to them by the courts, most youths still found themselves jailed with adults and punished in the same ways as adults.

The Juvenile Court

The development of the juvenile court followed the same logic as the establishment of the new institutions, namely that some individuals needed assistance rather than punishment to make them law-abiding, productive contributors to society. The first recognized individual juvenile court was established in Cook County (Chicago), Illinois, in 1899. The legislation that established the Illinois court reflected the general belief that juveniles needed assistance to overcome the disadvantages they faced in society and that they could be reformed through a system of benevolence rather than one that punished problematic behavior. In addition to responding to the concern over the poor and destitute, the new juvenile court also emerged as a result of the growth of scientific explanations for behavior, particularly those of psychology and sociology. These disciplines argued that the problems of youths could be addressed in ways other than by simple imposition of punishment by the criminal justice system. The new court also adopted a new vocabulary for its operations (Table 7.2).

Web Activity

Julian W. Mack was one of the leaders of the movement to establish a juvenile court and served as a judge in the Chicago juvenile court for many years. He described the role and methods of the court as one that assists parents in the proper ways to raise their children. You can read his seminal paper on the role of the juvenile court on the textbook's website (http://www.oup.com/us/labessentials).

The new juvenile court had jurisdiction over all youths aged 15 years or younger, no matter what the issue. The court operated in a very informal manner and avoided any resemblance to the adult court. Due process, attorneys, juries, and other elements of the adult system were excluded from the new juvenile system. The juvenile court was supposed to handle youths in a paternalistic manner and offer them help and assistance just like that found in a family. The court also relied on probation, rather than incarceration, for problem youths.

Table 7.2 Comparative Terminology Between Juvenile and Adult Systems

Juvenile	Adult
Adjudication	Conviction
Hearing	Trial
Aftercare	Parole
Commitment	Sentence
Delinquent	Criminal
Petition	Indictment
Custody	Arrest

The actual procedures and workings of the juvenile court generally reflected the character of the different judges and individuals working in the court.

The Philosophy of the System

Perhaps the greatest challenge to the growth of the juvenile justice system entailed the debate over the philosophy of the new court and the question of a juvenile's constitutional rights. The new juvenile court conformed to a philosophy that was diametrically opposed to the existing tenets of the adult criminal system. The juvenile system took the stand that youths were incapable of forming the *mens rea* (criminal intent) required for criminal acts. Instead, youthful deviant behavior was the result of forces that were beyond a juvenile's control. Alternatively, youths were simply too immature to understand the consequences of their behavior. Rather than take a strict legal response to juvenile misbehavior, which included concerns over the constitutional rights of youths, the juvenile court adopted the *parens patriae* philosophy that focused on protecting, nurturing, and training the youths so that they could make better decisions and avoid problems.

Parens patriae, or the state as parent, is based on the English Chancery Court, which was tasked with looking after the property rights of orphaned children, among other things (Table 7.3). The court was to act as a parent to those juveniles who were in need of assistance. *Parens patriae* opened the door to increased involvement in the lives of juveniles and their families. This is probably best exemplified in the passage of statutes specifically outlining status offenses. For example, the original Illinois statute establishing the juvenile court addressed criminal activity, dependency, and neglect. By 1903, however, the state added incorrigibility, curfews, and other status offenses to the court's mandate.

The *parens patriae* philosophy was not new to the juvenile court. Indeed, it had been used in an early court case in which a young girl was incarcerated against the wishes of her father. In *Ex parte Crouse* (1838), a woman asked the court to incarcerate her daughter because she was incapable of taking care of her.

Table 7.3 Important Contributors to the Growth of *Parens Patriae*

English Chancery Court (Middle Ages)	Basis of state intervention for welfare of children, particularly in terms of property matters.
Ex parte Crouse (1838)	Pennsylvania Supreme Court rules that *parens patriae* is sufficient basis for intervening in a child's life without parental consent.
People v. Turner (1870)	Illinois Supreme Court rules against *parens patriae* in favor of parental rights; largely ignored.
Commonwealth v. Fisher (1905)	Pennsylvania Supreme Court rules the court can intervene without impunity when the objective is to help the child.
Kent v. United States (1966)	*Parens patriae* is seriously questioned in light of the lack of adequate help being given by the juvenile court coupled with the lack of due-process protections given to youth.

The father objected and argued it was illegal to incarcerate a child without the benefit of a trial. The Pennsylvania Supreme Court, however, rejected the father's argument, stating that when a parent is incapable of doing his or her job, the state has a duty, under *parens patriae*, to step in and take action for the betterment of both the juvenile and the community. More important, the court noted that the rights of the parents are superseded by the rights and interests of society. This stance was reaffirmed after the initiation of the juvenile court in *Commonwealth v. Fisher* (1905). In this case, the Pennsylvania Supreme Court noted that when the objective of the state is not to punish or simply restrain a youth but, rather, to provide care and protection, the state has a right and duty to step in and take custody of a youth. In essence, if the intent is to help the youth, *parens patriae* allows the juvenile court wide latitude to intervene in the life of the youth and the family.

The *parens patriae* philosophy has remained the dominant view in the juvenile justice system. It was not until 1966 that the philosophy was seriously questioned in *Kent v. United States*. Although the U.S. Supreme Court did not rule specifically on the philosophy of the juvenile justice system, Justice Abe Fortas argued that

> there may be grounds for concern that the child receives the worst of both worlds: that he gets neither the protections accorded to adults nor the solicitous care and regenerative treatment postulated for children. (*Kent v. U.S.* [1966])

Justice Fortas was suggesting that the philosophy allowed the juvenile court unfettered involvement in the lives of juveniles without granting them due-process rights, despite the fact that the court was also failing to provide the help and care that the philosophy mandated. Changes in the juvenile justice system during the past 30 years show a gradual diminution of *parens patriae* in juvenile proceedings.

Despite *parens patriae's* continuing influence, other philosophical rationales also help drive juvenile justice. The General Purpose clauses for juvenile courts that appear in state statutes outline the primary intent or focus of the juvenile court. These clauses fall into five categories: (1) the Balanced and Restorative Justice orientation that focuses on the needs of all parties involved, including the youth and the victims; (2) the Standard Juvenile Court Act clauses that emphasize care, guardianship, and control of the youth; (3) the Legislative Guide clauses that focus on care, protection, supervision, and rehabilitation of children; (4) a Criminal Court orientation that focuses on deterrence, punishment, and accountability; and (5) traditional Child Welfare clauses in which the emphasis is on the best interests of the child. *Parens patriae* is a key in all of these but the criminal court orientation.

Web Activity

You can look at the general purpose clauses for your state and others at http://www
.ncjj.org/pdf/1State_Juvenile_Justice_Profiles_2005.pdf.

Critical Thinking Exercise

Research the general purpose clause for the juvenile court in your state.

DEFINING DELINQUENCY

The development of a separate system for handling problem youths also meant that a new set of laws and terminology was not far behind. Primary among these changes was the fact that "delinquency" replaced "crime" as the focus of the juvenile court. "Delinquency" did not exist prior to the establishment of the juvenile court. Youthful offenders had always been processed in the same criminal system as adult offenders. The juvenile court now handled youths under a different set of laws and policies.

One way to define **delinquency** is to simply use the **criminal law definition** of illegal behavior. In other words, a delinquent is any juvenile who violates the criminal code. Thus, a juvenile who commits a robbery, burglary, assault, or any other criminal offense is considered a delinquent. This definition is used throughout the United States.

There are also actions that are illegal only for persons of a certain status, such as juveniles. These are usually referred to as **status offenses**. Typical status offenses for juveniles include the use of alcohol or tobacco, curfew violations, truancy, disobeying one's parents, running away, or swearing. Adults who participate in any of these actions are not subject to sanctions by the criminal or juvenile justice systems. Different jurisdictions have different terms for status offenders. Common terms are "incorrigible," "unruly," "dependent," "PINS" (person in need of service), or "CHINS" (child in need of service). Some of these terms refer both to juveniles who have done something wrong and to youths who have been subjected to poor parenting or are victims of a crime and are in need of protection.

Critical Thinking Exercise

Look up the delinquency and status offense statutes for your state and at least two other states. How are they similar and different?

Web Activity

The legal definition of delinquent and unruly child for the state of Ohio can be found on the textbook website (http://www.oup.com/us/labessentials).

In defining delinquency, it is important also to note that the definition of a juvenile varies from jurisdiction to jurisdiction. In 41 states and the District of Columbia, a juvenile is anyone under the age of 18 years. Seven states define juveniles as those under age 17 years, and 2 states define juveniles as individuals under age 16 years. Although these ages set an upper limit for juvenile court jurisdiction, many states also set a minimum age for handling cases in the juvenile system. Thirty-three states have no minimum age, whereas 11 states set it at age 10 years, 4 states set it at age 7 years, 1 state sets it at age 8 years, and 1 state uses age 6 years as the minimum. In addition to the minimum age, there are often provisions whereby the juvenile system can retain jurisdiction over an individual who was adjudicated in the system but has since passed the age of majority. States accomplish this under what are generally known as **youthful offender statutes**.

Despite the existence of a separate system to handle youths, states also have provisions for handling juveniles in the criminal justice system. These provisions are known as **transfer** or **waiver**. Transfer, or waiver, is a process whereby someone who is legally a juvenile is determined to be beyond the help of the juvenile justice system. Thus, there is a need to invoke the adult criminal process to handle the youth and protect society. Most jurisdictions set a minimum age at which transfer can be invoked.

It should be evident that defining delinquency is not a straightforward endeavor. The definition varies greatly based on the age of the youth and the jurisdiction. This situation also leads to variation in the measurement of youthful misbehavior because the level of delinquency varies according to how the problem is defined.

Critical Thinking Exercise

Explore your state's statutes and find the definitions and guidelines for juveniles and transfer/waiver used by your state. How do they compare with what is presented here? Randomly pick one or two other states and compare those results to your state.

MEASURING DELINQUENCY

There are a number of different ways to measure delinquency, each of which produces a different picture of the delinquency problem. The two primary approaches to measuring delinquency are the use of official records and the administration of self-report surveys.

Official Measures

Official measures of delinquency are based on the records of various justice system agencies. The level of delinquency, therefore, reflects both the behavior of the juveniles and the activity of the agencies. Official statistics can be obtained from law enforcement, the courts, and corrections. The **Uniform Crime Reports** (UCR), which provides information on offenses coming to the attention of the police, is the most common. Unfortunately, because many crimes are not reported to the police and only a fraction of all crimes are cleared by arrest each year, little information is known about the offenders in most crimes. An inspection of cases in which an offender has been identified or arrested provides some insight into juvenile delinquency/criminal behavior. Arrest data by age for 2016 reveal that more than 680,000 juveniles were arrested, reflecting roughly 8 percent of all those arrested. The arrest data reveal that youths represented 10 percent of the arrests for the violent crimes of murder, rape, robbery, and aggravated assault and 14 percent of all property crime arrests in 2016.

The use of arrest data for measuring youthful offending is problematic mainly due to the focus on the Part I crimes listed in the UCR. There is a very skewed view of juvenile behavior if the focus is placed solely on crimes for which they have been arrested. What is missing are the many forms of misbehavior that are not reflected in the UCR.

Web Activity

Extensive UCR data can be found at https://ucr.fbi.gov/crime-in-the-u.s/2016/crime-in-the-u.s.-2016/topic-pages/persons-arrested for information on age, sex, race/ethnicity, and other factors related to offending.

Other sources of official delinquency data come from the courts and correctional system. Most youths reaching the courts enter after contact with law enforcement, although many also come from other agencies as well as direct from family referrals. In 2014, almost 975,000 youths reached the juvenile court for delinquency offenses and 100,000 status offenders appeared in courts. Compared to both police and court data, the number of youths who appear in correctional statistics is relatively small. Correctional data are typically presented as an average one-day count, with actual daily totals varying around figures. In 2015, public and private facilities combined held roughly 48,000 juveniles on a typical day (Sickmund et al. 2017), with public facilities holding roughly 69 percent of the youths.

Web Activity

Extensive correctional statistics can be found at http://www.ojjdp.gov/ojstatbb/ezacjrp.

Web Activity

Court statistics can be found at https://www.ojjdp.gov/ojstatbb/ezajcs/.

These data present a slightly different picture of juvenile offending. The key point to remember is that these figures reflect not only the behavior of the youths but also the behavior and decision-making processes of the agencies. In all official measures, the data fail to consider juvenile behavior that does not come to the attention of the juvenile justice system.

Self-Report Measures

Self-report measures attempt to gauge the level of delinquency by asking individuals to admit to their participation in deviant activity. Where official measures reflect information on those offenses that have been reported to the authorities or where an individual has been arrested, self-reports do not need any involvement of the criminal justice system.

Self-report surveys have a long history in juvenile justice. One of the earliest self-report surveys was developed by Short and Nye (1958) to tap the level of misbehavior by youths. Their survey asked youths to note the frequency with which they committed each of 24 items (Table 7.4). The items in the scale were dominated by status and minor property offenses, and it is common to see only a subset of the items used in analyses. Dentler and Monroe (1961) offered a similar self-report survey that focused on minor delinquent offenses.

Most self-report surveys uncover a great deal of delinquent activity. Indeed, various studies using scales such as that of Short and Nye (1958) show that virtually every juvenile is a delinquent. This is due to the many minor transgressions that appear in them. Defying parental authority and trying alcohol at some time are pretty universal activities for juveniles. Asking if the individual has "ever" committed an act contributes to the high levels of positive responses. Compared to official counts of delinquency, such self-reports show a great deal more deviance.

More recent self-report surveys, such as the **Monitoring the Future Survey** (MTF) and the **National Youth Survey** (NYS), include many more serious offenses that elicit significantly fewer positive responses. Both the MTF and the NYS include questions on hitting teachers, group fighting, use of weapons, robbery, and aggravated assault. Data from these projects reveal that few youths commit the more serious offenses.

Web Activity

Survey items from both the MTF and the NYS can be found on the textbook website (http://www.oup.com/us/labessentials).

Table 7.4 Short and Nye Self-Reported Delinquency Items

Defied parents' authority*
Driven a car without a driver's license or permit*
Skipped school*
Had a fist fight with one person
Ran away from home
School probation or expulsion
Drove too fast or recklessly
Taken little things (worth less than $2) that did not belong to you*
Taken things of medium value ($2–$50)
Taken things of large value ($50)
Used force (strong-arm methods) to get money from another person
Taken part in "gang fights"
Taken a car for a ride without the owner's knowledge
Bought or drank beer, wine, or liquor (including drinking at home)*
Bought or drank beer, wine, or liquor (outside your home)
Drank beer, wine, or liquor in your own home
Deliberate property damage*
Used or sold narcotic drugs
Had sex relations with another person of the same sex (not masturbation)*
Had sex relations with a person of the opposite sex
Went hunting or fishing without a license (or violated other game laws)
Taken things you didn't want
"Beat up" on kids who hadn't done anything to you
Hurt someone to see them squirm
*Commonly used items in subsequent self-report studies.

SOURCE: Short, J. F., and I. Nye. (1958). Extent of unrecorded delinquency: Tentative conclusion. *Journal of Criminal Law, Criminology and Police Science, 49,* 296–302.

Self-reports are especially useful for probing new behaviors that do not appear in police data or other official records. One major new topic receiving attention is **sexting**. Lounsbury, Mitchell, and Finkelhor (2011) note that sexting includes an array of behaviors. At the most basic level, sexting involves the transmission of sexual images across an electronic medium. The typical assumption is that this is by a cell phone, although it can be by email, social networks, online postings, faxing, or any electronic means. What makes it explicitly problematic is when it is done by or involves juveniles. Döring (2014) defines sexting as "the interpersonal exchange of self-produced sexualized texts and above all images (photos, videos) via cell phone or the internet."

Estimates of the extent of sexting are typically based on surveys of youths and young adults. These surveys may explore reports of being involved in sexting, or they may be victimization surveys in which respondents are asked if they have been the target of sexting. Based on self-report survey data, one study reports that almost 4 out of 10 youths claim to have sent sexually suggestive messages, whereas almost 20 percent have been involved in transmitting sexually oriented pictures (National Campaign to Prevent Teen and Unplanned Pregnancy 2009). Other surveys place the behavior as high as 50 percent and even higher by sexually active teens (Lee et al. 2015). Reports on receipt of sexual images reveal that roughly 7 out of 10 youths aged 16 to 18years have received sexts (Lee et al. 2015). Females more often send sexts, whereas males receive sexts more often than do females (Klettke, Hallford, and Mellor 2014).

The problem of sexting is multifaceted. The first concern is the blatant transmission of pornographic images, especially those involving children. The fact that it is being done by children and that they see no problem with this activity is a major concern. A second related concern is the use of such transmissions as a form of bullying between youths. The accompanying shame and embarrassment, along with the bullying, have led to suicide, attempted suicide, and assaultive reactions. These topics have been the focus of several national media reports. A third concern is that sexting has been tied to a range of other risk behaviors, such as heightened sexual activity and alcohol use, and emotional problems (Ševčíková 2016). A fourth concern is the fact that sexting is not easy for parents, teachers, and the juvenile justice system to see. It is an action that is easily hidden and, therefore, difficult to identify and address. In many jurisdictions, there is no clear legal definition of sexting, which makes it difficult to address except under laws defining pornography (Jolicoeur and Zedlewski 2010). The juvenile justice system must therefore use options not initially devised for this type of behavior between youths.

Critical Thinking Exercise

What measure of delinquency is the best, and why?

Like official data, self-report measures are not without fault. As already noted, many survey instruments tend to err on the side of recording numerous minor criminal acts and status offenses but often fail to tap into more serious actions. Exceptions to these instruments, such as the NYS and MTF, which include serious criminal acts, find results much more in line with those revealed in official arrest statistics. A second major problem with self-report data is the fact that most surveys are one-time efforts, which makes it difficult to know what changes (if any) are taking place over time.

THE JUVENILE COURT PROCESS

Most youths come to the juvenile court by way of the police. Other youths are referred to the court by parents, schools, or other agencies and individuals. In 2014, approximately 56 percent of all youths taken into custody were referred to the juvenile courts. Of these, 1 percent were sent directly to adult criminal court. Once a juvenile is referred to court, the case can follow a range of different paths through the system. Cases can be petitioned to court and handled in a formal capacity or not petitioned and subjected to informal interventions. Estimates of the number of delinquency cases and the movement of cases through the various alternative processes for 2014 are shown in Figure 7.1. In addition to these cases, another 100,000 status offense cases were petitioned to juvenile court.

No matter how youths reach the court, the process and decision points are the same. In general, there are five key stages in juvenile court processing: the detention decision, intake, transfer (or waiver), adjudication, and disposition. Within each stage, various issues and processes arise.

Detention

The initial decision to be made by juvenile court personnel is whether to hold a youth in custody or allow the youth to go home until further action is taken. A **detention** decision is the counterpart to the bail decision in adult court. The

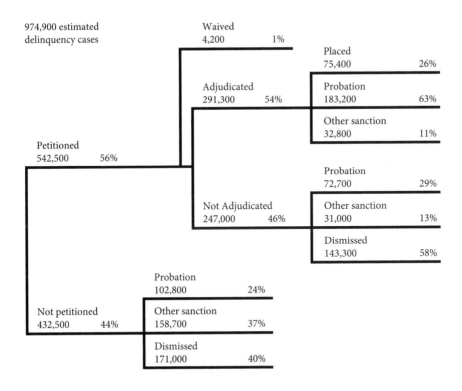

Figure 7.1 Juvenile court processing of delinquency cases, 2014.
SOURCE: Hockenberry, S., and C. Puzzanchera. (2017). *Juvenile court statistics*, 2014. Pittsburgh, PA: National Center for Juvenile Justice.

detention decision considers whether the individual will appear at a later date, whether the person is a threat to others, and whether the juvenile is in danger himself or herself. That is, detention is considered for the good of society *and* the good of the juvenile.

Detention decisions are initially made by probation officers or special detention workers, although the final decision on whether to continue detention is up to the juvenile court judge. The Model Juvenile Delinquency Act, a guideline for state codes, stipulates that a detention hearing be held within 36 hours. Critics of detaining youths who are at "high risk" for future offending generally claim that many youths who are held do not really constitute a threat and, therefore, the detention is a violation of their rights. Such preventive detention, however, has been declared constitutional by the U.S. Supreme Court (*Schall v. Martin* [1984]).

In 2014, approximately 212,900 (21%) of the delinquency cases involved detention. For status offense cases, roughly 7 percent involved detention. Most youths are released to their families. The choice of which youths to detain raises concerns for some observers. As a result, many courts now use risk-assessment instruments to base the detention decision on proven risk factors.

Web Activity

An example of a risk-assessment instrument, as well as a reference to other risk-assessment instruments, can be found on the textbook website (http://www.oup.com/us/labessentials).

The youths who are not released to their parents or guardians are placed into either secure or nonsecure detention facilities. **Secure detention** is the equivalent of the local jail for adults. While youths are in a locked facility, they must be isolated from adults, both physically and audibly. That is, youths are not supposed to be able to see or hear confined adults. In **nonsecure detention**, the youths may be placed in group homes, halfway houses, foster care, or other community-based alternatives. Youths in these facilities may still attend their normal schools and other functions as allowed by the court. Both secure and nonsecure detention facilities must provide food, a place to sleep, health care, educational programming, and appropriate treatment programs. Both the educational and treatment components respond to the *parens patriae* doctrine of helping youths rather than punishing them.

Because of the relatively short periods that most youths spend in detention, treatment interventions within the detention facilities are often very simplistic and do not address the underlying needs of the youths. Instead, the interventions tend to address the need to keep order in the facility. Perhaps the most common form of detention programming is a **token economy**. Under this approach, youths receive points or tokens for acting appropriately and lose them for inappropriate behaviors. The tokens are good toward extra privileges or purchases from a store or vending machine. Other interventions, such as counseling and vocational training, may appear in some facilities but are not very common due to the relatively short stay for many youths.

The cost involved in housing youths and providing for their constant care while in detention has led many jurisdictions to seek out alternative modes of supervision. **Day–evening centers**, one option, provide educational programming, treatment programs, or other activities during the day but send the youths home at night. This alleviates the need to provide beds, clothing, and three meals a day. The parents/guardians provide oversight at night. A second option is to use **home detention**, which involves ordering youths to remain at home at all times, unless given permission by the court to leave the premises. Youths are monitored by probation or court personnel through frequent visits, phone contacts, or even electronic monitoring devices. This is a cost-effective alternative to the use of a detention facility. A final alternative to detention is to allow youths to post **bail**, as in adult court. Although a seldom-used alternative, due mainly to the inability of most youths and their families to raise the required funds, bail is receiving greater attention as a method for handling serious youthful offenders.

The Intake Decision

The second major decision point in the juvenile court is intake. The **intake decision** is the juvenile system's counterpart to filing charges or a grand jury indictment in the adult system. It is at intake that the decision is made to file a petition with the court to hear the case or to handle the youth in another way. The petition alleges that a child is delinquent, neglected, abused, incorrigible, dependent, or otherwise in need of court intervention. The decision to file a petition is typically made by a probation officer or intake officer after he or she has reviewed the facts of the case, met with and talked to the youth and his or her family, gathered background information about the youth (including prior offending, school records, and so forth), and considered alternatives to formal court processing. Many jurisdictions mandate that all decisions to file or deny a petition be reviewed by a prosecutor in order to ensure that there is legal standing for the court to take action and guarantee that serious juvenile offenders are not moved out of the system. Despite the move to include prosecutorial oversight, fewer than half of all juvenile cases reaching the intake stage are *not* petitioned to the court.

Youths who are not petitioned to court are not simply let go by intake. Most of the time, some form of **informal adjustment** is mandated by the intake or probation office. An informal adjustment means that the youths will be required to participate in something short of a court procedure. Interestingly, almost 60 percent of the youths not petitioned to court were still placed on some form of probation or received some form of sanction (Hockenberry and Puzzanchera 2017). Alternatives may include making restitution or attending counseling or treatment programs. It is not unusual for such informal adjustments to require the participation of the parents and other family members, especially if counseling or treatment is mandated. These informal adjustments are an important part of the juvenile justice system and clearly fit the *parens patriae* philosophy of the court.

Two forms of specialty courts have developed in recent years to address special populations. The first of these, the **teen court** (or youth court), rests on the restorative justice philosophy, which seeks to help the offender, the victim, their families and friends, and society at large. In 2017, there were more than 1,050 teen court programs handling more than 100,000 cases (National Association of Youth Courts, 2017). These courts rely on youths to act as judges, attorneys, and jury members. The most common penalty from teen courts is community service, although writing apologies, composing essays on offending, and restitution are also common types of outcomes. Teen courts tend to be used effectively with status offenses and other minor transgressions. Currently, there is a lack of definitive evidence on their effectiveness (Butts, Roman, and Lynn-Whaley 2012).

The second specialty court is a **drug court**. Drug courts involve a strong collaboration among the judge, prosecutor, defense attorney, and drug treatment specialists. The goal is to address the youthful offending and the concurrent drug use. The courts use treatment, coordination of interventions, and intensive monitoring. Youths appear frequently so the judges can monitor their progress, offer encouragement, and admonish the youths if needed. There is frequent drug testing, with penalties for positive tests. Recent evaluations of drug courts show modest positive results. Mitchell et al. (2012) report that juvenile drug courts reduced recidivism from 50 percent to 43.5 percent.

The Transfer (or Waiver) Decision

One option available to the juvenile court when faced with a serious juvenile offender is to **transfer** or **waive** the youth to the adult system for processing. This is an important decision because the transfer means that the youth will be dealt with as an adult and will incur an adult criminal record if convicted. A criminal record may have serious ramifications for future employment opportunities, whereas a juvenile record is typically confidential and not subject to disclosure. In 2014, approximately 4,200 juveniles were waived to the adult criminal court (Hockenberry and Puzzanchera, 2017). This is significantly below the peak of 13,300 cases waived in 1994.

The traditional and most common method for transferring a juvenile is through **judicial waiver** (allowed in 47 states as of 2015). Judicial waiver is typically made at a hearing analogous to a preliminary hearing in adult court. At this hearing, the prosecutor asks the juvenile court judge to transfer the youth to the adult court for processing. The prosecutor must show probable cause that the juvenile committed the alleged offense. He or she must also convince the judge that the youth is not amenable to treatment in the juvenile system—that the juvenile justice system is not capable of helping the youth. This is typically demonstrated through past failures of the juvenile system to correct a problem or the particularly heinous nature of the offense.

Web Activity

A list of different forms of transfer can be found on the textbook website (http://www.oup.com/us/labessentials).

Concern over the increasing number and seriousness of juvenile crimes, particularly since 1990, has led to a greater reliance on two other types of transfer—prosecutorial waiver and legislative waiver. **Prosecutorial waiver** (or **direct file**) refers to the ability of prosecutors to directly file the case in adult court (possible in 15 states). The decision is at the sole discretion of the prosecutor within the boundaries set by state statutes. The third form of transfer is **legislative waiver** or **statutory exclusion**. Legislative waiver means that state legislatures determine that certain offenses or cases automatically go to adult court. Twenty-nine states have legislated immediate transfer to adult courts. The case is excluded from juvenile court processing by statute. The typical cases addressed by legislative waiver are serious personal offenses, such as murder, or those involving serious repeat offenders. **Once/always provisions**, which exist in 36 states, stipulate that once a youth is adjudicated as an adult, he or she will remain under the jurisdiction of the adult court for any future transgressions. Finally, 25 states allow for **reverse waiver**, where the adult court can return a waived youth to the juvenile system for processing.

Critical Thinking Exercise

Waiver protocols vary from jurisdiction to jurisdiction, and many jurisdictions allow for more than one type of waiver. The use of different forms of waiver by state can be found in the document at http://www.ncjj.org/PDF/MFC/MFC_Transfer_2008.pdf. Examine this information and discuss what it tells you about the use of waiver.

Although there was a clear policy shift in juvenile justice to call for harsher sanctioning of violent youths in the late 1980s and early 1990s, there has been a trend toward less punitive actions in recent years. Some states have moved to limit the use of waiver and to increase the possibility of reverse waiver. Several states have restored age 18 years as the minimum age for adult criminal court cases, and reverse waiver has become more prominent (Daugherty, 2013).

The impact of transferring youths to adult court on subsequent offending and crime rates is not clear. There is evidence that transfer has little or no deterrent effect (Jordan and Myers 2011; Mulvey and Schubert 2012). Those who are transferred tend to receive probation rather than being incarcerated or are released earlier than they would have been if kept under juvenile court jurisdiction (Fagan 1995). This may be due to the lack of appropriate places of confinement for youths who are convicted under adult statutes. They cannot simply be placed into adult correctional facilities with adults, but they are not under the jurisdiction of the juvenile correctional system. These results suggest that transferring youths to the adult system is not a panacea for the problem of youth crime.

Adjudication

Actual hearings in the juvenile court are referred to as the **adjudication** stage. During adjudication, the judge must determine whether there is enough evidence to support the petition and what remedy to use with the juvenile. This is comparable to finding guilt or innocence and sentencing in the adult court.

The adjudication stage in the juvenile court is supposed to look a great deal different from what is seen in an adult court. Under *parens patriae*, there is not supposed to be a determination of guilt or innocence. The actual fact that a crime may have been committed is secondary to the needs of the youth and his or her family. Due-process considerations of the admissibility of evidence, the use of hearsay evidence, the presence of attorneys, and similar issues are secondary to determining what is in the best interests of the child. The entire setting of a juvenile courtroom is often configured to suggest a non-adversarial proceeding. Indeed, during the early days of the juvenile court, attorneys were rarely included in the proceedings, with only the judge, the youth, his or her parents, and perhaps a probation or intake officer in attendance. Many hearings are held around a large conference table, and the judge does not wear judicial robes. It is common for the judge to ask all the questions, and the probation or intake officer offers most of the evidence.

This ideal process of juvenile procedure has undergone several changes during the past 30 years. Today, there is a greater emphasis on procedural rights in many cases, particularly those dealing with serious offenses. As a result, both prosecuting and defense attorneys are becoming more commonplace in juvenile court proceedings. The determination of guilt or innocence has also become more common. Many courts have adopted the trappings of adult court, with a judge's bench, judicial robes, defense and prosecution tables, and concern for the due-process rights of the youth. This movement may be due to the increasing levels of serious offending by youths.

The emergence of due-process concerns and the participation of attorneys in the juvenile court process lead to competing roles in the courtroom. The first is the **zealous advocate role** as found in the adult criminal court. The training of most attorneys and the move to more due-process concerns have resulted in attorneys fighting for their youthful clients, even when they know the child is guilty and in need of the help that could be provided by the court. The second role is the **concerned parent role**. This approach often leads attorneys to push youths to admit to petitions in order to secure the help and assistance of the court.

There is conflicting evidence on the effectiveness of defense attorneys in the juvenile court. First, many youths are not represented by attorneys because they do not understand their rights and often waive their right to representation out of ignorance of the law (Brooks and Kamine 2003). Second, where attorneys are used, their presence results in fewer dismissals and harsher outcomes, including out-of-home placement (Burruss and Kempf-Leonard 2002; Feld 1988; Guevara, Spohn, and Herz 2004). Finally, in many cases, the quality of representation is poor or ineffective (Brooks and Kamine 2003; Miller-Wilson and Puritz 2003). The participation of attorneys in the juvenile court setting, therefore, may not be beneficial for many youths.

Disposition

Once the court has determined that the facts of the petition are sufficiently supported, a **disposition** (the equivalent to a sentence in an adult court) is determined. Most often, the disposition reflects the *parens patriae* philosophy and seeks interventions and treatments that address the needs of the youth and the family. The judge pays a great deal of attention to the recommendations of the probation officers, social workers, psychologists, and others who have examined the youth. Counseling, educational programming, and treatment programs dominate most dispositions, and most of the time there is a strong desire to send youths home for treatment within the community. Indeed, the vast majority of youths are placed on some form of probation.

Many jurisdictions have moved to more punitive sanctions in recent years. This trend has been mandated in many places by legislative attempts to "get tough" on juvenile offenders by setting minimum sanctions that the juvenile courts must impose for some crimes. It is not unusual for jurisdictions to impose these harsher dispositions on older youths who have been involved in repeat offenses. A good deal of the concern is that these youths will continue their offending once they become adults and are no longer under the juvenile court's jurisdiction.

Jurisdictions also have developed systems of **blended sentencing** whereby the juvenile court or the adult criminal court imposes a sentence that can involve the juvenile or adult correctional system or both. Fourteen states have juvenile blended sentencing schemes, and 18 states have adult/criminal blended sentencing laws (Office of Juvenile Justice and Delinquency Prevention 2017). Blended sentencing addresses the loss of jurisdiction by the juvenile court before youths can be adjudicated or before treatment can be completed or the needs of young adults that cannot be met by the adult correctional system. Under blended sentencing, the court imposes dispositions that rely on both juvenile and adult systems. For example, a 17-year-old who is adjudicated in juvenile court may begin his or her disposition in a juvenile facility. Instead of simply being released when he or she turns age 18 years and the juvenile facility is no longer appropriate, the individual is automatically transferred to an adult facility and supervision by the adult court. Another possibility is for the 17-year-old to be sent directly to adult supervision after adjudication. Alternatively, a youthful adult offender (e.g., age 19 years) who is found guilty in adult court may be better served in a facility or program run by the juvenile court and, thus, sent to the juvenile system for help. Such blended sentencing is becoming more commonplace as society grapples with offenders who do not quite fit into one or the other system.

DUE PROCESS FOR JUVENILES

Juveniles share some, but not all, of the same constitutional rights as adults. Prior to the 1960s, the *parens patriae* philosophy ruled in the juvenile justice system and due-process rights were not a concern in the juvenile court. The 1960s and 1970s saw the growth of due-process protections for youthful offenders. The report of the President's Commission on Law Enforcement and the Administration of Justice (1967) raised serious questions about the juvenile court's handling of youths, its ability to deal with the increasing number of cases, and the need to protect both youths and society. During this period, the U.S. Supreme Court and state courts began to take a more active look at the operations of the juvenile justice system. Consequently, youths are now afforded some of the same constitutional rights that adults have in the criminal justice system. At the same time, the courts still recognize the *parens patriae* doctrine as the driving force when dealing with juveniles and have been reluctant to award full constitutional protections to youths in the juvenile justice system.

Four landmark Supreme Court cases opened the door to constitutional due-process protections for juveniles (Table 7.5). The first case to seriously question the *parens patriae* doctrine and the lack of due-process rights for juveniles was *Kent v. U.S.* (1966). In *Kent*, the U.S. Supreme Court was asked to examine the rights of a juvenile faced with transfer to the adult court. Kent was a 16-year-old boy accused of rape who had been waived to the adult court without benefit of a hearing, the assistance of counsel, or an explanation of why he was waived. The Supreme Court decided that the juvenile court judge had erred. Specifically, the court should have allowed Kent's attorney to review the evidence and be present at a hearing in order to refute the evidence and offer a counterargument to the court. The denial of counsel was a violation of Kent's Sixth Amendment rights. Furthermore, the Supreme Court ruled that the judge needed to set forth in writing the specific reasons why he transferred the case to the adult court. The *Kent* case is important for two reasons. First, it outlined the procedure by which transfer decisions must be made; no such procedure existed prior to this time. Second, and more important, the case established some due-process protections for the first time in juvenile procedures. Although the protections only applied to transfer decisions, they opened the way for further challenges to *parens patriae*.

Table 7.5 Landmark Supreme Court Decisions

Kent v. United States (1966)	Juveniles have certain due-process protections when the issue of waiver to the adult court is being considered, including the right to assistance of an attorney, the right to a hearing, and a written reason for why the waiver is granted.
In re Gault (1967)	When confinement is a possibility, youths have a right to an attorney, to know the charges, to confront witnesses, and to remain silent.
In re Winship (1970)	When confinement in a locked facility is possible, the court must use "proof beyond a reasonable doubt" as the standard, as opposed to the more common use of "preponderance of evidence."
McKeiver v. Pennsylvania (1971)	Youths do not have a right to a trial by jury, and jury trials are not needed for fair proceedings.

Web Activity

Excerpts from the court rulings for the landmark Supreme Court cases dealing with youths can be found on the textbook website (http://www.oup.com/us/labessentials).

The year after the *Kent* decision, the U.S. Supreme Court ruled in the case *In re Gault* (1967). In this case, a 15-year-old boy was accused of making obscene phone calls and was sentenced to the state training school until he became an adult. In essence, Gault was given a 6-year sentence for a crime that, for an adult, could only bring a $50 fine and two months in jail. The appeal, however, was not over the sentence; instead, the questions raised dealt with the procedure followed when imposing the sentence. Gault was taken into custody by the police without any notice being given to his mother. He was detained until his hearing one week later, at which he was denied the right to counsel, no specific charges were ever filed, the person making the accusation was not required to appear, and no transcripts of the proceedings were kept. The Supreme Court ruled that when there is a possibility of confinement, a juvenile does have certain rights, including the right to an attorney, the right to know the charges against him or her, the right to confront his or her accuser, and the right to remain silent (*In re Gault* [1967]). The Court specifically noted that the inclusion of due-process rights in juvenile court would not hinder the court's ability to act in the best interests of the child.

The rights of juveniles to due process were further enhanced in 1970 in the case *In re Winship*. In this case, a 12-year-old boy was confined to the state training facility for allegedly stealing $112 from a woman's purse. During the juvenile court hearing, the court adjudicated the youth delinquent using a "preponderance of evidence" criterion. The appeal dealt with whether this standard of proof was sufficient for incarcerating a juvenile. The U.S. Supreme Court noted that the higher standard of "beyond a reasonable doubt" as used in the adult court must also be used in juvenile proceedings when there is the possibility of committing a youth to a locked facility (*In re Winship* [1970]). The Court also questioned the use of "preponderance of evidence" based on its lack of accuracy and openness to interpretation.

Despite the growth of due-process considerations in juvenile court, not all constitutional rights afforded to adults are applicable to juveniles or the juvenile court. This was made evident only one year after *Winship* in the case *McKeiver v. Pennsylvania* (1971). In this case, the juvenile was denied the right to a jury trial and appealed to the U.S. Supreme Court for relief. The Supreme Court, however, sided with the lower courts and denied the appeal. It did this for several reasons. First, the Court ruled that there is no need for a jury trial to ensure fairness; bench trials are just as capable of ensuring fairness as a jury trial. Second, the Court did not want to turn the juvenile courts into an adversarial setting, and a jury trial would be much more adversarial. Third, the Court pointed out that the juvenile court was capable of fulfilling its mandate without giving full due-process rights to juveniles. Finally, although it did not mandate jury trials in juveniles cases, the Court did note that a jurisdiction could allow for juries if it desired to do so (*McKeiver v. Pennsylvania* [1971]).

These four cases are typically considered the most important cases for the juvenile justice system. They opened the door to review of the actions of the juvenile court and offered some constitutional protections to youths. At the same time, they limited the extent of those constitutional rights and reaffirmed the basic philosophical mandate underlying the juvenile system.

Web Activity

Since these cases were decided, many other challenges have been mounted on behalf of juveniles. See the textbook website (http://www.oup.com/us/labessentials) for a list of some other cases that further refine the rights of juveniles in the juvenile and criminal justice systems.

Throughout the court cases, there is an attempt to balance the rights of juveniles as individuals and citizens with the family and societal needs to protect and raise children to be law-abiding citizens. The growth of litigation over the rights of youths can be considered a direct result of changes in both the behavior of youths and societal responses to that behavior. As society and the juvenile justice system have taken new steps to address youthful misbehavior, particularly in terms of more adversarial proceedings and harsher forms of punishment, the courts have stepped in to outline appropriate safeguards for the rights of youths. In essence, the courts have established policy through the rulings they have handed down.

Critical Thinking Exercise

Should juveniles be given full constitutional protections? What would be the consequence of doing so? What would be the consequence of not doing so?

INSTITUTIONAL CORRECTIONS

Juvenile corrections takes a variety of forms, ranging from institutional and residential settings to probation and community-based alternatives. The primary goal throughout the juvenile corrections system is to help youths overcome the problems leading to misbehavior. The history of many correctional initiatives today dates back to the founding principles of the juvenile system. The early houses of refuge and reformatories set the stage for today's residential institutions, while probation has been a cornerstone of dealing with juveniles since before the first juvenile court was established.

Institutional and Residential Interventions

On the latest one-day count of juveniles in residential placement in 2014, more than 48,000 youths were being held in some form of residential facility, with more than 70 percent in public facilities and 29 percent held for offenses against persons (Hockenberry, Wachter, and Sladky 2016). Females constituted only 15 percent of those in facilities, and they are held for status offenses and technical violations more often than males.

State training schools are the juvenile justice system's equivalent of the adult prison. These schools house youths who are considered to be a risk to themselves and the community and who are beyond the help of community-based interventions. The actual setup of training schools varies greatly from place to place. Some closely resemble adult prisons, with high walls, fences, barbed wire, locked cells, and heavily regimented activities. At the other extreme are training schools built on the cottage design of the early reformatories. These institutions may be totally open, meaning there are no fences or locked doors to keep juveniles from escaping. The "guards" in these facilities may actually act more like parents than jailers.

The most important part of training schools is the degree of programming that is supposed to take place. Most training schools offer some combination of academic education, vocational training, and behavior modification. Academic education is required by law for all youths of school age who have not graduated from high school. Vocational training may be offered to older youths who have completed school or who are no longer required to go to school. **Behavior modification** is used ostensibly to teach youths about proper behavior through a system that rewards positive behavior and punishes poor behavior. Most institutions use a formal point system, or token economy. Beyond these three interventions, institutions may implement a wide range of additional programming. Individual, group, and family counseling sessions are popular interventions used in institutions, along with drug or alcohol programs, work release, vocational counseling, and job placement.

A key issue facing institutional programming is its effectiveness at reducing recidivism and helping the youths become productive members of society. Unfortunately, the evidence on effectiveness is mixed (Whitehead and Lab 2018). The reason for this is not entirely clear, although a large part of the problem may entail the degree to which the intervention is appropriately implemented and carried out (Schubert and Mulvey 2014). That is, did the institution deliver the treatment as it was meant to be delivered and at a level sufficient to bring about a positive change? Among effective programs are multisystemic therapy and those that incorporate proven principles and approaches such as cognitive–behavioral approaches. Some of the keys to effective programs is implementing interventions that are intensive and behavioral, target criminogenic need, match offenders to programs, and target risk factors (Andrews 2006; Andrews et al. 1990; Gendreau 1996).

Web Activity

References and materials addressing the effectiveness debate can be found on the textbook website (http://www.oup.com/us/labessentials).

Alternative Interventions

Traditional state training schools are not the only means of housing delinquents. Many youths are held in open facilities such as shelters, halfway houses, and group homes. These residents typically attend regular schools while receiving counseling and other interventions at the facility. One popular alternative has been the use of **boot camps**. Also known as a type of **shock incarceration**, boot camps are short-term programs that are supposed to handle first-time, nonviolent offenders. The camps are operated on a military model, with strict rules and discipline, physical training and conditioning, and counseling and education. The camps are intended to show youths that with hard work and self-discipline, they can succeed in life and do not need to turn to delinquent or criminal behavior. Unfortunately, the evidence shows that boot camps have little or no effect on recidivism (Aos, Miller, and Drake 2006; Lipsey 2009; MacKenzie and Freeland 2012). Boot camps are part of the more general trend to "get tough" on crime.

Another approach is **wilderness programs**, in which youths are placed in situations in which they must learn survival skills and rely on one another to succeed. These programs can be either short term or long term and can take a variety of forms, including sailing trips, wagon trains, or back-country camps. The underlying idea is to build self-esteem and show the youths that hard work and perseverance pay off. Implicit in the approach is that the skills and self-esteem developed in the program can be transferred back into the daily lives of the youths. Although research on these approaches is relatively limited, Lipsey and Wilson (1998) argue that wilderness experience programs have little or no impact on recidivism rates and that youths who participate in these interventions recidivate at comparable levels to those who are processed through other juvenile correctional programs. In addition, these programs can be very costly, and there have been problems, including serious injuries and even death.

Deinstitutionalization

One of the strongest policy recommendations made by the President's Commission in 1967 was to deinstitutionalize many of the youths held in secure juvenile facilities. One underlying rationale for this suggestion was the fact that many incarcerated youths were there for status offenses and not violations of the criminal law. A second argument was that there was little evidence that institutionalization was effective at correcting the problems of youths. Perhaps the strongest argument favoring **deinstitutionalization** was the belief that involvement in the formal justice system was criminogenic, meaning that youths would be more prone to criminal behavior after system intervention than before.

The move toward deinstitutionalization was codified in the 1974 Juvenile Justice and Delinquency Prevention Act. A major part of this legislation was to remove status offenders from any form of secure confinement. The rationale for this was twofold. First, mixing status offenders and serious delinquents has the potential of causing the status offenders more harm than good. Second, status offenders have committed no transgressions against other individuals; rather, they have exhibited behavior that may lead to further problems. Given the possible criminogenic effects of system intervention, it would be in the best interests of the youths to keep them out of any institutional placement. Interestingly, this legislation could not directly force states to deinstitutionalize status offenses because the states have the legislative authority over this matter. In order to influence the states, the legislation withheld federal monies from jurisdictions that failed to deinstitutionalize status offenders. In 2015, roughly 2,300 youths were held in residential facilities for status offenses, representing less than 5 percent of those in facilities (Sickmund et al. 2017).

Several states, including Massachusetts, Maryland, Missouri, California, Illinois, Ohio, New York, and Texas, have taken steps to close state training schools. Massachusetts incarcerates less than 15 percent of the youths sent to the state by the courts. California went from incarcerating 10,000 youths in 1996 to incarcerating 1,200 in 2010 (Bonnies et al. 2013). Nationally, the number of youths in residential placement dropped more than 50 percent between 1999 and 2015. Youths are now placed in alternative community programs or in settings run by private agencies under contract with the state authorities.

The deinstitutionalization movement has resulted in mixed outcomes. In terms of cost efficiency, the alternatives used in place of residential placement are significantly cheaper. The impact on recidivism, however, is not as positive. Various evaluations show that the recidivism rate has not significantly changed as a result of deinstitutionalizing youthful offenders. Although the move toward deinstitutionalization has been effective at reducing the numbers of youths in confinement, particularly status offenders, the move has not resulted in lower recidivism rates.

COMMUNITY INTERVENTIONS

At the outset of the juvenile justice system in 1899, community interventions were the preferred method for dealing with youths in need of assistance. There were no residential institutions under the control of the court, and the court relied on probation as the primary means of dealing with youths in need of help. Keeping juveniles at home and in the community was considered the best way of helping children.

Probation

The most common form of community intervention today is probation. Roughly 60 percent of all delinquent youths processed through the juvenile court end up being placed on probation. In addition, many more youths handled informally are also placed under some form of probation supervision.

Web Activity

Information on the adjudication offenses for youths placed on probation can be found on the textbook website (http://www.oup.com/us/labessentials).

Probation departments are active throughout the juvenile system and often fulfill the duties of intake, staff and administer local detention facilities, run informal intervention programs, develop social history reports (the juvenile system equivalent of a presentence investigation), and make recommendations to the judge on dispositions, as well as supervising and working with youths placed on probation. Much of the supervision revolves around making certain that the youths remain in school; obey the law; become involved in prosocial activities; as well as fulfill any orders to complete counseling, make restitution, or participate in other treatment programs. In general, probation in the juvenile justice system mirrors the process in the adult system. The major difference, however, should be a greater emphasis on providing treatment and aid to youths and a reduced interest in simply monitoring and enforcing rules.

Aftercare

Juvenile justice also has a form of parole, commonly referred to as **aftercare**. Aftercare differs from probation mainly by the fact that youths in aftercare have spent some amount of time in secure facilities and are being released back into the community. Many of the rules, regulations, and programming available in aftercare are identical to those found in probation, with supervision being the most important component. Due to the similarity between probation and aftercare, in many communities aftercare is provided by the probation department. Both probation and aftercare use many of the same treatment ideas, including reality therapy, behavior modification, an emphasis on educational achievement, and vocational training.

Reentry Concerns

Community supervision, particularly as aftercare, faces many problems with **reentry** for those youths returning to the community. Youths who have been separated from society need to be reintegrated to normal daily activities when they are released and return home. Studies on reentry programs and other interventions have not found a clear-cut or simple answer to what makes for successful reentry. However, the research does indicate some suggestions for success. First, mental health services can reduce recidivism. Second, mentoring is related to reduced recidivism, reductions in positive drug tests, and more connections to educational and employment services and mental health treatment (Nellis 2009).

Issues in Supervision

Although supervision appears to be a straightforward idea, there are a number of competing factors that make it a very difficult task for both probation and aftercare. The traditional view of supervision in the juvenile justice system has emphasized the *parens patriae* goals of providing benevolent assistance to youths and their families. Supervision is supposed to help youths identify problematic behavior and uncover means to overcome the problems and issues that push or pull them into delinquency. This approach is sometimes referred to as a "social worker" approach that attempts to find solutions to the problems underlying the behavior.

At the same time, there is a growing tendency to "get tough" with the youths. Rather than work to help youths, supervision becomes a means of watching for violations and sanctioning youths for additional transgressions. Supervision, therefore, is little more than another method used under a punitive model of juvenile justice. Probation officers and aftercare workers act as extensions of the police and seek to justify ways of placing youths into secure residential institutions.

An emerging middle ground for supervision is the balanced approach. Under this approach, probation or aftercare workers are responsible for addressing youths' needs while simultaneously taking the safety and security needs of the larger community into account. Typical responses under the balanced approach include restitution, community service, counseling, rehabilitation, and punishment. Officers are expected to identify the correct mix of the competing philosophies (*parens patriae*, retribution, restorative, etc.) to use with each youthful offender.

Although it may appear reasonable to use elements of a wide range of philosophies and approaches when addressing juvenile misconduct, this situation causes a great deal of anxiety for system workers. What is the correct approach to use with each individual juvenile? What interests are to be emphasized and when (e.g., youth or society)? What training is the most appropriate for the job? What does the community really want (e.g., retribution or rehabilitation)? How should the impact of supervision be evaluated (e.g., arrests, convictions, number of counseling sessions, or improved grades in school)? These and many other questions and issues form the basis for role confusion and discontent for many probation officers and aftercare workers.

Questions of the effectiveness of community interventions are similar to those found with institutional interventions. Many programs have exhibited positive results for some youths, especially when the program has been properly implemented and the proper amount of intervention has been applied. What has not been found is any one program that works all the time. In general, programs tend to be time and place specific.

SPECIAL TOPICS

The juvenile justice system must deal on a regular basis with a wide range of issues and topics related to youthful misbehavior. Some of the more prevalent issues are gang behavior, restorative justice, and capital punishment. There have also been calls to eliminate the juvenile justice system. Although space does not permit a full discussion of these issues, each is briefly addressed in the following paragraphs.

Gangs

Gangs have a long history in the juvenile justice system. A major reason for this is the observation that youths tend to commit offenses when in the company of other youths. Some authors have suggested a **group hazard hypothesis**, which claims that society responds to group transgressions more than to individual violations (Erickson 1973).

The study of juvenile gangs dates back to work done in Chicago in the 1930s. Since that time, a wide range of definitions for a gang have emerged, and writers have not settled on a single definition. Typical definitions include reference to a group that identifies itself as a gang, has a name, is recognized by outsiders as a gang, participates in criminal activity, and has some degree of permanence. Curry and Decker (1998) offer six elements as common to most definitions of a gang. First, there is typically a minimum number of members for the group.

Second, gangs typically have symbols that can be used to identify them, including certain clothing, colors, or hand signs. Third, gangs also are demarcated by both verbal and nonverbal forms of communication, such as hand signs and graffiti. Fourth, there is a degree of permanence to the gang, typically lasting a year or more. Fifth, gangs often claim territory. Finally, and perhaps most important, gangs are involved in criminal behavior.

Many jurisdictions have passed laws specifically dealing with gangs and gang behavior. Forty-four states and the District of Columbia have statutes defining a gang. Fourteen states define a gang member (National Gang Center 2016). Typical elements of statutory definitions are criminal activity, a pattern of criminal activity, a hierarchy or leadership structure, an alliance or understanding among members, and some common name or symbol (Barrows and Huff 2009).

Although not all gangs look alike, there are some common features of most gangs. Most gangs draw youths from the lower classes, are racially homogeneous, offer their members a sense of belonging and status, and are dominated by youths in their late teens. The degree of organization and the behavior of gangs vary considerably, although most gangs are involved in some type of criminal activity. Physical aggression or the willingness to use physical force has long been a cornerstone of gang activity, although in recent years this aggression has increasingly been expressed using firearms, resulting in the death of combatants. Drive-by shootings, or forays, have become a recognized part of gang violence in many cities.

The extent of gang membership is also difficult to assess. From 1996 to 2012, the National Gang Center conducted annual surveys to assess gang membership and activity. According to the 2012 survey, there are almost 30,000 active gangs with roughly 850,000 members operating in U.S. cities (Egley, Howell, and Harris 2014). The numbers of gangs and gang members vary greatly from area to area, but gangs appear in virtually all areas of the country.

Critical Thinking Exercise

Information on gangs and characteristics of gang members is routinely gathered by the National Gang Center. Examine the information from the National Youth Gang Survey at https://www.nationalgangcenter.gov/About/Surveys-and-Analyses.

Interventions with gangs have taken a variety of forms. In 1993, Spergel and Curry identified five common intervention strategies (Table 7.6): suppression, social intervention, organizational change and development, community organization, and opportunities. Although law enforcement respondents to a national survey indicated that opportunities provision was the most promising

Table 7.6 Gang Intervention Strategies

Suppression	Any form of social control in which the criminal justice system (police, courts, or corrections) or society attempt to impose formal or informal limits on behavior
Social intervention	Basically a social work approach to working with gangs in the neighborhoods (e.g., detached worker programs)
Organizational change and development	Altering the organizations that respond to gang problems, such as establishing gang units or offering specialized training to its personnel
Community organization	Mobilizing the community toward self-improvement and change, including both physical and social alterations
Opportunities provision	Recognizing the lack of meaningful jobs and the training needed to succeed, and taking steps to change the problems; education, vocational training, and job placement are elements

SOURCE: Spergel, I. A., and G. D. Curry. (1993). The National Youth Gang Survey: A research and development process. In A. P. Goldstein and C. R. Huff (Eds.), *The Gang Intervention Handbook*, 359–400. Champaign, IL: Research Press.

response to gangs, it is the least used. Suppression is the most common response but is considered the least effective (Spergel and Curry 1993). Vigil (2010) argues that effectively responding to gangs and gang problems requires a balanced strategy incorporating elements of prevention, intervention, and law enforcement. This means creating solutions that address the economies of the area, sociocultural factors surrounding youths, and the sociopsychological marginality of the youths (Vigil, 2010).

Among the methods used to address gangs and gang behavior are detached worker programs, statutory changes, deterrence strategies, and the G.R.E.A.T. program. **Detached worker programs** place gang workers into the community and free them from heavy paperwork and administrative responsibilities. The workers are supposed to spend time with the gangs and try to redirect their activities to those that are noncriminal. Although these programs are able to organize noncriminal activities and enhance contact with the gangs, there is evidence that they inadvertently increase gang cohesion among the members and actually make the gangs more attractive to youths.

Statutory changes attempt to make gang membership a crime, such as California's Street Terrorism Enforcement and Prevention Act of 1988 (the STEP Act). These statutes typically enhance civil penalties and injunctions against gang members associating with one another and congregating in public. Local jurisdictions may establish or enhance specialized gang units to enforce these new laws. Another innovative use of legal codes to fight gangs is to employ civil, rather than criminal, codes. **Civil abatement** procedures can be used to control or eliminate locations that gang members frequent or own (Cristall & Forman-Echols 2009). When an address is identified as a gang headquarters or hang-out, the police and civil authorities, including health departments and building code enforcement, will bring lawsuits in civil court against the owners that can result in eviction and/or property forfeiture. Injunctions against gang members can also be used to order them to stay away from the property. In a similar manner, **civil gang injunctions** involve court orders that prohibit certain behaviors linked to criminal activity. These orders may prohibit gang members from associating in public, marking territory, trespassing, loitering, or other similar activities. These injunctions are typically aimed at specific gangs/gang members, locations, and activities (Hennigan and Sloane 2013).

Deterrence strategies have received a great deal of attention in recent years. These typically involve suppression efforts along the lines of the **Boston Gun Project**, which used an approach called **pulling levers**. Pulling levers sought to deter behavior by taking a zero-tolerance response with regard to any transgressions by any member of a gang. The entire gang was held responsible for the acts of all its members. The Boston Gun Project resulted in a 63 percent reduction in homicides, a 25 percent reduction in assaults with firearms, and a 32 percent reduction in the number of shots fired (Braga et al. 2001). Replications of this approach in Indianapolis, Indiana, Cincinnati, Ohio, Stockton, California, and Lowell, Massachusetts, have found similar positive effects.

A final well-known intervention is the **G.R.E.A.T. (Gang Resistance Education and Training)** program, in which police officers teach anti-gang, anti-violence lessons in middle schools. The goal is to provide youths with the skills to identify high-risk situations and resist the peer pressure and allure to take part in gangs and gang activity. The program is geared toward increasing self-esteem, changing attitudes, and eliminating violent behavior. Conflict resolution is the key part of the program. A recent national evaluation of the program reports positive results, including increased refusal skills, better resistance to peer pressure, less gang membership, and more negative attitudes about gangs (Esbensen et al. 2013).

Unfortunately, the evidence on the effectiveness of interventions with gangs and gang members does not suggest strong positive results. Most methods appear to have little impact on criminal and deviant behavior. Some of the failure may be attributable to the fact that many programs fail to target the key causes of gangs and gang behavior and are poorly implemented. Indeed, most interventions tend to try to suppress gang behavior through arrest and prosecution rather than attacking the underlying causes of gangs and gang activity: the lack of social opportunities, the lack of jobs, poor education, and other key factors.

Restorative Justice

Given the recent debate over the proper goal of the juvenile justice system—whether to emphasize rehabilitation or punishment—it is not surprising that the idea of restorative justice has become more popular. **Restorative (reparative) justice** seeks to use interventions that return victims, offenders, and communities to their pre-offense states (Bazemore and Maloney 1994). The basic premise of restorative justice is that crime is the result of complex factors that are beyond the ability of the criminal code to address on its own. Restorative justice programs seek to bring offenders, victims, and various members of the community together to identify the types and levels of harm suffered, allow victims to express their concerns about the crimes and their losses, and allow offenders to explain why they committed the acts. The ultimate goals are to identify ways to repair the harm done to victims, help victims heal, restore communities to their pre-crime states, and reintegrate offenders into society.

Although restorative justice take various forms, **family group conferencing** (FGC) is especially targeted at youthful offenders. FGC came to prominence in 1989 when New Zealand removed all youths aged 14 to 17 years from formal court processing and mandated that they be diverted to conferencing (Kurki 2000). Facilitators lead family members, close friends, and other support groups of the victims and offenders through a discussion of the facts of the cases, the impact of the events on all parties, the feelings of all participants toward the actions and the offenders, and the development of mutually agreed-upon resolutions. FGC has become a part of police and pretrial diversion programs in many jurisdictions.

Evaluations of restorative justice show some promising results. Research uncovers high levels of satisfaction by those participating in FGC. However, the results are based only on those who volunteer to participate, so there is a built-in bias favoring FGC. In terms of recidivism, McGarrell et al. (2000) report a 40 percent reduction in recidivism for program youths compared to youths in regular juvenile justice programs. Similar recidivism findings appear in a range of other FGC evaluations. With the growing interest in using restorative justice approaches across the United States and other countries, it will be important to assess the potential of this approach.

Capital Punishment and Juveniles

The appropriateness of capital punishment for juveniles has been a matter of debate for several years. This is particularly true since the rise in lethal violence by youths in the late 1980s and early 1990s. Between 1973 and 2000, almost 200 individuals were sentenced to death for crimes committed when the offender was a juvenile, and 15 offenders were 15 years old at the time of the crime (Streib 2000). Prior to 2005, statutes allowing the imposition of the death penalty for individuals who committed their crimes when aged 16 or 17 years were permissible under the U.S. Supreme Court ruling in *Stanford v. Kentucky* (1989).

The legal status of the death penalty for youthful offenders was overturned in the case *Roper, Superintendent, Potosi Correctional Center v. Simmons* (2005). In the majority opinion, the Court noted that the "evolving standards of decency that mark the progress of a mature society" clearly indicate that imposing death on juveniles constitutes "cruel and unusual punishment" in violation of the Eighth Amendment. The Court noted that most states do not allow for the death penalty for juvenile cases, the majority of states with death penalty statutes for youthful offenders do not carry out the executions, and the prevailing international opinion is against the use of the death penalty for youths (*Roper v. Simmons* [2005]). After many years of debate, the death penalty is no longer an issue in relation to juvenile offenders.

Web Activity

Extensive information on the death penalty can be found on the Death Penalty Information Center's website at https://www.deathpenaltyinfo.org

---

THE FUTURE OF JUVENILE JUSTICE

A great deal of debate has occurred during approximately the past 30 years on the appropriate approach to dealing with problem youths and the form of the juvenile justice system. One major argument has been to "criminalize" juvenile court and to make it a scaled-down version of adult criminal court. A **criminalized juvenile court** would entail providing juveniles with all the procedural protections of criminal court. Thus, children would have the right to a jury trial and would have fully adversarial defense attorneys, not attorneys who often slip into the role of a concerned parent trading off zealous advocacy for promises of treatment. At the same time, it would be necessary to scale down penalties out of concern for the reduced culpability of children. The major problem with this suggestion is that it may not satisfy calls for a more punitive approach to juvenile offenders that imposes adult penalties for what some people perceive as adult offenses.

Critical Thinking Exercise

What impact would "criminalizing" the juvenile court have on youths and the juvenile justice system?

An alternative to basically eliminating the juvenile court is the idea of rebalancing the juvenile court (Bishop and Feld 2012). Rather than move toward a "get tough" approach, the court needs to balance *parens patriae* and the need to hold youths accountable for their actions. This argument fits with a softening of the "get tough" era. First, crime has declined and there are eased calls for harsh treatment of juveniles. Second, advances in both neuroscience and developmental psychology have provided scientific support for the proposition that youth are less mature and less responsible. Third, advocacy groups have worked to soften punitive demands of the "get tough" era. The National Research Council of the National Academies of Science recommends that juveniles be held accountable for offending but that condemnation, control, and lengthy confinement are not necessary to do so. Developmentally appropriate interventions should focus on implementing evidence-based programs and engage the youth's family and draw on neighborhood resources. There should also be an emphasis on procedural fairness and due-process rights.

One indication of the rebalancing has been a return to a lower bound of criminal court jurisdiction to age 18 years in several states. Other states have restricted the offense or offender criteria for transfer to the adult court (Daugherty 2013). Another indication is that the Supreme Court has ruled against life without parole sentences for youths convicted of non-homicide offenses (*Graham v. Florida*, 2010) and against mandatory life without parole sentences for juveniles (*Miller v. Alabama*, 2012).

Despite the calls for changes in juvenile justice, there remains an overriding belief in the need to help youths rather than punish them. Consequently, eliminating the juvenile justice system makes little sense. The adult system would have to make drastic changes if it were to assume responsibility for juvenile offenders. Many of the changes would probably mirror the current activities of the juvenile system. What is needed is a system that has the flexibility to guard the due-process rights needed to protect the accused and the power to use whatever intervention is in the best interests of both offenders and society. Clearly, the juvenile justice system will continue to undergo change, and that change may include moving closer to the adult system.

CONCLUSION

Juvenile offending raises special problems for society and agents of social control. Indeed, a separate system of justice has been in existence for more than 100 years to deal with problem youths. This system operates under a different philosophy from the criminal justice system, although many people have challenged the *parens patriae* philosophy in recent years. The juvenile system generally assumes that youths are in need of help rather than punishment and operates from the premise that the proper intervention can remove the causes of misbehavior. While many have called into question the effectiveness of the juvenile justice system and have called for more punitive responses to offending youths, others have argued for a more balanced approach that maintains *parens patriae* while emphasizing the safety of the community. It does not appear that the juvenile system is in danger of being abolished. Instead, it will continue to adapt to the competing demands being placed on it from various societal constituencies.

KEY WORDS

adjudication
aftercare
bail
behavior modification
blended sentencing
boot camps
Boston Gun Project
civil abatement
civil gang injunctions
concerned parent role
criminal law definition
day–evening centers
deinstitutionalization
delinquency
detached worker
 programs
detention
direct file
disposition
drug court

family group
 conferencing
G.R.E.A.T.
group hazard hypothesis
home detention
houses of refuge
informal adjustment
intake decision
judicial waiver
legislative waiver
Monitoring the Future
 Survey
National Youth Survey
nonsecure detention
nullification
once/always provisions
parens patriae
prosecutorial waiver
pulling levers
reentry

reformatories
restorative (reparative)
 justice
reverse waiver
secure detention
sexting
shock incarceration
state training schools
status offenses
statutory exclusion
teen court
token economy
transfer
Uniform Crime Reports
waiver
wilderness programs
youthful offender statutes
zealous advocate role

SUGGESTED READINGS

Empey, L. (1982). *American delinquency: Its meaning and construction*, Chapters 2–4. Homewood, IL: Dorsey Press.

Feld, B. (1993). *Justice for children: The right to counsel and the juvenile courts*. Boston, MA: Northeastern University Press.

Sickmund, M. (1994). *How juveniles get to criminal court: Juvenile justice bulletin*. Washington, DC: U.S. Department of Justice.

Torbet, P., R. Gable, H. Hurst, I. Montgomery, L. Szymanski, and D. Thomas. (1996). *State responses to serious and violent juvenile crime*. Washington, DC: Office of Juvenile Justice and Delinquency Prevention.

CHAPTER 8

Conclusion

CHAPTER OUTLINE

Criminal Justice and Discretion
Opioid Addiction and Responses
Technology and Social Media
Fiscal Austerity and Criminal Justice
Criminal Justice as a Processing System

After reading this chapter, you should be able to:

- Discuss how discretion is endemic throughout the criminal justice system
- Relate different points at which discretion appears
- Discuss the impact and challenges of opioid addiction on the system
- Outline technological changes impacting criminal justice
- Tell how fiscal austerity has affected the operations of the criminal justice system
- Discuss how criminal justice is a processing system influenced by different inputs

---

The criminal justice system is often viewed as a set of distinct subsystems included in addressing antisocial behavior in society. Indeed, each component contributes to social control. At the same time, similar themes/issues exist and emerge across the subsystems and impact the operations of the agencies and units that comprise the criminal justice system. Among these themes/issues are discretion, fiscal austerity, drug issues, and technology.

CRIMINAL JUSTICE AND DISCRETION

The criminal justice system is multidimensional, so we can think about it in different ways. For example, the system can be viewed as a series of interrelated discretionary decision points where citizens and criminal justice system actors make decisions about reported crimes and the future of suspects/defendants/offenders. For example, crime victims decide if they will report their victimization, police officers decide if they will arrest a suspect, prosecutors decide if (and how) to prosecute, and so on.

These decisions are made at different levels. At an individual level, each actor decides how to act, given a range of possible actions. There are usually multiple choices available to actors. Judges sentencing convicts usually choose from a range of supervision types (probation, intensive supervision probation, boot camps, or prison), the length of supervision, and the conditions (e.g., whether or not the convict will be required to attend substance abuse treatment as a condition of supervision).

Discretionary decisions are also made at an organizational or aggregate level. Jurisdictions rely on different balances of actions and options, and some may not have options that others do (e.g., boot camps or a secure detention facility for juveniles). For example, one jurisdiction may rely on community corrections options, such as probation and parole, to a greater extent than another. One court jurisdiction may plea bargain more cases than another.

Discretionary decision-making by actors is not without constraints. Both policy and substantive law limit and guide how these discretionary decisions are made by system actors. Decisions are also constrained and molded by local norms of appropriate behavior for actors. For example, police officers resort to physical force more often in some jurisdictions than in others. Most organizations exhibit informal, unwritten occupational norms of conduct for their employees, such as the police subculture. Because these norms and subcultures are unwritten, they are difficult to change via formal methods, such as changing a law, crafting a written organizational policy, or holding formal training programs. Although difficult to see and difficult to change, these informal norms have a powerful influence over system actors. At the end of the day, there is still significant latitude in discretionary decision-making despite the constraints imposed by policy, law, and local norms.

OPIOID ADDICTION AND RESPSONSES

The topic of drugs and crimes related to drugs has a long history in criminal justice. Indeed, at many points in time, "drugs" have been the cornerstone of both discussion and crime policy. It is easy to illustrate this point using events from the past half century. President Nixon identified drugs as one of the top issues facing the United States. Of particular importance was the rise in narcotic drug use coinciding with the return of military veterans from Vietnam. This became known as a "war on drugs." In the late 1980s and early 1990s, another war on drugs emerged focused largely on cocaine, crack cocaine, and the gang violence that accompanied the drugs. The recent past has seen the reemergence of an opioid epidemic that has led to significant numbers of deaths, largely due to the use of heroin laced with fentanyl.

Despite the recognition that drug use is a health and addiction problem, the criminal justice system remains on the front lines for addressing the problem. The police are the first ones called to address drug use and abuse, and corrections is faced with housing and treating convicted offenders. In between, the courts process drug users and drug crimes following statutes primarily aimed at punishment and deterrence.

Drug deaths have hit an all-time high, and the police are on the front line in responding to the problem. In 2016, there were roughly 64,000 opioid deaths in the United States, which reflects an increase of more than 20 percent from the previous year. Fentanyl deaths were up more than 500 percent during a three-year period, while heroin deaths increased roughly 400 percent from 2010 to 2016 (Katz 2017). The number of deaths from prescription opioids almost equals the number of deaths from heroin. On August 10, 2017, the opioid crisis was declared a national emergency.

The police are often the first responders to drug overdose situations. The police are expected to take appropriate action to assist overdose victims, despite the fact that they are not trained medical personnel (e.g., a doctor, nurse, or emergency medical technician). Due to the huge increase in opioid overdoses, some law enforcement officers have received training in the use of naloxone, which is a prescription drug that quickly reverses the impact of opioids, thus restoring normal respiration and reviving the person who has overdosed. The police typically use a nasal spray version of naloxone known as Narcan. It is not unusual for an overdose victim to need multiple administrations of Narcan to counteract the opioid's effect.

The growth in opioid addiction and the use of naloxone to counteract the impact of opioids have given rise to a number of questions and new problems. First, does the availability of an "antidote" prompt greater use of opioids? It is not unusual for the same individuals to be revived multiple times for an opioid overdose. This fact has prompted some to question whether the ready availability of naloxone actually increases the use of heroin and other opioids. Second, how many times should an individual be revived? The police often revive the same person multiple times. This has led some departments to set policies limiting the repeated revival of the same individuals. In turn, such limitations raise issues of how to maintain databases on past revivals that are readily accessible to officers on the street and how many doses of naloxone should be administered in a single overdose event. Both of these issues require law enforcement to develop new policies and procedures.

A third set of issues is related to the emergence of "good Samaritan" laws related to drug overdoses. These laws have emerged in more than 40 states and generally prohibit the arrest or prosecution of individuals in a drug overdose situation in which the crime would be considered a minor drug possession offense and the individual agrees to seek out assistance for his or her addiction. In Ohio (and many other states), this simply means the individual will seek out screening and referrals for treatment. Individuals who agree to this will have their case dismissed. Actually undergoing treatment is not a requirement, and follow-up to document the assessment and referral rarely takes place. This immunity from arrest and prosecution is typically limited (in Ohio, it can only happen twice). The major problems with this system are the inability to follow up on individuals' compliance (databases documenting these events typically do not exist) and the fact that individuals do not have to actually undergo treatment.

Although these issues with opioid overdoses and the use of naloxone appear to be problems that must be dealt with primarily by law enforcement, they actually impact the entire criminal justice system. The police are the first responders and make the first decisions on what to do. The prosecution and the court have the option of tracking and pursuing legal action and recommending/imposing appropriate sentences from punishment to treatment. Both correctional institutions and community corrections have to handle clients who are addicted and face treatment needs. Finally, society has to decide how to address drug use and addiction and to what extent the criminal justice system is to be on the front line of providing drug treatment to those who overdose on drugs.

TECHNOLOGY AND SOCIAL MEDIA

As discussed at different points in this text, technology plays an important role in criminal justice and is constantly evolving. This is not a new situation. The introduction of cars to police patrol was a giant step in using emerging technology. The move to radios from police call boxes is another early example of technology making a change in how the criminal justice system operates. The introduction of new technologies has increased in momentum since 2000 and can be seen throughout the operations of the criminal justice system—from the police to the courts and corrections.

The increase in the use of police body cameras is perhaps the most recognized enhancement in police technology in recent years. This move has been partly a response to the increased use of mobile phones by citizens to document police behavior and the use of force in police–citizen encounters. Many of those events have made their way onto the evening news and have prompted citizen disputes with police actions, sometimes involving violence. The police often point out that the citizen films fail to show the entire event and have responded by issuing body cameras and requiring officers to use them to document the entire encounters with citizens.

The police use both public media (i.e., television, radio, etc.) and social media to solve crimes and gain citizen support of their efforts. Crime Stoppers solicits the public for information about criminal events by showing pictures of wanted individuals or re-enactments of crimes (typically on television). There are roughly 1,200 Crime Stoppers programs throughout the world that have cleared more than 1.6 million cases since its inception in 1976 (Crime Stoppers International 2015). In recent years, social media such as Facebook, YouTube, Twitter, blogs, podcasts, and other tools have been used by police to solicit help to solve crimes. The International Association of Chiefs of Police (2014) notes that 94 percent of law enforcement agencies are using some type of social media to enhance their crime-solving abilities and to encourage public participation in prevention activities.

The courts have also embraced new technologies. Video arraignments and the use of distance technologies for other preliminary hearings are becoming commonplace in many jurisdictions. Instead of transporting accused individuals who are being held in jail to the courthouse for every hearing and appearance, the accused sits in a room at the jail that has been outfitted with a video camera while the judge (and often other court actors such as attorneys and court reporters) remains at the courthouse and the entire proceeding takes place "online." This saves time and cost associated with transportation and personnel time, and it allows for processing more cases. Another use of technology by the courts is to enhance the place of victims in the court process and proceedings. Given the orientation of the system to protect the rights of offenders, victims are often ignored or relegated to an afterthought. The system often fails to keep victims notified of important events regarding their cases, including case dates, sentencing hearings, and parole hearings. One major effort to address these problems has been the development of the Statewide Automated Victim Information and Notification (SAVIN) program. This system allows victims and witnesses to identify how (and if) they want to be kept notified about every event related to a case's processing. This system uses automated phone and email notifications.

The correctional system has also embraced technology. Perhaps the best example is the use of electronic monitoring systems (EMS). EMS technology is an enhancement of home confinement that responds to the lack of space to hold in jail everyone awaiting trial and the need for greater supervision for those released on probation or parole after conviction. This technology dates to the late 1980s, but it was initially limited due to the use of landline phone technology and the cost of the systems. Although cost is still a concern, the technology has advanced in a number of ways, making use of EMS more palatable. EMS are no longer tied to wired phone systems; they typically use wireless phone technology. Another recent innovation making EMS more useful is the coupling of EMS to global positioning system (GPS) technology. The use of GPS allows EMS to track the exact location of the individual in real time or retrospectively. EMS are used in countries throughout the world, and more than 110,000 individuals are on EMS in the United States (DeMichele and Payne 2009).

As technology changes, its impact on the criminal justice system will continue to grow. Advances in technology have increased in speed during the past several decades, and there is no indication that they will slow down. Indeed, it is likely the opposite will occur and impact individuals, agencies, and society in multiple ways. Certainly, the move to a cashless society has opened the way to new forms of theft, including general identity theft. The criminal justice system can also use the new technologies to improve its functioning and protect society.

FISCAL AUSTERITY AND CRIMINAL JUSTICE

Currently, two social forces intersect in ways that impose fiscal austerity on criminal justice systems. The first is economic: The fragile economy that resulted from, and persists beyond, the 2008 collapse in the financial sector has severely curtailed the tax revenues available to the public sector at all levels. The second is political: There is a broad movement to reduce public services that is partly ideological and partly a result of the economic crisis.

Privatization had made inroads into the state's monopoly over the criminal justice system well before the current economic crisis. Burgeoning prison populations resulted from the "get tough on crime" ideology of the 1980s and 1990s. One of the first resorts of states with excess inmate populations was to send their prisoners to other states with unused beds and cells. (This is slightly different from the informal policy of "bus therapy," sending troublesome prisoners from place to place to disrupt their criminal activities and social networks.) The rise of private prisons coincided with "outsourcing" in the private sector and the use of contractors for logistical support services (among others) by the military.

Sending prisoners to privately run facilities was not only consistent with the reigning political ideology of the time but also made it possible to shift costs away from the state. This can be done in many ways. First, shifting work to the private sector avoids the expensive pension systems of unionized state workers. Second, this shift moves other expenses (e.g., food and utilities) to a private bidding system outside public scrutiny. Third, the private sector can build facilities unencumbered by the demands of state bidding rules and regulations, thus speeding up the process and saving funds. In 2017, however, issues concerning safety and cost-effectiveness led to a federal decision to cease contracting with private prisons.

More recently, privatization has begun to affect policing as well. The use of private police officers tends to be an augmented service, with their jurisdiction overlapping that of the public police and sheriffs' departments. They are often employed by gated communities or resorts or other recreational areas. To date, none has played a significant role in municipal policing in any larger jurisdictions. Unlike their private security predecessors, however, private police are certified law enforcement officers, empowered by their respective state with powers of arrest. Although their jurisdiction tends to be linked contractually to the property rights of their employers, they are "real" police officers, better trained and more professional than the "rent-a-cop" stereotype of security guards.

To this point, "private" courts are restricted to the traditional tribal and ecclesiastical venues, not general criminal justice matters. The restorative justice movement often provides an alternative to public court proceedings, but always with the authorization of the courts. Prosecution remains a possibility should restorative efforts fail or one of the parties choose to withdraw from the process.

Fiscal austerity affects the entire criminal justice system, as well as the social agencies that work with system clientele. The federal largesse of previous decades has shriveled: Although operational grants are still available through the Bureau of Justice Assistance, and the National Institute of Justice still provides research and seed money for innovation, far fewer funds will be available for special projects such as DUI checkpoints.

Police are already taking drastic steps to maintain core services in the face of austerity. Many tasks once done by sworn officers have been "civilianized" or outsourced. Dispatch services are mostly performed by civilians, and in many cases they are regional rather than locality based. Crime scene security and prisoner transport duties are conducted by private companies. Increasingly, crime scene technicians are specialists rather than uniformed police officers.

State and local agencies are also affected by deferred maintenance programs, reduced training, fewer equipment upgrades, reduction in benefits, hiring freezes, and even layoffs. Prosecutors' offices have fewer equipment costs, but loss of investigator positions and clerical staff can curtail case preparation, in turn curtailing options for plea negotiations.

Fiscal austerity on the part of states and localities is already disrupting the traditional fixed-benefit pension systems of generations past, even though the private sector abandoned them decades ago. Although union contracts have held firm to the model because of their political clout, a tipping point may arrive when defined benefits give way to defined-contributions packages in the public sector as well. Another benefit issue is the cost of medical insurance, and that is also still in flux at the state and national levels. The attractiveness of benefits packages affects the pool of potential candidates, possibly mitigating other potential advantages (e.g., a better educated workforce in public service) of the contemporary jobless recovery.

It is not just the formal criminal justice agencies that are affected by economic austerity: The social services agencies that formally or informally are partners in the justice system are being affected as well. Victims' services, prisoner reintegration programs, and rehabilitation services are all vital to the overall effectiveness of the system. As the public's willingness to fund "soft" services deteriorates, there is a tendency to revert to the older investment in punishment as a crime deterrent, despite the lack of clear evidence of its effectiveness and the lack of funds to carry out punishment (whether incarceration or effective community supervision) on the scale called for in the "get tough on crime" era.

CRIMINAL JUSTICE AS A PROCESSING SYSTEM

How society controls crime is suggested by the different philosophies of criminal justice. These philosophies sometimes contradict each other, and most policies are usually a balance of different philosophies. Such contradiction is unavoidable in a democracy, but discretionary decision-making allows criminal justice actors to implement these sometimes competing policies while at the same time the system still functions. Usually, these philosophies are enacted by legislators as substantive laws. Procedural laws prescribe the methods by which governmental bodies may enact laws and are important because they limit many of the government's powers and thus dictate and constrain the creation and implementation of criminal justice policy. Lawmaking is in turn influenced and constrained by local politics, the media, and public sentiments and voting patterns.

Citizens are the true gatekeepers of the criminal justice system. When they choose to report crimes is a reflection of their belief/philosophy on what society should address. Their actions serve as the inputs for the system. Police officers and police agencies make discretionary decisions concerning what laws need to be enforced and when to make arrests. These decisions by police officers and agencies are influenced by the communities they serve and by laws and policies. Multiple courts and jurisdictions mean there are differences in the policies that are created and the decisions made. Prosecutors decide when to release an arrestee without charge or to press charges and when to engage in plea bargaining. Judges and defense attorneys, with their different backgrounds and institutional allegiances, influence the court process and the cases and sentences that result from court action. Prisons, jails, and community corrections all face different forces that influence their actions and beliefs about their roles. Their policies and decisions are influenced by the philosophies of criminal justice (e.g., the value of rehabilitation as opposed to incapacitation). These philosophies compete with each other for resources and sometimes contradict each other. Compromises often result as actors carry out competing mandates in their day-to-day work.

Discretion, fiscal austerity, emerging drug issues, and technology all play a role in the day-to-day processes of the different criminal justice components. At the same time, each agency/component brings issues, beliefs, and philosophies to the decision-making process. In the end, what we view as the criminal justice system is a complex web of social interactions among a myriad of system actors and the thousands of criminal justice organizations, as the system pursues multiple, competing, and sometimes contradictory goals. Philosophies are crafted into laws and policies, system actors strive to implement these laws and policies via their discretionary decisions, and all of this takes place within an ever-changing set of societal issues and demands.

GLOSSARY

actus reus The "act" of a crime, usually an overt act or act of omission.

adjudication In the juvenile court, the counterpart to finding guilt or innocence and sentencing in the adult court.

administrative law Law that is created and enforced by administrative bodies.

adversarial system A system, like the criminal justice system, in which two opposing parties (prosecution and defense) work with a neutral body (the judge) to determine the outcome of a case.

aftercare The juvenile justice system equivalent to adult parole.

alternative dispute resolution An alternative to the traditional criminal court, in which victims, offenders, and others work together to settle disputes outside of the criminal justice system.

appeal The opportunity for defendants to challenge their convictions, sentences, and other issues in order to ensure that their cases were handled properly.

appellate courts Courts that do not have the jurisdiction to conduct trials. They hear cases on appeal from lower courts; they do not hold trials.

appellate jurisdiction Courts with this jurisdiction hear cases on appeal from lower courts; they do not hold trials.

arraignment Stage of a criminal case in which defendants are required to enter pleas to the formal charges against them, usually after a **preliminary hearing** or **grand jury hearing**.

assembly-line justice Term used to describe the fast and efficient movement of cases in and out of the court system.

assigned counsel A court-appointed attorney paid on a case-by-case or hourly basis to act as defense counsel.

back-door options Early release options such as parole to relieve prison overcrowding.

background checks A standard part of the hiring process in any law enforcement agency. Telephone and in-person contacts with references, criminal history checks, and the like are made to ensure that candidates have the appropriate ethics, mentality, and skills to perform a job and to verify that all information provided by the candidates' applications is accurate.

bail   A system requiring a guarantee by defendants to return for court dates. Judges decide whether defendants must pay a certain amount of money to be released prior to trial or must be detained due to flight risk, public safety, and so forth.

bailiffs   Typically, law enforcement officers who maintain order in the courtroom.

beat integrity   The philosophy and administrative priority of assigning specific officers to specific beats for long periods of time to develop a comprehensive knowledge of the area and establish positive working relationships with the residents and merchants there; replaced an older system that moved officers around to many beats, frequently or haphazardly, in order to reduce the opportunities for corruption.

behavior modification   A system that rewards positive behavior and punishes poor behavior as a means of changing or controlling behavior; typical approach used in institutions.

bench trial   A trial without a jury, in which a judge hears the evidence and renders a verdict in a criminal case.

bills of attainder   Policies that allow the imposition of punishment without a trial. This type of policy is unconstitutional according to the U.S. Constitution.

blended sentencing   A disposition that relies on both juvenile and adult systems, such as when a youth begins his or her disposition in a juvenile facility and is automatically transferred to an adult facility after reaching the age of majority.

blue wall of silence   The term for the refusal of police officers to report misconduct of other officers, usually out of a misguided sense of solidarity or a fear of social ostracism and denial of assistance ("backup") on duty. The blue wall is usually composed of non-offending officers who know of elements of the misconduct but refuse to "rat" on or testify against other officers, regardless of the seriousness of the offense, thus thwarting effective investigation of police misconduct and crimes committed by police officers.

boot camps   Sometimes called **shock incarceration**, boot camps are short-term programs that are supposed to handle first-time, nonviolent offenders. They operate on a military model, with strict rules and discipline, physical training and conditioning, and counseling and education.

Boston Gun Project   This project used an approach called **pulling levers**. Pulling levers simply sought to deter behavior by taking a zero-tolerance response with regard to any transgressions by any member of a gang. The entire gang was held responsible for the acts of all its members.

broken windows   An informal theory of police responsibility for controlling low-level disorders and the relationship of disorder to more serious crime. First advanced by James Q. Wilson and George Kelling in an article in *The Atlantic Monthly* in 1982, the hypothesis asserted that order maintenance should be the primary police focus, not serious felony crime; reductions in serious crime would follow the reestablishment of civil order in the neighborhoods.

burden of proof Level of proof needed to find a defendant guilty of a crime, to issue search warrants, and so forth (e.g., to obtain a conviction, a prosecutor must prove his or her case "beyond a reasonable doubt").

campus-based academies Police recruit training facilities that function like college campuses and are frequently located on such campuses. The academies may be self-contained, giving instruction only to new police officers, or may be part of an academic degree course of study, typically a two-year associate's degree. The instructional curriculum is similar to that of stress academies, but without the military boot camp trappings.

case attrition Cases disappearing from the criminal justice system by being dropped, dismissed, and so forth.

case law Law created by judges through their interpretation of other types of laws.

chain of command A term referring to the command and supervision of the police organization. It is the sequence through which orders are given and information is relayed.

challenge for cause A method of removing jurors during jury selection for a legally prescribed cause (e.g., being a relative of the victim).

citizen patrols Patrols of an area by citizens acting as eyes and ears for the police.

civil rights movement A long-standing attempt by the African American community to overturn the legal and social restrictions of "Jim Crow" segregation and the social attitude prevalent among Whites that Blacks were inferior (a legacy of slavery). Although the movement has been ongoing since the end of Reconstruction, it was most visible and powerful in the 1950s and 1960s, when televised conflicts with White police galvanized both the movement and attempts to reform the police.

civilian review A special process of handling complaints against police officers by having civilian boards, or mixed police and civilian boards, review the facts and adjudicate the complaint; highly unpopular with police officers. Civilian review boards (CRBs) may work in concert with Internal Affairs or independent of it; the scope of authority given to a CRB is determined locally through the political process. CRBs emerged from strong feelings of dissatisfaction with police internal review of complaints against "their own."

Classical school Eighteenth-century philosophy that contends that humans possess free will and are rational and thus make choices about how to behave. Advocates consider behavior a process whereby people weigh the costs of their actions and the benefits they expect to receive.

classification Review in which the needs and risk of the offender are evaluated to determine the best placement of that individual within the prison system.

close security A security classification representing a middle ground between **maximum** and **medium security**. Facilities with this classification may be used for individuals convicted of violent offenses who do not require a maximum-security setting or disruptive inmates who do not pose as great a physical threat to inmates or staff.

collateral attack A type of appeal that allows a prisoner to challenge a conviction or sentence after the first appeal is over.

common law English-based law that was known throughout the country and applied by local judges through the use of precedent.

community corrections The various sanctions and forms of supervision that occur within the community rather than in an institutional setting.

community-oriented policing The term devised for a reform movement that arose in the mid-1980s to ease racial tensions and increase police effectiveness in minority neighborhoods. The thrust of the movement was to break down old prejudices by placing officers in regular contact with citizens in non-emergency settings, building better information about community events and conditions, building mutual trust, and creating effective problem-solving. The community-policing movement incorporates a wide range of tactical deployments, from walking beats to crime prevention activities and community organizing. One of the features that distinguishes community policing from traditional law enforcement is a focus on a range of noncrime problems broadly known as "quality-of-life issues," in which police advocacy and leadership play more important roles than law enforcement.

community supervision A general term to denote a variety of circumstances and sanctions requiring an offender to abide by specific conditions in order to remain in the community rather than being placed in an institutional setting.

CompStat A management initiative of the New York City Police Department (NYPD) under Commissioner Bill Bratton in the 1990s. Named for a column in a crime statistics database, CompStat involved the use of up-to-date crime information to reinvigorate the NYPD's command staff's commitment to crime reduction. It was also criticized for the sometimes adversarial nature of the central administration's challenges to the precinct commands. The term CompStat has become synonymous with data-driven approaches to crime control and police accountability.

concerned parent role This approach often leads attorneys to push youths to admit to petitions in order to secure the help and assistance of the court.

conditions of supervision The specific requirements imposed by a court or correctional authority that an offender must agree to and abide by to remain in the community.

confidentiality In self-report surveys, a condition in which the identity of a respondent is known by the researcher, but the researcher does not reveal that individual's identity. In confidential situations, the information from a respondent can be traced back to an individual. Note that confidentiality differs from anonymity.

consent decrees Formal contracts between the U.S. Department of Justice and local agencies or corporate entities to correct unlawful conditions. Usually an alternative to civil rights suits, consent decrees set out timetables and corrective measures to bring the agencies in line with acceptable practices.

constable An ancient English office of local police authority, with mandatory service on a rotating, annual basis under the 1285 Statute of Winchester; in contemporary America, a local office often attached to the court for service of papers and other writs; in modern-day England, a form of address to a police officer.

constitutional law Law that is found in the U.S. Constitution and the various state constitutions.

contract cities Local municipalities that contact with the county sheriffs for a specified number of hours of service. Contracts guarantee basic police services while relieving smaller cities of part of the expense of maintaining their own departments.

convict leasing A Southern development that spread throughout the United States, where inmates were contracted out to work in the stone quarries and coal mines during the industrial era of punishment.

correctional officers Individuals who supervise inmates in an institutional setting, sometimes referred to as guards.

corruption Generically, the misuse of a position of authority for personal gain. Police corruption in particular takes a variety of forms, from passive acceptance of gratuities to actively seeking bribes to accepting money from crime figures to destroy evidence or reveal police information. A subset, "corruption of noble cause," has emerged to describe the use of illegal means to achieve a legitimate crime-control end, with no personal benefit to the officers.

courtroom workgroup The collection of people who work in and around courthouses. The term *workgroup* is used because these people are employed by different organizations (prosecutor's offices, public defender's offices, probation, corrections, etc.) and the membership changes often, usually from one defendant's case to another.

crime-control model Philosophy of criminal justice that contends that the most important goal of the criminal justice system is to suppress crime. This goal is best achieved via the aggressive and quick apprehension, trial, and processing of criminals.

crime prevention A series of related actions, often promoted by the police, that reduce individual or collective risk of crime victimization. Target hardening through the use of locks or barriers, personal self-defense, property-marking records that reduce the resale value of stolen goods, collective actions such as Neighborhood Watch or other community organizing, educational programs in schools, and many more all fall under the crime prevention label.

crime rate The number of crimes committed (or reported to authorities), usually expressed as the number of events per 1,000 or 100,000 people (or residents) per year.

criminal law definition A delinquent is any juvenile who violates the criminal code.

cruel and unusual punishment Prohibits not only barbarous modes of punishment, such as the rack and thumb screws, but also any punishment that is grossly disproportionate to the crime at hand.

dark figure of crime   Term used by criminologists to refer to the total number of unreported crimes.

day–evening centers   Provide educational programming, treatment programs, or other activities during the day, but send the youths home at night.

day reporting centers   Nonresidential programs that require offenders to report on a daily or very frequent basis to a reporting center.

deadly force   That force that has the potential for causing the death of an individual being apprehended.

death penalty   Sanction that is reserved for the most serious offenders utilized in 38 states and in the federal system.

defense attorneys   Attorneys with the job of defending the accused against prosecution by the government.

deinstitutionalization   The release of individuals in secure care back into the community for supervision or outright release.

delinquency   Term referring to juvenile misbehavior that could refer to criminal acts or status offenses.

deprivation model   Explains the formation of prison subcultures and adaptation to the prison environment such that the nature and impact of an individual prison's culture over its residents will vary across prisons and among residents.

detached worker program   This type of program sought to place gang workers directly with the gangs in the communities. The workers were to spend time with the gangs and try to redirect their activities to noncriminal behavior.

detectives   Investigators who do not answer calls. Their time is spent interviewing witnesses and following up on leads in unsolved crime cases. Detectives may specialize in a certain type of crime (homicide, burglary, robbery, sex crimes, etc.) or conduct all kinds of criminal investigation.

detention   In the juvenile system, it is the counterpart to the bail decision in adult court.

detention centers   Facilities designed to hold a variety of offenders for a relatively brief period of time, usually for less than one year.

determinate sentencing   Also referred to as "flat" or "fixed" sentences, results in a defendant knowing how long his or her sentence will be when a judge imposes it.

deterrence   Contends that punishments should prevent crime by making potential offenders aware of the costs of crime. In effect, potential offenders will know that punishment will ensue if a crime is committed; thus, they will refrain from engaging in crime. Deterrence argues that the costs of crime outweigh its benefits.

deviance   Human behaviors or actions that are considered by others to be wrong, bad, or inappropriate.

discretion   It is not possible to write a law, or a rule, that will cover every possible situation the police might encounter. The police combine their knowledge with the array of verbal and nonverbal information that attends each unique situation, make an accurate judgment about what is going on (the "situational exigencies"), and decide on the proper response.

disposition The equivalent to a sentence in an adult court.

district courts The trial courts of the federal system.

diversion programs Programs available for some first-time, youthful, and/or nonviolent offenders that temporarily stop the prosecution of their cases in exchange for participation in preapproved programs. Upon successful completion of a program, the original charges are dismissed.

domestic violence courts Created to address a number of problems faced by the courts in domestic situations. For example, many domestic violence cases involve divorce proceedings and/or child custody issues, which can result in numerous cases being brought before different judges.

double jeopardy Constitutional provision that prohibits multiple prosecutions for the same offense.

drug courts Courts that focus on rehabilitation and treatment for drug offenders instead of criminal punishment.

dual court system Represented by the various state court systems and the federal courts. Individuals may be prosecuted by either state or federal courts (and sometimes both).

dual-disorder inmates Inmates who can be classified as having both substance abuse and mental health problems.

dual-entry tracks A term most often applied to progressive sheriffs' departments that hire separately for jail deputies and for patrol (road) deputies. It replaces the older "single-entry" system in which all deputies began their careers as jail deputies and then moved up to patrol. *See also* **single-entry tracks**.

due-process model As opposed to the **crime-control model**, a model of criminal justice that emphasizes procedures and guidelines that the government must follow in order to adjudicate defendants.

due-process revolution Term applied to a series of famous court cases that provided criminal suspects protections from the government. The due-process revolution began in the early 1960s.

electronic monitoring Use of technology to monitor offenders who are released into the community before trial or as a condition of a home-confinement sentence.

ex post facto A retroactive law that is prohibited by the U.S. Constitution.

excessive bail Unreasonably high bail, prohibited by the Eighth Amendment to the U.S. Constitution.

excessive fines Financial punishment deemed to be disproportionate to the offense, prohibited by the Eighth Amendment to the U.S. Constitution.

exclusionary rule A constitutional protection for citizens against unlawful police actions; the rule requires that any evidence obtained illegally must be excluded from criminal trials. Originally a federal-level rule only, it was applied to the states and to local police departments in the landmark 1961 Supreme Court decision *Mapp v. Ohio*.

family group conferencing (FGC) Includes family members, close friends, and other support groups of the victims and offenders in mediation conferences.

Facilitators lead the participants through a discussion of the facts of the cases, the impact of the events on all parties, the feelings of all participants toward the actions and the offenders, and the development of mutually agreed-upon resolutions.

felony Term applied to the most serious of crimes (including murder, robbery, and rape). Felonies usually carry a possible prison term of greater than one year.

field training (officers and programs) A process by which a newly hired police recruit makes the transition from academy learning to the street, under the tutelage and observation of an experienced police officer. Most programs involve a gradual increase in responsibilities, a formal grading process, and a series of tests on duty to determine whether the new officer is in fact an appropriate hire for the agency or should be dismissed because of conditions not revealed by the initial hiring process.

fines Punishment that requires payment of a monetary sum to the court. Usually used in conjunction with probation.

first responders Public employees in the emergency services who are the first to be called to the scene of an emergency, including fire and EMS (emergency medical services, ambulance, and first-aid workers). Police patrol officers are considered first responders, whereas detectives and other investigators are not.

force continuum A training guide for police use of force, linking police levels of force to specific actions by the citizens.

Foreign Intelligence Surveillance Act (FISA) court Federal court created by Congress in the Foreign Intelligence Surveillance Act of 1978. This court has jurisdiction over electronic surveillance of foreign agents.

Fourteenth Amendment Due process clause specifies that no state shall "deprive any person of life, liberty, and property without due process of law."

front-door options Community-based sanctions that are used to relieve prison overcrowding.

FTO field training officer. *See* **field training (officers and programs).**

Gang Resistance Education and Training (G.R.E.A.T.) Program involves using police officers to teach anti-gang, anti-violence lessons in middle schools. The thrust of G.R.E.A.T. is to provide youths with the necessary skills for identifying high-risk situations and resisting the peer pressure and allure to take part in gangs and gang activity.

general deterrence A subtype of deterrence theory that predicts that those contemplating the commission of a crime will be influenced by their understanding of the certainty and severity of the punishment and the speed at which that punishment will be administered. General deterrence contends that when laws entail sufficient certainty and severity and the punishment is quickly meted out, potential criminals will not commit crimes.

grand jury A proceeding featuring citizens who assess a prosecutor's evidence in order to determine if there is enough evidence to proceed to trial.

group hazard hypothesis The claim that society responds to group transgressions more strongly than to individual violations; thus, youth gangs are singled out for intervention more often than individual offenders.

habeas corpus Protection that allows defendants to challenge the legality of their confinement or incarceration.

halfway houses A term usually used to describe facilities that house recently released inmates or inmates in the transition process of approaching full release and that assist with their transition back into the community. May be privately operated or state-run.

HAZMAT An acronym for "hazardous materials," a broad category of harmful substances ranging from toxic chemicals to explosives and nuclear waste. First responders who respond to HAZMAT emergencies require special equipment and training.

home confinement The restriction of offenders to their residences except for preapproved activities. May be enforced by the use of various electronic monitoring equipment that can assist officials in knowing offenders' whereabouts. Also known as "house arrest."

home detention Involves ordering youths to remain at home at all times, unless given permission by the court to leave the premises.

houses of refuge Early institutions handling youths in need, particularly the poor, which focused on education, skill training, religious training, hard work, and discipline.

hung jury The term used when a trial jury cannot come to a unanimous verdict.

impartial trial Protection aimed at ensuring an unbiased and neutral jury at trial.

importation model Suggests that the skills, experiences, and attributes that individuals bring with them into a prison environment affect the prison culture and the ability of an individual to adjust to that environment.

incapacitation A philosophy of criminal justice that argues that the role of the criminal justice system is to separate or segregate criminals from the rest of society in order to protect it. If known criminals are removed from society, advocates argue, there will be less crime. Unlike **retribution**, incapacitation does not view segregation as a form of punishment. Incapacitation also differs from **rehabilitation** in that it does not necessarily advocate treating offenders.

incorporation The process of requiring states to adopt the protections found in the federal Bill of Rights.

indeterminate sentencing A sentencing scheme that is characterized by a range of punishments; the exact amount of time served is determined by the parole board.

industrial era The period in correctional history when inmates spent their confinement involved in private and state industry craft- or factory-oriented labor, worked on state-run canal and road projects, and even constructed prisons.

informal adjustment Decision to handle youths in a manner that does not involve full formal court processing.

informal social control One of two methods by which society and the other individuals who make up society influence behavior (the other method is called *formal social control*). Examples of informal social control include staring, scorn, the cold shoulder, shunning, and telling people that they are doing something wrong. Societies rely very heavily on informal social control to keep people in conformity.

initial appearance The first appearance of a defendant before a judge after arrest, when the defendant is notified of the charges against him or her, a bail decision, and the right to counsel. Also known as *first appearance*.

intake decision The juvenile system's counterpart to filing charges or a grand jury indictment in the adult system; at intake the decision is made to file a petition with the court to hear the case or to handle the youth in another way.

intensive supervision probation A form of probation (or parole) that requires more frequent contacts between offenders and their supervising officers than regular probation and typically involves more conditions of supervision.

intermediate sanctions A general term used to describe a variety of sanctions that fall between regular probation and jail or prison in severity.

Internal Affairs A special investigative unit within a police department, charged with investigating complaints against police officers. The current trend is toward redefining the unit as an "Office of Professional Responsibility" or similar title; other, less printable names are applied to it by police officers under investigation.

jails Facilities designed to hold a variety of offenders for a relatively brief period of time, usually less than one year.

john details A form of sting operation directed against street prostitution in which undercover police officers pose as prostitutes to arrest "johns," men who solicit prostitutes for sex.

judges Individuals who are considered neutral figures among the courtroom workgroup. They make a number of decisions ranging from issuance of warrants to sentencing defendants.

judicial review The power of courts to declare laws unconstitutional.

judicial waiver Requires a waiver hearing in front of a judge who determines the suitability of removing the case to the adult court.

jurisdiction The authority of a court to hear a case; for instance, appellate courts have jurisdiction over appeals, but not trials.

jury trial *See* **trial by jury**.

just deserts Appropriate punishment for a crime; an element of retribution.

justification A defense to criminal liability that states that an offender was justified in committing a crime (e.g., self-defense).

Kansas City Preventive Patrol Experiment The first randomized test of police patrol's effectiveness as a deterrent of crime; preliminary results indicated that the number of police officers had little or no impact on crime or citizens' perceptions. Subsequent developments in the field, notably the Minneapolis Hot Spots of Crime experiment, have refocused the issue with different results.

law compliance The voluntary observance by citizens of the requirements of law.

law enforcement The application of deterrence, rapid response, investigation, arrest, and prosecution against those who would or do violate the criminal law. Also applied to violators of traffic laws and local ordinances.

legal aid A form of appointed counsel that is considered nonprofit and is usually found in larger cities.

legislative waiver/statutory exclusion The legislature has dictated, through a statute, that certain youths must be tried in the adult court—the juvenile court is excluded from hearing the case.

mala in se Behaviors that are considered inherently bad and must be prohibited and punished (e.g., murder).

mala prohibita Behaviors that are considered problematic but not necessarily bad (e.g., gambling).

master jury list A list of individuals in the community deemed eligible for jury service, usually those who are registered voters or who possess a driver's license. **maximum-security prisons** A prison classification that represents the highest level of security in many states, typically holding the most violent and disruptive prisoners in those jurisdictions without supermax facilities. Movement within such facilities is limited.

medium-security prisons A classification of prisons that hold a diverse inmate population and can have a variety of architectural styles. Inmates may have some degree of movement within the institutions during certain times of the day and participate in a range of activities.

mens rea The intent or "guilty mind" behind the commission of a crime.

mental capacity A defense to criminal liability in which offenders' mental states can reduce or absolve them of liability (e.g., insanity).

mental health courts Courts that work with corrections officials and the community to assist defendants who suffer from mental illness.

merit selection A from of judicial appointment in which a state governor selects a judge to serve a specified amount of time (usually one year) and asks voters to either retain or replace the judge at the end of that period.

minimum-security prisons A prison classification representing the most open and least restrictive type of institution. These facilities can house prisoners convicted of nonviolent offenses, those who pose a minimal security risk, and those nearing final release and allow the greatest freedom of movement for housed inmates.

Minneapolis Domestic Violence Experiment Project that provided evidence that arrests had a greater deterrent effect on subsequent marital violence than police believed, forging a new police response to a widespread social problem.

misdemeanor A class of less serious crimes, usually involving punishment of less than one year in prison. Misdemeanors often have different levels of seriousness (misdemeanor one, misdemeanor two, etc.).

M'Naghten rule Under this rule, individuals must prove that they were in such a state of mind that they could not know what they were doing or that they did not know that what they were doing was wrong.

Monitoring the Future Survey A self-report survey that includes many more serious offenses than earlier self-report surveys and elicits significantly fewer positive responses. It includes questions on hitting teachers, group fighting, use of weapons, robbery, and aggravated assault.

multi-jurisdictional task forces Composite organizations made up of representatives of law enforcement personnel from many agencies across a wide geographical area that may include representatives from state and federal agencies. Task forces concentrate on crime problems that extend far beyond the jurisdictional boundaries of any single agency, such as organized crime, drug distribution networks, and counterterrorist intelligence work. Sometimes called *regional task forces, multi-jurisdictional* is the current preferred term, recognizing federal and state participation.

mutual aid Formal agreements between and among police agencies to assist each other in times of need. A system of legal compacts that provide law enforcement authority and civil protection to officers who are called upon to assist in jurisdictions other than their own.

National Youth Survey (NYS) Self-report survey that included many more serious offenses than other surveys and elicited significantly fewer positive responses.

Neighborhood Watch An organization for citizens to work together for community-based self-help activities.

net widening Term used to describe circumstances in which a correctional program is inadvertently used for a larger or different population than the one originally intended.

new-generation jails (NGJs) Newer facilities, often built to replace or modify existing jails, that house fewer inmates in what are known as pods or modules that contain anywhere from 16 to 30 separate cells with one or two inmates per cell.

new-offense violations Criminal offenses that violate offenders' community-supervision sanctions.

nonpartisan election A method of electing state judges in which candidates do not indicate a party affiliation on the ballot.

nonsecure detention The placement of youths in group homes, halfway houses, foster care, or other community-based alternatives to a secure facility.

nullification Refusal to enforce the law and sanctions against children.

official statistics One of three types of data society gathers on crime. Official statistics are gathered by or from criminal justice institutions and usually involve crimes brought to the attention of these institutions. The most famous of these official statistics are the FBI's Uniform Crime Reports (UCR), which record the number of crimes reported to the police and the number of arrests police make. *See also* **self-report statistics** and **victimization studies**.

once/always provision   Once a youth has been adjudicated in adult court, the youth is permanently under the adult court's jurisdiction.

order maintenance   A form of police activity that targets conduct that is less serious than predatory crime but still disturbs the quality of life of citizens. Generally low-level police interventions encourage law compliance, but law enforcement techniques may be used when necessary to ensure general compliance with expected forms of conduct, such as "local rules" about the use of parks, loud music, self-expression through graffiti, and a wide range of other social expectations and violations.

original jurisdiction   Jurisdiction in which a court serves as the entry point for cases, typically for initial appearances, trials, and so forth.

pains of imprisonment   Deprivations faced by inmates to varying degrees while imprisoned, such as the loss of liberty, deprivation of goods and services, barring of heterosexual relations, limitations on autonomy, and concerns over personal security.

parens patriae   Basic philosophy of the juvenile court emphasizing a role of the state as parent. The philosophy grew out of the English Chancery Court, which was tasked with looking after the property rights of orphaned children, among other things.

parole supervision   The supervision of offenders who have been released from correctional institutions prior to the completion of their maximum terms of incarceration and must abide by their conditions of supervision to remain in the community. Used in jurisdictions with indeterminate sentencing.

partisan election   A method of electing state judges in which candidates indicate a party affiliation on the ballot.

patrol   A form of police deployment that puts officers on the streets as a visible presence, both to deter criminals and reassure law-abiding citizens and to discover crimes and unsafe conditions that require police intervention. Although most patrolling is done in police cars, other types of patrol, such as motorcycles, bicycles, and foot patrols, are common.

penitentiary era   The period in correctional history when a formal penal system was developed that relied heavily on incarceration as punishment.

peremptory challenge   A method of removing jurors from the jury pool in which the prosecutors or defense attorneys do not specify reasons for the removal.

plea bargain   An agreement between the prosecutor and defense attorney, approved by the judge, in which a defendant pleads guilty to a charge in hopes of lenient treatment.

police academy   The "boot camp" for new or prospective police officers. A formal training setting in which the basic knowledge, skills, and responsibilities of police service are taught through formal instruction. Two models exist: **stress-based academies**, which emulate many features of the military boot camp, and **campus-based academies**, in which the training regimen is often integrated into an associate's degree program on the campus.

police subculture An outgrowth of studies of police in the 1960s, the concept of a "police subculture" assumes a broad allegiance to various philosophical beliefs and common concerns: danger, challenges to authority, political conservation (reactionary, in the 1960s), and the general division of the world into good and bad, with the police as a "thin blue line" separating tax-paying civilization from the anarchy of the criminal classes. In light of wholesale changes in the police occupation, including the inclusion of women and minorities and the changes in philosophy of **community-oriented policing** and **problem-oriented policing**, the assumptions of this notion are now being challenged.

political era A reference to the 19th-century climate under which the American police developed in the cities. Also known as the "patronage era" because of its corrupt politics. Notable for the low quality of police recruits and for the general absence of crime control as a police duty.

Positivist school The Positivist school of criminal justice contends that human behavior is influenced by external conditions and situations that are beyond individuals' control; things such as poverty and abusive parenting influence the likelihood that a child will grow up poor and abusive as well.

postconviction review A form of appeal undertaken after the first appeal of right in which defendants challenge the constitutionality of the case process.

power shifts Special time slots, usually spanning the late evening and early morning hours, when additional police officers are on duty to handle expanded call load. Power shifts are often volunteer slots, selected by officers because of the greater likelihood of activity. They tend to be permanent or semipermanent hours, although some flexibility is possible in many agencies.

precedent The judicial practice of relying on previous decisions to make current ones, in order for the law to be stable and consistent.

precincts Administrative division of police agencies containing multiple beats and patrol areas; refers to both a specific geographical area and the police personnel assigned to it. A feature of larger communities where central command is cumbersome, precinct organization allows for more responsive policing services and a tighter chain of command for everyday operations. Both patrol and investigative services may be precinct based, although support services and some investigative units may operate from a single, central command center.

preliminary hearing The stage in a criminal case in which a judge determines if there is enough evidence against a defendant to proceed to trial. Used in place of a grand jury if a grand jury is not convened.

presentence investigation A report produced at the request of the court to assist in determining the most appropriate sentence for a particular offender.

preservice training In some states, individuals are permitted to seek their police officer certification by putting themselves through a police training academy before being hired by an agency; completion of the training does not give them police powers, however, which are only bestowed once they are hired by a municipality or other jurisdiction.

President's Commission on Law Enforcement and the Administration of Justice A widespread investigation of the deficiencies and needs of the criminal justice system in America ordered by President Johnson. Its February 1967 report, *The Challenge of Crime in a Free Society*, galvanized reform efforts and contributed to the passage of the 1968 Omnibus Crime Control and Safe Streets Act and to the creation of the Law Enforcement Assistance Administration.

preventive detention Detention of a defendant pending trial because of a perceived risk to public safety.

principle of legality A principle of law that requires the existence of a law that prohibits conduct before a person can be found guilty of it.

prison A facility designed to hold offenders who have been convicted and sentenced to more than one year of incarceration of felony offenses.

prison programs Organized instruction designed to help offenders with rehabilitation, educational, and vocational needs and to guide the structure and activities involved in inmates' daily routines.

prison violence Coercive actions, threats made, and physical assaults against and between those living and working in prison.

prisoner reentry A general term used to denote a prisoner's transition from an institutional setting and the challenges in that process.

private police Uniformed security services that function as police protection for local interests. Some employ officers who have completed state-mandated police certification; others do not. The authority for private police typically derives from the property rights of their employers, but there are special legal provisions in some cases. Campus police officers serving colleges and universities, the Port Authority Police of New York and New Jersey Port Authority, railroad police, and others operate under particular legislative authorization.

private prison A correctional facility that is managed and operated by a private corporation.

pro bono A form of legal representation in which attorneys volunteer their time without compensation.

pro se A form of legal representation in which defendants serve as their own attorneys in court proceedings.

probable cause This standard is difficult to define, but the U.S. Supreme Court, in *Brinegar v. United States* (1949), provided a definition: Probable cause exists when "the facts and circumstances . . . [and] . . . reasonably trustworthy information [are] sufficient in themselves to warrant a man of reasonable caution in the belief that an offense has been or is being committed."

probation A form of community supervision in which an offender is allowed to remain in the community but must abide by certain restrictions, such as finding employment or abstaining from alcohol use.

problem-oriented policing An informal theory of police effectiveness first articulated by Herman Goldstein in 1979, which criticizes the police efforts at crime control as incident-based and emphasizing the means over the ends. It proposes the use of broader analysis to link multiple events that stem from common sources, redefining them as "problems" and bringing a wide spectrum of police and community resources to bear on the sources of the problem. The tactical equivalent is known as "problem-solving," and both are united under the acronym POP.

procedural law The "how" of the law that outlines procedures that government officials must follow when adjudicating defendants.

property marking Prevention technique in which owners mark their property for protection and return of the property if stolen.

prosecutorial waiver The decision to try a juvenile in the adult court is made by the prosecutor, who has sole discretion in the matter.

prosecutors Attorneys who represent the state against the accused in criminal cases and are responsible for charging defendants and presenting evidence of their guilt.

public defender A type of appointed counsel who provides indigent defense services only.

public trial Criminal proceeding open to the public, which acts as a "watchdog" over government practices. The right to a public trial is guaranteed by the Sixth Amendment to the U.S. Constitution.

pulling levers Pulling levers simply sought to deter behavior by taking a zero-tolerance response with regard to any transgressions by any member of a gang. The entire gang was held responsible for the acts of all its members.

punishment Response given to those who violate group norms, rules, and laws.

racial profiling A contested practice, denied by the police but asserted by minority communities, in which police aggressively stop Black and Hispanic motorists for trivial reasons in order to view and try to search their cars for drugs. It is premised upon an unsupported belief that minorities are more involved in the illegal drug trade than Whites.

rebuttal The chance to refute any evidence given by the other side.

reentry The transition period of persons soon to be or recently released from prison/jail back into the community. It involves providing services and assistance to these returning individuals and their families.

reform era The period in correctional history when a more humanitarian approach to the practice of incarceration was advocated. Practices such as purposeful labor, vocational and educational training, early release, and rewards for good behavior were utilized.

reformatories Early institutions for handling youths that largely supplanted houses of refuge. They focused on education, religious training, hard work, and discipline. **regional task forces** *See* **multi-jurisdictional task forces**.

rehabilitation A philosophy of criminal justice that views criminals as "broken" and seeks to "repair" them by reformation and treatment. According to supporters of rehabilitation, once reformed, criminals will no longer engage in crime. Examples of rehabilitation include drug treatment, mental health counseling, and job training.

rehabilitation era The period in correctional history that focused on the needs of individual offenders and relied less on prisons to carry out criminal sanctions. The medical model of treating offenders as if their offending was an illness that could be cured predominated the thinking of this era.

residential community correctional program A general term used to describe a facility that houses offenders (typically for six months or less) who were either sentenced to or placed in the program as a condition of their community supervision. There is a considerable diversity in the populations served by these programs, the types of programs available, and the freedom of movement afforded residents.

restorative (reparative) justice Programs that use interventions to return victims, offenders, and communities to their preoffense states. They generally involve the voluntary participation of offenders, victims, and community members in seeking an outcome acceptable to all parties. Also known as *reparative justice.*

retribution A philosophy based on the belief that criminals should be punished because they have violated the law and that the criminal justice system exists to punish wrongdoers. Punishment should be commensurate with the harm committed by the criminal (an "eye for an eye"), which is in accord with the beliefs of those who follow the Classical school. Retribution, however, does not punish in order to prevent potential criminals from committing crime. Rather, advocates of retribution argue that punishment is the proper and just thing for a society to do, regardless of its effectiveness in preventing crime.

retributive era The period in correctional history when the response to law violators was more severe penalties and decreasing support for rehabilitative efforts, including lengthier prison sentences, more punitive sanctions such as "three strikes, you're out," and attempts to limit the discretion of judges and correctional administrators who make decisions on sentence lengths.

reverse waiver Return by the adult court of a waived youth to the juvenile system for processing.

right to counsel Protection guaranteed by the Sixth Amendment to the U.S. Constitution that allows certain defendants the right to have attorneys assist them in their defense.

rotating shifts A means of providing around-the-clock police coverage in a manner that is fair to all employees. The burden of working the difficult hours of the midnight shift and weekends and the benefits of working days are equally distributed by assigning officers to work each shift in turn for a set period of time, then "rotating" or moving to another shift: days to evenings to midnights and then back to days to begin the cycle again. Rotating shifts tend to be defined in terms of weeks or months (usually no more than three months at the longest). Disruption of the "internal clock" of the body's circadian rhythm is one of the negative effects of rotating shifts. The alternative is **steady shifts** of longer duration.

safe havens Homes or businesses where youths can go for safety when they feel threatened, typically on the way to or from school.

school resource officers Sworn police officers who are assigned to schools or networks of schools, on either a full- or part-time basis. School resource officers usually work in uniform and monitor safety situations in the schools in addition to performing community-relations work with school-age children and with other school groups.

secure custody Involves several components: Prisons must ensure that they are physically secure and can prevent the likelihood of escape and the introduction of contraband into the institution; reduce the occurrence of inmate assaults on staff; limit the frequency of inmate-on-inmate violence; and secure the efficient functioning of an institution.

secure detention The equivalent in the juvenile system of the local jail for adults.

self-incrimination Protection found in the Fifth Amendment to the U.S. Constitution that specifies that an individual cannot be forced to confess to involvement in criminal activity.

self-report statistics One of three types of data collected on crime. Self-report statistics are gathered by asking people to report the number of times they have committed a crime during a set period of time. Self-report statistics are often better at discovering unreported crimes, victimless crimes, less serious crimes, and crimes where arrest is unlikely. *See also* **official statistics** and **victimization studies**.

sentencing guidelines Sentencing structures utilized in some states to determine sentences based on the offenses committed, the defendants 'prior records, and other information in order to create more fairness and equity in sentencing.

service An umbrella term for a wide range of police assistance to citizens (e.g., directions, emergency transportation, and escorts of funeral processions) that do not fall under either **law enforcement** or **order maintenance**.

sexting Involves the transmission of sexual images across an electronic medium.

sheriff The chief law enforcement officer of a country. Also, an ancient office, first developed in England. Also, an elected position and an office established in the state constitution of many states. Sheriffs' departments provide general policing services, court security and services, and correctional facilities of the country jail, although not all sheriffs' departments provide all three services.

shock incarceration Something used interchangeably with **boot camps** but can also refer to a program in which judges or correctional authorities are given the authority to grant early conditional release (often after less than 180 days' incarceration) to low-risk offenders who had been originally sentenced to a term of incarceration and place them on a form of community supervision for the remainder of their sentences.

single-entry tracks A phrase referring to the practice of starting all sworn employees of an agency at the same level: patrol officer in police departments and frequently jail officer in sheriffs 'departments. *See also* **dual-entry tracks**.

special conditions Conditions of community supervision that are tailored to the risks or needs of particular offenders and that are not used for all offenders in a jurisdiction. Common examples include drug treatment, work toward obtaining a GED, sex offender counseling, and the payment of restitution to a victim.

specialized prisons Facilities that primarily house inmates with specific characteristics that pose unique challenges to institutions, such as substances abusers, sex offenders, and mentally handicapped or psychiatric prisoners.

specific deterrence One of the two types of deterrence. Specific deterrence refers to the deterring effect of punishing a particular offender and argues that offenders who are punished for a crime will be less likely to commit that crime again because they will remember the punishment they received the first time. *See also* **general deterrence**.

speedy trial Protection found in the Sixth Amendment to the U.S. Constitution that guarantees that defendants have their trials commence within a certain amount of time after arrest.

split sentences Prisoners serve a period of probation following their release.

standard conditions Conditions of community supervision that are required for all offenders placed on community supervision in a given jurisdiction. Common examples include remaining law-abiding, reporting to their supervising officers as directed, and notifying their officers of changes in residence.

state patrols/highway patrols Primarily enforce traffic laws on state highways; they have police powers and training but no general police jurisdiction.

state police Police who have standard law enforcement duties and general jurisdiction throughout the state.

state training schools The juvenile justice system alternative to adult institutions.

status offense An action that is illegal only for juveniles. Typical status offenses include the use of alcohol or tobacco, curfew violations, truancy, disobeying one's parents, running away, and swearing.

statutory exclusion The legislature has dictated, through a statute, that certain youths must be tried in the adult court—the juvenile court is excluded from hearing the case.

statutory law The most common type of law, created by legislative bodies. Crimes and punishments are examples of statutory law.

steady shifts A means of providing around-the-clock police coverage that allows the body to adjust to shift work over longer periods, typically from six months to a year. Shift assignments are usually voluntary or assigned on a seniority-based lottery system. Officers spend a longer time on one shift.

sting operations Anti-crime tactics in which police officers pose as criminals in order to arrest other criminal actors and discredit criminal market areas. Sting operations include officers posing as drug dealers in known drug locations, posing as prostitutes in areas known for street prostitution or gay cruising, posing as fences for stolen property, and impersonating other market-driven criminal enterprises.

stress-based academics Police recruit training facilities that function in a manner similar to military boot camps, with a heavy emphasis on physical training, regimented military-style discipline, and residential settings. The instructional curriculum is similar to that of the alternate model, campus-based academics, which forgo the boot camp style of inducing stress in favor of other values.

strict liability Crimes that do not require **mens rea**, or intent, for an individual to be held liable.

substantive law The "what" of the law. Describes what the law is rather than how the law should be enforced (i.e., **procedural law**).

supermax prisons The most restrictive and secure prisons in the country, generally reserved for the most incorrigible and dangerous prisoners in a correctional system.

supervised release A term of supervision following a prisoner's mandatory release from prison. Although similar to parole, it is used in jurisdictions with **determinate sentencing** and does not involve a discretionary release by the parole authority.

supervision violations Violations of a condition of supervision. Depending on the seriousness of the violations, may result in consequences ranging from informal warnings to eventual revocation of offenders' community supervision and possible prison sentences.

technical violations Violations of conditions of supervision that do not involve the commission of new criminal offenses. Common examples include failure to pay financial conditions, failure to attend required treatment programs, or drug tests that indicate the use of illegal or prohibited substances.

teen courts (or youth courts) Courts based on the restorative justice philosophy, which seeks to help the offender, the victim, their families and friends, and society at large. These courts rely on youths to act as judges, attorneys, and jury members.

token economy Method for controlling or rewarding behavior in juvenile facilities. Youths receive points or tokens for acting appropriately and lose them for inappropriate behaviors. Tokens are good toward extra privileges or purchases from a store or vending machine.

transfer or waiver Process whereby youths are sent to the adult court for processing. It may take various forms, including judicial waiver, prosecutorial waiver, statutory exclusion/legislative waiver, or demand waiver.

transinstitutionalization Process whereby the mentally ill were first placed in secure confinement in a hospital setting, released, and then reconfined under the authority of the criminal justice system (i.e., prisons).

trial by jury Criminal proceedings heard by a jury made up of a defendant's peers. The right to a trial by jury is guaranteed by the U.S. Constitution but only applies to defendants facing six months' or more incarceration.

trial courts of general jurisdiction Usually, courts that handle felony trials.

trial courts of limited jurisdiction Courts that handle the early stages of criminal cases, such as first appearances, bail hearings, and so forth, as well as other cases such as traffic violations and minor civil actions.

troops Administrative divisions of a state police or state patrol agency, corresponding to "precincts" in local police departments. It refers to both a specific geographical area and the police personnel assigned to it.

Uniform Crime Reports (UCR) The most common official source of information on offending and offenders. The UCR reflects offenses that come to the attention of the police.

use of force A general power of the police, used to gain compliance when other measures such as persuasion and direction fail. Use of force is a broad term covering any physical contact initiated by police against a resisting citizen, from a guiding hand to a firm restraining grip; to the application of chemical sprays, stun guns, or impact weapons such as the nightstick; to the use of firearms. Use of firearms and some applications of impact weapons fall under the special category of **deadly force**, that which can produce death or serious bodily injury.

venire A group of individuals called for jury duty. After receiving a summons in the mail, these individuals must report to court for jury selection.

victimization studies One of the three types of crime data collected. Victimization studies ask people if they have been victims of a crime during a certain time period, and they mitigate some of the problems encountered by **official statistics** and **self-report statistics**.

victimless crime Class of crime in which there is no individual directly victimized, including crimes such as illegal drug use or underage drinking.

vigilantes Historically, groups of citizens on the American frontier who acted in concert to protect life and property against outlaws in the absence of formal law enforcement. In modern use, a pejorative term for those who "take the law into their own hands" rather than assisting authorized law enforcement.

voir dire The questioning of potential jurors during jury selection to screen out those who may not be appropriate (e.g., those who may be biased against the defendant or who may be relatives of the victim).

waiver A process whereby someone who is legally a juvenile is determined to be beyond the help of the juvenile justice system (also known as **transfer).**

wilderness programming Programs in which youths are placed in situations in which they must learn survival skills and rely on one another to succeed. Can be either short term or long term and can take a variety of different forms, including sailing trips, wagon trains, or back-country camps. The underlying idea is to build self-esteem and show the youths that hard work and perseverance pay off.

youthful offender statutes Provisions whereby the juvenile justice system can retain jurisdiction over individuals who were adjudicated in the system but have since passed the age of majority.

zealous advocate role Emulate the role of an attorney found in the adult criminal court. The training of most attorneys and the move to more due-process concerns has resulted in attorneys fighting for their youthful clients, even when they know the child is guilty and in need of the help that could be provided by the court.

REFERENCES

Abadinsky, H. (1997). *Probation and parole: Theory and practice*, 6th ed. Upper Saddle River, NJ: Prentice Hall.

Adams, K. (1992). Adjusting to prison life. In M. Tonry (Ed.), *Crime and justice: A review of research*, 275–360. Chicago: University of Chicago Press.

Aday, R. (2003). *Aging prisoners: Crisis in American corrections*. Westport, CT: Praeger.

Alemagno, S., E. Shaffer-King, P. Tonkin, and R. Hammel. (2004). *Characteristics of arrestees at risk for co-existing substance abuse and mental disorder*. Washington, DC: National Institute of Justice.

Alm, S. A. (2015). HOPE Probation and the new drug court: A powerful combination. *Minnesota Law Review, 99,* 1665–1696.

American Civil Liberties Union. (2012). *At America's expense: The mass incarceration of the elderly*. Retrieved from https://www.aclu.org/files/assets/elderlyprisonreport_20120613_1.pdf.

American Law Institute. (1962). *Model Penal Code*. Philadelphia: American Law Institute.

Anderson, J. (2003). *Public policymaking: An introduction*. Boston: Houghton Mifflin.

Andrews, D. A. (2006). Enhancing adherence to risk–need–responsivity: Making quality a matter of policy. *Criminology and Public Policy, 5,* 595–602.

Andrews, D. A., and J. Bonta. (2006). *The psychology of criminal conduct*. Cincinnati, OH: Anderson.

Andrews, D. A., I. Zinger, R. Hoge, J. Bonta, P. Gendreau, and F. Cullen. (1990). Does correctional treatment work? A clinically relevant and psychologically informed meta-analysis. *Criminology, 28,* 369–404.

Aos, S., M. Miller, and E. Drake. (2006). *Evidence-based public policy options to reduce future prison construction, criminal justice costs, and crime rates* (Washington State Institute of Public Policy Report No. 06-10-1201). Olympia, WA: Washington State Institute for Public Policy. Retrieved from http://www.wsipp.wa.gov.

Applegate, B., R. Surette, and B. McCarthy. (1999). Detention and desistance from crime: Evaluating the influence of a new generation jail on recidivism. *Journal of Criminal Justice, 27,* 539–548.

Argersinger v. Hamlin, 407 U.S. 25 (1972).

Arnold, E., P. Valentine, M. McInnis, and A. McNeece. (2000). Evaluating drug courts: An alternative to incarceration. In L. Mays and P. Gregware (Eds.), *Courts and justice: A reader,* 419–431. Prospect Heights, IL: Waveland.

Atkins v. Virginia, 536 U.S. 304 (2002).

Austin, J. (2014, April 5). *Key trends in national crime, arrests and jails* [Video file]. Retrieved from https://www.youtube.com/watch?v=kAKat5OPA18.

Austin, J., and J. Irwin. (2001). *It's about time: America's imprisonment binge,* 3rd ed. Belmont, CA: Wadsworth Thompson.

Barrows, J., and C. R. Huff. (2009). Gangs and public policy: Constructing and deconstructing gang databases. *Criminology and Public Policy, 8,* 675–704.

Batson v. Kentucky, 476 U.S. 79 (1986).

Bayens, G., J. Williams, and J. Smykla. (1997). Jail type makes a difference: Evaluating the transition from a traditional to a podular, direct supervision jail across ten years. *American Jails, 11,* 32–39.

Bazemore, G., and D. Maloney. (1994). Rehabilitating community service: Toward restorative service sanctions in a balanced justice system. *Federal Probation, 58,* 24–35.

Beck, A., and L. Maruschak. (2001). *Mental health treatment in state prisons, 2000.* Washington, DC: Bureau of Justice Statistics.

Belknap, J. (2001). *The invisible woman: Gender, crime, and justice.* Belmont, CA: Wadsworth.

Bennett, T., K. Holloway, and D. Farrington. (2008). The statistical association between drug misuse and crime: A meta-analysis. *Aggression and Violent Behavior, 13,* 107–118.

Berman, M. (2017, July 28). Trump tells police not to worry about injuring suspects during arrest. *The Washington Post.*

Bernfeld, G. A., D. P. Farrington, and A. W. Leschied (Eds.). (2001). *Offender rehabilitation in practice: Implementing and evaluating effective programs.* New York: Wiley.

Biderman, A. D., and A. J. Reiss. (1967). On exploring the "dark figure" of crime. *The Annals, 374*(1), 1–15.

Bishop, D. M., and B. C. Feld. (2012). Trends in juvenile justice policy and practice. In B. C. Feld and D. M. Bishop (Eds.), *The Oxford handbook of juvenile crime and juvenile justice,* pp. 898–926. New York: Oxford University Press.

Bittner, E. (1970). *The functions of the police in modern society: A review of background factors, current practices, and possible role models.* Cambridge, MA: MIT Press.

Black, D. (1981). *The manners and customs of the police.* New York: Academic Press.

Blackstone, W. (2002). *Commentaries on the laws of England.* Chicago: University of Chicago Press.

Blumstein, A. (1995). Crime and punishment in the United States over 20 years: A failure of deterrence and incapacitation? In P. Wikstrom, R. Clarke, and J. McCord (Eds.), *Integrating crime prevention strategies: Propensity and opportunity,* 123–140. Stockholm, Sweden: National Council for Crime Prevention.

Blumstein, A., and A. Beck. (1999). Population growth in U.S. prisons. In M. Tonry and J. Petersilia (Eds.), *Prisons,* 17–62. Chicago: University of Chicago Press.

Bond, B. (2001, April). Principals and SROs: Defining roles. *Principal Leadership,* 51–55.

Bonnies, R. J., R. L. Johnson, B. M. Chemers, and J. A. Schuck (Eds.). (2013). *Reforming juvenile justice: A developmental approach.* Washington, DC: National Academies Press.

Bonta, J., S. Wallace-Capretta, and R. Rooney. (2000). A quasi-experimental evaluation of an intensive rehabilitation supervision program. *Criminal Justice and Behavior, 27,* 312–329.

Bottomley, K. (1990). Parole in transition: A comparative study of origins, developments, and prospects for the 1990s. In M. Tonry and N. Morris (Eds.), *Crime and justice: A review of research*, 319–374. Chicago: University of Chicago Press.

Bottoms, A. (1999). Interpersonal violence and social order in prisons. In M. Tonry and J. Petersilia (Eds.), *Prisons*, 205–282. Chicago: University of Chicago Press.

Braga, A. A., D. M. Kennedy, A. M. Piehl, and E. J. Waring. (2001). *The Boston Gun Project: Impact evaluation findings*. Washington, DC: National Institute of Justice.

Breed v. Jones, 421 U.S. 519 (1975).

Brinegar v. U.S., 338 U.S. 160 (1949).

Brooks, K., and Kamine, D. (2003). *Justice cut short: An assessment of access to counsel and quality of representation in delinquency proceedings in Ohio*. Columbus: Ohio State Bar Association.

Brown, M. K. (1981). *Working the street: Police discretion and the dilemmas of reform*. New York: Russell Sage Foundation.

Brown, T. M. L., S. A. McCabe, and C. Wellford. (2007). *Global positioning system (GPS) technology for community supervision: Lessons learned*. Falls Church, VA: Noblis. Retrieved from https://www.ncjrs.gov/pdffiles1/nij/grants/219376.pdf.

Bureau of Justice Statistics. (2017). *NCVS victimization analysis tool*. Accessed December 9, 2017, from https://www.bjs.gov/index.cfm?ty=nvat.

Burke, P. (1995). *Abolishing parole: Why the emperor has no clothes*. Lexington, KY: American Probation and Parole Association.

Burruss, G. W., and K. Kempf-Leonard. (2002). The questionable advantage of defense counsel in juvenile court. *Justice Quarterly, 19,* 37–68.

Button, D. M., M. DeMichele, and B. K. Payne. (2009). Using electronic monitoring to supervise sex offenders: Legislative patterns and implications for community corrections officers. *Criminal Justice Policy Review, 20,* 414–436.

Butts, J. A., J. K. Roman, and J. Lynn-Whaley. (2012). Varieties of juvenile court: Non-specialized courts, teen courts, drug courts, and mental health courts. In B. C. Feld and D. M. Bishop (Eds.), *The Oxford handbook of juvenile crime and juvenile justice*, 606–635. New York: Oxford University Press.

Carp, R., and R. Stidham. (1990). *Judicial process in America*. Washington, DC: Congressional Quarterly Press.

Carp, R., R. Stidham, K. Manning, and L. Holmes. (2017). *Judicial process in America*. Thousand Oaks, CA: CQ Press.

Carroll, L. (1974). *Hacks, Blacks, and cons*. Lexington, MA: Lexington Books.

Carson, E. A. (2015). *Prisoners in 2014*. Washington, DC: Bureau of Justice Statistics.

Carson, E. A., and Anderson, E. (2016). *Prisoners in 2015*. Washington, DC: Bureau of Justice Statistics.

Carson, E. A., and W. J. Sabol. (2012). *Prisoners in 2011*. Washington, DC: Bureau of Justice Statistics.

Casey, P., and D. Rottman. (2005). *Problem-solving courts: Models and trends*. Williamsburg, VA: National Center for State Courts.

Center for Substance Abuse Treatment. (2005). *Substance abuse treatment for adults in the criminal justice system* (Treatment Improvement Protocol (TIP) Series 44). Rockville, MD: Substance Abuse and Mental Health Services Administration.

Clark, J. (2009, June 30). *U.S. and Europe jointly establish cyber-crime force*. Retrieved from https://www.wsj.com/articles/SB124632958157771629.

Clear, T., and H. Dammer. (2003). *The offender in the community*. Belmont, CA: Thompson Wadsworth.

Clear, T., P. Harris, and S. Baird. (1992). Probationer violations and officer response. *Journal of Criminal Justice, 20,* 1–12.

Cohen, S. (1985). *Visions of social control.* Cambridge, MA: Polity Press.

Coker v. Georgia, 433 U.S. 584 (1977).

Commonwealth v. Fisher, 213 Pa. 48 (1905).

Cooper v. Pate, 378 U.S. 546 (1964)

Conley, J. (1980). Prisons, production, and profit: Reconsidering the importance of prison industries. *Journal of Social History, 14,* 257–275.

Corbett, R. P., Jr. (2015). The burdens of leniency: The changing face of probation. *Minnesota Law Review, 99,* 1697–1733.

Covey, R. (2008). Fixed justice: Reforming plea bargaining with plea-based ceilings. *Tulane Law Review, 82,* 1237–1290.

Crank, J. P. (1998). *Understanding police culture.* Cincinnati, OH: Anderson.

Crime and Justice Institute. (2004, April 24). *Implementing evidence-based practice in community corrections.* Retrieved June 1, 2009, from https://nicic.gov/implementing-evidence-based-practice-community-corrections-principles-effective-intervention.

Crime Stoppers International. (2015). https://csiworld.org

Cristall, J., and Forman-Echols, L. (2009). *Property abatements—The other gang injunction: Project T.O.U.G.H* (National Gang Center Bulletin 2). Washington, DC: Bureau of Justice Assistance.

Cullen, F. T., S. M. Manchak, and S. A. Duriez. (2014). Before adopting Project HOPE, read the warning label: A rejoinder to Kleiman, Kilmer, and Fisher's comment. *Federal Probation, 78*(2), 75–77.

Curry, G., and S. Decker. (1998). *Confronting gangs: Crime and community.* Los Angeles: Roxbury.

Daugherty, C. (2013). *State trends: Legislative victories from 2011–2013 removing youth from the adult criminal justice system.* Washington, DC: Campaign for Youth Justice.

Death Penalty Information Center. (2017). *Death penalty in flux.* Retrieved from https://www.deathpenaltyinfo.org/death-penalty-flux.

DeMichele, M., and B. Payne. (2009). *Offender supervision with electronic technology: Community corrections resource,* 2nd ed. Washington, DC: U.S. Department of Justice. Retrieved from http://www.appa-net.org/eweb/docs/APPA/pubs/OSET_2.pdf.

Dentler, R. A., and L. J. Monroe. (1961). Social correlates of early adolescent theft. *American Sociological Review, 26,* 733–743.

Ditton, P. M. (1999). *Mental health and treatment of inmates and probationers.* Washington, DC: U.S. Department of Justice. Retrieved from https://www.prisonlegalnews.org/media/publications/bojs_mental_health_and_treatment_of_inmates_and_probationers_1999.pdf.

Döring, N. (2014). Consensual sexting among adolescents: Risk prevention through abstinence education or safer sexting? *Cyberpsychology, 8.* Accessed July 1, 2017, from https://doi.org/10.5817/CP2014-1-9

Downing, R. (2011). *Cybersecurity: Protecting America's new frontier.* Retrieved from https://www.gpo.gov/fdsys/pkg/CHRG-112hhrg71238/html/CHRG-112hhrg71238.htm.

Duff, R. A. (2003). Probation, punishment, and restorative justice: Should altruism be engaged in punishment? *Howard Journal of Criminal Justice, 42,* 181–197.

Egley, A., J. C. Howell, and M. Harris. (2014). *Highlights of the 2012 National Youth Gang Survey*. Washington, DC: Office of Juvenile Justice and Delinquency Prevention. Accessed June 1, 2017, from https://www.ojjdp.gov/pubs/248025.pdf.

Erickson, M. (1973). Group violations and officials delinquency: The group hazard hypothesis. *Criminology, 11,* 127–160.

Esbensen, F., D. W. Osgood, D. Peterson, T. T. Taylor, and D. C. Carson. (2013). Short- and long-term outcome results from a multisite evaluation of the G.R.E.A.T. program. *Criminology and Public Policy, 12,* 375–412.

Ex parte Hull, 312 U.S. 546 (1941).

Ex parte Crouse, 4 Wheaton (Pa.) 9 (1838).

Fagan, J. (1995). Separating men from the boys: The comparative advantage of juvenile versus criminal court sanctions on recidivism among adolescent felony offenders. In J. Howell, B. Krisberg, J. Hawkins, and J. Wilson (Eds.), *A sourcebook: Serious, violent, and chronic juvenile offenders,* 238–260. Thousand Oaks, CA: Sage.

Faiver, K. (1998). *Health care management issues in corrections.* Lanham, MD: American Correctional Association.

Federal Bureau of Investigation. (2012). *Crime in the United States, 2010.* Retrieved March 21, 2012, from https://ucr.fbi.gov/crime-in-the-u.s/2010/crime-in-the-u.s.-2010.

Feld, B. C. (1988). *In re Gault* revisited: A cross-state comparison of the right to counsel in juvenile court. *Crime and Delinquency, 34,* 393–424.

Feld, B. C. (2013). Adolescent criminal responsibility, proportionality, and sentencing policy: *Roper, Graham, Miller/Jackson* and the youth discount. *Law and Inequality, 31,* 263–330.

Fletcher v. Peck, 10 U.S. 87 (1810).

Florida Department of Corrections. (2017, July). Florida's community supervision population: Monthly status report. Retrieved from http://www.dc.state.fl.us/pub/spop/2017/spop-2017-07.pdf.

Fontaine, J., D. Gilchrist-Scott, J. Roman, S. Taxy, and C. G. Roman. (2012). *Supportive housing for returning prisoners: Outcomes and impacts of the retuning home—Ohio Pilot Project.* Washington, DC: Urban Institute, Justice Policy Center. Retrieved from https://www.urban.org/research/publication/supportive-housing-returning-prisoners-outcomes-and-impacts-returning-home-ohio-pilot-project

Freedman, E. B. (1984). *Their sisters' keepers: Women's prison reform in America, 1830–1930.* Ann Arbor, MI: University of Michigan Press.

Gaes, G., T. Flanagan, L. Motiuk, and L. Stewart. (1999). Adult correctional treatment. In M. Tonry and J. Petersilia (Eds.), *Prisons.* Chicago: University of Chicago Press.

Gaes, G., and W. McGuire. (1985). Prison violence: The contribution of crowding versus other determinants of prison assault rates. *Journal of Research in Crime and Delinquency, 22,* 41–65.

Galassi, A., E. Mpofu, and J. Athanasou. (2015). Therapeutic community treatment of an inmate population with substance use disorders. *International Journal of Environmental Research and Public Health, 12,* 7059–7072;

Garofalo, J., and M. McLeod. (1988). *Improving the use and effectiveness of Neighborhood Watch programs (NIJ Research in Action series).* Washington, DC: National Institute of Justice.

Gendreau, P. (1996). The principles of effective intervention with offenders. In A. T. Harland (Ed.), *Choosing correctional options that work: Defining the demand and evaluating the supply,* 117–130. Thousand Oaks, CA: Sage.

Gideon v. Wainwright, 372 U.S. 335 (1963).

Glaze, L. E., and D. Kaeble. (2014). *Correctional populations in the United States, 2013* (NCJ No. 248479). Retrieved from https://www.bjs.gov/content/pub/pdf/cpus13.pdf

Gleicher, L., S. M. Manchak, and F. T. Cullen. (2012). Creating a supervision tool kit: How to improve probation and parole. *Federal Probation, 77*(1), 22–27.

Gottfredson, M., and D. Gottfredson. (1988). *Decision-making in criminal justice: Toward the rational exercise of discretion*. New York: Plenum.

Gowdy, V. (2001). Should we privatize our prisons: The pros and cons. In E. Latessa, A. Holsinger, J. Marquart, and J. Sorenson (Eds.), *Correctional contexts: Contemporary and classical readings*, 198–208. Los Angeles: Roxbury.

Graham v. Florida, 560 U.S. (2010).

Gray, M. K., M. Fields, and S. R. Maxwell. (2001). Examining probation violations: Who, what, and when. *Crime and Delinquency, 47*(4), 537–557.

Gregg v. Georgia, 428 U.S. 153 (1976).

Guevara, L., C. Spohn, and D. Herz. (2004). Race, legal representation, and juvenile justice: Issues and concerns. *Crime and Delinquency, 50,* 344–371.

Guyot, D. (1979). Bending granite: Attempts to change the rank structure of American police departments. *Journal of Police Science and Administration, 7*(3), 253–284.

Haas, K., and G. Alpert. (1989). American prisoners and the right of access to the courts: A vanishing concept of protection. In L. Goodstein and D. MacKenzie (Eds.), *The American prison: Issues in research and policy*, 65–87. New York: Plenum.

Hagan, J., and R. Dinovitzer. (1999). Collateral consequences of imprisonment for children, communities, and prisoners. In M. Tonry and J. Petersilia (Eds.), *Prisons*, 121–162. Chicago: University of Chicago Press.

Hammett, T. (1998). *Public health/corrections collaborations: Prevention and treatment of HIV/AIDS, STDs, and TB*. Washington, DC: National Institute of Justice.

Harer, M., and D. Steffensmeier. (1996). Race and prison violence. *Criminology, 34,* 323–355.

Harland, A. (1998). Defining a continuum of sanctions: Some research and policy development implications. In J. Petersilia (Ed.), *Community corrections: Probation, parole, and intermediate sanctions*, 70–79. New York: Oxford University Press.

Harmelin v. Michigan, 501 U.S. 957 (1991).

Harris, M. (1996). The goals of community sanctions. In T. Ellsworth (Ed.), *Contemporary community corrections*, 13–33. Prospect Heights, IL: Waveland.

Hartwell, S. (2010). Ex-inmates with psychiatric disabilities returning to the community from correctional custody: The forensic transition team approach after a decade. In S. Burns (Ed.), *New approaches to social problems treatment*, 263–283. West Yorkshire, UK: Emerald Group Publishing.

Hawkins, R., and G. Alpert. (1989). *American prison systems: Punishment and justice*. Englewood Cliffs, NJ: Prentice Hall.

Hemmens, C., J. Worrall, and A. Thompson. (2004). *Significant cases in criminal procedure*. Los Angeles: Roxbury.

Hennigan, K. M., and D. Sloane. (2013). Improving civil gang injunctions: How implementation can affect gang dynamics, crime, and violence. *Criminology and Public Policy, 12,* 7–42.

Hindelang, M., T. Hirschi, and J. Weis. (1979). Correlates of delinquency: The illusion of discrepancy between self-report and official measures. *American Sociological Review, 44,* 995–1014.

Hockenberry, S., and C. Puzzanchera. (2017). *Juvenile court statistics, 2014.* Pittsburgh, PA: National Center for Juvenile Justice.

Hockenberry, S., A. Wachter, and A. Sladky. (2016). *Juvenile residential facility census, 2014: Selected findings.* Washington, DC: Office of Juvenile Justice and Delinquency Prevention. Retrieved from http://www.ncjj.org/Publication/Juvenile-Residential-Facility-Census-2014-Selected-Findings-.aspx.

Horwitz, A. (2010). The costs of abusing probationary sentences: Overincarceration and the erosion of due process. *Brooklyn Law Review, 75*(3), 753–790.

Hughes, T., and D. J. Wilson. (2002). *Reentry trends in the United States.* Washington, DC: U.S. Department of Justice, Bureau of Justice Assistance. Retrieved from https://www.bjs.gov/content/reentry/reentry.cfm.

In re Gault, 387 U.S. 1 (1967).

In re Winship, 397 U.S. 358 (1970).

International Association of Chiefs of Police. (2014). *2013 social media survey results.* Retrieved from http://www.theiacp.org/SearchResults/tabid/87/Default.aspx?Search=social%20media%20survey%20results.

Irwin, J. (1980). *Prisons in turmoil.* Boston: Little, Brown.

Jacobs, J. (1982). Sentencing by prison personnel: Good time. *UCLA Law Review, 30,* 217–270.

Jacobson, M. P., Schiraldi, V., Daly, R., and Hotez, E. (2017). *Less is more: How reducing probation populations can improve outcomes* (Papers from the Executive Session on Community Corrections). Retrieved from https://www.hks.harvard.edu/centers/wiener/programs/criminaljustice/research-publications/executive-session-on-community-corrections/publications/less-is-more-how-reducing-probation-populations-can-improve-outcomes.

James, D. J., and L. E. Glaze. (2006). *Mental health problems of prison and jail inmates.* Washington, DC: U.S. Department of Justice.

Johnson, H., and N. Wolfe. (1996). *History of criminal justice*, 2nd ed. Cincinnati, OH: Anderson Publishing.

Johnson, R. (2002). *Hard time: Understanding and reforming the prison.* Belmont, CA: Wadsworth.

Jolicoeur, M., and E. Zedlewski. (2010). *Much ado about sexting.* Washington, DC: National Institute of Justice.

Jones, M., and J. J. Kerbs. (2007). Probation and parole officers and discretionary decision-making: Responses to technical and criminal violations. *Federal Probation, 71*(1), 9–15.

Jordan, K. L., and Myers, D. (2011). Juvenile transfer and deterrence: Re-examining the effectiveness of a "get tough" policy. *Crime and Delinquency, 57*(2), 247–270.

Joyce, N. (1992). A view of the future: The effects of policy on prison population growth. *Crime and Delinquency, 38,* 357–368.

Justice Center. (2008). *Mental health courts: A primer for policy makers and practitioners.* New York: Justice Center/Council of State Governments.

Kaeble, D., and T. P. Bonczar. (2016). *Probation and parole in the United States, 2015* (NCJ 250230). Retrieved from https://www.bjs.gov/content/pub/pdf/ppus15.pdf.

Kaeble, D., and L. E. Glaze. (2016). *Correctional populations in the United States, 2015* (NCJ 250374). Retrieved from https://www.bjs.gov/content/pub/pdf/cpus15.pdf.

Katz, J. (2017, June 5). *Drug deaths in America are rising faster than ever. New York Times.* Retrieved from https://www.nytimes.com/interactive/2017/06/05/upshot/opioid-epidemic-drug-overdose-deaths-are-rising-faster-than-ever.html.

Kempinen, C. A., and M. C. Kurlycheck. (2003). An outcome evaluation of Pennsylvania's boot camp: Does rehabilitative programming within a disciplinary setting reduce recidivism? *Crime and Delinquency, 49,* 581–602.

Kent v. U.S., 383 U.S. 541 (1966).

Kleiman, M. A. R. (2015). Substituting effective community supervision for incarceration. *Minnesota Law Review, 99,* 1621–1630.

Kleiman, M. A. R. (2016). Swift–certain–fair: What do we know now, and what do we need to know? *Criminology & Public Policy, 15*(4), 1185–1193.

Klettke, B., D. J. Hallford, and D. J. Mellor. (2014). Sexting prevalence and correlates: A systematic literature review. *Clinical Psychology Review, 34,* 44–53.

Klingele, C. (2013). Rethinking the use of community supervision. *Journal of Criminal Law and Criminology, 103*(4), 1015–1069.

Klingele, C. (2015). What are we hoping for? Defining purpose in deterrence-based correctional programs. *Minnesota Law Review, 99,* 1631–1663.

Klockars, C. (1985). *The idea of police.* Newbury Park, CA: Sage.

Kurki, L. (2000). Restorative and community justice in the United States. In M. Tonry (Ed.), *Crime and justice: A review of research,* Vol. 27. Chicago: University of Chicago Press.

Kyllo v. U.S., 533 U.S. 27 (2001).

Lab, S. D. (2016). *Crime prevention: Approaches, practices, and evaluations,* 9th ed. New York: Routledge.

Langan, P., and D. Levin. (2002). *Recidivism of prisoners released in 1994.* Washington, DC: Bureau of Justice Statistics.

Larkin, P. J. (2015). Swift, certain, and fair punishment: 24/7 Sobriety and HOPE: Creative approaches to alcohol- and illicit drug-using offenders. *Journal of Criminal Law and Criminology, 105*(1), 39–94.

Latessa, E. J., S. J. Listwan, and D. Koetzle. (2013). *What works (and doesn't) in reducing recidivism.* New York: Routledge.

Latessa, E. J., and L. Travis. (1992). Residential community correctional programs. In J. Byrne, A. Lurrigo, and J. Petersilia (Eds.), *Smart sentencing: The emergence of intermediate sanctions,* 166–181. Newbury Park, CA: Sage.

Lattimore, P. K., D. L. MacKenzie, G. Zajac, D. Dawes, E. Arsenault, and S. Tueller. (2016). Outcome findings from the HOPE demonstration field experiment: Is swift, certain, and fair an effective supervision strategy? *Criminology & Public Policy, 15*(4), 1103–1141.

Lee, M., T. Crofts, A. McGovern, and S. Milivojevic. (2015). *Sexting among young people: Perceptions and practices* (Trends and Issues in Crime and Criminal Justice No. 508). Canberra, Australia: Australian Institute of Criminology.

Lipsey, M. W. (2009). The primary factors that characterize effective interventions with juvenile offenders: A meta-analytic overview. *Victims and Offenders, 4,* 124–147.

Lipsey, M. W., and D. Wilson. (1998). Effective intervention for serious juvenile offenders: A synthesis of research. In R. Loeber and D. Farrington (Eds.), *Serious and violent juvenile offenders: Risk factors and successful interventions, 313–344.* Thousand Oaks, CA: Sage.

Lounsbury, K., K. J. Mitchell, and D. Finkelhor. (2011). *The true prevalence of "sexting."* Durham, NH: University of New Hampshire, Crimes Against Children Research Center.

Lowenkamp, C. T., A. W. Flores, A. M. Holsinger, M. D. Makarios, and E. J. Latessa. (2010). Intensive supervision programs: Does program philosophy and the principle of effective intervention matter? *Journal of Criminal Justice, 38,* 368–375.

Lowenkamp, C. T., and E. J. Latessa. (2005). Increasing the effectiveness of correctional programming through the risk principle: Identifying offenders for residential placement. *Criminology & Public Policy, 4*(2), 263–290.

Lowenkamp, C. T., E. J. Latessa, and A. M. Holsinger. (2006). The risk principle in action: What have we learned from 13,676 offenders and 97 correctional programs? *Crime and Delinquency, 52,* 77–93.

Lowenkamp, C. T., E. J. Latessa, and P. Smith. (2006). Does correctional program quality really matter? The impact of adhering to the principles of effective interventions. *Criminology and Public Policy, 5*(3), 575–594.

Lurigio, A. J., A. Rollins, and J. Fallon. (2004). The effects of serious mental illness on offender reentry. *Federal Probation, 68*(2), 45–52.

Lurigio, A. J., and J. Petersilia. (1992). The emergence of intensive probation supervision programs in the United States. In J. Byrne, A. Lurigio, and J. Petersilia (Eds.), *Smart sentencing: The emergence of intermediate sanctions,* 3–18. Newbury Park, CA: Sage.

MacKenzie, D. L., and H. Donaldson. (1996). Boot camp for women offenders. *Criminal Justice Policy Review, 21,* 21–43.

MacKenzie, D. L., and R. Freeland. (2012). Examining the effectiveness of juvenile residential programs. In B. C. Feld and D. M. Bishop (Eds.), *The Oxford handbook of juvenile justice,* 771–798. New York: Oxford University Press.

Maguire, K., and A. Pastore. (2006). *Sourcebook of criminal justice statistics* [Online]. Retrieved March 22, 2012, from https://www.albany.edu/sourcebook

Mai, C., and R. Subramanian. (2017). *Price of prisons 2015: Examining state spending trends, 2010–2015.* New York: Vera Institute of Justice.

Makarios, M., and E. J. Latessa. (2013). Developing a risk and needs assessment instrument for prison inmates. *Criminal Justice and Behavior, 40*(12), 1449–1471.

Maltz, M. (1999). *Bridging gaps in police crime data: A discussion paper from the BJS Fellows Program.* Washington, DC: U.S. Department of Justice.

Mancini, M. (1978). Race, economics, and the abandonment of convict leasing. *Journal of Negro History, 63,* 339–340.

Mapp v. Ohio, 367 U.S. 643 (1961).

Marbury v. Madison, 5 U.S. 137 (1803).

Marciniak, L. M. (1999). The use of day reporting as an intermediate sanction: A study of offender targeting and program termination. The Prison Journal, 79(2), 205–225.

Martin, C., D. E. Olson, and A. J. Lurigio. (2000). *An evaluation of the Cook County Sheriff's Day Reporting Center Program: Rearrest and reincarceration after discharge.* Chicago: Illinois Criminal Justice Information Authority. Retrieved from http://www.icjia.org/assets/pdf/researchreports/An%20Evaluation%20Rearrest%20and%20Reincarceration%20After%20Discharge.pdf.

Martinson, R. (1974). What works? Questions and answers about prison reform. *The Public Interest, 42,* 22–54.

Maruna, S., and R. Immarigeon (Eds.). (2004). *After crime and punishment: Pathways to offender reintegration.* Portland, OR: Willan.

Maruschak, L. M. (2004). *HIV in prisons and jails, 2002.* Washington, DC: U.S. Department of Justice.

Mastrofski, S. D., J. B. Snipes, and A. E. Supina. (1996). Compliance on demand: The public's response to specific police requests. *Journal of Research in Crime and Delinquency, 35*(3), 269–305.

McBride, D., and C. VanderWaal. (1997). Day reporting centers as an alternative for drug-using offenders. *Journal of Drug Issues, 27,* 379–397.

McCleary, R. (1992). *Dangerous men: The sociology of parole,* 2nd ed. New York: Harrow & Heston.

McCollister, K., M. French, M. Prendergast, E. Hall, and S. Sacks. (2004). Long-term cost effectiveness of addiction treatment for criminal offenders. *Justice Quarterly, 21,* 559–679.

McCulloch v. Maryland, 17 U.S. 316 (1819).

McGarrell, E. F., K. Olivares, K. Crawford, and N. Kroovand. (2000). *Returning justice to the community: The Indianapolis juvenile restorative justice experiment.* Indianapolis, IN: Hudson Institute.

McGuire, J. (2001). What works in correctional intervention? Evidence and practical implications. In G. A. Bernfeld, D. P. Farrington, and A. W. Leschied (Eds.), *Offender rehabilitation in practice: Implementing and evaluating effective programs,* 25–43. New York: Wiley.

McKeiver v. Pennsylvania, 403 U.S. 528 (1971).

McMann v. Richardson, 397 U.S. 759 (1970).

Mendoza, M. (2011). *AT IMPACT: 35,000 worldwide convicted for terror.* Retrieved from http://www.sandiegouniontribune.com/sdut-ap-impact-35000-worldwide-convicted-for-terror-2011sep03-story.html.

Miller-Wilson, L. S., and P. Puritz. (2003). *Pennsylvania: An assessment of access to counsel and quality of representation in delinquency proceedings.* Washington, DC, and Philadelphia: American Bar Association Juvenile Justice Center and Juvenile Law Center in collaboration with the National Juvenile Defender Center and the Northeast Juvenile Defender Center. Retrieved from http://www.jlc.org/sites/default/files/publication_pdfs/PA%20Assesment%20of%20Access%20to%20Counsel.pdf.

Miller v. Alabama, 132 S. Ct. 2455 (2012)

Mitchell, K. J., D. Finkelhor, L. M. Jones, and J. Wolak. (2012). Prevalence and characteristics of youth sexting: A national study. *Pediatrics, 129,* 1–9.

M'Naughten's Case, 8 Eng. Rep. 718 (1843).

Morgan, K. (1996). Factors influencing probation outcome: A review of the literature. In T. Ellsworth (Ed.), *Contemporary community corrections,* 327–340. Prospect Heights, IL: Waveland.

Morris, N., and D. Rothman. (1995). *The Oxford history of the prison.* New York: Oxford University Press.

Morris, N., and M. Tonry. (1990). *Between prison and probation: Intermediate punishments in a rational sentencing system.* New York: Oxford University Press.

Mulvey, E. P., and C. A. Schubert. (2012). *Transfer of juveniles to adult court: Effects of a broad policy change in one court.* Washington, DC: Office of Juvenile Justice and Delinquency Prevention.

National Association of Youth Courts. (2017). https://www.youthcourt.net

National Campaign to Prevent Teen and Unplanned Pregnancy. (2009). *Sex and tech: Results from a survey of teens and young adults.* Retrieved from https://powertodecide.org/what-we-do/information/resource-library/sex-and-tech-results-survey-teens-and-young-adults.

National Education Association. (2016). *Ranking of the states 2015 and estimates of school statistics 2016.* Retrieved from http://www.nea.org/home/66703.htm.

National Gang Center. (2016). *Brief review of federal and state definitions of the terms "gang," "gang crime," and "gang member."* Accessed June 4, 2017, from https://www.nationalgangcenter.gov/Content/Documents/Definitions.pdf.

National Institute of Corrections. (2011). *Special challenges facing parole* (NIC 024200). Washington, DC: U.S. Department of Justice.

National Institute of Justice. (2003). *Correctional boot camps: Lessons from a decade of research.* Washington, DC: U.S. Department of Justice.

National Institute of Justice. (n.d.). *Restorative justice.* Retrieved from https://www.nij.gov/topics/courts/restorative-justice/welcome.htm

Nellis, A. (2009). *Back on track: Supporting youth reentry from out-of-home placement to the community.* Washington, DC: Juvenile Justice and Delinquency Prevention Coalition: The Sentencing Project.

Neubauer, D., and H. Fradella. (2014). *America's courts and the criminal justice system.* Stanford, CA: Stanford University Press.

New York State Division of Criminal Justice Services. (2008). *New York State probation population: 2007 profile.* Albany: NY Office of Justice and Research Performance. Retrieved from http://www.criminaljustice.ny.gov/pio/annualreport/nys_probation_report2007_profile.pdf.

Newman, S. A., J. A. Fox, E. A. Flynn, and W. Christeson. (2000). *America's after-school choice: Prime time for juvenile crime, or enrichment and achievement.* Washington, DC: Invest in Kids.

Niederhoffer, A. (1967). *Behind the shield: The police in urban society.* New York: Doubleday.

O'Connell, D. J., J. J. Brent, and C. A. Visher. (2016). Decide Your Time: A randomized trial of a drug testing and graduated sanctions program for probationers. *Criminology & Public Policy, 15*(4), 1073-1102.

Office of Juvenile Justice and Delinquency Prevention. (2017). *Statistical briefing book.* Retrieved from https://www.ojjdp.gov/ojstatbb

Ohio Department of Rehabilitation and Corrections. (2007). *Best practices tool-kit: Sex offender assessment and treatment.* Retrieved June 1, 2009, from https://kb.osu.edu/dspace/handle/1811/30140.

O'Neal v. Vermont, 144 U.S. 323 (1892).

Osterman, M. (2009). An analysis of New Jersey's Day Reporting Center and Halfway Back Programs: Embracing the rehabilitative ideal through evidence based practices. *Journal of Offender Rehabilitation, 48*(2), 139–153.

Packer, H. (1968). *The limits of the criminal sanction.* Stanford, CA: Stanford University Press.

Padgett, K. G., W. D. Bales, and T. G. Blomberg. (2006). Under surveillance: An empirical test of the effectiveness and consequences of electronic monitoring. *Criminology and Public Policy, 5,* 61–91.

Palko v. Connecticut, 302 U.S. 319 (1937).

Paparozzi, M. A., and M. DeMichele. (2008). Probation and parole: Overworked, misunderstood, and under-appreciated: But why? *Howard Journal of Criminal Justice, 47*(3), 275–296.

Paparozzi, M. A., and P. Gendreau. (2005). An intensive supervision program that worked: Service delivery, professional orientation, and organizational supportiveness. *The Prison Journal, 85,* 445–466.

Pease, K. (1999). The probation career of altruism. *Howard Journal of Criminal Justice*, *38*, 2–16.

People v. Turner, 55 Ill. 280; 1870 Ill.

Petersilia, J. (1997). Probation in the United States. In M. Tonry (Ed.), *Crime and justice: A review of research*, 149–200. Chicago: University of Chicago Press.

Petersilia, J. (1998). A crime control rationale for reinvesting in community corrections. In J. Petersilia (Ed.), *Community corrections: Probation, parole, and intermediate sanctions*, 20–28. New York: Oxford University Press.

Petersilia, J. (2002). Community corrections. In J. Wilson and J. Petersilia (Eds.), *Crime: Public policies for crime control*, 483–508. Oakland, CA: Institute for Contemporary Studies.

Petersilia, J. (2003). *When prisoners return home: Parole and prisoner reentry*. New York: Oxford University Press.

Petersilia, J., and S. Turner. (1993). *Evaluating intensive supervision probation/parole: Results of a nationwide experiment (Research in Brief: National Institute of Justice)*. Washington, DC: U.S. Department of Justice.

Pew Center on the States. (2008). *One in 100: Behind bars in America 2008*. Retrieved February 4, 2012, from http://www.pewtrusts.org/~/media/legacy/uploadedfiles/wwwpewtrustsorg/reports/sentencing_and_corrections/onein100pdf.pdf.

Pew Center on the States. (2011). *State of recidivism: The revolving door of America's prisons*. Washington, DC: The Pew Charitable Trusts.

Pew Charitable Trusts. (2014). *Max out: The rise in prison inmates released without supervision*. Retrieved from http://www.pewtrusts.org/en/research-and-analysis/reports/2014/06/04/max-out.

Pisciotta, A. (1994). *Benevolent repression: Social control and the American reformatory-prison movement*. New York: New York University Press.

Pollock, J. (2004). *Prisons and prison life: Costs and consequences*. Los Angeles: Roxbury.

President's Commission on Law Enforcement and the Administration of Justice. (1967). *The challenge of crime in a free society*. Washington, DC: U.S. Government Printing Office.

Prins, S. J., and L. Draper. (2009). *Improving outcomes for people with mental illnesses under community supervision: A guide to research-informed policy and practice*. New York: Justice Center/Council of State Governments. Retrieved from https://csgjusticecenter .org/wp-content/uploads/2012/12/Community-Corrections-Research-Guide.pdf.

Prison Fellowship International, Centre for Justice and Reconciliation. (2012). *Restorative justice*. Retrieved from http://www.restorativejustice.org.

Reaves, B. A. (2013). *Felony defendants in large urban counties, 2009—Statistical tables* (NCJ 243777). Retrieved from https://www.bjs.gov/content/pub/pdf/fdluc09.pdf.

Reaves, B. A. (2015). *Local police departments, 2013: Personnel, policies and practices*. Washington, DC: Bureau of Justice Statistics. Retrieved from https://www.bjs.gov/content/pub/pdf/lpd13ppp.pdf.

Reider, L. (1998). Towards a new test for the insanity defense: Incorporating the discoveries of neuroscience into moral and legal theories. *UCLA Law Review, 46*, 289–342.

Rembar, C. (1989). *The law of the land: The evolution of our legal system*. New York: Simon & Schuster.

Riley v. California, 573 U.S. 132 (2014).

Roper, Superintendent, Potosi Correctional Center v. Simmons, 543 U.S. 551 (2005).

Rose, D., and T. Clear. (2003). Incarceration, reentry, and social capital: Social networks in the balance. In J. Travis and M. Waul (Eds.), *Prisoners once removed: The impact of incarceration and reentry on children, families, and communities*, 313–342. Washington, DC: Urban Institute Press.

Rosenbaum, D. P. (1987). The theory and research behind Neighborhood Watch: Is it a sound fear and crime reduction strategy? *Crime and Delinquency, 33,* 103–134.

Rothman, D. (1971). *The discovery of the asylum.* Boston: Little, Brown.

Rothman, D. (1980). *Conscience and convenience: The asylum and its alternatives in progressive America.* Boston: Little, Brown.

Samaha, J. (2012). *Criminal procedure.* Belmont, CA: Wadsworth/Cengage.

Schall v. Martin, 467 U.S. 253 (1984).

Schubert, C.A. & Mulvey, E.P. (2014). Behavioral health problems, treatment, and outcomes in serious youthful offenders. Washington, DC: Office of Juvenile Justice and Delinquency Prevention.

Schwartz, B. (1992). *The great rights of mankind: A history of the American Bill of Rights.* Madison, WI: Madison House.

Scott, D., and J. Kunselman. (2007). Social justice implications of domestic violence court processes. *Journal of Social Welfare and Family Law, 29,* 17–31.

Scott v. Illinois, 440 U.S. 367 (1979).

Sellin, J. (1976). *Slavery and the penal system.* New York: Elsevier.

Ševčíková, A. (2016). Girls' and boys' experience with teen sexting in early and later adolescence. *Journal of Adolescence, 51,* 156–162.

Sexton, G. (1995). *Work in American prisons: Joint ventures with the private sector.* Washington, DC: National Institute of Justice.

Sheenan, R., G. McIvor, and C. Trotter (Eds.). (2011). *Working with women offenders in the community.* New York: Willan.

Sheldon, R. (2001). *Controlling the dangerous classes: An introduction to the history of criminal justice.* Needham Heights, MA: Allyn & Bacon.

Short, J., and I. Nye. (1958). Extent of unrecorded delinquency: Tentative conclusions. *Journal of Criminal Law, Criminology, and Police Science, 49,* 296–302.

Shy, Y. (2004). *Mandatory minimum sentencing in Massachusetts: Alternative approaches.* Retrieved November 2, 2004, from http://www.cjpc.org/mandatory-minimum-in-other-states.html

Sickmund, M., T. J. Sladky, W. Kang, and C. Puzzanchera. (2017). *Easy access to the census of juveniles in residential placement.* Retrieved from https://www.ojjdp.gov/ojstatbb/ezacjrp.

Skolnick, J. H. (1966). *Justice without trial: Law enforcement in democratic society.* New York: Wiley.

Slate, R. (2000). Courts for mentally ill offenders: Necessity or abdication of responsibility? In L. Mays and P. Gregware (Eds.), *Crime and justice: A reader,* 432–450. Prospect Heights, IL: Waveland.

Smith, D., and C. Visher. (1981). Street-level justice: Situational determinants of police arrest decisions. *Social Problems, 29,* 167–177.

Smith, R. E. (2001). *What future for "public safety" and "restorative justice" in community corrections?* (Papers from the Executive Sessions on Sentencing and Corrections, No. 11). Washington, DC: National Institute of Justice. Retrieved from https://www.ncjrs.gov/pdffiles1/nij/187773.pdf.

Smith, S., and C. DeFrances. (1996). *Indigent defense*. Washington, DC: U.S. Department of Justice, Office of Justice Programs.

Spergel, I. A., and G. D. Curry. (1993). The National Youth Gang Survey: A research and development process. In A. P. Goldstein and C. R. Huff (Eds.), *The gang intervention handbook*, 359–400. Champaign, IL: Research Press.

Stanford v. Kentucky, 492 U.S. 361 (1989).

Streib, V. (2000). *The juvenile death penalty today: Death sentences and executions for juvenile crimes, January 1, 1973–June 30, 2000*. Ada: Ohio Northern University, Claude W. Pettit College of Law.

Strickland v. Washington, 446 U.S. 668 (1984).

Sykes, G. (1958). *The society of captives*. Princeton, NJ: Princeton University Press.

Taxman, F. S. (2008a). *No illusions: Offender and organizational change in Maryland's proactive community supervision efforts. Criminology & Public Policy, 7(2), 275–302.*

Taxman, F. S. (2008b). *To be or not to be: Community supervision de'ja' vu. Journal of Offender Rehabilitation, 47(3), 209–219.*

Tonry, M. (1990). Stated and latent functions of ISP. *Crime and Delinquency, 36*, 174–191.

Tonry, M. (1999). *The fragmentation of sentencing and corrections in America: Sentencing and corrections: Issues for the 21st century* (Papers from the Executive Sessions on Sentencing and Corrections, No. 1). Washington, DC: NIJ. Retrieved from https://pdfs.semanticscholar.org/2bdc/15e94992ca7ff67c10d579821ec8280532fd.pdf.

Tonry, M., and M. Lynch. (1996). Intermediate sanctions. In M. Tonry (Ed.), *Crime and justice: A review of research*, 99–144. Chicago: University of Chicago Press.

Travis, J. (2004). Reentry and reintegration: New perspectives on the challenges of mass incarceration. In M. Pattillo, D. Weiman, and B. Western (Eds.), *Imprisoning America: The social effects of mass incarceration, 247–268*. New York: Russell Sage.

Travis, J. (2005). *But they all come back: Facing the challenges of prisoner reentry*. Washington, DC: Urban Institute Press.

Travis, J., and M. Waul (Eds.). (2003). *Prisoners once removed: The impact of incarceration and reentry on children, families, and communities*. Washington, DC: Urban Institute Press.

Treatment Advocacy Center. (2014). *The treatment of persons with mental illness and jails: A state survey* [Abridged]. Retrieved from http://www.treatmentadvocacycenter.org/storage/documents/treatment-behind-bars/treatment-behind-bars.pdf.

Treglia, S. (2011). *Are international cybercrime laws a hopeless fantasy?* Retrieved from https://www.law.com/jsp/article.jsp?id=1202534084454.

Trotter, C. (2006). *Working with involuntary clients: A guide to practice*. Thousand Oaks, CA: Sage.

Trupin, E. (2001). *City of Seattle, Seattle Municipal Court, Mental Health Court, Evaluation Report*. Retrieved from https://www.pdffiller.com/23748671-MHReportpdf-Mental-Health-Court-Evaluation-Report-City-of-Seattle-seattle-Various-Fillable-FormsUnited States v. Finley*, 477 F.3d 250 (5th Circuit 2007).

United States v. Jones, 132 S.Ct. 945 (2012). Slip opinion retrieved from http://www.supremecourt.gov/opinions/11pdf/10-1259.pdf

United States v. Perrine, 518 F.3d 1196 (2008).

United States v. Salerno, 481 U.S. 739 (1987).

United States v. Smith, 155 F.3d 1051 (9th Circuit 1998).

U.S. Department of Education, Policy and Program Studies Service. (2016). *State and local expenditures on corrections and education: A brief.* Retrieved from https://www2.ed.gov/rschstat/eval/other/expenditures-corrections-education/brief.pdf.

U.S. Department of Justice, Civil Rights Division. (2015). *Investigation of the Ferguson Police Department.* https://www.courts.mo.gov/file.jsp?id=95274.

Vaas, A., and A. Weston. (1990). Probation day centres as an alternative to custody. *British Journal of Criminology, 30,* 189–205.

Van Voorhis, P. (1994). *Psychological classification of the adult male prison inmate.* Albany: University of New York Press.

Vanstone, M. (2008). The international origins and initial development of probation. *British Journal of Criminology, 48,* 735–755.

Vigil, J. D. (2010). *Gang redux: A balanced anti-gang strategy.* Long Grove, IL: Waveland.

Visher, C. A., and J. Travis. (2011). Life on the outside: Returning home after incarceration. *Prison Journal, 91*(3), 1025–1195.

von Hirsch, A. (1998). The ethics of community-based sanctions. In J. Petersilia (Ed.), *Community corrections: Probation, parole, and intermediate sanctions,* 89–98. New York: Oxford University Press.

Walker, S. (1993). *Taming the system: The control of discretion in criminal justice, 1950–1990.* New York: Oxford University Press.

White, R., and H. Graham. (2010). *Working with offenders: A guide to concepts and practice.* New York: Willan.

White, T. F. (2005). *Re-engineering probation towards greater public safety: A framework for recidivism reduction through evidence-based practice.* Retrieved June 1, 2009, from http://www.ct.gov/opm/lib/opm/cjppd/cjresearch/projectbehaviorhealth/resources/20050401studyreengineerprobationcssd.pdf.

Whitehead, J., and S. Lab. (2018). *Juvenile justice: An introduction,* 9th ed. New York: Routledge.

Wilson, D. B., D. L. MacKenzie, and F. N. Mitchell. (2005). *Effects of correctional boot camps on offending: A Campbell Collaboration systematic review.* Retrieved from https://www.campbellcollaboration.org/library/effects-of-correctional-boot-camps-on-offending.html.

Wilson, J. A., and R. C. Davis. (2006). Good intentions meet hard realities: An evaluation of the Project Greenlight reentry program. *Criminology and Public Policy, 5*(2), 303–338.

Wilson, J. Q. (1968). *Varieties of police behavior.* Cambridge, MA: Harvard University Press.

Wodahl, E. J., R. Ogle, and C. Heck. (2011). Revocation trends: A threat to the legitimacy of community-based corrections. *Prison Journal, 9*(2), 207–226.

Wooldredge, J. D. (1994). Inmate crime and victimization in a southwestern correctional facility. *Journal of Criminal Justice, 22,* 367–381.

Zalman, M., and L. Siegel. (1997). *Criminal procedure.* Florence, KY: Cengage.

Zimmer, L. (1986). *Women guarding men.* Chicago: University of Chicago Press.

Zupan, L. (2002). New generation jails. In *Encyclopedia of Crime and Punishment,* 1089–1092. Thousand Oaks, CA: Sage.

INDEX

act of omission, 31
actus reus, 31
adjudication
 court system and, 83, 85–86
 stage in juvenile court process, 201, 202–203
administrative agencies, 28
administrative law, 28
ADR (alternative dispute resolution), 113
adversarial system of justice, 84
African Americans
 police use of force against, 23, 75–76
 in prison demographics, 131
aftercare
 for juvenile offenders, 211
 post-boot camps, 168
 for substance abuse problems, 139–140
age, as defense to criminal liability, 38
aggravated burglary, 34
aging and elderly inmates, 140–142, 141f, 150
Alcohol, Tobacco, Firearms and Explosives
 Bureau (ATF), 63
alcohol- and drug testing equipment, 164b
alibi, 106
Alm, J., 174b–175b
alternative dispute resolution (ADR), 113
American Civil Liberties Union, 140
American Correctional Association, 122
Andrews, D. A., 148–149
Antifa movement, 58
appeal, 110
appellate courts, 84, 87–88, 110, 144. See also state
 court systems; U.S. Courts of Appeal; U.S.
 Supreme Court
appellate jurisdiction, 84, 87–88
Apple iCloud hack, 41
Argersinger v. Hamlin, 97
arraignment, 102, 104, 114, 224
arrests. See also policing and law enforcement
 due to domestic violence, 19
 good Samaritan laws, for drug overdose and,
 222–223
 of juveniles, 193
 police discretion and, 19, 21, 56, 72, 103–104,
 221, 227

UCR reports and, 193
 use of official statistics and, 11–12
 warrantless, 51, 100
arson, 34, 63
Article III judges, 93–94
Assange, Julian, 42–43
assault, 33
assembly-line justice, 103–104
assigned counsel, 98
Assistant U.S. Attorneys, 96
asylums, 142
ATF. See Alcohol, Tobacco, Firearms and Explosives
 Bureau (ATF)
Atkins v. Virginia, 49
attorneys/defense attorneys. See also prosecutors
 appointed attorneys, 97–99
 contract system, 98–99
 district attorneys, 96
 juvenile courts and, 202, 203
 private attorneys, 97, 98
 role of, 97
 within courtroom workgroups, 19–20
Auburn Prison, New York, 119–120, 122, 123
Augustus, J., 154–155
Australian penal system, 129, 155

back-door options, 126
background checks, 68
bail, 49, 100, 101, 199
bail bondsmen, 101
bailiffs, 99–100
balanced approach, within juvenile justice system,
 211–212
Batson v. Kentucky, 105
beat integrity, 66
beats, in police patrols, 66
Beccaria, Cesare, 6
behavior modification, 207–208
bench trials, 104, 206
Bill of Rights and Amendments, 44–51, 44b–45b.
 See also specific Amendments
bills of attainder, 44
Bittner, E., 23, 55
Black Lives Matter, 75

blended sentencing, in juvenile courts, 203–204
blue wall of silence, 76
body-worn cameras, by police, 22, 75, 79, 223
bonds, 101
Bonta, J., 148–149
boot camps, 109, 153, 158*t*, 167–168, 178, 208
Boston Gun Project, 215
bounding, in victimization studies, 14
breaking and entering, 34
Brinegar v. United States, 46
British penal system, 129, 155, 166, 189, 189*b*
Brockway, Z., 156
broken windows initiatives, 59
Brown, Michael, 23, 58, 75
bullying, 196
burden of proof, 106
Bureau of Justice Statistics. *See* U.S. Justice
        Department
burglary, 33, 34, 65, 191
bus therapy, 225
"but for" causation, 32

California
    court structure, 90, 91*b*
    Street Terrorism Enforcement and Prevention
        Act (1988), 214
    three-strikes law, 108
campus-based academies, 69
Canadian penal system, 129
capital punishment, 7. *See also* death penalty
career paths, within law enforcement, 67–71
    field training, 69
    hiring process, 68–69
    promotion, 69–71
Carp, R., 88, 95
case attrition, 103–104, 105*f*
case flow, in criminal justice system, 18*f*
case law, 29
case management technology, 113–114
Casey, P., 112
cash bonds, 101
causation, 32–33
cause in fact, 32
celerity, defined, 8
cell phones, 21–22, 51, 79, 223
chain gangs, 123
chain of command, in law enforcement, 65–67
challenge for cause, in jury selection, 104
charge/count bargain, 103
checks and balances system, 14–20
    crime control vs. due process and, 15
    discretion and, 16–17
    four C's of criminal justice system and, 17, 19–20
    individual liberty vs. societal civility and, 14–15
    as loosely coupled system, 16
    as mix of ideologies, 15
children. *See also* juvenile courts; juvenile justice
        system
    historically as property, 186
    mandatory reporting of suspected abuse of, 19
    safe havens for, 56
    school safety, 56, 70
circuit courts, 87
circuit riding, 87
circumstantial evidence, 106
cities/towns

crime counts/rates, 10
    local ordinances as policy, 5
    mayoral power within executive branch, 29
citizen patrols, 56
citizens. *See also* civil rights; privacy rights
    crime reports by, 17
    as gatekeepers of system, 227
    involvement in judicial merit selection, 94–95
    monitoring of police denial of civil rights, 76
    within four C's of criminal justice system, 17, 19
    within loosely coupled system, 16
civil abatement, 214–215
civil gang injunctions, 215
civilian review, 77
civility, 14–15
civil law, 30, 40, 86
civil rights, 57, 76–77, 80, 125, 145–146
Classical school, 6, 7, 118
classification, 124, 132–133, 146, 147–149
clerks of court, 100
close security, 133
cocaine/crack cocaine, 35, 222
coercive force. *See* use of force, by police
Coker v. Georgia, 49
collateral attacks, 110
collateral bonds, 101
common law, 27, 29, 90
Commonwealth v. Fisher, 189*b*, 190
community correctional facilities, 158*t*
community corrections, 152–183. *See also* com-
        munity supervision; parole; probation
    best practices, 180
    defined, 153
    effectiveness of, 177–179
    history of, 154–156
    incapacitation and, 9
    intermediate sanctions, 109, 153, 159, 161–169,
        177–178
    jurisdiction and, 153–154, 157, 159
    post-release supervision and reintegration,
        169–171
    restorative justice and, 159*b*–160*b*
    sanctions, 157–158, 158*t*
    swift-certain-fair policies, 174*b*–175*b*
community interventions, for juvenile offenders,
        210–212
community-oriented policing, 59, 77
community service work (CSW), 130, 134, 158*t*,
        162, 200
community supervision
    effectiveness of, 177–179
    history of, 154
    offender responsibilities, 172
    officer responsibilities, 172–173
    prevalence of, 131
    rehabilitation and, 8
    special-needs populations, 175–176
    supervision violations, 174, 174*b*–175*b*
    technological advances, 163–164, 164*b*
    types of release and, 169–170
compassionate release, 141–142
CompStat, 59
concerned parent role, 202
concurrent cause, 32
conditions of supervision, 172, 173, 174
confidentiality, in surveys, 13

conjugal visits, 136–137
consent decrees, 76–77
constables, 61
constitutional law, 28
constitutions, 28, 39, 50
continuous signaling devices, 163–164
contract cities, 66
contract system, of indigent defense, 98–99
convict leasing, 123–124
Cooper v. Pate, 144
cops, within four C's of criminal justice system, 19.
    See also policing and law enforcement
correctional officers, 134, 135, 143, 145
corrections, in four C's of criminal justice system,
    19–20. *See also* community corrections;
    institutional corrections
corruption, 17, 66, 72, 76
counsel, right to, 48
county government. *See also* jails; sheriff
    departments; sheriffs
    local prosecutors, 96–97
    public defenders, 98
county police, 60
court administrators, 100
CourTools, 114
court reporters, 100
courtroom workgroups, 19–20
court system, 82–115. *See also* federal court system;
    sentences and sentencing; state court systems;
    specific courts and types of actors
    actors in system, 93–100
    appeal, 110
    basic tenets of, 83–85
    history of federal courts, 85–89
    history of state courts, 89–93
    initial stages to formal charging, 100–104
    movement of cases through, 100–110, 105f
    sentencing, 106–110
    specialized courts, 110–112
    trials, 44, 48, 50, 104–106, 206
    use of technology, 23, 74–75, 113–114, 224
    victim involvement, 21, 112–113
    within four C's of criminal justice system, 19–20
Crank, J. P., 71
Crawford, John, 75
crime. *See also specific acts*
    defined, 3–4
    mala in se vs. mala prohibita, 4, 30, 32
    measurement of, 9–14
    witness videos of, 22, 23, 74–75
crime-control model, 15, 85
crime laboratories, 80
crime prevention, 56
crime rate, defined, 10
crime scene technicians, 226
crime statistics
    CompStat, 59
    explanation of, 9–10
    measurement of crime, 9–14
    NIBRS, 11, 12b
    official statistics, 11–12, 192–194
    self-report statistics, 12–13, 194–196, 195t
    victimization studies and, 13–14
Crime Stoppers, 223–224

criminalized juvenile court, 217
criminal justice, overview, 1–24, 220–227
    checks and balances, 14–20
    crime, defined, 3–4
    discretion and, 221
    fiscal austerity and, 225–226
    measurement of crime, 9–14
    philosophies of, 6–9, 226–227
    as processing system, 226–227
    recent trends in, 20–23
    sequence of events in case flow, 18f
    types of policy, 4–5
criminal justice actors. *See also specific types of
    actors*
    defined, 16
    discretion and, 16–17, 19–20
criminal law. *See also* defenses to criminal liability
    history of U.S., 27
    procedural law and, 30, 43–49
    sources of, in U.S., 27–29
    substantive law and, 30–33, 40–43
criminal law definition, of illegal behavior, 191
criminogenic needs, in classification, 148
Crofton, W., 155
crowdsourcing, 22
cruel and unusual punishment clause, 49, 216
CSW. *See* community service work (CSW)
Curry, G. D., 212, 213–214, 214b
cybercrime, 21–22, 40–42, 51, 78–79

D.A.R.E. *See* Drug Abuse Resistance Education
    (D.A.R.E.)
dark figure of crime, 10, 14
day–evening centers, for juvenile offenders, 199
day reporting centers (DRCs), 158t, 165–166
DEA. *See* U.S. Drug Enforcement Administration
    (DEA)
deadly force, 23, 37, 74
death penalty
    death row wings of prisons, 158t
    for drug offenses, 35
    juvenile justice system and, 186, 216–217
    for most serious offenders, 109
    for murder, 33, 109
    U.S. Supreme Court on, 49
Decker, S., 212, 213–214
defense attorneys. *See* attorneys/defense attorneys
defenses to criminal liability, 36–39
    excuses, 37–38
    justification and self-defense, 37
    mental capacity, 38–39
deinstitutionalization, 77, 142, 209–210
delinquency. *See also* juvenile courts; juvenile
    justice system
    defined, 191–192
    jurisdiction and, 192
    measurement of, 192–196, 195t
Dentler, R. A., 194
deprivation model, 136–137
detached worker programs, 214
detectives, 69–70
detention
    immigration control and, 58–59
    juvenile courts and, 197–199, 207–208

pretrial, 109
preventive, 101
detention centers, 58, 129–131, 210
determinate sentencing, 107, 125, 128, 147, 169–170
deterrence
    as crime prevention, 56
    elements of, 8
    in penitentiary era, 122
    as philosophy of punishment, 7–8
    prison reform and, 145, 146
deviance, defined, 3
direct cause, 32
direct evidence, 106
direct file, 201
direct-supervision jails, 147
discretion
    by criminal justice actors, 16–17, 19–20, 221
    criminal justice system and, 221
    four C's of criminal justice system and, 17, 19–20
    in police arrest decisions, 19, 21, 56, 72, 103–104, 221, 227
    in use of coercive force by police, 55
disposition, in juvenile courts, 203–204
district courts, 86, 87, 96, 145–146
diversion programs, 173
domestic terrorism, defined, 42
domestic violence, arrests due to, 19
domestic violence courts, 112
Doring, N., 195
double jeopardy, 47
DRCs. See day reporting centers (DRCs)
drones, 78–79
Drug Abuse Resistance Education (D.A.R.E.), 70
drug courts, 111, 139, 200
drug offenses, 35, 72–73, 79–80, 108–109, 119, 125, 146, 221–223. See also specific illegal drugs
drug-related deaths, 222
drug tests, 164b, 173
drug treatment, 111, 139–140, 222–223
dual court system, 83–84
dual-disorder inmates, 143
dual-entry tracks, in sheriff departments, 67–68
due-process clause, for states, 50–51
due-process model, 15, 85
due process rights, for juvenile offenders, 202–203, 204–207, 205t, 218
duress, 38

early release on medical parole, 141–142
Eastern State Penitentiary, Philadelphia, 122, 123
economic issues
    community control due to, 79
    correctional budget shortfalls, 126, 129, 149, 180
    impacts of war on crime/drugs efforts, 149–150
    privatization, 134, 225–226
    probation caseloads and, 161
e-court, 113–114
education expenditures, compared to corrections expenditures, 128, 129
Eighth Amendment, 45b, 49, 216
electronic bracelets, 163–164
electronic monitoring systems (EMS), 51, 80, 109, 163–164, 164b, 178, 224
Elmira Reformatory, New York, 123, 155–156

embezzlement, 34
employment, post-release, 171
employment services, 211
EMS. See electronic monitoring systems (EMS)
en banc proceedings, 87–88, 93
English law. See common law
Espionage Act (1917), 42–43
European Electronic Crime Task Force, 41
Evarts Act (1891), 87
evidence, 106
excessive bail, 49
excessive fines, 49
exclusionary rule, 46
excuses, as defenses to criminal liability, 37–38
executive branch
    executive orders as policy, 5
    law-creation ability, 29
Ex parte Crouse, 189–190
Ex parte Hull, 144
ex post facto, constitutional provision, 44

Facebook, 21, 51, 224
family group conferencing (FGC), 216
FDA. See Food and Drug Administration (FDA)
Federal Bureau of Investigation (FBI)
    hiring practices, 68
    jurisdiction of, 62–63
    Uniform Crime Reports, 11, 193
federal court system. See also U.S. Courts of Appeal; U.S. District Courts; U.S. Supreme Court
    actors in system, 93–94, 96
    appeals, 110
    congressional creation of lower courts, 86
    history of, 85–89
    impacts of PRLA, 145–146
    interpretation of laws, 26
    public policies and, 5
    tenets of, 83–84
federal judges, 93–94
federal law enforcement, 61–63. See also specific agencies
Federal Law Enforcement Training Centers (FLETC), 62, 68
felonies
    available sanctions, 157–159, 158t
    defined, 4
    grand jury hearings, 102
    pleading guilty to, 100, 102–103
    probation and, 157, 161, 177
    three-strikes laws, 108, 125
female offenders/inmates
    boot camps as inappropriate for, 167
    conjugal visits and family "homes" on site, 136–137
    the differential response, during reformatory era, 120–121
    the equalization response, in twentieth century, 121
    increase of, 119, 133
    in juvenile residential placement, 207
    the neglect response, in penal codes, 119–120
    violence within women prisons, 135
fentanyl and carfentanyl, 80, 222
FGC (family group conferencing), 216

Fields, M., 177
Field Training Officer (FTO) program, 69
Fifth Amendment, 45*b*, 47, 144
fines, 109, 158*t*, 162
Finkelhor, D., 195
First Amendment, 44*b*
first responders, 64
fixed sentencing. *See* determinate sentencing
flat sentencing. *See* determinate sentencing
fleeing felon rule, 74
FLETC. *See* Federal Law Enforcement Training
    Centers (FLETC)
Fletcher v. Peck, 50
flight risk, 101
Food and Drug Administration (FDA), 28
force continuum, 73–74, 74*b*
forensic technologies, 62–63
Fortas, Abe, 190
foster care, 198
four C's of criminal justice system, 17, 19–20
Fourteenth Amendment, 45*b*, 50–51, 144
Fourth Amendment, 44*b*, 46–47
Fradella, H., 87, 92, 97, 104, 110
front-door options, 126
FTO. *See* Field Training Officer (FTO) program

gang activity and interventions, 42, 56, 212–215,
    214*b*, 222
Garner, Eric, 75
general deterrence, 7
general needs, in classification, 148
Georgia, Seven Deadly Sins law, 108
geriatric units, in prisons, 140–142
get-tough movement, 109, 124–125, 126, 129, 138,
    149–150, 227
Gideon v. Wainwright, 29, 97
globalization, 80
global positioning system. *See* GPS surveillance
good Samaritan laws, for drug overdose, 222–223
good-time credit, 136, 145, 149
governmental control of justice
    distrust of and local control, 16
    principle of legality, 30
    public policies, 5
GPS surveillance, 79, 80, 164*b*, 224
Graham v. Florida, 218
grand juries, 47, 75, 96, 98, 102, 199
grand jury hearings, 102
Gray, M. K., 177
G.R.E.A.T. (Gang Resistance Education and
    Training) program, 214, 215
Gregg v. Georgia, 49
group hazard hypothesis, 212
group homes, 198, 208
gubernatorial appointment of judges, 95
Guyot, D., 72

habeas corpus, 44, 110
habitual offenders, 9, 108, 157
halfway houses, 166, 171, 198, 208
harm, 32–33
Harmelin v. Michigan, 49
Hawaii, HOPE-style probation, 174*b*–175*b*
HAZMAT, 66, 70

heroin, 222
highway patrols, 61
HIV/AIDS, in prison population, 138–139, 150
home detention, 199
Homeland Security Act (2002), 42
homicide, 10, 33, 65, 146, 215
HOPE-style probation, 174*b*–175*b*
hospice facilities, in prisons, 142
house arrest/home confinement, 109, 163–164, 224
houses of refuge, for juveniles, 187
hung jury, 106

ICE. *See* U.S. Immigration and Customs
    Enforcement (ICE)
immigrant communities, 58–59, 77–78
impartial trials, 48
impending, defined, 37
importation model, 137
imprisonment. *See* institutional corrections; prison
incapacitation model. *See also* deterrence
    economic issues and, 79
    in penitentiary era, 122
    in prisons, 145, 146
    as protection of society, 8–9
    sentencing and, 107
incarceration. *See also* institutional corrections;
    prison
    as form of retribution, 7
    rates of, 127–129, 149, 170
    shock incarceration, 158*t*, 167, 208
incorporation, 50–51
indeterminate sentencing, 107, 155
indigent defense, 97–98
individual liberty vs. societal civility, 14–15
industrial era, 123–124
informal adjustment, in juvenile courts, 199–200
informal social control, 3–4, 5
information, 102
initial appearance, 100, 102
inmate rights, 144–146
innocence, presumption of, 84
In re Gault, 205, 205*t*
In re Winship, 205–206, 205*t*
insanity defense, 37, 38–39
institutional corrections, 116–151
    classification systems and, 124, 132–133, 146,
        147–149
    custody and security within, 134–135
    economic issues and, 79
    eras of punishment, 121–127
    female offenders/inmates, history of, 119–121
    future directions for, 149–150
    history of punishment, 117–127
    inmate rights within, 144–146
    jails, 129–131
    overcrowding, 79, 126, 128, 146, 156
    prison management and discipline, 135–136
    prison subculture and coping, 136–137
    prison types, 132–134
    rehabilitation programs, 8, 137
    size and costs of imprisonment, 127–129, 127*f*
    special offender populations, 138–144
    state laws on operations, 20
    violence within, 135–136, 146–147

institutional corrections, for juvenile offenders, 207–210
intake decisions, in juvenile courts, 199–200
intelligence-led policing, 59
intensive supervision probation (ISP), 109, 158*t*, 161, 162–164
intent, 31–32, 38
intermediate courts of appeal, 92
intermediate sanctions, in community corrections, 109, 153, 159, 161–169, 177–178
Internal Affairs, 70
International Association of Chiefs of Police, 224
international crime, 62
Internet and cybercrime. *See* cybercrime
involuntary intoxication, 37–38
Irish penal system, 155
ISP. *See* intensive supervision probation (ISP)
ISP officers. *See* probation officers

jails
    function of, 109, 129–131
    inmate demographics, 131
    mentally ill inmates, 131
    new-generation (NGJs), 130–131, 147
    number in U.S., 129
    sentencing and, 158*t*
J.C. Penney, 124
john details, 70
Jostens, 124
judges
    approval of arrest warrants, 100
    bail amounts, 49
    bench trials, 104, 106
    check and balance role of, 16
    creation of courtroom policies, 20
    declaration of hung jury, 106
    in early court system, 27, 29, 87
    federal appointment of, 93–94
    in juvenile courts, 202–203
    role of, 93–95
    in state court systems, 90–91, 92, 94–95
    three-judge panels, 87–88, 92
    within courtroom workgroups, 20
judicial branch. *See also* federal court system; state court systems; *specific courts*
    court rulings as public policy, 5
    law-creation ability, 29
judicial review, 50
judicial waivers, 200
Judiciary Act (1789), 63, 86, 87
juries. *See also* grand juries; trial by jury
    challenge for cause in selection of, 104
    hung jury, 106
    peremptory challenge in selection of, 104–105
    role of, 100
jurisdiction
    appellate courts, 84, 87–88
    applicable laws and, 26
    court system definition, 84
    definition of delinquency and, 192
    of FBI, 62–63
    original, 86, 88
    in state court systems, 90–91, 92
    within policing and law enforcement, 60–65

jury consultants, 114
just deserts, 7, 125, 164*b*
justification, as defense to criminal liability, 37
juvenile courts, 84, 196–204
    adjudication stage, 201, 202–203
    case flow, 197*f*
    detention, 197–199
    disposition, 203–204
    history of, 188–189
    intake decisions, 199–200
    official statistics, 192–194
    referrals to, 196–197
    transfer/waiver decisions, 192, 200–202, 218
Juvenile Justice and Delinquency Prevention Act (1974), 209
juvenile justice system, 184–219. *See also* juvenile courts
    age and intent, 38
    balanced approach with, 211–212
    boot camps, 168
    community interventions, 210–212
    comparative terminology with adult systems, 188*b*
    death penalty and, 186, 216–217
    delinquency concept within, 191–192
    development of, 186–191
    due process rights, 202–203, 204–207, 205*t*, 218
    early institutions, 187
    gangs and, 56, 212–215, 214*b*
    history of, 186–191, 187*b*
    institutional corrections, 207–210
    Juvenile Investigations units, 70
    measurement of delinquency, 192–196, 195*t*
    parens patriae philosophy of, 189–191, 189*b*, 198, 199–200, 202, 203, 204, 211, 217
    reform debates, 217–218
    restorative justice and, 159*b*–160*b*, 200, 215–216

Kansas City Preventive Patrol Experiment, 59
Kent v. United States, 189*b*, 190, 204, 205*t*
kidnapping, 33, 62, 108
King, Rodney, 74
Knapp Commission (1970s), 72
Kunselman, J., 112
Kyllo v. United States, 78

larceny/theft, 31, 33, 34
law, overview of, 25–52
    defenses to criminal liability, 36–39
    function of laws, 4
    history of law in U.S., 27
    incorporation, 50–51
    procedural criminal law trends, 51
    procedural law, 30, 43–49
    rule of law, 27
    sources of law in U.S., 27–29
    substantive criminal law trends, 40–43
    substantive law, 30–33
    types of crimes, 33–36
    victim's rights, 39
law-and-order approach. *See* get-tough movement
law compliance, 54–55
law enforcement. *See* policing and law enforcement
legal aid, 99

legality, principle of, 30
legislative appointment of judges, 95
legislative branch, 28
legislative waiver/statutory exclusion, 201
liability
    act of omission and, 31
    actus reus and, 31
    defenses to criminal, 36–39
    degrees of, 33–34
    mens rea and, 31–32
    mental capacity and, 38–39
    strict liability, 32
Lipsey, M., 209
loitering, 4, 34, 215
Los Angeles Rampart Division CRASH scandal
    (1990s), 72
Louisiana, common law in, 27
Lounsbury, K., 195
Lynch, M., 177
Lyon Brothers Manufacturing Company, 124

Maconochie, A., 155
macro-level policies, 5
mala in se crimes, 4, 30
mala prohibita crimes, 4, 30, 32
mandatory minimum sentences, 108, 129, 138, 140
manslaughter, 10, 33
Mapp v. Ohio, 46
Marbury v. Madison, 50, 88
marijuana, 13, 35, 80, 84
Marshall, J., 88
Martinson, R., 125
master jury list, 104
maximum-security prisons, 133, 136
Maxwell, S. R., 177
McCulloch v. Maryland, 88
McDonald, Laquan, 75
McGarrell, E. F., 216
McKeiver v. Pennsylvania, 205t, 206
McMann v. Richardson, 99
mediation, 113
medical marijuana, 84
medical model, in rehabilitation, 124
medical parole, 141–142
medical treatment, for special offender populations,
    138–144
medium-security prisons, 133
mens rea, 31–32
mental capacity, as defense to criminal liability,
    38–39
mental health courts, 111–112, 176
mental health treatment, 111–112, 143, 176, 211
mental illness, 77, 131, 133, 139, 142–144, 171, 176
mentoring, 211
merit selection, of state judges, 94–95
micro-level policies, 5
minimum-security prisons, 133
Minneapolis Domestic Violence Experiment, 59
misdemeanors
    alternative dispute resolution (ADR), 113
    defined, 4
    jail sentences, 109
    pleading guilty to, 100, 102
    probation and, 157, 177

Mitchell, K. J., 195, 200
M'Naghten rule, 38–39
Model Juvenile Delinquency Act, 198
Monitoring the Future Survey (MTF), 13, 194, 196
Monroe, L. J., 194
Morgan, K., 177
Mullen Commission (1980s), 72
multi-jurisdictional task forces, 62
municipal police agencies, 60
murder
    bail decision and, 101
    in crime statistics, 10
    death penalty, 109
    in early English common law, 27
    first-degree, 101
    first-degree/aggravated, 30, 33, 109
    intent/mens rea and, 31–32
    juvenile arrests for, 193
    legislative waivers for, 201
    as mala in se crime, 4, 30
    sentences for, 33, 108, 109
mutual aid compacts, 60

nanotechnology, 79
Napoleonic Code, 27
Narcan/naloxone treatments, 80, 222–223
National Center for State Courts, 114
National Crime Victimization Survey (NCVS),
    13–14
National Gang Center, 213
National Institute of Justice, 226
National Prison Association, 122, 124, 155
National Research Council of the National Acad-
    emies of Science, 218
National Youth Survey (NYS), 194, 196
Native Americans, tribal police/courts, 60, 63, 225
NCVS (National Crime Victimization Survey),
    13–14
necessary, defined, 37
need principle, in classification, 148
Neighborhood Watch, 56
net widening, 168–169, 178
Neubauer, D., 87, 92, 97, 104, 110
new-generation jails (NGJs), 130–131, 147
New Jersey Plan, 85–86
new-offense violations, 174, 177, 178
New York (state)
    court structure, 91, 91b
    crime statistics (2010), 10
    NYPD and corruption, 72
    NYPD and crime reduction, 59
New York County Lawyers' Association, 98
New Zealand, FGC program, 216
NIBRS (National Incident-Based Reporting
    System), 11, 12b
Ninth Amendment, 45b
Nixon, Richard, 221
nonpartisan election, of state judges, 94
nonsecure detention, 198
no true bill issuance, 102
nullification, 186
Nye, I., 194, 195t
NYS. *See* National Youth Survey (NYS)

Office of Professional Responsibility, 70
official statistics, 11–12, 192–194
Ohio
    court structure, 90, 91b
    Public Defender Commission, 5, 28
once/always provisions, 201
O'Neil v. Vermont, 49
opioid crisis, 80, 221–223
opportunities provision, as gang intervention
        strategy, 213–214, 214b
order maintenance, 55, 56, 59
organized crime, 72
original jurisdiction, 86, 88
overcrowding
    of court system, 90, 102–103
    of jails, 130
    of prisons, 79, 126, 128, 146, 156

Packer, H., 15, 85
Pad, The, 72
pains of imprisonment, 136
Palko v. Connecticut, 50
parens patriae philosophy, of juvenile justice system,
        189–191, 189b, 198, 199–200, 202, 203, 204,
        211, 217
parole. *See also* community corrections
    early release on medical parole, 141–142
    effectiveness of, 179
    hearings for, 21, 136
    history of, 125, 126+, 155–156
    jurisdiction and, 157, 159
    limiting to one year, 149
    in reform era, 123
parole boards, 174
parole officers, 20, 166
parole supervision, 153, 170
partisan election, of state judges, 94
patrols, by police, 56, 66
penitentiaries. *See* institutional corrections; prison
penitentiary era, 122
pension systems, 226
People v. Turner, 189b
peremptory challenge, in jury selection, 104–105
personal crimes, 33
Petersilia, J., 177
Philadelphia, crime statistics (2010), 10
philosophies of criminal justice, 6–9, 226–227
    Classical school, 6, 7, 118
    deterrence and punishment, 7–8
    incapacitation and punishment, 8–9
    Positivist school, 6–7
    rehabilitation and punishment, 8
    retribution and punishment, 7
plea bargains
    in deterrence approach, 8
    as form of retribution, 7
    incidence and characteristics of, 102–103
police academies, 68–69
Police Activity League volunteers, 56
police brutality, 23, 73–76
police unions, 76
policing and law enforcement, 53–81. *See also*
        arrests; use of force, by police
    career paths within, 67–71

case attrition practice, 103–104, 105f
community-oriented policing, 59
corruption within, 17, 66, 72, 76
education and training for officers, 68–69, 70
harassment and racial profiling, 72–73
hiring processes, 68–69
intelligence-led policing, 59
Internal Affairs, 70
law enforcement role, 55–56
opioid crisis and, 222–223
order maintenance role, 56, 59
organization and chain of command, 65–67
police brutality, 23, 73–76
police subculture, 71–72, 76–77
police work shifts, 67
private police, 64, 225–226
problem-oriented policing, 59
promotions within, 69–71
restricted procedural rights and, 51
school education programs, 70, 215
service role, 56–57
societal roles and eras of, 57–59
specialization of tasks, 65–66
special needs communities and, 77–78
specialty teams/units, 70
structure and jurisdictions, 60–65
sworn officers vs. civilian personnel, 65, 226
use of official statistics and, 11–12
use of social media in investigation, 22
use of technology, 22, 75, 79, 223–224
within four C's of criminal justice system, 19
policy and criminal justice, 4–5
pornography, 195–196
Port Authority of New York and New Jersey
        Police, 61
Positivist school, 6–7
postconviction review, 110
post-release supervision and reintegration, 169–171
power shifts, in police work, 67
precedent, 27
precincts, in police departments, 66
preliminary hearings, 102
prescription opioids, 221–223
presentence investigation, 172–173
preservice training, in police work, 68
presidential campaign (2016), alleged hacking, 41
President's Commission on Law Enforcement and
        the Administration of Justice (1967), 204, 209
President's Task Force on 21st Century Policing, 23
pretrial detention, 109
preventive detention, 101
principle of legality, 30
prison. *See also* institutional corrections; *specific
        prisons by name*
    as available sanction, 108–109, 158t
    types of, 132–134
    women-only, 120, 121, 135
prisoner reentry/reintegration, 170–171.
        See also community supervision
    economic issues and, 79
    effectiveness of, 179
    era of, 125–127
    programs and assistance, 126–127
prisoner rights movement, 144–145, 146

Prison Litigation Reform Act (PLRA) (1995), 145–146
prison programs, 8, 137, 145, 179
prison riots, 23, 124, 135
prison violence, 135–136, 146–147
privacy rights, 51, 78–79, 80, 164b
private police, 64, 225–226
private prisons, 109, 133–134
privatization, 134, 225–226
PRLA. See Prison Litigation Reform Act (PLRA) (1995)
probable cause, 46, 51, 102
probation. See also community corrections
    community supervision and, 177
    defined, 158t
    effectiveness of, 178
    as form of retribution, 7
    function of, 109
    history of, 124, 126, 154–155
    HOPE-style (Hawaii), 174b–175b
    jurisdiction and, 157
    for juvenile offenders, 203, 210
    sanctions for violation of, 175b
    split sentences, 169
    as term of conditional supervision, 161
    unsupervised, 161
probation officers
    community supervision and, 172–173
    day reporting centers and, 166
    diversion programs and, 173
    history of, 155
    for juvenile offenders, 200, 211–212
    presentence investigation, 172–173
    role of, 20, 99–100, 153, 161
    supervision violations and, 174, 174b–175b
problem-oriented policing, 59
pro bono, 99
procedural law, 30, 43–49, 51
procedural rights, 50, 202
process model. See four C's of criminal justice system
programmed contact devices, 163
Prohibition, 72
property crimes, 34, 119, 193
property marking, 56
pro se, 99
prosecutorial waiver, 201
prosecutors. See also attorneys/defense attorneys
    check and balance role of, 16
    chief prosecutors, 96–97
    federal prosecutors, 96
    juvenile courts and, 202
    role of, 95–96
    state and local prosecutors, 96–97
prostitution, 11, 35, 70
protection, defined, 37
proximate cause, 32
public defenders, 98
public order crimes, 34–35
public policies, defined, 4–5
public safety vs. individual rights, 51
public trials, 48
pulling levers approach, as gang intervention strategy, 215

punishment. See also institutional corrections; sentences and sentencing
    Beccaria on, 6
    deterrence approach to, 7–8
    history of, 117–127
    incapacitation approach to, 8–9
    rehabilitation approach to, 8, 124–125
    retribution approach to, 7
punishment amendment. See Eighth Amendment

racial prejudice, 75–76
racial profiling, 72–73, 77
rape, 4, 27, 30, 32, 33, 49, 108, 193, 204
reasonable, defined, 37
rebuttal, 106
recidivism rates
    boot camps and, 168, 178, 208
    community corrections and, 177–179
    deinstitutionalization and, 210
    disproportionate incarceration and, 128
    domestic violence courts and, 112
    drug treatment programs and, 140
    HOPE-style probation and, 175b
    intermediate sanctions and, 178
    for juvenile offenders, 211, 216
    mental health treatment and, 112
    new-generation jails and, 131
    rehabilitation and, 125
    special-needs populations and, 176
    treatment programs and, 178
    wilderness programs and, 209
    within three years of release, 126, 170
reentry, defined, 125–126. See also prisoner reentry/reintegration
reentry, for juvenile offenders, 211
reformatories, for juveniles, 187
reform era, 122–123
regional task forces, in law enforcement, 66
rehabilitation
    as alternative to punishment, 8, 124–125
    in prisons, 8, 137, 145
    in reform era, 122–123, 146
    sentencing and, 8, 107
rehabilitation era, 124–125
release, types of, 169–170
remote alcohol detection devices, 164b
residential community correctional programs, 153, 166–167
residential interventions, for juvenile offenders, 207–208
responsivity principle, in classification, 148–149
restitution, 113, 200
restorative (reparative) justice
    community corrections and, 159b–160b
    defined, 113
    juvenile justice system and, 215–216
    victim involvement in court system and, 21, 100, 112–113, 224
retained counsel, 97
retribution, as philosophy of punishment, 7
retributive era, 125
revenge, in earlier centuries, 5
revenge porn, 22
reverse waivers, 201

Rice, Tamir, 75
RICO (Racketeering Influenced and Corrupt
    Organization), 40
right to counsel, 48
Riley v. California, 79
riots. *See* prison riots
risk-assessment instruments, 198
risk principle, in classification, 148
robbery, 4, 27, 33, 34, 62, 65, 108, 191, 193
Roman Catholic Church, 117
Roper, Superintendent, Potosi Correctional Center v.
    Simmons, 49, 216–217
rotating shifts, in police work, 67
Rothman, D., 156
Rottman, D., 112
rule of law, defined, 27

safe havens, 56
sanctions. *See also specific types of sanctions*
    in community corrections, 157–158, 158*t*
    defined, 157
    intermediate sanctions, 109, 153, 159, 163–171,
        177–178
    prison as, 108–109, 158*t*
    for probation violations, 175*b*
    in sentencing, 108–109
    types of correctional, 158*t*
SAVIN program, 224
Scalia, Antonin, 49
Schall v. Martin, 198
school resource officers, 56, 70
Scott, D., 112
Scott v. Illinois, 97
Second Amendment, 44*b*
Second Chance Act (2008), 127
secure custody, 134–135
secure detention, 198
self-defense, 37
self-incrimination, 47
self-report, 12–13, 194–196, 195*t*
self-representation, 99
sentence bargain, 103
sentences and sentencing. *See also* death penalty
    available sanctions, 108–109
    blended sentencing for juvenile offenders,
        203–204
    get-tough movement and, 125, 126, 129, 138
    guidelines for, 107–108, 149
    habitual offenders and, 9, 108, 157
    indeterminate vs. determinate, 107
    mandatory minimum sentences, 108, 129, 138,
        140
    for probation violations, 175*b*
    proportionality in, 49
    rehabilitation plans and, 8, 107
    sentence bargain, 103
    split sentences, 169
    victim impact statements, 21
sentencing guidelines, 107–108, 149
Serpico, Frank, 72
service role, of police, 55, 56–57
Seventh Amendment, 45*b*
sex offenders, under community supervision, 164*b*
sexting, 195–196

sheriff departments, 57, 61, 66, 67–68, 225
sheriffs, 16, 60
shock incarceration, 158*t*, 167, 208. *See also* boot
    camps
shoplifting, 33
Short, J. F., 194, 195*t*
single-entry tracks, in sheriff departments, 67
Sing Sing Prison, New York, 123
Sixth Amendment, 45*b*, 48, 204
smart-on-crime strategies, 129
Snapchat, 21
Snowden, Edward, 43
social intervention, as gang intervention strategy,
    213, 214*b*
social media, 21–22, 51, 223–225
social/political tensions, 58–59, 124–125
social worker approach, 211–212
societal civility, 14–15
Sony Pictures hack, 41
special conditions, in community supervision, 172,
    173
specialized courts, 110–112, 200
specialized prisons, 133
special offender populations, 138–144
    aging and elderly inmates, 140–142, 141*f*, 150
    community supervision and, 175–176
    inmates and HIV/AIDS, 138–139, 150
    inmates and mental illness, 133, 139, 142–144,
        176
    inmates and substance use, 139–140, 150
special police forces, 61
specific deterrence, 7
speedy trial right, 48
Spergel, I. A., 214*b*
split sentences, 169
standard conditions, in community supervision, 172
Standard Juvenile Court Act, 190
Stanford v. Kentucky, 216
state constitutions, 28, 39, 60
state court judges, 94–95
state courts of appeal, 92
state court systems, 89–93
    annual caseload, 90
    California court structure, 90, 91*b*
    courts of appeal, 89, 90, 92
    judicial election or appointment, 94–95
    New York court structure, 91, 91*b*
    Ohio court structure, 90, 91*b*
    public defenders, 98
    public policies and, 5
    state prosecutors, 96
    supreme courts, 90, 92–93
    trial courts of general jurisdiction, 92
    trial courts of limited jurisdiction, 90–91
state laws. *See also specific states and laws*
    crime reporting, 19
    degrees of criminal liability based on, 33–34
    on gang activity, 212
    General Purpose Clauses for juvenile courts, 190
    good Samaritan laws, for drug overdose, 222–223
    on prison operations, 20
    three-strikes laws, 9, 108, 125
    youthful offender statutes, 192
state patrols, 61

state police, 61, 66
state supreme courts, 89, 92–93
state training schools, for juvenile offenders, 207–208, 209
Statewide Automated Victim Information and Notification (SAVIN) program, 224
statistics. *See* crime statistics
status offenses, 189, 191, 197, 198, 200, 207, 209
statutory exclusion, 201
statutory law, 27–28
statutory rape, 32
steady shifts, in police work, 67
Stewart, Martha, 35*b*–36*b*
Stidham, R., 95
sting operations, 70
Street Terrorism Enforcement and Prevention Act (California/1988), 214
stress-based academies, 68–69
Strickland v. Washington, 99
strict liability, 32
subcultures
    of police and law enforcement, 71–72, 76–77
    of prison life, 136–137
substance abuse, 139–140, 150, 171. *See also* drug offenses; opioid crisis
substantial capacity test, 39
substantive law, 30–33, 40–43
suicide, 146, 196
supermax prisons, 132
supervised release, 169–170
supervision violations, in community supervision, 174, 174*b*–175*b*, 177–179
suppression, as gang intervention strategy, 214, 214*b*, 215
surveillance. *See* electronic monitoring systems (EMS); GPS surveillance
SWAT/SRT (Special Response Team), 70
swift-certain-fair policies, 174*b*–175*b*
Sykes, G., 136

technical violations, in community supervision, 174, 174*b*–175*b*, 177, 178
technology. *See also* crime statistics
    community supervision, 163–164, 164*b*
    court operations, 23, 74–75, 113–114, 224
    cybercrime, 21–22, 40–42, 51, 78–79
    ethical issues and, 164*b*
    forensic technologies, 62–63
    law enforcement, 75, 223–224
    nanotechnology, 79
    security of data due to, 64
    social media, 21–22, 51, 223–225
    substantive criminal law trends, 40–42
    U.S. Supreme Court on warrants and, 79
    video technology, 22, 23, 74–75, 114, 163, 195–196, 224
teen courts, 200
telescoping, 14
Tennessee v. Garner, 74
Tenth Amendment, 45*b*
terrorism, 42–43
    civil liberties and, 80
    creation of DHS, 62

intelligence fusion centers and, 59
    use of social media in, 22
Third Amendment, 44*b*
Third Generation, 124
three-strikes laws, 9, 108, 125
token economy, in juvenile detention, 198–199, 207–208
Tonry, M., 177
transfer decisions, for juvenile offenders, 192, 200–202, 218
transinstitutionalization, 142
trespass, 34, 73, 215
trial by jury. *See also* juries
    constitutional right to, 44, 48, 50, 104
    for juvenile offenders, 206
    movement of cases through, 104–106
trial courts of general jurisdiction, 92
trial courts of limited jurisdiction, 90–91
trial rights amendment. *See* Sixth Amendment
trials
    bench trials, 104, 206
    in state court systems, 90–91, 92
tribal police/courts, 60, 63, 225
troops, in state police, 66
true bill of indictment, 102
Trump, Donald, 41, 57
Trump presidential campaign (2016), alleged Russian hacking, 41
Twitter, 21, 224

UCR. *See* Uniform Crime Reports (UCR) (FBI)
undercover officers, 70
underreporting of crime, 9–10, 13, 14, 19
Uniform Crime Reports (UCR) (FBI), 11, 193
United States (U.S.). *See also specific states and federal agencies*
    age distribution of inmates, 141*f*
    anti-terrorism efforts, 42–43
    correctional budgets, 128
    cost of incarceration per person, 128–129
    dual court system, 83–84
    gang members and activity, 213
    history of law in, 27
    individuals under correctional supervision, 127–128, 127*f*
    inmates with mental illness, 111, 143
    juvenile arrests, 193
    juveniles in residential placement, 207
    as loosely coupled criminal justice system, 16
    number of district courts, 86
    number of inmates, 108
    number of police and law enforcement agencies in, 60
    offenders in correctional supervision, 109, 153, 156, 161
    opioid deaths, 222
    prisoners released annually, 169
    sources of law in, 27–29
United States v. Finley, 51
United States v. Perrine, 51
United States v. Salerno, 101
United States v. Smith, 51
unreasonable search and seizure, 46

use of force, by police, 23, 37, 55, 71, 73–76, 74*b*
U.S.A. Patriot Act, 42, 51
U.S. Attorney General, 96
U.S. Attorneys, 96
U.S. Bureau of Indian Affairs, 63
U.S. Bureau of Justice Assistance, 226
U.S. Coast Guard, 62
U.S. Congress
    creation of lower federal courts, 86
    law-creation ability, 26
    restrictions on habeas corpus, 110
U.S. Constitution. *See also specific Amendments*
    Article III provisions, 86, 93–94
    Bill of Rights and Amendments, 44–49, 44*b*–45*b*
    bills of attainder provision, 44
    ex post facto provision, 44
    habeas corpus, 44
    on Indian tribes as sovereign entities, 63
    law creation powers, 26
    procedural law based on, 43–44
    right to trial, 44, 48, 50, 104
    supremacy of, 28
U.S. Courts of Appeal, 87–88, 89
U.S. Customs and Border Protection, 58–59, 62, 68
U.S. District Attorney, multi-jurisdictional task
    forces, 62
U.S. District Courts, 86, 87, 96, 145–146
U.S. Drug Enforcement Administration (DEA),
    63, 68
U.S. Education Department, Policy and Program
    Studies Service, 128
U.S. Homeland Security Department (DHS), 42, 62
U.S. Immigration and Customs Enforcement (ICE),
    58–59, 62, 77–78
U.S. Justice Department, 62. *See also* Federal Bureau
    of Investigation (FBI); U.S. Drug Enforcement
    Administration (DEA)
    Bureau of Justice Statistics, 13–14, 119
    federal prosecutors, 96
    lawsuits against police departments, 76–77
    on RICO statute, 40
U.S. Marshals Service, 63
U.S. Office of Justice Programs, Office of
    Community Oriented Policing Services
    (OJP OCOPS), 58
U.S. Secret Service, 62, 63
    European Electronic Crime Task Force, 41
U.S. Supreme Court
    annual caseload, 89
    on court-appointed counsel, 97–98
    cruel and unusual punishment clause, 49, 216
    on death penalty, 49
    on denial of bail, 101
    on effective assistance of counsel, 99
    establishment and role of, 88–89
    on incorporation and judicial review, 50
    on inmate rights, 144
    landmark decisions, 204–206, 205*t*
    law-creation ability, 29
    on medical treatment for special offender popu-
        lations, 138
    on probable cause, 46
    restrictions on habeas corpus, 110

rulings affecting juvenile justice, 198, 204–206,
    205*t*, 216–217, 218
    on use of lethal force, 74
    on warrants and technology, 79
U.S. Transportation Safety Administration, 62
U.S. Treasury Department, 62. *See also* Alcohol,
    Tobacco, Firearms and Explosives Bureau
    (ATF)

Varieties of Police Behavior (Wilson), 55
venire, 104
victim-centered system, 5
victimization studies, 13–14
victimless crimes, 13
victims
    advocates for, 100
    of cybercrime, 21–22
    as gatekeepers of criminal justice, 21
    involvement in court system, 21, 100, 112–113,
        224
    live-streaming of crimes in progress, 22
    notification laws and, 21
    restitution for, 113, 200
    restorative justice and, 159*b*–160*b*
    rights of, 39
    SAVIN program and, 224
    of violence and corruption in prison
        subculture, 145
Victoria's Secret, 124
video technology
    for arraignment and hearings, 114, 224
    in electronic monitoring, 163
    sexting and, 195–196
    social media postings and, 22
    use by witnesses to alleged crimes, 22, 23, 74–75
Vigil, J. D., 214
Virginia Plan, 86
vocational training and education, 124, 207
voir dire, 104
voluntary intoxication, 38
von Hirsch, A., 164*b*

waiver decisions, for juvenile offenders, 192,
    200–202
war on drugs, 125, 139, 146, 149–150, 221–222.
    See also drug offenses; *specific drugs*
warrantless arrest, 51, 100
warrants
    for arrest, 100
    for GPS devices, 79
    judicial approval of warrants for, 100
    to search individual's home, 46
    for search of cell phones incidental to
        arrest, 79
    U.S. Supreme Court on, 79
white-collar offenses, 35–36
    Martha Stewart case, 35*b*–36*b*
White supremacy groups, 58
Wickersham Commission (1931), 124
WikiLeaks, 42–43
wilderness programs, 208–209
William the Conqueror, 27
Wilson, D., 209

Wilson, J. Q., 55
witnesses
  in court proceedings, 100, 104, 106
  protection of endangered federal, 63
  SAVIN program and, 224
  Sixth Amendment and, 48
  victims as witness for the state, 113
  videos of alleged crimes, 22, 23, 74–75

women-only prisons, 120, 121, 135. *See also* female
  offenders/inmates

youthful offender statutes, 192
YouTube, 51, 224

zealous advocate role, 202
zero tolerance, 215